EUROPEAN COMMUNITY TOURISM LAW AND POLICY

Marc McDonald et al.

Faculty of Tourism and Food,
Dublin Institute of Technology

BLACKHALL
Publishing

Blackhall Publishing Ltd
27 Carysfort Avenue
Blackrock
Co Dublin,
Dublin 8

Typeset by
Gough Typesetting Services
Dublin

Printed by Colorbooks Dublin

ISBN 1 842180 53 3

European Community Tourism Law and Policy

TABLE OF CONTENTS

PREFACE

Despite the fact that the Treaty of Rome does not provide for a tourism policy of any kind to be followed by the European Community, the activities of the Community have a significant impact on tourism. They embrace all dimensions of tourism and operate both directly and indirectly.

To deal with its peculiar involvement in tourism the Community has tried and arguably failed to adopt a consistent, integrated approach and instead has had to do with a variety of sectoral approaches – market, environmental, cohesion, consumer and so on - in which tourism and its concerns have generally not been central. To compound matters tourism also falls into the pit of unresolved relationships between the Community and member states and every direct Community initiative involving tourism has had to run the gauntlet of the subsidiarity principle, not an easy challenge.

Law plays an important role in Community approaches to tourism primarily because the Community, as the unique supranational creature it is, uses legal measures as the basis for all its activities and also because both prescriptive rights and duties and legal frameworks are commonly used instruments of Community policy relevant to tourism.

So sectoral is the Community approach to tourism that it is difficult to form an overview of either the range of Community interactions with tourism or the potential that a more comprehensive approach to tourism might hold.

This therefore provided the first impetus for the writing of this text. If it is difficult for those with an interest in the area to develop a global perspective on Community legal and policy impacts on tourism, how can a vision of the added value, to use a Commission phrase, which a comprehensive approach might permit, be developed?

The second impetus resulted from the absence of any attempt to gather in the one place a representative selection of Community legal and policy literature which tells the story of the Community's witting or unwitting involvement in tourism. There is no shortage of critiques or evaluations of Community policy in tourism. But what is in short supply is storytelling which allows Community sources, so far as is practicable, to tell the tale themselves over the longer period, that is since the Community started taking an interest in tourism, and in a way which is hopefully illuminating for tourism professional and student alike.

For various reasons including the specialist nature of the focus, we have had to make choices as to which dimensions of Community involvement in tourism we would cover. Thus, while we cannot claim a comprehensive treatment of the topic, we do claim a valid representation of most of the main areas where law plays a major role in Community interaction with tourism. Changes made to the Treaty of Rome by the Treat of Nice have been included, although as of the end of 2002 the Treaty is not yet in force.

The writers of the contributions come from different member states and different academic backgrounds. Over the period of collaboration we have managed to work out and apply a generally consistent framework to the presentation of the material. It would not have been either right or desirable to attempt a rigidly identical structure and the reader will notice differences of approach and presentation. The general guiding principle has been to judiciously select informative extracts from both policy and legal Community sources and link them with an informed and sometimes critical commentary. The range of particularly indirect Community material relevant to tourism is of course enormous and in places it has not been possible to present it in the detail that might be wished. But this too is consistent with our overall aim. We wish to provide the reader with a taste for the nature and degree of Community legal and policy involvement in tourism and then propel him/her on a research path through the referenced sources.

Collaboration on this text has been made possible through Socrates funding channelled through the European Tourism University Partnership, an academic network championed by Paul Constable of the University of Savoie, Chambery, France. To both Socrates and Paul a deep debt is owed. Each of our contributor/participants also deserves special thanks. The initial stages of our collaboration were not easy and it took some time to identify what we hope is the unique focus of our approach. The end was only reached because each contributor made the extra effort.

So specialised was our task that we had to go outside the ETUP network in search of collaborators. A special thanks is due to Susanne Storm, Denis Ketel, Jan-Willem Proper and Willem Buijs for recognizing the value of what we were trying to do and for so committedly supporting it.

Thanks are also due to Bruce Carolan, Gerry Dunne and Bernadette Quinn for reading various chapters and making helpful comments. We are particularly grateful to Rheinhard Klein, Head of the Tourism Unit in the Enterprise-Directorate-General of the European Commission, who read a final draft of the text, for his helpful suggestions. The European Documentation Centre in the Berkeley Library in Trinity College Dublin and the information service of the European Commission offices in Dublin were hugely useful in tracking down Community material.

Marc Mc Donald, marc.mcdonald@dit.ie
April 2003

LIST OF CONTRIBUTORS

Arrant Arruti: University of Deusto, Bilbao, Spain.

Willem Buijs: DTV Consultants, Breda, The Netherlands.

Dennis Ketel: NHTV, formerly of Breda University of Professional Education, The Netherlands.

Marc McDonald: Dublin Institute of Technology, Dublin, Ireland.

Ariane Portegies: NHTV, Breda University of Professional Education, The Netherlands.

Jan-Willem Proper: NHTV, Breda University of Professional Education, The Netherlands.

Susanne Storm: University of Southern Denmark, Odense, Denmark.

LIST OF ABBREVIATIONS AND TERMS

A	See PE A.
Acquis	Collective term for entire body of Community legal rules and administrative decisions.
AGBG	German Civil Code.
C	Commission documents.
Cabotage	Provision of transport services between two points in another state.
CE	Commission.
CI	Community initiative.
CMLR	Common Market Law Reports.
CNS	Legislative procedure involving Council acting in consultation with Parliament.
COD	Legislative Procedure involving Council acting in co-decisions in co-decisions with Parliament.
COM	Communication from Commission.
COR	Committee of the Regions.
COREPER	Committee of Permanent Representatives of governments of Member States.
CRS	Computer reservation system.
CSL	Council.
CSF	Community Support Framework.
CTP	Common transport policy.
E	European Community Treaty/Rome Treaty.
EEA	European Economic Area (Community plus Norway, Iceland, Liechtenstein).
EAGGF	European Agricultural Guidance and Guarantee Fund.
EAP	Environmental Action Programme.
EC	European Community.
ECR	European Court Reports.
EIA	Environmental Impact Assessment.
EIB	European Investment Bank.
EP	European Parliament.
ERDF	European Regional Development Fund.
ESC/CES	Economic and Social Committee.
ESF	European Social Fund.

EUR-LEX	Internet database of Community legislative acts.
Ex-ante	Prospective.
Ex-post	Retrospective.
EYT	European Year of Tourism.
GDP	Gross domestic product.
GNP	Gross national product.
Ha	Hectare.
IATA	International Air Transport Association.
Ibid	Same footnote reference as immediately above, different page number.
IGC	Inter-governmental conference.
IMO	International Maritime Organisation.
Interreg	Community initiative under cohesion policy.
Intra-Community	Inside the Community.
ISPA	Instrument for structural policies for pre-accession.
LAG	Local action group.
LA's	Local authorities.
Leader	Community initiative under cohesion policy.
MECU	Millions of European currency units (before euro).
MS	Member State.
MTE	Mid-term evaluation.
NUTS	Nomenclature of Territorial Statistical Units.
OFT	Office of Fair Trading (UK).
OJ	Official Journal of the European Communities.
OJ C	C series of Official Journal contains official non-legislative material produced for publication.
OJ E	OJ available only electronically.
OJ L	L series of Official Journal contains official Community legal measures, including regulations, directives and decisions produced for publication.
OP	Operational Programme.
PE	Parliament document.
PE A	Final version of Parliamentary Committee report document presented to Parliament for adoption.
PE T	Parliament documents recording opinions/resolutions/decisions adopted by parliament during a legislative procedure.
Philoxenia	Proposed tourisms multi annual action plan.
PSO	Public service obligation.
Re	Concerning.
Schengen	Luxembourg village on the River Moselle where aboard

	a cruise boat the Agreement and Convention on the gradual abolition of internal border controls were signed.
Schengen acquis	Collective term for Agreement, Convention, accession agreements and executive committee decisions/declarations dealing with removal of internal border controls.
SDR	Special drawing rights.
SEC	Commission Secretariat internal working document.
Secondary legislation	Collective term for regulations, directives, recommendations and decisions.
SF	Structural Funds.
SPD	Single Programming Document.
SYN	Legislative procedure involving Council acting in co-operation with Parliament.
Supra	Exact same footnote and page reference as immediately above or exact same footnote reference as more than one footnote above.
T	See PE T.
TEC	Travaux en cours/work in progress.
TEN-T	Trans-European network transport.
Third country	Country outside European Community.
Tort	Private law wrong.
Transparency	Availability of information to enable average EU citizen understand a Community process.
Transpose	Implement nationally.
UNTS	United Nations Treaty Series.
Urban	Community initiative under cohesion policy.

TABLE OF CASES AND DECISIONS

TABLE OF CASES

TABLE OF DECISIONS

TABLE OF LEGISLATION

IRELAND

INTERNATIONAL CONVENTIONS

INTERNATIONAL TREATIES

Treaty of Rome 1957—*contd.*

Treaty of Rome 1957—*contd.*

TABLE OF REGULATIONS

TABLE OF DIRECTIVES

CHAPTER 1

INTRODUCTION[1]

This book examines how a range of law and policy aspects of tourism are dealt with by an supranational[2] organisation comprised of states and their citizens – the European Community. Its main purpose is to increase awareness and understanding of the role of Community laws and related policies in the tourism sector of the Community.

This chapter identifies the topics covered in this book and puts them into a context. It firstly presents a brief overview of the Community and its institutions. Secondly, it explains the particular focus of the book under the following headings:

- the European Community and international bodies.
- the added value of Community legal involvement in tourism.
- the importance of law in Community involvement in tourism.
- the role of policy in Community law.

To support this approach, a short note on each of the chapters is provided to illustrate the link between the context and the topics chosen. Areas that are not covered in the book are identified and the reasons for their omission briefly explained.

Finally, the chapter explains the particular way the material in the book is presented and how the book goes beyond the legal and tourism material available on the Community's extensive web sites.

OVERVEW OF THE EUROPEAN COMMUNITY, THE EUROPEAN UNION AND THE INSTITUTIONS

The European Community was formed in 1958 by an agreement between

---

[1] Marc McDonald.

[2] An international organisation affects only states, whereas a supranational organisation affects states and their citizens.

six states[3] – the Treaty of Rome/Rome Treaty.[4] Thereafter as each new state joined,[5] it agreed another treaty with the Community, called a Treaty of Accession. Under this, each state agreed to be bound by the Rome Treaty and by Community law, usually over a transitional phase, and to change its domestic legal and administrative framework accordingly. The same procedure, albeit preceded by a more formalised enlargement process,[6] is being used with the current applicant states from Central and Eastern Europe.

To change the Treaty of Rome a new treaty must be agreed among the Member States. This has happened a number of times[7] and has increased the areas the Community can be active in and reformed the institutions, and the ways Community decisions are reached.

The European Union was created by the Treaty on European Union 1992, signed in Maastricht (Maastricht Treaty)[8] as amended by the Treaty on European Union signed in Amsterdam in 1997 (Amsterdam Treaty)[9] and the Nice Treaty.[10] The European Union is related to the European Community in that the same States belong to both; the same institutions run both; and both form part of the same push towards greater integration among the same states. Seen from a distance they can be easily confused. But they serve the goal of European integration in different ways and this is highly significant.

The Community provides the framework for integration in economic and social matters, while the Union is a looser framework for co-operation on diverse matters not covered by the Community, such as foreign and security matters, home affairs and judicial co-operation. Acts can only be taken by the Union with the agreement of all the States, whereas under the Community framework majority voting often takes place and Member States must further share power with the European Parliament. Thus, under the Union power rests entirely with the states, while this is decidedly not the case under the Community.

The Treaty on European Union does not now directly impact on tourism. When first enacted in 1992 it did. Important issues connected with the entry

---

[3] Belgium, France, Germany, Italy, Luxembourg, and the Netherlands.

[4] Signed in Rome, March 25, 1957, entered into force January 1, 1958. Throughout this text the current version of the Treaty establishing the European Community 1958, that is the Treaty as amended, is referred to as the Treaty of Rome/Rome Treaty.

[5] Denmark, Ireland and the UK in 1972; Greece in 1981; Portugal and Spain in 1986; Austria, Finland, Sweden in 1995.

[6] See website http://www.europa.eu.int/pol/enlarg/index_en.htm.

[7] See p. 21.

[8] Signed February 7, 1992, entered into force November 1, 1993.

[9] Signed October 2, 1997, entered into force May 1, 1999.

[10] Signed February 26, 2001, in force since February 1, 2003. For the text of the treaties establishing the European Union, see http://www.europa.eu.int/abc/treaties_en.htm.

and movement of non-EU nationals as tourists as well as immigrants were within its scope, but these were transferred to the Rome Treaty and thus the Community framework by the Amsterdam Treaty in 1999.Tourism aspects of this are dealt with in chapter 4.

The Treaty of Rome created institutions, separate from those of the Member States, to secure the objectives of the Community laid down in the Treaty. The principal institutions are the Parliament, the Council, the Commission, the Court of Justice and the Court of Auditors. Only the Parliament is genuinely democratic in that the citizens of the Member States directly elect it. The Council represents the governments of the Member States and for a long time was the primary force within the Community. Increasingly the Council now shares the vital power to make laws with Parliament. The Commission, whose members are appointed by common accord with the Member States and the approval of Parliament, is the Community body that oversees the observance and implementation of Community policies and laws and has the responsibility and capacities to monitor observance of Community law both by states and individuals.

The Commission has another vital role. All initiatives for new legal measures within the Community must begin with a proposal from the Commission. This means that neither the Council nor Parliament can initiate new laws or adopt new policies without the Commission. Before exercising this highly significant power of initiative, the Commission is obliged to prepare the ground carefully

The Treaty of Rome is the basic or constitutional law of the European Community. However, the Treaty also allows the institutions of the Community to make regulations and directives and these too are treated as laws, the essential difference between them being that a regulation once made can directly affect the legal rights of individuals and businesses, while a directive is addressed to governments requiring them to make their own laws to implement what the directive says.

Community laws begin life in proposal form only after much consultation and discussion by the Commission both with states and affected parties. The proposal usually goes simultaneously to Parliament and the Council both of whom debate and consider the proposal through a series of readings. If there is no agreement on the contents of a measure, the Treaty provides for a conciliation procedure involving both institutions under which their representatives form a committee and either work out some shared view or the measure falls.

The Community uses law in a variety of ways. The Treaty itself fixes what the Community and its institutions can actually do. Regulations and directives can have the significant effect of actually forcing states to change their laws and ways of administration. The Community also uses laws to directly impact on ways individuals and businesses operate, say, when deciding to approve a merger between two large businesses or fining a business for anti-competitive activities. The Community also uses law to simply record its decisions.

Since law is relied on so much by the Community, the need for a court to conclusively determine the meaning and application of these laws is clear. Thus the Treaty also creates a Court of Justice and Court of First Instance, both of which in different ways have the task of delivering definitive rulings of whether Community law has been breached, say by a Member State or a company, or determining what a law means.

The spending of Community funds represents a huge part of Community activities. Ensuring that these funds are properly spent and monitoring the relevant safeguards applied both by the other Community institutions and the beneficiaries of funds spent, are matters of great legal importance and for this reason a further Community body was created – the Court of Auditors. This is not a court in the typical sense. It conducts the audit of the Community income and expenditure and determines if principles of sound financial management have been applied.

Thus, the core activities of the European Community are adopting policies, making laws, disbursing funds, ensuring compliance with Community laws. But the Treaty only created the various institutions and provided powers to make laws in order to achieve certain definite objectives. These are the real kernel of the Community and are set out initially in the Treaty in general terms and later in more detail, although much is still left for amplification by laws and policies.

At its widest the Community's objectives are a closer union of the European peoples. Among the chief ways of achieving this are creating a common market, creating economic and monetary union, promoting regional cohesion, creating Union citizenship, banning non-nationality discrimination and devising and implementing a range of common polices and other measures. The specific ways this wide range of objectives impact on tourism form the subject mater of this book.

The listing and detailing of objectives in the Rome Treaty is somewhat unique compared with how state constitutions are usually written. These are more concerned with creating institutions of state, empowering them and creating appropriate balances of power between them. Beyond declaring the broad nature of the state, state constitutions do not usually go much into detail regarding the type of policies the state should pursue. That is left to the elected governments and law makers.

Of necessity the position is different with a supranational organisation like the European Community which is given such extensive means for realising its ambitious objectives. States agreeing to a new international organisation naturally feel a pressing need to define why it is created and what areas or topics it can be active in. Every act the new body takes must then reflect those choices and a particular perspective, both legal and policy, must be developed to understand how it approaches its tasks. Legal competence, that is the authority to act, is a key issue not only in relation to the Treaty of Rome generally, but especially in relation to tourism, where as will be seen in Chapter 2, most Community acts affecting tourism are not based on the reference to tourism in the Treaty.

The European Community is not the only organisation of European states with potential relevance to tourism. The Council of Europe[11] is another such body. However, it does not compare with the European Community in terms of its actual impact on tourism, whether by virtue of the rules it makes, the scope of its legal competence to promote policies or the availability of its own financial resources.

Council of Europe

The Council of Europe is different from the European Community and the European Union. It is an organisation of European States that provides at best a framework for states to promote best political practice at European level on any of a wide range of governmental and inter-governmental issues. It acts only by unanimous agreement among the states. With the exception of human rights, it has a much lesser impact on citizen's lives. It has no capacity to make binding rules which impact on individual citizens or on states opposed to those rules and it has little or no resources to effect change along desired lines.

Inter-Governmental Bodies

There are a host of what can be called inter-governmental bodies whose actions can impact on tourism, such as the World Tourism Organisation,[12] the United Nations Educational, Social and Cultural Organisation,[13] the United Nations Environmental Programme,[14] the World Trade Organisation – GATS,[15] the International Civil Aviation Organisation,[16] the World Maritime Organisation,[17]

---

[11] See generally, website http://www.coe.int/portalT.asp.

[12] See http://www.world–tourism.org.

[13] See http://www.unesco.org/whc/nwhc/pages/home/pages/homepage.htm.

[14] http://www.unep.org.

[15] http://www.wto.org.

[16] See http://www.icao.int.

[17] See http://www.imo.org/index.htm.

the Inter-governmental Organisation for International Carriage by Rail[18] and the Inter-national Institute for the Unification of Private Law (Unidroit).[19] Some of these are topic specific, dealing only with issues like international air or maritime transport, while others have a sectoral remit, like the World Tourism Organisation which, unlike the European Community, has limited capacity and resources to effect change.

What principally distinguishes these bodies from the European Community in terms of law and tourism is that their member states cannot be forced to adhere to the international agreements which they sponsor, these bodies usually act by unanimity, their rules bind only governments and have no capacity to independently impact on individuals. Nor do these bodies or the agreements they sponsor permit the raising of own resources that go beyond administrative housekeeping or are large enough to enable them to significantly influence activity within and between their State members.

ADDED VALUE OF COMMUNITY INVOLVEMENT IN TOURISM LAW

This section addresses the question – what would trans-national tourism law and policy among the Community Member States be like if there was no European Community?

It is clear there would be much state co-operation. The various free travel arrangements which existed before some States joined the Community, such as among the Nordic states[20] or between the UK and Ireland,[21] would still exist. So too would co-operation on specific traveller issues like air,[22] ferry/cruise[23] and rail[24] carrier liability for injury to passengers and their luggage and hotelier liability for loss/damage to hotel residents property.[25] States would have

---

[18] See http://www.otif.org/e/index.htm.

[19] See http://www.unidroit.org/english/presentation/pres.htm.

[20] Nordic Passport Convention allowing travel without passports.

[21] The common travel area between Ireland and the UK is not based on an agreement between both States but on a series of domestic measures which permit travel without passport between both states. See also Protocol 3 to the Treaty of Rome as amended, OJ C 340/97, 10.11.97.

[22] ICAO, Convention for the Unification of Certain Rules for International Carriage by Air, Warsaw 1929/Montreal 1999.

[23] IMO, Convention relating to the Carriage of Passengers and their Luggage by Sea, Athens 1974.

[24] Intergovernmental Organisation for International Carriage by Rail (OTIF), Convention concerning International Carriage by Rail, Berne 1980/Vilnius 1999.

[25] Council of Europe, Convention on the Liability of Hotel–Keepers concerning the Property of their Guests, 590 UNTS 81, Paris 1962.

continued to make bilateral and multilateral agreements with each other to provide a legal framework for international passenger air travel. Attempts would still have been made to facilitate international travel[26] and to streamline/loosen/regulate border checks to facilitate tourist or personal movement generally[27] and would no doubt have developed. Unidroit had already succeeded in promoting model uniform rules for adoption by states on contracts between tour operators/travel agents and customers,[28] though it has so far failed with a similar endeavour with hotel contracts.[29] Attempts would also have been made at world level to promote trade in services, including tourism services under the aegis of the World Trade Organisation and the 1994 General Agreement on Trade in Services (GATS).[30] European states in particular would have continued to use the framework of the Council of Europe to promote best practice in areas relevant to tourism, like conservation of wildlife and natural habitats[31] and the protection of the archaeological[32] and architectural[33] heritage. Efforts at world level through the 1972 Convention concerning the Protection of the World Cultural and Natural Heritage to protect heritage sites of world importance[34] would also have continued.

---

[26] League of Nations, Convention and Statute on Freedom of Transit, 7 LNTS 11, Barcelona 1921; UN Convention for the International Carriage of Passengers and Luggage by Road, 163 UNTS 34, Geneva 1974; UN Customs Convention on the Temporary Importation of Private Road Vehicles, 282 UNTS 249, New York 1954; UN, Convention on the Taxation of Road Vehicles for Private Use in International Traffic, 339 UNTS 3, Geneva 1965; UN Customs Convention on the Temporary Importation for Private Use of Aircraft and Pleasure Boats, 319 UNTS 21, Geneva 1956; European Agreement concerning the temporary provision of medical care to persons during temporary residence, Geneva 1983; UN Convention concerning Customs Facilities for Tourism, 276 UNTS 191, New York 1954; UN Additional Protocol to the 1954 Convention concerning Customs Facilities for Touring relating to the Importation of Tourist Publicity Documents and Material, 276 UNTS 191, New York 1954.

[27] Council of Europe, European Agreement on regulations Governing the Movement of Persons between Member States of the Council of Europe, 315 UNTS 139, Paris 1957; Council of Europe, European Agreement on Travel by Young Persons on Collective Passports between the Member Countries of the Council of Europe, 544 UNTS 19, Paris 1961; WTO, Draft Convention to Facilitate Tourist Travel, Visits and Stays, Budapest 1989.

[28] Unidroit, International Convention on Travel Contracts, Brussels, 1970.

[29] Unidroit, the Hotelkeepers Contract, Secretariat Memorandum, 67th session, February 1988.

[30] WTO, GATS and Tourism – Implications of the General Agreement on Trade in Services, Madrid 1995.

[31] Council of Europe Convention on the Conservation of European Wildlife and Natural Habitat, ETS104, Berne 1979.

[32] Council of Europe, European Convention on the Protection of the Archaeological Heritage, ETS 143, Valetta 1992.

[33] Council of Europe, Convention for the Protection of the Architectural Heritage of Europe, ETS 121, Granada 1985.

[34] For the text and details concerning this Convention, see http://www.unesco.org/whc/nwhc/pages/doc/main.htm.

International networks for promoting new ideas on tourism and its impacts, such as the World Conservation Union[35] and ECO trans,[36] and designed to feed into national and international governmental processes would have evolved.

But all of these international initiatives would still not have matched the tourism achievements (good and bad) of the European Community. This is because, despite the weaknesses documented over this book's chapters, the Community has:

- a far greater level of ambition in what it is trying to do,
- a far greater level of legal powers to try and do it,
- a far greater capacity to react speedily to changing circumstances, and
- a far greater amount of its own financial resources.

The greater ambition of the European Community, which transcended previous levels of inter-governmental cooperation, is the promotion of European integration by a variety of means, and particularly for the purposes of this book, by the establishment of a common market in goods and services related to tourism. The stress here is significant. It is not tourism in itself, but tourism as part of the common market, as an economic activity, which forms the basis for significant Community action impacting tourism. This point and its relevance to the legal rights of tourists is further developed below.

This sideways view of tourism derives both from the still largely economic focus of the Treaty of Rome (amply documented in the course of the book) and also from historical factors which can be briefly elaborated here. Although it represents an ideal means for promoting European consciousness among European citizens, tourism played little direct or conscious role in the creation of the common market. In the late 1950s, tourism was still largely national in character and the opportunities for foreign travel were generally limited. Over time tourism in Europe has been utterly transformed from an elite to a mass phenomenon. Improved and more affordable means of transport and accommodation, new marketing techniques, such as the package holiday, greater amounts of leisure time and disposable income, have all contributed to this. As the demand and supply sides of tourism have grown in importance, policy makers, the trade and citizens have increasingly questioned whether a sideways approach to tourism at Community level remains appropriate.

---

[35] See http://www.iucn.org.
[36] See http://www.ecotrans.org/Englishfr.htm.

Common Market and Tourism

The creation of a common market is the main objective laid down in the Treaty establishing the European Community (Treaty of Rome) which impacts on tourism, although flanking measures, such as cohesion policy, competition rules and consumer protection – designed to ensure the operation of the common market does not lead to undesirable concentration of activities and resources – also significantly impact on tourism.[37]

The words 'common market' are used by the Treaty in a global economic sense to describe an area of broadly equal trading opportunity across the territory of the Community for all goods and services. This area is/should be free of national rules and administrative practices which unjustifiably impede the capability of sellers and buyers to operate. Expressed simply, the idea is to create the same trading conditions between Madrid and Malmo as exist between Madrid and Malaga.

Within the common market there clearly are different markets. Within tourism itself there are a wide range of markets, both geographic and product. Chapter 9 details a number of such markets, including, for example, the tour operator market which can divide into short haul and long haul, city break, beach, weekend, summer and so forth.

This text uses the words 'common market' or 'tourism common market' in an elastic manner to cover either:

- the general idea of free trading opportunity or (as the context will indicate),
- a specific individual market.

It is usually used when talking about a state law, which continues to protect a national market against outride penetration.

Although the common market remains the central focus of legal activity by the European Community in tourism, revisions to the Rome Treaty have added new qualitative dimensions to Community attempts to remove state obstacles to the common market. If a Community response to an obstacle will impact on consumers then it must adopt a high level of protection. More generally Community measures must respect the principle of sustainable development, that is matching environmental impacts with the long-term carrying capacity of the environment.

The addition of new dimensions to Community measures means that the

---

[37] In larger terms, the common market is a stage in a process of principally economic and possibly ultimately political integration among Member States. This wider process, running from free trade and customs union to monetary union and closer forms of political co-operation, lies beyond the tourism focus of this book.

Community's areas of activity and goals are multi-faceted, sometimes difficult to reconcile and help explain the broad scope of the material covered in this book. Tourism provides useful illustrations of what some would see as policy conflict at Community level, especially in the tourism /environment area, where continued belief in the appropriateness of tourism as a driver of regional regeneration, and the channelling of Community funds into tourism infrastructure, comes up against the idea of sustainable development.

The scale of the Community's actual and potential involvement with tourism made it inevitable that the question would be asked – why not take a more coherent and focused approach to tourism? Why not create a Treaty framework which would permit the Community to adopt a more holistic approach to tourism?

The question was certainly asked. As the latter part of Chapter 2 shows the early 1990s were a period of debate and optimism regarding increased direct Community involvement in tourism, based principally on the hope of strengthened Treaty references. Ultimately, however, nothing happened because of the opposition of a number of Member States, principally the tourist exporting states, who feared the financial and other consequences of Community activism in this area. One consequence of this short sighted view is that the Community has continued to focus on tourism primarily from a common market perspective with particular emphasis on enterprise and employment potential. This has left it ill-equipped to address what may be emerging as the greatest challenge facing international tourism into the 21st century – managing if not reversing ever increasing demand for tourism.

IMPORTANCE OF LAW IN EUROPEAN COMMUNITY INVOLVEMENT IN TOURISM

Agreements between sovereign states are considered law in the sense that in reaching agreement a state considers itself bound to adhere to the outcome. Further, in order for the parameters of action under an agreement to be understood, the agreement has to be in writing and will usually provide for some internal mechanism to ensure adherence. When a particular agreement goes further, as the Treaty of Rome does, and establishes a new supranational entity it must of course provide a statement of the aims and objectives of that entity and also provide the means by which the entity will achieve those objectives. That in turn requires the creation of institutions, the definition of their roles and powers, balances to be struck between those institutions and the founding states. It further requires the clear establishment of the means by which those institutions can act. Those means will naturally be accorded the status of laws.

Thus it is of the very essence of the European Community, and this book is founded on this insight, that the Community cannot operate without law. The central role of law in the creation and life of the European Community operates at two levels – the Treaty itself as the basic or constitutional law of the Community (also called the primary law) and the Community's legal measures (regulations, directives, decision, recommendations – also called the secondary law) which the Community's institution adopt when attempting to achieve Treaty objectives.

What adds to the central role of law in the Community's life is that those who drafted the Treaty drew their inspiration from continental legal traditions, which, more than the legal traditions of Ireland and the United Kingdom, require formal documentary frameworks for administrative actions and decisions. Even small scale budgetary allocations within the Community require the use of some formal legal instrument to secure adoption, as do decisions taken by the Commission, most of which under Community law must be published in the Community's official journal or otherwise.[38] In effect, everything the Community does must in some manner or means be expressed through legal instruments.

IMPORTANCE OF POLICY IN EUROPEAN COMMUNITY TOURISM LAW

Community laws as much as national laws are written binding reflections of policy decisions by law-makers. Policy is inevitably present in the construction and making of a law. But once made judges and lawyers generally prefer not to take policy considerations into account when interpreting a law because of the fear that it brings them too close to the subjective political choices which underpin the law. Their preference is that once a law is made, in whatever shape or form, the process of extracting meaning from it should be a matter of interpreting the law in the light of accepted methods of text interpretation, any overriding legal principles and the views expressed in any previous similar cases. This they believe provides for better dispute settling and public acceptability of judicial decisions.

However, this approach is not possible when interpreting the Rome Treaty and more particularly the Community's secondary laws. There are a number of reasons for this.

---

[38] This ensures a high degree of transparency, which is the ability of citizens to follow in document/web form the activities of the Community's institutions, which in turn results in the extensive information and database resources mentioned below being maintained by the Community.

The Challenge of Legal Interpretation

Firstly, while the Treaty is a binding legal document, it represents an agreement between states on a huge range of policy matters which in many cases are expressed in the widest possible political and economic language which is not susceptible to easy or neat legal interpretation. The alternative, to use either lengthy legal provisions or provisions which place a premium of word interpretation, would not have suited the economic nature of what was being attempted. Thus, the interpretation of the Treaty requires a larger recourse to policy reasoning, that is reasoning by reference to the underlying purposes of a measure, than judges and lawyers are traditionally comfortable with.

Secondly, it is possible to read the Treaty structure in a relatively logical manner which starts with the motives of the Treaty makers expressed in the Preamble, moves onto extremely general statements of the Community's objectives in Articles 2 and 3 and then elaborates on these ultimate objectives through a whole series of intermediate and sub-intermediate objectives, again spelt out in varying degrees of detail. Means are then provided in relation to the different types and levels of objectives. Such a construction makes it difficult to see any one part of the Treaty in isolation from the rest.

Thirdly, the Treaty itself requires that the reasons for a law must be stated in the law. Article 253 states that regulations, directives and decisions:

> shall state the reasons on which they are based and shall refer to any proposals or opinions which are required to be obtained pursuant to this Treaty.

The reasons for a law, set out in its Preamble, are inevitably expressed as policy statements. Further, the underlying proposals and opinions, collectively know as the preparatory documents (*travaux preparatoires*), will also be full of policy statements and are these too can be referred to when interpreting a measure.[39]

A purposive approach to legal interpretation is the outcome of the emphasis on policy matters. This means that interpretation difficulties are not usually resolved by nit-picking word meanings, but by identifying the underlying policy and approving the interpretation which favours that.

Economic Participation and Legal Interpretation

Another somewhat special (at least for lawyers) approach to the interpretation of Community law is needed. This arises principally from the primarily but not exclusively economic focus of the Rome Treaty.

---

[39] An illustration of this is found in *Club–Tour v. Garrido* [2002] E.C.R. I–4051. See p. 290.

Ordinarily private laws, that is laws dealing with individuals, focus on individual rights and construct entitlements based on those rights. Those rights are human or basic rights based on concepts of the importance of the individual in society. Their use can be regulated in accordance with the public good.

European Community law, however, while acknowledging the role of human rights as a backdrop in the constitutional traditions of the Member States, focuses primarily on the common market and on economic activity generally and thus both on the role of persons as participants in the common market and on whether the operation of the common market impedes or facilitates the ability of persons to participate in and gain the benefit of the market. Participating in the market them becomes a central legal concern.

A tourist participates in the common market as a consumer of tourism products. Under Community law this means a lot. The tourist has a legal right to do all things necessary to receive tourism services and act as a tourist, such as travel, bring money, visit museums etc. This provides a distinct perspective from which to examine state laws which control availability of services and ensure that any national restrictions can only stand on legitimate public policy grounds that do not act in a disproportionate manner.

In short, a tourist has rights under Community law, not because of any human/ social right to free movement or recreation or participation in cultural life, but because of the tourist's ability/desire to purchase tourism services, which are part of the common market in tourism services and in turn part of the wider common market. This may seem like a strange way of claiming a right to act as a tourist. Additionally, any protection the tourist receives under Community law as a consumer is given not out of any universal concept of fairness towards the individual, but of a fairness concept related to the proper operation of the common market and the optimum distribution of benefits under that Market. Thus, ultimately tourist rights and protections are based on economic status, not human status.

Community law also makes demands on the public law frameworks and administrative practices of Member States. These demands operate in proportion to the extent to which these frameworks and practices facilitate the operation of the common market and also in proportion to the extent to which any national restrictions on Community rights are within proper public policy exceptions recognised by the Treaty and, very importantly, do not operate disproportionately.

Community demands on Member State laws can be very wide ranging, focusing on any state inspired or related cost which can affect a tourism business or which can lessen the ability of the tourist to participate in the common market. This can include even something as seemingly innocuous as discriminatory museum admission charges.[40] Whether a cost is state inspired or related and

---

[40] See p. 36.

whether it distorts the common market becomes a critical issue of legal interpretation as it decides whether a state is failing to meet its obligations under Community law.

Two hypothetical examples may help illustrate how this participatory angle on the common market applies to the legal interpretation of Community law.

A 19 year old tourist visits another Member State on a weekend city break and is refused service in a pub because the barman belies he/she is under 18. The barman refuses to accept the tourist's passport as proof of age, preferring instead to see a locally issued age card (which the tourist cannot obtain because he/she does not know about it or has not time to get it) the production of which is the only defence local law allows to the seller. It is certainly arguable that the tourist can claim a breach of a Community law on the basis of being wrongfully denied a common market service and more latterly on the basis of denial of free movement rights based on Union citizenship. Community law only requires a passport to enter another state and this presumes a passport is enough to avail of services there. While an age restriction of consuming liquor can be regarded as within the realm of Member State power to restrict access to services on public policy grounds, the state law must only act proportionately and the local age card is not the only way age can be proved. A passport can just as easily do it.

A budget hotel chain wishes to avail of its common market right to establish a hotel is another Member State. One of the key features of this hotel chain is that it does not provide bathrooms en-suite and is thus able to offer budget rates. The local law in the other state requires each hotel bedroom to have a bathroom en-suite and denies use of the word hotel and thus entry to the hotel market. It is certainly arguable that the national law can be seen as denying the Community law right of establishment and thus distorting the common market. Different legally binding minimum standards for hotels mean differing costs are imposed on competing hotel operators. The national law may also operate disproportionately. Making it compulsory for all hotels to have bathrooms en-suite is not the least restrictive way to achieve the objective of providing modern hotels. This can also be achieved by giving a lower grade to hotels without en-suite bathrooms so that tourist can easily see who provides en-suite bathrooms and the budget chain would not be prevented from accessing the hotel market. Thus, the national law would probably be considered to operate disproportionately and the Member State would be failing to comply with Community law.

CHAPTER OVERVIEW

This section presents a brief overview of the focus and contents of each chapter. It is intended as an opportunity to see the books' focus on Community tourism law and policy in its entirety and to note how different areas link into each other and the overall theme.

Chapter 2 – Treaty of Rome and Tourism

This chapter examines the relevance of the Treaty of Rome to tourism in both its direct and indirect forms. It also examines the role, which the Court of Justice plays in developing the indirect relevance of the Treaty to tourism. A number of core Community law concepts, such as proportionality and subsidiarity, which have become so important in shaping the nature of Community intervention in tourism and other areas are then described. The fact that tourism is not dealt with more ambitiously in the Treaty has been the subject of much debate over the years. The latter part of this chapter focuses on this debate and seeks not only to provide a record of its central issues, but also to reinforce an understanding of the centrality of the Rome Treaty in this whole area.

Chapter 3 – Tourism in the Institutions, Laws and Decision-Making Procedures of the Community

Because of the central importance of the Community's institutions in the life of the Community, this chapter uses tourism examples to explain the role and powers of Parliament, Council, Commission, Court of Justice, Court of Auditors, Economic and Social Committee and the Committee of the Regions. The chapter also describes the different types of laws which the Community can make and outlines some of the procedures currently used to link the institutions when making Community laws which impact on tourism.

Chapter 4 – Free Movement and Tourism

This chapter focuses firstly on what free movement means and its central role in tourism. It then examines the legal measures that underpin the degree of free movement so far achieved within the Community and the scope for residual state controls over free movement of tourists. The chapter also notes the unfinished business, that is the areas affecting free movement and tourism which remain to be dealt with at Community level and still impede tourist flows, (external border formalities and checks, removing internal border controls etc) and particularly tourist movement originating outside the Community.

Chapter 5 – Community Transport Policy and Tourism

This chapter focuses on the many different dimensions to transport, which facilitate the movement of tourists across the Community. After noting the Treaty provisions dealing with transport issues, the chapter outlines the pressures which, ever increasing passenger transport demand imposes both on transport infrastructures and the environment. The attempt of the Community to create a transport network which is designed to facilitate cross border transport, including tourist movement, is then described. Finally, the later half of the chapter focuses on the different transport modes and tourism, outlining the broad thrust of Community legal involvement in market liberalisation and qualitative dimensions such as passenger safety and carrier liability in the event of accidents.

Chapter 6 – Community Cohesion Policy and Tourism

This chapter examines the legal framework used to promote cohesion/regional development. It begins by noting the Treaty basis for Community actions and for the creation of structural funds used to support projects. It then identifies and examines each of the basic principles that guide the use of Community funding to promote regional development, including concentration, programming, additionality and evaluation. Throughout the chapter short references are made to the specific impact of funded measures on tourism projects.

Chapter 7 – Community Consumer Protection and Tourism

This chapter begins by noting how the Treaty mandates the Community to adopt a high level of consumer protection in its attempts to prevent distortions of the common market. It then focuses on four distinct areas of business practice which impact negatively on tourist's commercial interests – package holidays, air delay, timeshare and unfair contract terms – and describes the Community legal responses to these practices, including possible future reforms.

Chapter 8 – Community Competition Policy and Tourism

This chapter describes the vital role played by competition law in ensuring that the competitive benefits of the tourism common market are freely enjoyed. The overarching role of Treaty provisions is firstly described and then the contents of secondary laws are examined. This examination draws on the many tourism cases which have been decided by the Commission. It shows how Community competition law tries to regulate competition among the larger operators by, firstly, either banning anti-competitive agreements or allowing them under conditions if they are globally beneficial; secondly, by prohibiting abusive behaviour by dominant market players; thirdly by monitoring mergers and other concentrating activities which might limit new entrant access to a market or create undue dominance in a market or fix prices. The chapter closes with a brief look at how competition law controls the aids that states can give to tourism enterprises and the dangers this can pose to the common market in tourism services.

Chapter 9 – Environment Policy and Tourism

Through the extensive documentation in the area, this chapter traces how the Community's interest in the negative environmental impacts of tourism has grown in proportion to the extent of those impacts. It outlines the Treaty basis for Community attempts to protect the environment and explains the legal basis for the limited success of Community attempts to deal with the negative environmental impacts of tourism. While much of the huge body of Community environmental law can be of indirect relevance to tourism, the chapter focuses on specific areas that hold particular relevance to tourism – environmental impact assessment, strategic environmental assessment and the conservation of wildlife of European importance.

PRACTICALITIES

The chapter outline above indicates the extent of the book's coverage. The areas covered are chosen not only for their relevance but also because the law impact in each one is particularly significant. As can be seen from the periodic overviews of Community activities affecting tourism[41] published by the Commission, overall Community relevance to tourism is considerably wider than this.

It would not, however, have been feasible to attempt a wider coverage in a text such as this. The balance between the areas to be covered and achieving an appropriate level of coverage means that the book's focus had to be confined to

---

[41] For the most recent see Commission, Report on Community Measure affecting tourism, COM (2000) 3000, 15.3.02 availableathttp://www.europa.eu.int/comm/enterprise/services/tourism/tourism–publications/documents/commmeas_en.pdf . See also Commission, Report on Community measures affecting tourism, COM (2001) 171 final, 28.3.01; Commission, Report on Community measures affecting tourism, COM.(97) 332 final, July 1997; Commission, Staff Working Paper on Community actions affecting tourism, SEC(97) 1419, 11.7.97; Commission, Report on Community measures affecting tourism, COM(94) 74 final, 6.4.94.

areas where Community law goes beyond being a mere vehicle for expressing Community activity affecting tourism and is extensively or significantly used to impact on tourism.

Thus, while Community measures to support small and medium sized enterprisers, tax and fiscal policies, third world development, culture, monetary union and employment, enlargement to mention a number, are important areas of Community activity which have tourism impacts, the particularly law expression of these impacts is not considered to be as extensive as the areas chosen and for this reason are not dealt with.

Presenting the Material

In the age of the internet and an abundance of information about the Community a brief note on how the book is presented. The presentation is not, generally speaking, the typical descriptive/discursive treatment of a topic.

The text consists principally of selected extracts taken from the Community's extensive electronic and paper information resources, supplemented in places by a more descriptive account. These extracts mostly explain the thinking behind particular Community laws and are chosen because they aptly reveal some important dimension of Community law and policy on an issue. The extracts are linked with an informed narrative which helps the sequencing of the topics presented.

Most chapters begin with a short introduction to the overall Community policy treatment of an area and its relationship with tourism. This is followed by an account of how the Community's fundamental law, the Treaty of Rome, deals with the area and how the particular initiatives impacting on tourism can be traced back to relevant Treaty provisions. Thereafter the different law and policy tourism dimensions of the topic are explored through the Community's own resources. Finally, there is a brief chapter conclusion.

For students, a set of learning objectives is set out at the end of the introduction to each chapter to assist in recognising the level of understanding expected after engaging with the material. At the end of each chapter there are a series of questions designed to test student comprehension of the material. The latter require recourse to some of the source material referred to in the text.

The alternative approach to the one adopted is the traditional descriptive and possibly analytical presentation which links into existing academic writing. While very aware of the merits of this approach, the reason it was not adopted is that, after initial exploration, the team of collaborators concluded, such was the richness of legal information on Community tourism and such was the usually uncomplicated language in which it was expressed, a more appropriate approach would be to let the material speak for itself by making extensive use of original extracts and quotes. It is not often it can be done, but here was an instance where readers could form an introductory understanding of an area without the need for a dominant intermediary between the reader and the material. Further, such was the quality of the material that one risked little in terms of critical insight. The Community' institutions adopt robustly independent positions and the material contains much insightful criticism.

A further reason for the predominantly extract-driven approach is that the book seeks to address in the most appropriate manner the considerable under-appreciation of the role and importance of law in the tourism life of the European Community. Few third level institutions offer course modules in European Community tourism law and even fewer non-law academics have sought to develop a perspective on this issue. The emphasis in module delivery often tends to be on the policy side, but at such a general level that little understanding is gained of the central role of law in how the Community operates. Given such a deficit, it was felt the greater initial need is for material that sketches the broad range of the legal dimension and not one that seeks a higher level of critical insight.

Community Websites

Much Community material detailing law and policy aspects of tourism is available in one shape or form on the Community's websites, the addresses of which are provided in the different chapters. The Community's overall website at http://www.europa.eu.int permits ready access to the web homepages of the different institutions, activities and information sources.

The existence of so much material on the Community's websites represents both a challenge and an opportunity and is dealt with as follows.

This book does not reproduce the text of Community laws. This is easily accessed through EUR-LEX at http://europa.eu.int/eur-lex/en/search/index.html.

Where necessary only short extracts are reproduced in this text. Much detail concerning the nature of Community institutions and general policies is also better accessed through the institutions and policies websites.

This book's opportunity lies in the shortcomings of these websites. The tourism website maintained by the Enterprise Directorate General focuses on over viewing recent developments, statistics, publications and broad concerns and does not present a wider or specifically legal perspective on Community involvement in tourism. Other Commission directorates produce more documents of legal relevance to tourism, but these are sometimes available on Community web pages for short periods and thereafter are only accessible in paper form. For some time now the tourism unit has produced helpful and synthesizing documents generally summarising Community activates affecting tourism,[42] but these too are removed after a period. Further, while individual older documents can sometimes be accessed through the Community web pages, much material is only available in paper form. In fact there is no single electronic or paper source which seeks to draw together tourism material from the range of areas covered in this book and present it with a distinct law and policy perspective. This is the opportunity this book seeks to take advantage of.

---

[42] See n.41 above.

Chapter 2

THE TREATY OF ROME AND TOURISM[1]

INTRODUCTION

One cannot overestimate the importance of the Treaty of Rome for European Community involvement in tourism. This Treaty, more formally called the Treaty establishing the European Community, was signed in Rome on March 25, 1957 (hence Treaty of Rome/ Rome Treaty) by the six founder Member States and came into force on January 1, 1958. It has been amended a number of times by other treaties (Singe European Act,[2] Maastricht/Amsterdam/Nice Treaties[3]), each time parts of the original Treaty being removed and new parts inserted.

The Treaty of Rome is an international agreement between sovereign states. Its very first Article created a new type of supranational body.

> By this Treaty, the High Contracting Parties (founder Member States) establish among themselves the EUROPEAN COMMUNITY.

Because the Treaty creates the Community, it follows that it forms the legal basis or source of lawful authority for anything the Community wants to do and further, in the way the Treaty is written, it defines the permitted fields of action for European Community involvement in tourism. Thus, the European Community can only do what the Treaty of Rome says it can do. Understanding the meaning and interpretation of Treaty references to tourism, direct and indirect, explicit and implicit, and the reasoning behind those references and their limitations, and understanding the working principles which have evolved to help the interpretation of the Treaty, is therefore essential for developing an understanding of the unique way the European Community impacts on European tourism. The Community can only be as effective or ineffective in dealing with tourism within the Community as Treaty references permit.

Although tourism is mentioned in the Treaty of Rome, it is not as will be

---

[1] Marc McDonald.
[2] In force since July 1, 1987.
[3] See also p. 2.

seen, a strong reference. The main relevance of the Treaty to tourism lies in its indirect references, that is to references to general aspects of economic activity of which tourism is an important part. The role of the extensive number of indirect references to tourism has been exploited over the years with varying degrees of enthusiasm by Community institutions and received considerable confirmation in a series of decisions by the Court of Justice that have creatively applied Treaty references to tourism activities.

The way the Treaty deals with tourism both directly and indirectly has provoked much controversy over the years. Much of this debate forms part of the wider debate over the role of the Community which plays out against the variable desires of Member States to retain greater power over various activities. Specific debate over the most appropriate role for the Community in tourism (and how that should be expressed in the Treaty) has been spasmodic and inconclusive. Given the complex nature of tourism as simultaneously a business activity, a leisure/recreational activity and an environmental impact and given also the uniquely local nature of most tourism impacts, this is not surprising.

As will be seen, the considerable excitement of the early 1990s gave way to keen disappointment over the failure by the Member States to agree a more dynamic Community involvement in tourism – mediated of course through the Treaty. Community ambition for tourism is currently modest and is seen mainly through indirect activities. All of this is developed further in this chapter.

Tourism and the Treaty of Rome

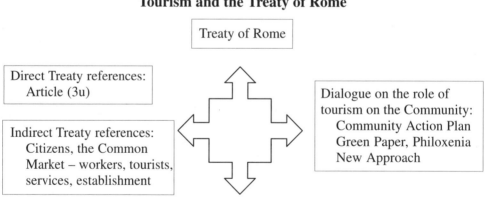

Treaty of Rome

Direct Treaty references:
Article (3u)

Indirect Treaty references:
Citizens, the Common
Market – workers, tourists,
services, establishment

Dialogue on the role of
tourism on the Community:
Community Action Plan
Green Paper, Philoxenia
New Approach

Core Concepts of Community Law:
Competence and subsidiarity,
Ban on Nationalist discrimination,
Proportionality,
Transparency/legal certainty,
Powers to act

Learning Outcomes:

After reading/studying this chapter, the student should:

- understand the central importance of the Treaty of Rome for tourism and how that role operates both directly and indirectly,
- appreciate the role of the Court of Justice in developing the relevance of the Treaty to tourism,
- understand how the common market and the fundamental principles of Community law shape Community measures affecting tourism,
- trace the debate among Community institutions regarding the inclusion of stronger references to tourism in the Treaty.

These learning outcomes will be addressed through the following main headings:

> Treaty References directly related to Tourism.
> Treaty References indirectly related to Tourism.
> Interpretation of Treaty References to Tourism by the Court of Justice.
> Community Dialogue on the role of Tourism in the Treaty.

TREATY REFERENCES DIRECTLY RELATED TO TOURISM

The provisions of the Treaty of Rome are divided into parts, titles, chapters, sections, and articles (where applicable). The importance of any given area for the Community (as opposed to Member States individually) is reflected in how the area is presented within this hierarchy of reference, the actual words used and underlying policy analysis.

The nature of the Treaty (an international agreement between otherwise sovereign states) involves setting:

- ultimate and penultimate/intermediate objectives, the latter being both objective and means for achieving an ultimate objective, like the common market,
- identifying activities or measures which can be undertaken to advance the objectives,
- conferring powers to undertake the activities, and
- identifying the legal basis in the Treaty for decision making as regards the activity or measure.

The European Community has no explicit competence in the field of tourism.

Tourism has neither a chapter nor title of its own in the Treaty of Rome. Nor is it made the subject of a common or other type of policy. Instead it is briefly mentioned in Article 3 (as instead by the Maastricht Treaty) which states:

> For the purposes set out in Article 2 the activities of the Community shall include ... (u) measures in the spheres of energy, civil protection and tourism.[4]

This reference is not generally considered to authorise significant Community action regarding tourism. According to the Commission:[5]

> Article [3u], in which tourism is mentioned in the Treaty for this first time, simply expresses the desirability of extending the activities of the Community to include the spheres of ... tourism for the purpose of achieving the objectives of Article 2. The Community can only take specific action on the basis of Article [308].

The generally expressed objectives set out in Article 2, which are reproduced below, are the ultimate Community objectives, and are economic and social in nature and not tourism specific. This makes it difficult to identify and evaluate actions which can be taken under Article 3u with a view to contributing to Article 2 objectives. Further, as will also be seen, the absence of any specific legal basis in the Treaty for actions taken under Article 3u has given rise to discussion as to what the appropriate general basis for tourism actions is.

The 1992 Maastricht changes to the Treaty of Rome left open the question whether stronger Treaty references might in the future be made to tourism. The Member States agreed (Declaration No 1 to the Maastricht Treaty on European Union which became part of the Rome Treaty):

> The Conference declares that the question of introducing into the Treaty establishing the European Community Titles relating to the spheres referred to in Article 3 [u] of that Treaty will be examined, in accordance with the procedure laid down in Article N (2) of the Treaty on European Union on the basis of a report which the Commission will submit to the Council by 1996 at the latest.

> The Commission declares that Community action in those spheres will be pursued on the basis of the present provisions of the Treaties establishing the European Communities.

---

4 The text of Article 2 is on p. 26.
5 Green Paper on the role of the Union in the Field of Tourism, COM(95)97 final, 14.4.95, p.20.

Article N(2) of the Maastricht Treaty of European Union developed this commitment.

> A conference of representatives of the governments of the Member States shall be convened in 1996 to examine those provisions of this Treaty for which revision is provided.

Such a conference took place in the run up to the Amsterdam Treaty and did not result in any change to the above text. The latter part of this chapter outlines the dialogue within the Community regarding the role of tourism in the Treaty and the Community.

TREATY REFERENCES INDIRECTLY RELATED TO TOURISM

Although the direct reference to tourism in the Treaty is minimal, there are many references in the Treaty which indirectly effect different aspects of tourism. This is because tourism is not an area of social and economic activity separate from others. Rather, in keeping with the economic focus of the Treaty, tourism is an activity which:

- touches the wider vision of the Community (common market, cohesion, subsidiarity, nationality discrimination and proportionality),
- avails of fundamental economic and citizenship pre-requisites (workers, citizens, capital, services including transport), and
- uses important public goods (culture, environment) in a wide range ways.

Since the Treaty of Rome is written in such a way as to be centrally concerned with both the generality and specificity of social and economic life in the Community, Treaty references to these wider issues are vitally relevant to understanding Community competence and involvement in tourism.

Since other chapters in this text focus specifically on some of these areas, it is enough at this stage to briefly explain a number of core Treaty principles or concepts which hugely determine the nature and extent of Community actions affecting tourism. These concepts concern:

- common market and tourism.
- competencies and subsidiarity.
- the ban on nationality discrimination.
- proportionality.
- transparency and legal certainty.
- powers to act.

Common Market and Tourism

Under the Treaty of Rome the three related primary obligations of the European Community are to establish a common market for goods and services, establish an economic and monetary union and implement common policies or activities listed in Articles 3 and 4. These obligations are not ends in themselves but are the primary means of attaining a range of desirable policy objectives set out in Article 2. This Treaty scheme of objectives and obligations can be seen in the way Article 2 is expressed.

> The Community shall have as its task, by establishing a common market and an economic and monetary union and by implementing common policies or activities referred to in Articles 3 and 4, to promote ... a harmonious, balanced and sustainable development of economic activities, a high level of employment and of social protection ... sustainable and non-inflationary growth, a high degree of competitiveness and convergence of economic performance, a high level of protection ... of the quality of the environment ... the raising of the standard of living and quality of life, and economic and social cohesion and solidarity among Member States.

Among the activities listed in Article 3 and elaborated elsewhere in the Treaty of relevance to tourism (examined in more detail in the various chapters in this book) are the internal market[6] dealing with free movement, a common transport policy, a competition system for ensuring competition in the internal market is not distorted, the strengthening of economic and social cohesion, a policy in the sphere of the environment and a contribution to the strengthening of consumer protection.

Elements of the common market

The Treaty of Rome makes clear that the elements of the common market are rights to free movement regarding goods, persons, services and capital. This is elaborated in Title III of the Treaty which lists establishment as a further element of the common market. While free movement for persons as tourists, tourism workers and tourism service providers are crucial elements in the tourism common market and Chapter 3 is devoted to this, the closely related services and establishment freedoms need to be distinguished.

---

[6] The phrase 'internal market' in the Treaty of Rome is connected with the completion of the Common Market in the early 1990s. For convenience this text uses the wider phrase 'common market'.

The freedom to provide tourism services in another Member State involves movement to the other state and the temporary provision of services there. The freedom of establishment involves the freedom to move to another Member State to take up an occupation as a self-employed person on the same terms as a host state resident, regardless of whether the commercial activity takes place inside or outside the Community.

In *Commission v. UK*[7] the Court of Justice held that the UK had failed to comply with its Treaty obligations when it signed an air transport agreement with the US which conferred benefits on UK nationals but not on nationals from other Member States who exercised the establishment freedom in the UK. Even if nationals from other Member States could not rely on the services freedom to fly between the UK and the US (because the services freedom can only operate in the Community) the establishment freedom is different and covers participating in commercial activities on the same footing as local nationals and can thus posses effects which reach beyond the Community.

The essence of the service freedom is temporary presence in the other state which in turn means that state should not make the temporary service provider subject to the same laws as a permanent service provider established there. Otherwise the service freedom is absorbed by the establishment freedom and lost.

In *Commission v. France*[8] a French law obliged anyone wishing to act as a tour guide in certain parts of France to obtain a French licence. This meant the temporary service provider was in fact being treated the same as a person seeking to set up a business in France. The Court of Justice stated:

> In particular, the Member State cannot make the performance of he services in its territory subject to observance of all the conditions required for establishment; were it to do so the provisions securing freedom to provide services would be deprived of all practical effect.

Many tourism activities, such as hotels, involve the provision of services, yet are permanent in nature and can be legitimately made subject to state laws governing the right of establishment. It seems likely (though it has not been the subject of a Court of Justice ruling) that opening a hotel in another state involves

---

[7] Case C–466/98. Judgment delivered on November 5, 2002.
[8] [1991] E.C.R. I–659, 685.

the establishment freedom rather than the service freedom, even though accommodation services are by definition temporary, because the accommodation will be provided on a permanent or at least an indefinite basis.

Obstacles and Distortions

The tourism common market, if one can use that term, much like other markets is not something that was created overnight in 1958 and has remained undisturbed. The legal framework to enable it to operate had to be created and once created it has to be maintained.[9] The Treaty envisaged (reading Articles 2 and 3 together) that creating the common market would mean removing state obstacles to its operation. The key driver of the common market is therefore the removal of obstacles to the free movement of the elements of economic activity.

Two broad approaches are used to remove obstacles to the operation of the tourism common market:

- initial measures to remove national obstacles to entry to controlled tourism activities,
- on-going measures to remove obstacles to the common tourism market as and when they arise.

Initial obstacles

A major thrust of Community measures supporting the tourism common market has been ensuring access to the various tourism markets, particularly passenger transport markets, traditionally controlled by state laws. Chapter 6 on transport recounts how the need to obtain national authorizations to operate transport services in other states has been gradually removed by Community legislation, with the most recent example being the opening of domestic ferry services to operators from other Member States. The opening of national air passenger transport markets to Community competition in 1992 played a major role in stimulating tourist movement in the Community.

---

[9]   A legal framework on its own does not mean that tourists/tourism businesses actually increase their cross–border tourism activities. While the framework has certainly benefited tourists, the picture is less clear for tourism businesses who in many cases still operate within national markets. This is evident both from marketing campaigns which are targeted at nationals of one state only and by Commission competitive analysis in competition cases which confirm that important tourism markets are still predominantly national in character – see p. 353.

On-going obstacles and distortions

The on-going operation of the common market in tourism can be subject to distortion from a variety of sources. New goods and services spurred by technological, environmental or competitive pressures are constantly developing. Governments respond with new legislation which can cause market distortions. If a state law or action or even inaction affects costs borne by tourism competitors based in different markets, it can distort the tourism common market. State aids to industry, different national standards, a new state law enacted with the best of motives, say dealing with the effects of a new technology, can cause distortions. Conversely a failure to make a state law when other states make them can distort trading conditions in a market. Even tangential issues, for example, safety considerations affecting ferry transport can result in a market distortion. If one state ratifies a new international safety convention and another does not, the result is different levels of cost associated with the different safety measures. Operators in the ratifying state may have to bear higher costs than operators in the non-ratifying state. This can distort the market.

All of these pressures and national responses work constantly to disrupt the common market in tourism. Community measures are and will always be required to ensure the common market is maintained. As will be seen, a great deal of new Community law impacting tourism originates from this need.

Removing obstacles

Community law uses either of two approaches to removing obstacles (initial or on-going) to the operation of the common market:

- approximation/harmonisation, that is replacing national rules with Community ones, though often with varying degrees of uniformity, as with package travel or,
- compelling Member States to recognize compliance with services laws in an originating Member State, that is full or part recognition of qualifications/ certificates obtained in another Member State, as with some types of tour guides.

The section in Chapter 6 dealing with air transport shows how the Community has been active in removing obstacles. Other Community policies, such as consumer protection, dictate a higher level of protection than might be available under national policies, thus also favouring approximation. Package travel is one area examined in this book which falls into this category.

Not every distortion of the common market results in a Community law being made to remove it. Whether a Community law is passed depends whether a significant distortion is found and significantly on the political will of a large number of players, particularly in the Council of Ministers. For many years up to the early 1990s many State barriers remained to the operation of the tourism common market. This was due to a lack of agreement within the Council of Ministers on Commission proposals. It was not difficult for states to grandly agree the object of a common market in the Treaty but detailed proposals to give it life was a different matter.

The Treaty itself foresaw this reality by providing for complex rules on voting within the Council of Ministers. Such rules implicitly acknowledge the scope for both action and inaction on proposals to remove obstacles to the operation of the common market.

One area where arguably distortions still remain concerns the common market for hotel services. There are no harmonized rules regarding the minimum legal requirements for operating a hotel and Member States definitions vary. There is no common grading system for hotels across the Member States. This means that a three star in one country might not mean the same in another. Liability rules which decide when a hotel must pay compensation for theft of resident property also vary significantly across Member States. None of these differences has yet provoked Community action presumably because the issue is not considered significant enough and because any proposals might not attract sufficient political support in the Council of Ministers.

External dimension to the common market

The common market has an external as well as an internal dimension. That is, the trading conditions operating internally in the market can be influenced by the external market place. Equally, trading conditions based on internal market rules can be effected by any relevant external market rules, such as may be found in agreements between a Member and non-Member State.

Perhaps the most obvious area in tourism where external conditions influence the internal market concerns air passenger transport into and out of the Community. Passenger flights within the Community by Community airlines are governed by Community rules, but there are no express Community rules governing flights into the Community from outside. Member states have traditionally negotiated separate bilateral deals with non-Member States which set the legal framework for air passenger services between them.

In the mid 1990s a number of Member State negotiated separate but similar 'open skies' agreements with the United States. These considerably liberalized air passenger traffic between the US and the individual Member State, involving many areas, including wider spread of geographic services, and a system of mutual disapproval of air fares. An important element of these agreements permitted drop-off and pick-up at stops before and after the state in question. By concluding a series of these agreements with Member States US carriers were thus able to operate intra-Community flight services, that is fly from one Community airport to another. By definition such agreements were also national in character, that is they allowed each side to ban flights for airlines controlled by nationals of states not party to the agreement.

The Commission consistently opposed such bilateral agreements believing they distorted the operation of the common market in air passenger services which had been created by liberalisation in 1992.

> Liberalisation [the creation of an internal passenger market] has addressed so far only air services within the boundaries of the European Union … there is not yet freedom to provide services between our Member States and countries outside Europe. These routes are still regulated by the traditional system based on bilateral [country to country] agreements. Under such a bilateral agreement, air service between two signatory countries can be operated by airlines that are majority owned and controlled by nationals of those countries … A particularly negative consequence … is that European airlines normally cannot fly to non Member States from any point in the EU but only from the territory of their home Member State. This creates an asymmetry that clearly disadvantages European airlines in comparison to their competitors. … In the view of the Commission 'open skies' agreements constitute a major distortion of the internal market … since they grant 5th freedom rights [rights to pick up and put down on purely internal Community routes] within the Community to US airlines and discriminate between Community carries on ground of nationality. …[10]

In legal proceedings taken by the Commission against a number of Member States,[11] the Court of Justice in 2002 agreed that once a common market rule either governed a market issue or affected non-Union citizens operating in the Community, an individual Member State no longer had a legal competence to make an international rule which covered the same matter, even if the content of both rules was the same. Henceforth only the Community was competent to make external agreements affecting the rule.

The Court examined existing common market rules on passenger air transport to see if the issues they covered were also covered in the bilateral agreements

---

[10] Commission, The European Airline Industry: From Single Market to World–Wide Challenges, COM(1999) 182 final, 20.5.99, p.18.

[11] *Commission v. Denmark*, C–467/98; *Commission v. Sweden*, C–468/98; *Commission v. Finland*, C–469/98; *Commission v. Belgium*, C–471/98; *Commission v. Luxembourg* C–472/98; *Commission v. Austria*, C–475/98; *Commission v. Germany*, C–476/98. Judgment in all cases delivered on November 5, 2002.

which Member States had made with the US. It identified a number of such rules dealing with the setting air fares and the operation of CRSs which also applied to non-Union citizens. The Court concluded in the case of, for example, Denmark that:

> it must be held that , by entering [its open skies agreement with the United States] concerning air fares and rates charged by carriers designated by the United States of America on intra-Community rotes [and] concerning CRSs offered for use or used in Danish territory ... Denmark has failed fulfil its obligations under Article 5 ... of the Treaty ...[12]

The result of these cases is likely to lead ultimately to a Commission brokered approach to passenger air services between the Community and other states, including the US.[13] More generally, they indicate that when the Community makes rules affecting the tourism common market, Member States cannot continue to operate existing or make new agreements with non-Member States which cover the same topics. The key question will be whether sufficiently clear common market rules exist.

COMPETENCIES AND SUBSIDIARITY

When the signatories to the Treaty of Rome established a new supranational body, the European Community, they raised a whole series of new issues regarding their relationship with the new entity and particularly what the new body could do in its own, what it could do acting with the Member States and what is could not do at all. These questions had to be addressed in the Treaty and the way they are dealt with both individually and globally has a vital bearing what the Community can legally do.

Clearly for its core tasks, such as the establishment of the common market, the Community is given exclusive competence to act. This means at least in legal theory the Community does not depend on Member State agreement to act, though if states oppose a proposal in the Council of Ministers (their representative body) it might not be adopted. For other areas competence can be shared in widely varying ways depending on the language used. Contrast the following words in the Treaty:

> The Community shall have as its task ... [Article 2, and] The Council

---

[12] At para. 140. A further ground relating to nationality discrimination is dealt with at p. 38.
[13] Commission, Communication on the consequences of the Court judgments of November 5, 2002 for European transport policy, COM(2002) 649 final, 19.11.02.

may, acting by a qualified majority, decide whether, to what extent and by what procedure appropriate provisions may be laid down for sea and air transport … – Article 80(2).

Given the vague nature of some Treaty provisions and the specific and variable nature of others and the wide scope for differing views as to how far the Community's competence extends, the issue of more precisely dealing with relative competence has over time assumed greater importance in the life of the Community. Tourism as will be seen, has gotten caught up in this.

For areas not exclusively conferred on the Community, subsidiarity is the current explicit concept used in the Treaty for resolving questions of competence. According to Article 5:

> In areas which do not fall within its exclusive competence, the Community shall take action, in accordance with the principle of subsidiarity, only if and insofar as the objectives of the proposed action cannot be sufficiently achieved by the Member States and can therefore, by reason of the scale or effect of the proposed action, be better achieved by the Community.

> Any action by the Community shall not go beyond what is necessary to achieve the objectives of the Treaty.

Direct tourism actions based on Article 3u do not fall within the exclusive competence of the Community. Therefore it is an area of shared competence with the Member States and any actions the Community may wish to take in this area are subject to the subsidiarity principle. As will be seen this has proved a significant impediment to greater direct Community involvement in tourism. Tourism effects are primarily local or regional and on many occasions can to a significant degree be addressed by Member States themselves. Identifying the remaining areas where the scale or effect of proposed actions can be better achieved by the Community is the key challenge the Community constantly faces.

Subsidiarity also has a procedural dimension following from the elaboration of the subsidiarity principle in Protocol 30 to the Amsterdam Treaty:

> For any proposed Community legislation, the reasons on which it is based shall be stated with a view to justifying its compliance with the principles of subsidiarity and proportionality; the reasons for concluding that a Community objective can be better achieved by the Community must be substantiated by qualitative or, wherever possible, quantitative indicators.

Protocol 30 even extends the influence of subsidiarity to the formulation of

Commission proposals for action. According to paragraph 9:

> the Commission should:
>
> > – except in cases of particular urgency ... consult widely before proposing legislation and wherever appropriate publish consultation documents;
> > – justify the relevance of its proposals with regard to the principle of subsidiarity; wherever necessary, the explanatory memorandum accompanying a proposal will give details in this respect ...

Among the consultation steps which can therefore be required are publishing a consultation or green paper, perhaps a white paper, and a follow-up communication, commissioning reports and surveys including a Eurobarometer survey, holding different types of meetings, open meeting/round table/forum. When the Commission states that it 'wants to prepare the ground thoroughly and build consensus before making proposals'[14] we can see not only a pragmatic desire to ensure greater acceptability of its proposal, but also compliance with the Treaty.

Subsidiarity also forces the Commission when it publishes a proposal to raise and answer questions like:[15]

- How are the Proposals related to the Community's obligations?

- Is the Proposal within an area of exclusive Community competence or is competence shared with Member States?

- What is the Community dimension to the problem?

- What is the most effective solution comparing the means of Member States and the Community?

- What would be the cost of inaction by the Community?

- What actions are available to the Community? (recommendations, financial support, legislation etc)

- Which is the most appropriate type of legal measure? – a uniform regulation or a directive setting out general objectives and leaving the detailed execution to the Member States?

---

[14] Commission Memo 02/135, 11.6.02.

[15] As in Proposal for a Council Directive on the effects of certain plans and programmes on the environment, COM(96) 511 final, 4.11.96; Explanatory Memo, pp. 8–11. See also Proposal for a Council Directive on Conditions for the Operation of Regular Ro/Ro Ferries and High Speed Passenger Craft Services in the Community, COM(98) 71 final, 18.2.98.

An example of how a tourism proposal sought to comply with this is to be found in a Commission proposal in 1996 for a multi-annual programme to assist European tourism. In the explanatory memorandum,[16] the Commission rationalised the proposal by claiming it was:

> justified in that Community actions to assist European tourism, in accordance with the principle of subsidiarity, are in the interest of both the European Union and the member States and respond to the expectations of both the industry and the tourist.

> All actions provided for in this proposal have a common denominator: they are not, or cannot be, satisfactorily undertaken at local, regional or national level. In addition they aim to make other Community measures more cohesive. All the actions proposed will give added value.

> The proposal integrates the results of the consultation on the Green Paper …… .

Further attempts to strengthen the influence of the subsidiarity principle seem likely to emerge from the current Convention on the Future of Europe, and may include a formal role for national parliaments to express reasoned opinions on whether proposed measures respect the principle.[17]

Subsidiarity and proportionality are also significant drivers, along with the promotion of competitiveness and sustainable development, of the attempt by the Community to ensure better Community law-making by systemizing improved consultation and impact assessment in the preparation of proposals for Community laws.[18] Systemize means creating a common administrative framework within the Commission of procedures and guidelines for processing proposals for laws. The desire to improve law-making is connected to ensuring greater public acceptability of Community laws and arises from the complexity and wide impact of some Community measures. According to the Commission,[19] 'It will use the consultations and impact assessment ... in order to rally support for its proposals.'

---

[16] Proposal for a Council Decision on a First Multi–annual Programme to Assist European Tourism 'Philoxenia' 1997 – 2000, COM(96) 168 final, 30.4.96, p. 4.

[17] European Convention, Conclusion of Working Group I on the principle of subsidiarity, CONV 286/02, 24.9.02.

[18] Commission, Communication on simplifying and improving the regulatory environment, COM (2001) 726 final, 5.12.01. See also DG Enterprise Working Paper, Business Impact Assessment Pilot Project, Final Report, March 2000.

[19] Commission, Communication on Action Plan 'Simplifying and Improving the Regulatory Environment', COM(2002) 278 final, 5.6.02, p.5.

Ban on Nationality Discrimination

> Within the scope of application of this Treaty, and without prejudice to
> any special provisions contained therein, any discrimination on grounds
> of nationality shall be prohibited – Article 12.

This guiding principle of Community law operates to deny legitimacy to any
Member State (or Community) action which differentiates between nationals
of different states. Both the Commission in its role as guardian of the treaties
and the Court of Justice, as the ultimate authority for deciding issues of
Community law, play important roles in relation to ensuring that nationality
differentiation does not affect tourism activities.

Pricing is one area where the ban on nationality discrimination has relevance
to tourism. Tourists from perceived wealthier states may be charged higher
prices for the same services than local residents. This can happen in the private
or the public sector. Such practises clearly involve nationality discrimination,
though private sector discrimination is more usually controlled by national
legislation.

In 1991 under the heading *Financial Discrimination Against Tourists,* a
Committee of the European Parliament:[20]

> deplored that in some Member States (such as Greece, Italy and Spain)
> there is flagrant discrimination against tourists, who are charged much
> higher prices for certain services (museum visits, for example) than
> nationals of these States. The principle of non-discrimination which is
> one of the foundation stones of the EEC Treaty is totally opposed to
> such practices.

Pricing discrimination can also happen regarding access to public attractions,
in particular museums.

In *Commission v. Spain*[21] the Commission complained to the Court of Justice
about a Spanish law which allowed free entry to public museums in Spain
one day a week to Spanish citizens, Union citizens resident in Spain and all
persons under 21, but all other adults including all other Union citizens had
to pay. The Court of Justice held that:

---

[20] EP, Opinion of the Committee on the Environment, Public Health and Consumer Protection
on Tourism and the Consumer, A3–0155/91/Part B, p.40.
[21] [1994] E.C.R. I–911, 920.

> It follows ... that the Spanish rules on admission to State museums entail discrimination affecting only for foreign tourists over 21 years of age which, for Community nationals, is prohibited ... and ... Spain has thereby failed to comply with its obligations...

> While visiting Venice, a British pensioner noticed he had to pay the full price for admission to the Doge's Palace, whereas Italian pensioners were entitled to a reduction. The Commission agreed that there had been a violation of the Treaty (Articles 49 and 12): freedom to provide services and discrimination on the basis of nationality or residence), and began infringement proceedings against Italy. The Italian authorities undertook to amend relevant national legislation that applies to many state and municipal museums so that reduced admission prices are extended to all EU citizens of pensionable age. This case also opened up the question of reduced prices for other categories of visitors (e.g. students, school children, etc), and the Commission will monitor the revision of the national legislation to ensure that it complies with Community law.[22]

Prohibited discrimination also applies to refusal of entry to a visitor facility based even indirectly on nationality.

> An Irish Petitioner complained that while on holiday in France, he was refused entry to visit a naval base in Brest, while his wife and children of French nationality were not. The facility was advertised in the local tourist office and at the entrance to the base in terms which presented it as a tourist attraction. Entry was refused on the ground that Ireland was not a signatory to the Schengen Convention which deals with the removal of internal border checks within the Community. Since there was no objective link between whether a Member State had agreed to remove internal border controls and entry to a visitor facility at a French naval base, the refusal was based on nationality discrimination. The French authorities have since issued instructions that there should be no discriminatory treatment between Community citizens who wish to visit such establishments and revised arrangements are now in place.[23]

More generally, discrimination on ancillary matters affecting the safety of tourists

---

[22] EP, Committee on Petitions, Petition 922/98.
[23] *Ibid.*, Petition 900/99.

in another Member State is prohibited under the Treaty. For example, if a public scheme to support tourist victims of crime applied only to some tourists from some Member States and not others, that would infringe the Treaty ban. Further, any victim compensation scheme must also avoid nationality discrimination.

> In *Cowan v. Tresor Public*,[24] a British tourist was mugged outside a Paris Metro station by an assailant who escaped. The French criminal injures compensation scheme applied only to persons resident in France. The Court of Justice held that a person protected under Community law as a tourist (recipient of tourism services) was entitled to equal treatment as regard any matters which affected his ability to exercise his freedom to receive tourism services. This included an entitlement to receive compensation if mugged.

Non-Union citizens (third country tourists) are also protected by the ban on nationality discrimination. Article 12 of the Treaty quoted above is not confined to discrimination against Member State nationals. The key words at the start 'Within the scope of this Treaty' indicate that the ban applies to nationality discrimination which obstructs the operation of the common market. Discriminating against third country tourists necessarily involves discrimination against suppliers of tourist services who are thereby prevented from supplying services to such tourists.

In the tourism context this means that public museums or other state visitor attractions, such as a naval base advertised as a visitor attraction, which applies different admission practices or entry conditions to third country tourists may infringe the Treaty.

The principle of equal treatment between citizens of different nationality also applies to the exercise of the services and establishment freedoms in the tourism common market.

> In *Commission v. UK* in 2002[25] the Court of Justice ruled that an international agreement between the US and the UK regarding air passenger services between both states involved nationality discrimination because Community airlines were not treated the same as UK airlines. The agreement allowed the US:
>
> > to revoke, suspend or limit the operating authorizations or technical permission of an airline designated by the United Kingdom but of which

---

[24] [1989] E.C.R. I–907.
[25] Case C–466/98. Judgment delivered on 5.11.02. Similar proceedings were taken against other Member States – see p. 31.

> a substantial part of the ownership and effective control is not vested in that Member State or its nationals ... by contrast, it is clear ... that the United States of America is in principle under an obligation to grant the appropriate authorisations ... to airlines of which substantial part of the ownership and effective control is vested in the United Kingdom or its nationals. ... It follows that Community airlines may always be excluded from the benefit of the [US/UK agreement] while that benefit is always assured to United Kingdom airlines. Consequently, Community airlines suffer discrimination. ...[26]

PROPORTIONALITY

This hugely important principle is frequently cited by the Court of Justice when assessing the compatibility of Member State laws with a provision in the Treaty, a regulation or a directive. It requires that state measures adopted to advance some permitted national object are clearly needed to achieve that goal, go no further than is necessary to go and produce the least restrictive effects.

The principle is also used to guide the lawfulness of administrative decisions taken by Community institutions and indeed the policy justification and lawfulness of Community laws, such as regulations and directives, themselves.

For a legal principle which has become so central to all aspects of Community law it may seen surprising that the Treaty does not as such mandate its application, although it is referred to in the Treaty protocol on subsidiarity. However, it would seem that indirectly the Treaty does warrant its central role in Community law and policy. This is because of the nature of the Treaty and the way it is set out, that is by listing objectives which the Community must pursue. In listing objectives the focus naturally turns to the measures or actions intended to achieve them and critically on the relationship between both, that is whether the measures/actions can be causally and properly linked/related to the objectives.

Thus, in Article 253 the Treaty requires Community laws to identify the reasons on which they are based. This is developed in the Council's Rules of Procedure by a requirement that Community laws must indicate the Treaty and any other relevant provisions on which they are based.[27] Consequently, if a measure cannot logically be adequately related to a Treaty provision, then the measure by definition acts disproportionately and cannot be valid under Community law.

---

[26] *Ibid.*, para. 47.
[27] See p. 82.

Equally, any Member State measure intended to implement a Community regulation or directive or decision, is also (ultimately) trying to implement some Treaty objective. It too can be tested by the policy or rule of proportionality.

> In *Italy v. Commission*[28] Italy sought reversal of a Commission decision prohibiting implementation of an Italian law which sought to move some air passenger traffic from an older Milan airport, Linate to a new one, Malpensa. Acting under the authority of Regulation 2408/92 the Commission decision relied on the disproportionate impact of the Italian law in terms of its greater effects on some air carriers, even though the Regulation did not actually mention the proportionality rule. In rejecting the Italian appeal the Court of Justice upheld the Commission's reliance on the proportionality principle.
>
> > as the Court has held in previous decisions, in interpreting a provision of Community law it is necessary to consider not only its wording but also the context in which it occurs and the objects of the rules of which forms part.
>
> The present context involved dealing with a Member State purporting to use a power of restriction on air carriers freedoms based on a Community regulation based in turn on a Treaty provision. The Court declared that: "In order that such restrictions may be authorised under Regulation No 2408/92, they must be justified and, in particular, proportionate to the purpose for which they were adopted."[29]

TRANSPARENCY AND LEGAL CERTAINTY

Transparency is related to democracy. Citizens develop allegiance to an institution if they can see what it does and how it does it. Thus, Article 255 of the Treaty gives citizens a right of access to Community documents with certain exceptions. From a narrower legal perspective, however, the related principles of transparency and legal certainty require disclosure of the reasoning underlying Community actions. In the case of a decision (by the Commission of Court of Justice/First Instance) it means that the reasons which led to the decision must be fully disclosed so that a person affected by it can have fuller confidence in its

---

[28] [2001] E.C.R. I–385.
[29] For further detail on this case, see p. 202.

correctness and can better decide on a future course of action. In the case of an administrative practice (used by a Community institution) it means that parties potentially affected by the way the institution discharges its duties know the criteria used by the institution in reaching its decisions and can adopt their behaviour accordingly.

This is particularly relevant to Community competition policy and cohesion policy and will be seen in the relevant chapters. In both areas the Commission publishes notices and guidelines indicating how it interprets Community law. This helps applicants/undertakings decide if they satisfy relevant legal criteria or come within some legal exemption. It also helps states decide if they comply with some aspect of Community law, and how calculations required under a Community law should be made.

These principles also govern Member States' implementation of Community law. States can be required to enact a new law to ensure that the Community law is clearly and obviously being applied. Changing a national administrative practice would not be enough.

POWERS FOR ACTIONS TO IMPLEMENT TREATY OBJECTIVES

To understand the importance of the issue of a power to act, it is necessary to firstly address the subtle distinction between Community competence in an area and Community power to act in an area. The general reader might be forgiven for assuming they mean the same thing. If the Treaty says the Community has power to act, that should mean it has authority to act. However, at the risk of causing misunderstanding, the Treaty separates both concepts. The reason it does this is that the power to act has a bearing on the choice of procedure for adopting a measure and crucially on whether qualified majority voting or unanimity among the Member States in the Council of Ministers is required.

This is relevant to tourism in the following way. Article 3u of the Rome Treaty, it will be recalled, only permits direct Community activities in tourism if they advance wider Community objectives set out in Article 2. Article 3u does not, however, contain a power to take the acts it permits. However, this is not unusual. The same happens elsewhere in the Treaty. The Treaty deals with the issue globally in Article 308 (formerly 235) which provides:

> If action by the Community should prove necessary to attain, in the course of the operation of the common market, one of the objectives of the Community and this Treaty has not provided the necessary powers, the Council shall, acting unanimously on a proposal from the Commission and after consulting the European Parliament take the appropriate measures.

In the few tourism-specific measures taken by the Community this provision was expressly relied on. For example, in the Preamble to the Council Decision on a Community action plan to assist tourism in 1992,[30] the Council stated that:

> Having regard to the Treaty establishing the European Economic Community, and in particular Article 235 ... Whereas the Treaty does not provide for any powers for the adoption of this decision other than those mentioned in Article 235...

From a practical point of view Article 235 is a less-than-ideal basis for power to take Community actions affecting tourism since it requires unanimity among the Council. As will be seen unanimity has been impossible to achieve for many tourism actions at Community level.

By contrast, the power to take Community action on a proposal that indirectly affects tourism, though the tourism impact may nonetheless be significant, is often made explicit in the relevant Treaty provision. Such provisions often make clear that the exercise of this power does not require unanimity among Council members. This is particularly true of Community measures to create and safeguard the common market, many of which impinge on tourism. Much of the power to take measures to achieve the internal market is set out in Article 95(1) (formerly 100a) which states:

> The Council shall, acting in accordance with the procedure referred to in Article 251 and after consulting the Economic and Social Committee, adopt the measures for the approximation of the provisions laid down by law, regulation or administrative action in Member States which have as their object the establishment and functioning of the internal market.

The decision-making procedure set out in Article 251 requires the Council to act by qualified majority only.

The Article 95 power was used in the Council Directive on Package Holidays,[31] the Preamble to which recites:

> Having regard to the Treaty establishing the European Economic Community, and in particular Article 100a thereof ...

> Whereas one of the main objectives of the Community is to complete the internal market, of which the tourist sector is an essential part ...

---

[30] OJ L 231/26, 13.8.92.
[31] OJ L 158/159, 13.6.90.

Whereas the establishment of common rules on packages will contribute to the elimination of … obstacles and thereby to the achievement of a common market in services …

INTERPRETATION OF TREATY REFERENCES TO TOURISM BY THE COURT OF JUSTICE

The direct and indirect references in the Treaty establishing the European Community (Treaty of Rome) to tourism recited above form the legal basis of actions by Community institutions when exercising their functions under the Treaty.

Many of these references merely identify in wide terms the areas of Community competence, and provide appropriate powers to act, but only rarely indicate that the Community must act. The realm or scope for discretion for interpretation and actions by the law and policy making institutions of the Community is therefore very wide. If the political will particularly among Member States for activities in any given area is not strong then no specific proposal or measure will emerge. From the range of measures and policies outlined in the various chapters of this book, it will be seen that the Community has been active in adopting measures and laws relevant to tourism

However, the responsibility for furthering economic integration within the Community does not rest solely with the law and policy making institutions (Parliament, Council, Commission) of the Community. Under the Treaty (and discussed further in Chapter 3), a specific Community institution, the Court of Justice, is given ultimate power for determining the meaning and relevance of Treaty references to tourism (and indeed all other references and Community laws).

On two broad fronts the Court interprets Community law with the possibility that its decisions can expand or limit the relevance of the Treaty and its secondary laws to tourism. The first one, which is of immediate concern in this chapter, arises when interpreting the Treaty itself and the second which will be seen in the other chapters arises when interpreting the Community's secondary laws in ways which determine their relevance to tourism. Once the court rules a Treaty provision has a particular meaning or application, that interpretation becomes binding on all.

So far Court of Justice rulings have been important in widening the relevance of the Treaty to tourism. These rulings were made without reliance on the reference to tourism in Article 3u. The Court's interpretations have focused principally on Article 49 and on two specific issues arising from this – the tourism service provider's freedom to provide services and the protection of tourists who travel to another Member State to receive tourism services. These have resulted in a variety of national restrictions affecting tourist service providers and tourists being declared incompatible with Community law. In reaching its decisions the Court of Justice relied on the principle of proportionality, which, it will be recalled, requires, among other things, that Member State restrictions on Community freedoms must be a proportionate means of advancing some legitimate national policy, and also on the ban on nationality discrimination.

Tourism Service Providers

The principal case law illustration of the application of Article 49 to tourism is found in the tour guide cases, a series of Treaty infringement proceedings taken by the European Commission against France, Italy and Greece[32] respectively; similar proceedings were taken against Spain [33] over similar requirements in national law which required tour guides accompanying foreign tours to possess a local licence to act as a guide. In each case using similar language the Court of Justice upheld the Commission complaint that the national rules infringed the right to provide services guaranteed in Article 59 of the Treaty, that is the national rule wrongfully denied a Community freedom. [34]

Tourists

The freedom of Community citizens to act as tourists has been held deductively to lie within Article 49 and thus within the scope of the Treaty of Rome. The Court of Justice reached this important conclusion in 1984 in an Italian case, *Luisi and Carbone v. Ministero del Tesoro.*[35] The Court focused on the logical corollaries of the protection of service providers in Article 49 and concluded:[36]

> It follows that the freedom to provide services includes the freedom, for the recipients of services, to go to another Member-State in order to receive a service there, without being obstructed by restrictions … and that tourists … are to be regarded as recipients of services.

Since this pronouncement the Court of Justice has relied on this reasoning in three cases to declare various national restrictions that affected tourist movement

---

[32] [1991] E.C.R. I– 659, 709, 727.
[33] *Commission v. Spain* [1999] E.C.R. I–923.
[34] Discussed further at p. 170.
[35] [1984] E.C.R. 377.
[36] *Ibid.*, p.403.

incompatible with Community law. These restriction related to criminal injures compensation schemes, entry to museums and life expulsion of a tourist from another Member State. These cases are more fully explored in Chapter 3 dealing with the free movement of tourists and tourism workers.

COMMUNITY DIALOGUE ON THE ROLE OF TOURISM IN THE TREATY

Between 1958 and 1992, despite the absence of any reference to tourism in the Treaty, the European Community adopted many legal and other measures centrally or significantly affecting tourism. This was done on the basis of Treaty references to other dimensions of economic activity (highlighted above). A 39 point list of Community measures affecting tourism was set out in 1984 in an Annex to the Initial Guidelines for a Community Policy on Tourism.[37]

During the 1980s and into the mid-1990s the increasing economic and other impacts of tourism in the Community and a fear that insufficient account was being taken of tourism in the formation of other Community policies lead to demands for the inclusion of stronger references to tourism in the Treaty and thus a widening of Community competence and responsibility in this area. The Commission and the Council were lukewarm about these demands, while Parliament, the Economic and Social Committee and more latterly the Committee of the Regions were generally in favour.

Dialogue among Community institutions about direct competence in tourism centres around five main events:

- a Community policy on tourism in 1982.
- a Community Action Plan to assist tourism in 1992.
- the first and only mention of tourism in the Treaty in 1992.
- the Commission Green Paper on the role of tourism in the Community in 1995 and the attempt to strengthen the Treaty reference to tourism.
- the proposed Philoxenia programme in 1996.

Dialogue grew more intense in the early and mid-1990s due to ultimately unsuccessful attempts to secure stronger Treaty references to tourism. In this respect, events since Philoxenia are only of slight relevance since debate has largely died away.

The constant key element in Community dialogue regarding strengthened Treaty references to tourism has been identifying and assessing the extra

---

[37] OJ C 115/27, 30.4.84.

dimension or added value which greater Community involvement in tourism might bring. Underlying this has been a search for consensus on the appropriate Community, governmental and private sector levels at which different tourism issues should best be addressed. The minimum realm of uncontested activity has embraced:

- improved tourism information,
- greater exchanges among, and improved consultation/co-ordination between Commission departments whose activities impinge on tourism and,
- greater evaluation of Community actions.

Beyond this the Member States divided between those for whom tourism is economically important, that is suppliers of the product, and those who primarily provide the tourists.

The following account of the dialogue between the institutions focuses merely on the general role of the Community in tourism and the Treaty. It is important to note that it is not intended either as a general account of Community policy towards tourism or as an account of policy developments in specific areas like regional development, environment, consumer protection etc which are dealt with in the different chapters.

Getting Interested in Tourism

The initial question which Community commentary on tourism had to address was whether tourism was even an issue of Community competence and concern. In its first dedicated commentary on tourism in the Community in 1982,[38] before the word tourism was inserted into the Treaty in 1992, the Commission identified[39] the indirect relevance of Treaty provisions to tourism:

> Article 2 of the Treaty of Rome assigns to the European Community the task of promoting closer relations between the States which belong to it. Tourism can assist the Community to achieve this goal and, by bringing the peoples of Europe into contact, it buttresses the edifice of European integration.
>
> Tourism is also an important economic activity in the spirit of Article 2 of the Treaty. It provides jobs for 4 million people in the Community and its indirect effect on employment is considerably greater. It contributes to

---

[38] Commission, Communication on initial Guidelines for a Community Policy on Tourism COM(82) 385 final, 1.7.82; OJ C 115/2, 30.4.84.
[39] *Ibid.*, p.1.

balance of payments stability between the northern European peoples and those of the south and assists in the development of the poorest regions of the Community. Special attention should therefore be paid to promoting its harmonious development through out the Community.

A further measure of the importance of tourism to the Community is the large number of Community policies which, directly or indirectly, have a bearing on it. These range from the free movement of persons and the freedom to provide tourist services, through passenger transport to regional development and the protection of the environment. To give further stimulation to tourism within the Community, a 'tourist dimension' should be given to these so that the needs of tourism are taken into account when decisions are taken and Community actions implemented.

The Council of Ministers responded in 1984[40] by also acknowledging the role which tourism can play in achieving the Community objectives set out in Article 2 and declared:[41]

tourism is an important activity for the integration of Europe and affects or is affected by many of the Community's activities,

The Council welcomed:

the Commission's initiative in drawing attention to the importance of tourism ... and emphasizes the need for the tourist dimension to be taken more fully into consideration in the Community' decision-making process and the need for consultation between the Member States and the Commission on matters relating to tourism and invites the Commission to present proposals to it in the field of tourism ... respecting the peculiarities of the national policies. ...[42]

Pursuant to this the Council established by Decision 86/664[43] an advisory committee to be serviced by the Commission to facilitate exchange of information, consultation and co-operation on tourism matters among Member States. In the Preamble to its Decision after citing Article 2 of the Treaty and its list of objectives and noting that tourism "can help achieve these objectives", the Council declared:

---

[40] Resolution on a Community policy of tourism in 1984, OJ C 115/1, 30.4.84.

[41] *Supra.*

[42] *Supra.*

[43] Council Decision 86/664 Establishing a Consultation and Co–operation Procedure in the Field of Tourism, OJ L 384/52, 31.12.86.

consultation is a useful means of facilitating cooperation between the Member States and the Commission with a view to achieving the objectives of the Treaty.

From the outset the Commission adopted a realistic, perhaps unduly realistic, view of what could be done regarding tourism at Community level. In its 1982 commentary[44] when it sought to map out what was possible by reference to what had been done indirectly before then, the Commission showed an early awareness of the limits of potential Community action.

> The main responsibility for tourism lies with the Member States. The past twenty years have shown that both the public and the private sectors of the economy in the Member States have succeeded in adopting themselves to a tourism whose expectations have grown in line with its numbers. While it is true that the existence of the Community has given them a favourable context which it could improve still further by adopting a number of common rules and by better coordination of its activities in the field of tourism, it should not go too far in seeking to coordinate national policies because each of these reflects the very different situations of the Member States. Nor should it try to solve problems that could better be dealt with at national or even regional level.[45]

Both the Economic and Social Committee (ESC) and Parliament were unhappy with the narrow scope of the Commission's ambition, though they welcomed the signs of interest. The Economic and Social Committee[46] after noting that:

> the Commission's intention is not to replace national policies but to pinpoint a number of priorities in certain spheres on which action might be proposed.

went on to admonish the Commission over its narrow ambition:

> there is no need for reticence in presenting the Council with recommendations over and above those envisaged in the Guidelines. ...The Committee in fact considers that in view of the extensive range of activities which tourism covers, the Guidelines could give a significant political impetus to the achievement of an authentic Community internal market.[47]

---

[44] Commission, Communication on Initial Guidelines for Community Policy on Tourism, COM(82) 385 final, 1.7.82.

[45] *Ibid.*, p.11.

[46] ESC, Opinion on the Initial Guidelines for a Community Policy on Tourism, CES (84) 4, 26.10.83.

[47] At p.1.

Parliament for its part emphasised the importance of tourism for the individual and society as a whole, and in its first specific resolution on tourism[48] grandly declared its support for:

> the principle of promoting tourism through Community measures within the framework of a global Community policy.

As Community interest in tourism increased during the mid-1980s, Community ministers for tourism and the Commission began holding regular informal meetings in order to exchange information on tourism policy and discuss approaches to Community action, though the first formal meting of tourism ministers only took place in December 1988. A specific budget for tourism spending only became available to the Commission from 1986 due to pressure from Parliament. A Parliament resolution in 1987 which lead to 1990 being declared European Year of Tourism, noted the large range of mainly indirect Community actions affecting tourism and recognised:[49]

> with satisfaction that tourism is finally developing into an area of Community policy as a basis for further and specific Community action.

Within Parliament there were greater and lesser degrees of impatience with the slow progress towards a consistent Community approach to tourism. In an Opinion in 1991 one Committee outlined, as it saw it, the consequences of a lack of a focused Community involvement in tourism:[50]

> Hitherto the growth of tourism has been left to the natural course of events, the interplay of economic forces and often only to speculation. This has led to distortion in the development of the sector, accompanied by an increasing concentration of tourism in certain geographic areas and during certain periods, serious shortcomings in facilities (in particular water supply, sewage and depuration plants, health services, transport and road conditions), and blatant damage to and even out-and out attacks on the land and the artistic and historical heritage, which has in too many cases fallen into neglect. This has given rise to a discrepancy between the quantity and the quality of tourism and the amount of attention devoted to the legislative and administrative problems involved in proper management of the problem.

---

[48] Resolution on Community Policy on Tourism, OJ C 10/282, 16.1.84.

[49] EP, Resolution on Facilitation, Promotion and Funding of Tourism in the European Community, OJ C 49/159, 22.1.88.

[50] EP, Opinion of the Committee on Social Affairs, Employment and the Working Environment on the social aspects of tourism, A3–0155/91/Part B, p.29.

In another resolution in 1991 Parliament[51] drew attention to the wide range of Community involvement in tourism both directly and indirectly and to the need for a fundamental examination of the Community's role:

> the radical changes in the external and internal environment of the European Community should prompt a re-examination of the Community 's policy for tourism and the development of tourism into a major sphere of Community activity ... the European Year of Tourism should be the starting point for this intensive examination of the current policy of the Community's tourism policy and for its development into a major field of the Community' activities.[52]

In the lead-up to the Maastricht Treaty, Parliament boldly called:

> on the Intergovernmental Conference on Political Union to consider immediately the incorporation *expressis verbis* of tourism into the Treaties as an essential flanking policy for the creation of Economic and Monetary Union, even if the rules governing the free movement of persons, goods, services and capital in the internal market also embrace tourism.[53]

Action Plan to Assist Tourism

In response to the build up of interest in a more focused Community approach to tourism the Commission produced a proposal in 1991 for a decision on a Community action plan to assist tourism.[54] The ambition of the proposal lay in the use of existing Community competences in tourism through limited direct measures. It was a modest way of showing what the Community could do without antagonising those with reservations.

> In defining these measures and the ways of implementing them, the Commission will fully respect the principles of subsidiarity; its priority role will be to coordinate national policies and actions and initiate new measures, mainly on the basis of exchanges and the demonstration of innovatory practises. ...[55]

The Commission also noted that: "The Member States themselves attach varying

---

[51] EP, Resolution on a Community Tourism Policy, OJ C 183/74, 15.7.91.

[52] *Ibid.*, p.75.

[53] *Ibid.*, p.78.

[54] Commission, Community Action Plan to assist Tourism, COM(91) 97 final, 24.4.91.

[55] *Ibid.*, p.2.

importance to tourism in the context of their economic and social development".[56]

In a commentary[57] on the Commission's proposal the Economic and Social Committee expressed disappointment at its narrow ambition and even attributed some of the problems of European tourism to the limited Community approach.

> The Community has hesitated in preparing and adopting a tourism policy which can (a) establish a basic reference framework and (b) provide guidelines for, in particular, the application of other sectoral policies and regional development; this hesitation has proved damaging for balanced development in this sector. ... The drop in quality of tourism and the over concentration of tourists in some areas ... together with environmental damage particularly in the coastal and mountain areas .... are all explained to a considerable extent by (a) a wide spread lack of knowledge of the features and requirements of tourism and (b) the lack of self-regulating mechanisms. ...

> The Committee endorses the proposed measures but feels that they are insufficient   and doubts their effective capacity to respond to the sector's needs or contribute significantly to removing the negative factors affecting European tourism. ... Hitherto, Community action on tourism has resulted almost solely from measures introduced under other policies or aimed at other sectors, which have a knock-on beneficial effect on tourism. It is true that tourism's increasingly close links with other activities means that measures for developing these other activities in the end also benefit tourism. However, tourism has now assumed an importance and scale that warrant separate treatment. Tourism must be given the status of a fully fledged policy, being both autonomous and complementary to other policies, particularly environment, regional development, employment, culture and transport. ... For this reason it is vital that, when the Treaty of Rome is next revised, express reference be made to tourism.[58]

In 1992 the Member States did take notice of the increasing importance of tourism in the Community. As already indicated, in the Maastricht Treaty they agreed a new reference to tourism in the Rome Treaty, but it was probably the minimum of what might have been hoped for and did no more than make explicit what was happening anyway.

---

[56] *Ibid.*, p.3.
[57] ESC, Opinion on the Community Action Plan to Assist Tourism, OJ C 49/43, 24.2.92.
[58] *Ibid.*, p.45.

When the Council of Ministers approved the Commission's proposed Action Plan[59] also in 1992 it did so in language which indicated the Council's satisfaction with the Commission's view of the limited role of the Community in tourism under the Treaty.

> Community action regarding tourism should take the form of a strengthening of the horizontal approach to tourism in the Community and national policies, and of the implementation of specific measures .. that approach should also include coordination of the measures undertaken by Commission departments which affect tourism. ...

> Measures to be implemented under the action plan must comply with certain criteria in particular the need to comply with the subsidiarity principle [60]

Half way through the Action Plan in 1994, the Economic and Social Committee[61] in a wide ranging commentary linked the narrow scope of the Action Plan with the local nature of tourism and the limited reference to tourism in the Treaty. However, it welcomed the wider 'horizontal' approach of the Plan, in which all Community actions affecting tourism and not just direct measures are deemed relevant.

> When expressing a view on Community policy for the tourist industry one must always bear in mind that the primary responsibility – including that for taking any initiatives in this important economic sector – lies at national or local level, depending on the set-up in the Member States. It is for this reason too that the Community has only limited powers in the area and that the Commission has been burdened with a highly limited mandate by the Council in the action programme. As a result, only a very limited budget is available directly for tourism policy and so the Tourism Department within DG XXIII is very limited in scope.[62]

> Its 'horizontal' approach means that the interests of the industry and those of the consumer are to become an integral part of the decision-making process in all relevant policy areas. The economic, social and cultural importance of tourism makes such integration both desirable and right in every way. ... The [first Commission report on the implementation of the 1992 Action Plan] of April 1994 on Community measures affecting tourism

---

[59] Council Decision 94/421 on a Community Plan to Assist Tourism OJ L 231/26, 13.8.92.
[60] *Supra.*
[61] ESC, Opinion on Tourism, CES (94) 1021, 15.9.94.
[62] *Ibid.*, p.2.

continues this line. It reports on activities in policy areas outside the direct scope of the action programme where Community measures or financial resources geared to tourism are applied. But the ESC thinks that the common tread is too often missing. It sees one prime cause for this: the lack of an adequate legal basis in the Treaty for a full-blown Community tourism policy.

6. From a horizontal and specific tourism policy to an express basis for a treaty.

In [its 1991 Opinion] the ESC said that tourism should be given a proper place of its own in a future revision of the Treaty of Rome.

The Treaty of Maastricht has been a disappointment in this respect as tourism has been given only a very limited place – Article3[u] – is one of the EU's fields of activity … which is totally out of keeping with the sector's actual and potential importance to economic development. As well as this prosperity aspect, one must not overlook the welfare aspect which is so characteristic of the tourism industry.

The European parliament has also spoke out on this matter. It calls upon the Commission to draw up a White Paper on how tourism policy can best be incorporated into the European Union Treaty when that Treaty is next amended … It may be thought extremely useful to give right now the political signal that is needed if a place is to be found for a tourism policy in a future treaty.[63]

Further criticism of the Action Plan was made by an external evaluator in 1996 who cited fragmented measures, confusion between objectives and measures, overlapping measures, over ambition given limited resources, lack of continuity over the period. In accepting these criticisms[64] the Commission linked some of the failings cited by the evaluator to the clash of views over tourism policy and the lack of clear guidance at Treaty level as to what the purpose of Community action in tourism should be.

The Commission broadly agrees with these criticisms. The Commission views the Plan however as the outcome of a long discussion which resulted in a number of competing priorities. Tourism policy as such does not exist

---

[63] *Ibid.*, p.9.
[64] Commission, Report of the evaluation of the Community Action Plan to assist tourism 1993–95, COM (96) final, 30.4.96.

and a specific tourism 'strategy' at EU level is at a formative stage. The differing views and priorities of the member States; the complex nature of the different interests associated with tourism; the lack of previous specific actions at EU level; the subsidiarity principle; and the requirement for unanimity within the Council all served to shape the Plan. [65]

Lead-up to 1996 IGC

Dialogue on the role of tourism in the Community and the Treaty quickened in the run up to the 1996 intergovernmental conference (IGC) on treaty revision and the obligation imposed by Declaration No. 1 to the Maastricht Treaty on the Commission to produce a report on a possible treaty title on tourism.

Research commissioned by Parliament[66] took a cautious and ultimately prophetic view of the possibilities. After outlining the arguments in favour of an EC tourism policy, the report dealt with arguments against such a policy.

> most EC Member States are essentially strong competitors in the tourism field and it can be argued that a coherent and effective policy framework which takes account of subsequent rivalries would be very difficult to conceive.[67]

Further,

> The most powerful arguments against a more developed EC tourism policy centres on the sector's 'diffuseness' across policy areas (i.e. transport, environment, taxation etc) and diversity of the tourism industry across Member States. The core of these arguments, which suggest strong roles for Member Sates national tourism authorities and for individual specialised inputs from relevant DGs, is valid. An effective and workable EC tourism policy requires these roles to be 'integrated' into an overall framework, while simultaneously ensuring that boundaries and responsibilities are clearly recognised and defined.[68]

However, the Community could still have a role, "provided this role is well-defined and very carefully constructed". According to the Report:

---

[65] *Ibid.*, p.2.
[66] EP, Working Paper, the Role of the Community in regard to Tourism and Regional development, Regional Policy Series, October 1993.
[67] *Ibid.*, p.111.
[68] *Ibid.*, p.112.

there is scope to develop an EC 'Tourism Policy Framework'. Such a framework would largely maintain the status quo in that the bulk of policy decisions … are taken at Member State regional level. There are a number of reasons for preferring a loose policy 'framework' over the establishment of a fully detailed EC tourism policy. Firstly, in this period of 'subsidiarity' the policy mood in the Community is to avoid over-centralisation. Secondly, tourism is a fast changing industry in which policy is best viewed as on-going concept. Thirdly, reflecting the diversity of the industry, a 'common' tourism policy covering the sector in all Member States is unrealistic. [69]

Despite the cautious note struck about Community involvement in tourism, Parliament itself continued in early 1995 to demand a stronger Treaty reference:

The forthcoming revision of the Treaty on European Union cannot postpone consolidation of a Community policy in tourism and … this must be embraced wholeheartedly.

and called:

for the forthcoming revisions of the Treaty on European Union in 1996, whilst abiding by the principle of subsidiarity, to include a specific title on tourism containing a specific, multidisciplinary and multidimensional European tourism policy which incorporates and constitutes environmental, economic, social, employment and cultural criteria in its planning.[70]

COMMISSION GREEN PAPER ON THE ROLE OF THE UNION IN THE FIELD OF TOURISM

Two reasons lead the Commission in 1995 to produce a discussion document, Green Paper on the role of the Union in the field of tourism.[71] The first is that under the Amsterdam Treaty the Commission was obliged to prepare a report for the intergovernmental conference to decide whether to include a title on tourism in the Rome Treaty. The second was the need, resulting from the subsidiarity principle, to focus debate, in advance of any possible Treaty revision, on a clearly identified role for the Community in specific tourism matters.

---

[69] *Ibid.*, p.113.
[70] EP, Resolution on the Report from the Commission on Community Measures Affecting Tourism, OJ C 18/160, 23.1.95.
[71] COM(95) 97 final, 4.4.95.

The Green Paper was divided in three sections – reviewing previous Community actions affecting tourism, identifying the added value in policy terms which Community involvement in tourism could bring, and finally and crucially suggesting future options for Community involvement in tourism. Only the second and third sections are of relevance here.

The Green Paper firstly sought to explain why tourism had not previously been accorded more recognition under the Treaty:

> as a result of the complex nature of the field of activity which the notion of tourism encompasses, the diversity of national approaches and the interaction of tourism and numerous other Community policies, the Treaty does not enter into the same degree of detail as regards specific objectives and implementation procedures for Community measures in the field of tourism as it does, for example, with … culture … or … consumer protection.[72]

Yet the Treaty remained central. Under the heading *A RESPONSE TO THE OBJECTIVES SET OUT IN THE TREATY ON EUROPEAN UNION*, the Commission noted the central role of Article 2 of the Treaty in defining the Community's basic objectives, including promoting economic and social progress and also economic and social cohesion, and linked it into Article 3u.

> The extension of the Community's responsibilities to tourism in Article 3[u] thus makes explicit the measures already carried out to assist tourism under the various Community policies for attaining *the objectives of the Treaty.*[73]

The Commission then catalogued how tourism serves other Treaty goals, such as:

– reducing the differences between levels of development in the various regions:

> Tourism can assist in bringing about a better distribution of activities and jobs in the Union, thus contributing to the desirable aim of redressing the imbalance between the regions in the Community. …

– promoting sustainable and non-inflationary growth respecting the environment. The very nature of tourism with its reliance on public

---

[72] *Ibid.,* p.3.
[73] *Ibid.,* p.12.

goods such as landscapes, culture, heritage, leisure faculties, transport infrastructure means that:

> tourism is a field of action ready-made for implementing sustainable development[74]

– promoting integration through Article 6 (formerly 130, r (2)) which insists that:

> environmental protection requirements must be integrated into the definition and implementation of other Union policies.[75]

– promoting European identity and citizenship:

The exercise of [Union] citizenship is defined by a certain number of rights, one of the foremost being that of moving and travelling freely within the territory of the Member States of the Union ... In the case of the majority of European citizens, this right of abode and freedom of movement will be exercised in the context of tourism... In the context of this search for ways of establishing the meaning of citizenship as instituted by the Treaty, tourism is an area which should be explored....[76]

– contributing to the management of structural and technological change and the development of small and medium sized enterprises:

> The Community could also help businesses adapt to structural and technological change by promoting the creation of a legislative and administrative environment likely to promote the development of tourist demand or stimulate adaptation to changes in supply.[77]

But the greatest challenge facing greater Community involvement in tourism (and any Treaty reference) arose from the varying needs of the different actors in tourism:

> Real awareness of the equal value of the three dimensions of tourism [enterprise growth, tourist satisfaction and heritage protection] and of the need to offer combined responses requires the active involvement of all the players concerned. ... However, it is hard to see how such involvement can be provoked or stimulated if Community action does not have a high

---

[74] *Ibid.*, p.14.
[75] *Supra.*
[76] *Ibid.*, p.15.
[77] *Ibid.*, p.17.

profile. ... Clearly, a number of policies and measures implemented by the Member States or the Community already contribute, at different levels, to satisfying certain of the interest represented in tourism. However, more often than not, this happens in a fragmented fashion, and this can be an obstacle to the balanced and sustainable growth of tourism. ... Member States' responses to the complexity of the interests at stake in tourism seem to vary, depending on whether the country is principally a sender/generator or receiver/beneficiary of tourist flows. Taking the Union as a whole, this is often characterised by a North/South divide.[78]

The four options listed in the Commission Green Paper were doing nothing, continuing or increasing present levels of activity (both under the Treaty provisions) and creating a new Community tourism policy.[79]

Option 1

I. Reducing or Eliminating Specific Community Actions

Since the three poles around which the interests of tourism can be said to revolve are served by existing Community policies, one possible option would be to rule out from the start any specific action as regards tourism. It could, in other words, be argued that the field of tourism is sufficiently or even fully covered by individual measures which, although scattered, have proved to be reasonably effective. ... Action to develop tourism in the Community could, then, be envisaged independently of a specific coordinating exercise, simply through proper application of existing policies designed to meet broader objectives or to cater for areas other than tourism

   Given the lack of a suitable framework, a comparison of practises at the various levels (Community, national, regional and local) and an exchange of best results would obviously not be feasible under this option.

Option 2

II. Retaining the Current Framework and Level of Intervention

The lack of a specific basis for tourism in the Treaty establishing the European Community did not prevent the Commission from presenting and the Council from approving, under Article 235 [now 308], a Community Action Plan to assist tourism, once a number of measures had been identified.

---

[78] *Ibid.*, p.18.
[79] *Ibid.*, pp. 19–22.

... The Community Action Plan of July 1992 is positive in that it provides a base for organising cooperation between Member States and stimulating dialogue with industry and the sectors concerned... The active participation of all the Member States in the actions tested as part of the plan has ... given a real indication of the advantages of transnational cooperation as a tool for tourism growth and European integration. Since effective dialogue between all the parties concerned and at the various administrative levels ... is seen as the backbone of an effective Community plan, the actions provided for are founded on cooperation between different operational administrative levels, without interfering with the latter's own powers of initiative...This is mainly a matter of facilitating the comparison of national and regional tourism initiatives with the aim of encouraging exchanges and common actions. ...

Option 3

III. Strengthening Community Action Via The Existing Treaty

[The Community Action Plan to assist tourism in 1992] was not sufficient to ensure that the full potential of tourism and related actions was harnessed to the benefit of the Union's measures.... One possible response to this insufficiency might perhaps be to strengthen existing measures with an impact on tourism .. and to increase the funding allocated to them. ...

The Community could, within the framework of the Treaty, increase its support for efforts to achieve greater growth and competitiveness in the tourist industry, assist in improving the safety and well-being of tourists and, finally, accord priority to encouraging the protection and proper use of the natural and cultural heritage ....

Option 4

IV. Towards a Community Tourism Policy?

The question of increased Community intervention to assist tourism has been raised on a number of occasions over the past few years. The demand for such intervention itself raises the following questions. Could the Community play the part of information disseminator and act as an interface between the Union and the various parties concerned ... thus allowing the Member States to consult each other in liaison with the Commission and, where necessary, to coordinate their actions with a view to balancing the diverse interests at play in the field of tourism? If it could indeed play such a part, the Commission could also take any initiative it considered useful in promoting this coordination.

> It is also possible to envisage a Community policy, complementary to the policies of the Member States, which could be drawn upon in defining the other Community actions with a potential impact on tourism. Would a Community policy along these lines generate a demonstrable Community response able to meet the need for balanced conservation of the triads of interests underlying tourism and for the integration of these interests in a logic of sustainable development?

Only Options 1 and 4 would have involved changing the Treaty, the former by removing the word tourism and the latter probably by inserting a new title on tourism.

ESC Response

In line with its previous enthusiasm for a stronger Community policy the ESC favoured the fourth option. In an Opinion on the Green Paper,[80] it firstly reiterated its views about the inadequate way the Treaty of Rome dealt with tourism.

> The inadequacy of the present treaty on this subject arises not only from the lack of a legal basis, but also from the fact that the Treaty does not clarify either the specific objectives or the implementing procedures for Community measures in the tourism sector. ... Once again the European Parliament ... and the Economic and Social Committee ... have deplored this state of affairs, stressing the need for tourism be given the full status of a Community policy at the forthcoming Intergovernmental Conference.[81]

The Committee specifically rejected an approach based merely on better integration of tourism into existing Community activities.

> The incorporation of tourism in other Community programmes and policies is a necessary, but not a sufficient, condition; it does not necessarily comply with the logic of overall development of tourism to develop all its potentialities fully, as the ESC and the European Parliament have frequently stressed.[82]

Commenting in turn[83] on each of the four Options identified in the Commission's Green Paper, the ESC thought the First one excludes:

---

[80] ESC, Opinion on the Commission Green Paper, CES 976/95, 14.9.95.
[81] *Ibid.*, p.2.
[82] *Ibid.*, p.4.
[83] *Ibid.*, pp.9–11.

any form of coordination since there would be no specific reference framework for tourism.

The Second Option was not much better since it:

entails maintenance of the current framework and level of intervention … and thus leaves unresolved the question of the Commission's political authority in the field of tourism … and limits the aims and scope of co-operation.

The Third Option:

calls for a strengthening of Community action via the existing Treaty … Political legitimacy in the field of tourism will still be out of the question although instruments currently in operation will be bolstered in terms of resources, if not objectives. What is lacking with this option is something which can only be given by political legitimacy, viz. more closely coordinated measures in order to give Community action a higher profile and create a multiplier effect for the added value of each of the separate policies

After further discussion the ESC concluded it had:

no doubt of the need for a fully-fledged, effective Community policy on tourism, as spelt out in Option IV of the Green Paper. … On the basis of Option IV of the Green Paper the Commission should … define the overall framework, guidelines and coordinating measures which, alongside autonomous initiatives, are needed to ensure that the most important activities engaged in as part of a Community tourism policy are effective in achieving the objectives of the Union, while at the same time complying with the principle of subsidiarity

As part of its own contribution to the debate the Committee then proposed:[84]

that the following new title be added to the Treaty:

Tourism
The Community and the Member States shall be responsible for creating the necessary pre-conditions for maintaining and improving the competitive

---

[84] *Ibid.*, p.11.

capacity of the Community tourism sector. To that end, their actions shall aim to:

- achieve close coordination between Community and Member State policy in the tourism sector;

- develop joint measures by the Community and the Member States to ensure that the Community tourism sector is able to stand up to worldwide competition;

- strike a balance between the interests of the industry and those of the consumer, with due regard for the principle of sustainable development predicated on conservation of the cultural and national heritage.

In order to achieve the aims set out in paragraph 1 above, the Commission shall ensure that tourism policy is integrated and co-ordinated with all aspects of Community policy.

This was not the only suggestion for a new Treaty title dealing with tourism in the debate following publication of the Green Paper. Another suggestion was put forward by a variety of tourism interests[85] and is reproduced below. Both attempts reflect the same key policy elements involving an overall objective of improving Community tourism competitiveness through sub-objectives which included cooperation and consultation, better integration of tourism into other Community policies and measures relating to consumer and environmental protection.

Article W

The Community and the Member States shall ensure that conditions exist for the competitiveness and sustainable development of Community tourism.

To this end, their actions should be aimed at:
> modernising tourism;
> removing barriers to the free movement of tourists;
> attaining a high level of tourist protection, assistance and information and accessibility to Community tourism;
> improving the operation and performance of the tourist industry and the quality of its services.

---

[85] A Proposal by the AIT and FIA to the Intergovernmental Conference, Community Tourism Policy: The Integration of Tourism in the Treaty. Available at www.europa.eu.int.en/agenda/igc–home/index.htl, 16.4.01.

Article X

Member States shall consult and exchange information with each other in liaison with the Commission and, where necessary, shall co-ordinate their action. The Commission may take any useful initiative to promote such coordination.

Article Y

The Community shall contribute to the achievement of the objectives set out in Article W through measures adopted pursuant to other provisions of this Treaty, particularly [those relating to consumer protection, trans European networks, industry and environment] action taken through the Structural Funds;

specific action which supports and supplements the policy pursued by the Member States.

Article Z

The Council acting by qualified majority on a proposal form the Commission, and after consulting the Economic and Social Committee and the Committee of the Regions may decide, according to procedure mentioned in Article 189b, on specific measures in support of the action taken in the Member States to achieve the objectives set out in Article W.

Parliament's Response

In its response to the Commission Green Paper[86] the European Parliament also supported the Fourth Option and considered:

> that a sustainable Community tourism policy should seek to accomplish the objectives set out in Article 2 [and] focus its efforts in intra-Community tourism and international tourism, in accordance with the principle of subsidiarity.[87]

Parliament acknowledged Option 3 had some merit, but not enough:

> At a time when subsidiarity has become something of a watchword for all new initiatives at Union level, this third option certainly has its attractions.

---

[86] Report on the Commission's Green Paper on the Role of the Union in the Field of Tourism, PE 215.091, 25.1.96.

[87] *Ibid.*, p.6.

As the Commission itself points out, simply retaining the existing framework would not rule out Commission initiatives to strengthen the internal coordination of its activities in order to make them more coherent with tourism. However, ...the time is right to go a step further and to establish a Community Tourism Policy with its own Title in the treaty and Chapter in the Budget. For only this would enable the Commission to assume the role ... as a centre for the dissemination of information and 'best practise' between the many parties concerned ... as a coordinator, at Union level, of the actions of these many parties interested [in tourism] as well as with other Community actions with an impact on tourism – and as an initiator of common policies where appropriate. ... [88]

At the core of this Community Tourism Policy should be the tourist and the environment.

Tourism policy as w hole must unquestionably be centred around tourists themselves and their environment.[89]

Parliament's Committee on the Environment, Public Heath and Consumer Protection was particularly critical of how tourist and environment concerns were dealt with in the Green Paper.

The Green Paper on Tourism should therefore have included not only a definition of the sector's specific concerns, but also guidelines in the following areas: social and labour issues, the environment, culture, protection of tourists as consumers. ... There can be no hiding the fact that the Green Paper is threadbare and hollow, nor that it is bereft of any innovative spark in so important an area – intimately linked as it is to the concept of Union citizenship and constituting, as it does, a primary source of wealth and employment. For the nth time, the Green Paper cites the established programmes under way ... etc, while evading any specific commitment in these and other areas, as if it were frightened either of the Council, whose disinclination to tackle the tourist sector is well known, or perhaps of the opinion of certain tourism lobbies which advocate leaving things exactly as they are in the sector as soon as there is any question of attempting to place tourists and their surroundings at the centre of any Community tourist policy.[90]

---

[88] *Ibid.*, p.20.
[89] *Ibid.*, p.5.
[90] *Ibid.*, p.24.

In the same report another of Parliament's Committee's cited the added competitive pressures faced by tourism businesses resulting from the world-wide liberalisation of trade in service, including tourism services, brought about by the General Agreement on Trade in Services 1993 (GATS), as also justifying enhanced Community involvement in tourism:

> A further reason why a Community policy is necessary is the provisions of the General Agreement on Trade in Services [including tourism services, made] recently within the framework of the GATT negotiations, have caused problems of competitiveness for the Community tourist industry ... the problem is particularly acute because most Community tourist enterprises ... are small and medium-sized undertakings.[91]

Committee of the Regions' Response

Contrary to the enthusiasm of Parliament and the Economic and Social Committee for Option 4 of the Green Paper, the Committee of the Regions (COR) rejected it[92] for the same reasons as some states opposed it and which led ultimately, as will be seen, to the Green Paper's failure to bring about any change in the Treaty.

Reflecting membership concerns that most tourism issues were peculiarly suited to local responses, the Committee accepted the case for some limited role for the Community and tried to identify it.

> The COR takes the view that a more active, better-coordinated EU contribution is necessary to cope with the dynamic development of tourism and the scope for tourist activities, particularly because of tourism's complex links to many areas within the EU's remit.

> The COR does not, however, believe that over and above the provisions of the existing EU policies, there is a need to establish a legislative basis for an EU tourist policy.

> Nevertheless, it is necessary that those initiatives which are implemented at Community level should have a transparent coherent basis giving EU action the necessary legitimacy, and hence making it both coordinated and effective. ...

---

[91] *Ibid.*, p.13.
[92] COR, Opinion on the Commission Green Paper on the Role of the Union in the Field of Tourism, 376 (95), 16.11.95.

The COR stresses that EU involvement in tourism must be based on the subsidiarity principle. Moreover, any attempt to create a common European image could only serve to submerge the individual and cultural identities which Member States and local and regional authorities at present highlight in their destination marketing.[93]

Thus, the Committee:

supports the idea of setting transparent and coordinated guidelines for those tourist activities which are carried out at EU level;

recommends the establishment of a basis to ensure that the Union takes greater account of the specific interests in the area of tourism in connection with planning and implementation of other Community policies;

does not believe that this necessarily requires amending the current legislative basis or giving the EU more powers in this area; ...

urges the Commission to base its report, to be submitted to the Council ... on the principles of partnership, complementarity and subsidiarity and stresses the local authorities' responsibility and potential in action to develop tourism;

believes that the proposals contained in section CIII (strengthening Community action via the existing Treaty) constitute the soundest basis for the Commission's future work, since option CIII gives a clear political signal that the present legal basis (Article 3 ....) is adequate for the Union to reach all of the above mentioned goals.[94]

Other Responses

Of the 12 Member States who are recorded in the briefings on the 1996 Inter-Governmental Conference[95] as expressing an opinion on the Green Paper Options, none favoured Option I, four favoured Option II, four favoured Option III and four favoured Option IV.

Regarding the Member States positions, most of the opinions that are expressed call for political recognition of Community action on tourism, both in terms of substance (by strengthening resources) and in terms of

---

[93] Para. 11.

[94] *Ibid.*, para. 22.

[95] White Paper on the 1996 Inter–Governmental Conference, Volume III, Part two – provisional version, N. 30 Briefing on the Tourism and the 1996 IGC, p.507.

form (by including a specific title in the treaty), while complying with the principle of subsidiarity. Only Denmark, France and Sweden have not expressed any definite opinion. The comments of the other Member States range from a minimalist approach (D, UK) to a maximalistic approach (B, IRL, FR, I). Although it had not come out in favour of the latter position, one Member State (L) indicates that it would make no objection. There is reason to wonder whether, if certain guarantees can be given, the position of some other countries could be revised upwards, either to option 3 (NL) or option 4 (FIN, P). This does not seem to be the case at present for two other countries (E, A).[96]

Consultations promoted by the Commission[97] among interested parties made it at least possible:

to identify common ground in the discussion on what a Community policy should not be about: wresting away anything that is better handled at national, regional or local level/laws and regulations not meeting the needs of industry/bureaucracy and red tape/excessive Community control/fixing anything that isn't broken/over centralised control of promotion and marketing/causing harm to the pluralism and diversity that is the strength of Europe's image/promoting unfair or biased competition. ... A large majority of the contributions from the industry reflect a wish to strengthen Community action on tourism. More specifically, the majority European organisations taking part in the Commission's consultation meetings with the industry even advocate including a title in the Treaty.[98]

Following wide ranging consultations, the conclusion to rather brief Report finally submitted by the Commission to the Council of Ministers in accordance with Declaration No.1 of the Treaty on European Union firstly set the background[99]:

When the Treaty on European Union was being negotiated a number of Member States wanted the Treaty to contain new chapters on ... tourism. ... In the end the Treaty incorporated [a promise to study the matter at the next IGC]

---

[96] *Ibid.*, p.489.

[97] Commission, Consultation on the Basis of the Green Paper – A Step further towards Recognition of Community Action to Assist Tourism. Forum on European Tourism, Brussels, 1995.

[98] *Ibid.*, p.7.

[99] Commission, Report on Civil Protection, Tourism and Energy, SEC(96) 496 final, 3.4.96, p.1.

Then followed a brief account of existing indirect tourism actions, followed by an evaluation which was hardly more than a further description of recent activities. In conclusion, the Commission avoided any preference and merely noted some possibilities:[100]

> At present there are no specific bases for Community action in the three fields under discussion.
>
> While it is true that this lack of specific legal bases has not prevented the Community from undertaking and implementing a number of measures in these fields, the measures in question have had to be based either on the general provisions of the Treaty and/or those relating to its sectoral policies or on Article 235 of the Treaty. Such action could be stepped up within the existing framework of the Treaty.

But the Commission was mindful of the pitfalls associated with this approach.

> It must be borne in mind, however, that action based on Article 235 of the Treaty is likely to become much more difficult, if not impossible, in an enlarged Community in which unanimity would still be required for taking decisions.
>
> Furthermore, the continuity and coherence of Community action in the fields concerned could be facilitated by inserting into the Treaty provisions which would make such action more efficient and more visible. ...
>
> The Commission nevertheless wishes to point out that it is not asking for new powers. It will therefore be for the Conference to announce its position on this question.

What ultimately matters in treaty revisions are the views of the Member States (since the Treaty is made by them). Given the Commission's equivocal position and despite the support of various Community institutions, some states and interested groups for a stronger Treaty reference to tourism, some members states remained unconvinced of the need for enhanced Treaty references (and as events subsequently proved, were even unsupportive of continuing existing Community activity). Since unanimity is required for any change, the refusal of a few meant that no change was made regarding tourism by the Amsterdam Treaty.

---

[100] *Ibid.*, p.6.

Philoxenia

Shortly after it published the Green Paper without waiting the outcome of the IGC, the Commission sought to continue previous direct but limited Community involvement in tourism by presenting to the Council a proposal for a multi-annual programme, titled 'Philoxenia', to assist European tourism.[101] Paying due deference to the subsidiarity principle and based of necessity on Article 235, the Philoxenia proposal identified four broad areas of action which satisfied the demanding Treaty requirements of subsidiarity:

- improving tourism knowledge,
- improving the legislative and financial environment for tourism,
- raising tourism quality,
- increasing the number of tourists from third countries.

A modest enough proposal, such was the negative light in which Community involvement in tourism was then held by some Member States, that even after significant sliming down, it failed to secure the unanimous agreement needed for its approval by the Council under Article 235 and was not proceeded with. The grounds of opposition were conflict with the principle of subsidiarity and the level of funding proposed. According to the Budget Committee of Parliament:[102]

> While taking the view that common action to promote tourism as a factor in economic and social development is desirable, the Committee on Budgets pointed out nevertheless that this proposal raises two major problems from the outset, that of subsidiarity and that of the effectiveness of the resources proposed seen in relation to the objectives to be attained.

> On the first point, the question is to ascertain whether an area like tourism, which, in most Member States, is decentralised for operational reasons at regional and local levels, needs to be covered by Community action.

> From a budgetary point of view, given the limited resources available and the oft-repeated wish that they should be concentrated on specific areas in order to boost their effectiveness, the … committee takes the view that the resources proposed by the Commission are not enough, on their own, to finance the development of tourism on a genuinely effective scale … [while]

---

[101] Commission, Proposal for a Council decision on a First Multi–annual Programme to Assist European Tourism, 'Philoxenia' 1997–2000, COM(96) 168 final, 30.4.96.

[102] European Parliament, Opinion of the Committee on Budgets, A4–0298/96, p.42.

the indicative internal breakdown of resources in relation to the objectives highlights their fragmentary nature which is likely to leave Community funding at a level below the critical mass of effectiveness for the measure in question, as a result, could not be obtained. ...

As for the remaining measures, promotion campaigns [the projected allocations] create a financing requirement of close on ECU 12 m (out of a total of ECU 25m) for the promotion of tourism and hence justifying the fears expressed above concerning the role to be played by the Union in a field very broadly covered by subsidiarity.

In the end, according to the Commission:

despite intensive discussion and changes resulting from it, [Philoxenia] did not find the unanimous support in the Council of Ministers, and finally was withdrawn by the Commission in April 2000.[103]

A New Approach

With the failure to secure Council support for the Philoxenia proposal, Commission commitment to funded programmatic tourism action appears to have largely died.

The development of a fully-fledged European policy for the tourism and leisure industry seems to have come to a dead end.[104]

But this of course did not, indeed could not, mean the end of Community interest in tourism. Following the lack of success with Philoxenia the Commission reoriented its interest away from direct tourism measures towards the impact of tourism on other Community policies, particularly employment[105] and enterprise. However, activities since 1998, while important for tourism policy, are of limited relevance to the role of tourism in the Treaty. In the following section, while some of these activities are noted, the emphasis will be on continuing calls for an enhanced Treaty role for tourism.

At the outset of the new millennium, Community policy now treats tourism

---

[103] Commission, Report on Community Measures Affecting Tourism 1997/99, COM(2001) 171 final, 28.3.01, p.5.
[104] ESC, Own Initiative Opinion on European Tourism Policy, CES 323, 24.3.99, p.1.
[105] Commission, Report on Community Measures Affecting Tourism, COM(2001) 171 final, 28.4.01, p.5.

more as a product and less as a recreational need or social entitlement. Its challenges are economic ones, such as:

> increasing the basic knowledge of this economic activity, increasing the competitiveness of its businesses and improving the sustainable development of tourism in the EU and its contribution to job creation.[106]

Among the ways of improving an understanding of how tousism operates and its economic impacts, are the improved collection of tourism statistics and satelitte tourism accounts.[107] Directive 95/57[108] is a rare example of a specific tourism measure intended to address the knowledge challenge by establishing a harmonised system for the collection of tourism statisics. The Treaty of Rome is sufficiently elastic to accommodate, even promote, a new role for tourism as a means for promoting the Rome Treaty's enterprise objectives.

> Article 3(u) of the Treaty establishing the European Community provides for Community action to comprise measures in the field of tourism for the purposes set out in Article 2 of the Treaty. ... More specifically, tourism contributes to a large extent to the objectives of enterprise policy. The diversity of products and services, the different locations and the development of the market towards a sustainable tourism, open to everyone, will lead to the creation of new markets for innovative enterprises, especially SMEs.[109]

Thus in the future Community action in tourism will continue to be dictated by the absence of stronger Treaty references to tourism and the lack of Member State interest in stronger direct actions. What is left is the realm of consultation, information and best practice. A great deal has taken place in this regard in recent years, including the holding of the annual European Tourism Forum. Industry expects the Commission to better reflect its concerns and particularly to effectively operate the business impact assessment[110] of proposed legal measures which affect tourism. The Commission continues to emphasise the importance of sustainable tourism and the promotion of the UNEP Agenda 21, as will be seen in Chapter 9.

---

[106] Commission, Communication on Working together for the Future of European Tourism, COM(2001) 665 final, 13.11.01, p.3.

[107] http:europa.eu.int/comm/enterprise/services/tourism/index_en.htm.

[108] OJ L 29/32, 6.12.95.

[109] *Ibid.*, p.6.

[110] Enterprise DG, Tourism and Impact Assessment. Discussion Document prepared for ETF, 10.12.02. See also p. 35.

Other Community institutions such as Parliament, the Economic and Social Committee and the Committee of the Regions, while supportive of current Commission's activities, have not abandoned their long-held views on the need for a coherent Community focus on tourism and greater guidance in the Treaty itself.

The Council of the Regions, which along with the Economic and Social Committee has produced some the clearest thinking about Community tourism, still wants a specific Community tourism policy embedded in the Treaty. In 1999 in a wide ranging opinion[111] it outlined the difficult background which Community involvement in tourism has had to contend with and concluded, as if the issue was still an open one, that tourism deserved to be treated as a priority issue at Community level.

> at the moment Member States' interest in tourism is not equally great from a social and economic point of view; differences exist, and it is clear there are differences as to whether they favour more or less Community intervention. A crucial difference tends to be the level of demand in each country ...certain Member States probably do not want Community intervention – regulatory or otherwise – in their tourism markets, on the grounds that a totally free market functions perfectly; it may be that they do not wish more Community funds to be allocated to the tourism sector in the Member States than are already being provided through the structural funds. Thus these countries have reservations, in the sense that they would like to restrict Community intervention (reflecting the current trend in the EU), or on financial grounds, fearing that new funding will be required. At the same time, other Member States are calling for more Community interest and intervention (because they believe that there are distortions in the functioning of the tourism market, e.g. excessive power of tour operators).

> The European Union has therefore not yet managed to introduce a Community tourism policy in a treaty revision, a deficit that we feel needs to be rectified as soon as possible. The European Union should therefore be enabled, as part of its remit, to provide appropriate support for the tourism policy pursued by Member States and by regional and local authorities. Bearing in mind that Community policies are being formulated in areas that have implications for tourism – e.g. consumer protection, environmental protection and transport – sufficient account should be taken

---

[111] COR, Opinion on the Role of Local and Regional Authorities in Tourism Development and the Impact of European Union Measures in the Sphere of Tourism, COR 157/98 final, 13.7.99.

of the justified concerns of the European tourism industry so as to ensure competitiveness on the international tourism market. ...

Tourism is thus often required to bear costs and adapt to conditions that have no relations to its needs. ... The lack of a tourism policy is also making it impossible to define jointly goals and measures specific to tourism, e.g. the objective of social justice, while satisfying the legitimate expectations of the general public regarding the right to holidays and leisure for everybody.[112]

Matters seem unlikely to change under any new European Constitution. The proceedings of the Convention on the future of Europe, intended to plot a future legal framework for the Union and the Community, may have consequences for future Community involvement with tourism. Tourism was not mentioned in the first draft of a new Constitution,[113] though efforts are being made to change this. However, even if successful any new reference seems unlikely to be much of an improvement on the present.

CHAPTER CONCLUSION

This chapter details the ways in which current Treaty provisions and core legal concepts influence Community actions in tourism. It also details the long course of attempts to bolster the degree of Community involvement in tourism through strengthened Treaty references. There is little doubt that the complex nature of tourism and the uncertain consequences of any strengthened references in the Rome Treaty have stymied the capacity of the Community to contribute in any focused dynamic way to European tourism. In any event, the desire to accommodate the social and recreational needs of European citizens sits uncomfortably with the ruling economic focus of the Rome Treaty. As the Community becomes increasingly aware of the negative environmental and transport consequences of the endless nurturing of tourism supply and demand, it may ultimately be forced to re-think its attitude to Treaty references to tourism, as much to deal with the complex issue of sustainable demand for tourism, as promoting competitiveness. A failure to include a specific task of promoting sustainable tourism in the new European Constitution will be a significant missed opportunity.

---

[112] *Ibid.*, pp. 6–7.

[113] Mainly it would seem because of the absence of complimentary articles detailing the types of competencies and powers needed to make a tourism reference meaningful. COM 375/1/ 02, p. 15.

Undergraduate questions:

1. The absence of a specific title or chapter in the Treaty of Rome dealing with tourism has not prevented the Community from taking action in this area.

   Explain:

2. Explain how the Commission Green Paper on the role of the Union in the field of tourism identified the 'added-value' which Community involvement in tourism can bring.

3. Describe how the Court of Justice has adapted non-tourism references in the Treaty of Rome to the tourism industry.

Postgraduate questions:

1. Consider whether the nature of tourism makes it difficult for the European Community to develop its activities in this area.

2. In the end the Treaty of Rome was not amended at the Inter-Governmental Conference preceding the Amsterdam Treaty to include a stronger reference to tourism.

3. Consider whether this means that there is now only a weak basis for any Community action in this area.

4. Attempt to draft a new title in the Treaty of Rome or the proposed European Constitution providing for greater Community involvement in tourism. Explain the reasoning behind your choice.

CHAPTER 3

TOURISM IN THE INSTITUTIONS, LAWS AND DECISION-MAKING PROCEDURES OF THE EUROPEAN COMMUNITY[1]

INTRODUCTION

The most fundamental provision of the Treaty establishing the European Community (Treaty of Rome) dealing with the institutions of the European Community is Article 7 which states that:

1. The Tasks entrusted to the Community shall be carried out by the following institutions:

   – a European Parliament,
   – a Council,
   – a Commission,
   – a Court Of Justice,
   – a Court Of Auditors.

Each institution shall act within the limits of the powers conferred upon it by this Treaty.

2. The Council and the Commission shall be assisted by an Economic and Social Committee and a Committee of the Regions acting in an advisory capacity.

Later parts of the Treaty spell out the necessary details concerning each institution.

The general nature of these institutions, the procedures they adopt in reaching decisions and the types of legal measures they can adopt is described in this chapter. The task is made easier by the fact that a great deal of general and topical information about the composition and workings of the institutions of

---

[1] Marc Mc Donald.

the European Community is available from the institutions website pages which are accessible through the Community web home page:

http://www.europa.eu.int

The reader is encouraged to make use of these web sites for most factual information about Community institutions. The 'added value' of this chapter lies in its attempt to sketch the Community's institutions, laws and procedures through tourism illustrations.

The enlargement of the European Community, after adoption of the Nice Treaty, will have particular consequences for the make-up of the Community's institutions and the vital issue of balances of power within the various institutions. Particularly affected will be the balance of power between the Council of Ministers and the Member States and the Community. However, these important consequences will not have any exceptional impact on tourism and for this reason will not be further addressed. For further information about enlargement, readers should access the Community enlargement web page at:

http://www.europa.eu.int/pol/enlarg/index_en.htm

Tourism and the Community's Institutions

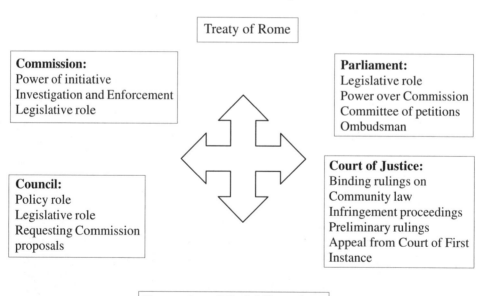

Tourism: Decision-Making Procedures and Community Laws

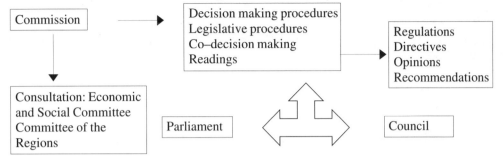

Learning Outcomes:

After reading this chapter, the student should:

- appreciate the way in which the institutions and bodies of the Community are relevant to tourism,
- appreciate the distinct roles of the Community's institutions,
- understand the differences between Community laws as they pertain to tourism,
- be able to follow the procedures used by Community institutions in arriving at tourism related decisions using the co-decision procedure.

These outcomes will be addressed through the following main headings:

> Policy Introduction to Community Institutions.
>
> Types of Community Laws.
>
> Outline of Community Institutions.
>
> Community Decision-Making Procedures.

POLICY INTRODUCTION TO THE INSTITUTIONS OF THE EUROPEAN COMMUNITY

The ambitious objectives and policies of the European Community are often expressed in the Treaty of Rome in vague and general terms. In earlier versions of the Treaty the primary and technocratic focus of these goals was the creation of a Common Market among the economies of the Member-States. This provided a powerful backdrop to the initial creation in the Treaty of Community institutions tasked with diverse responsibilities for translating general Treaty aspirations into concrete achievements.

Central Role of Member-State Governments

If one had to start from scratch to construct appropriate Community institutions a number of underlying realities would become apparent. Firstly, the creation of powerful institutions by the Treaty of Rome to exercise pooled sovereignty in economic matters was a new departure in international relations. While, Member States clearly wished the Community to succeed, they also proceeded cautiously in surrendering power to unknown entities so as to protect "vital national interests."

Thus, it is not surprising that the Community and its institutions were originally and today still are, in large measure, constructed in a way that real power within the Community, that is the power to take or, as importantly, refuse to take legislative decisions, is retained by the Member-States exercisable through the Community institution which represents them – the Council of Ministers.

Power within Council of Ministers

Even within the Council of Ministers member-states do not act in a collective manner, unlike the Commission. They do not have identical interests. The larger and smaller states, the more advanced and less developed states, northern and southern states frequently have different views on policy matters, and each state's views are of course conditioned by its experiences and state of economic development.

A second reality which the Treaty therefore deals with concerns the way decision-making is arrived at within the Council so as to prevent domination by any state or bloc of states. This is treated as primarily a voting matter and has lead to the development of subtle voting rules, an issue which is briefly discussed further below.

Institutional Balance Between Council and Commission

If the Council of Ministers was initially going to be the most powerful Community institution (albeit one where Member States could be expected, at least initially, to reflect "selfish" national interests within a Community context) a different institution – the Commission – was required to provide the initiative and momentum for attaining Treaty goals, one which would seek to drive fledgling Community, as opposed to Member-State, interests.

Defining the relationship between Council and Commission then became a vital matter since the Commission needed real powers and functions particularly if the Common Market was to be realised. A delicate balance between Council and Commission was therefore constructed involving, as will be seen, the interesting device of withholding from the Council the power to determine its own agenda and initiate proposals for action and reserved it to the Commission.

The importance of the Commission lies in the breath of tasks conferred on it. It could have been, but was not, made directly electable by the citizens of the Member-States (the Council could never be electable since it is designed to represent the governments of the states). Consequently, the Commission suffers from a "democratic deficit", though it tries to partly remedy this by making its actions as transparent and understandable as possible. Maintaining a full and informative website is part of this. As the Community evolves, greater attention will be paid to ways of making the Commission more democratically accountable to the peoples of Europe.

Finding a Role for the Parliament

The authors of the original Treaty of Rome nevertheless appreciated that some democratic input into Community institutions would be needed if citizens were to develop any loyalty to Community ideals and institutions.

The Treaty therefore provides for the election and operation of a third Community institution, initially called an Assembly and now called a Parliament. Since this body did not initially and still does not have the power to either initiate to enact legislation on its own, it was always going to be difficult to devise appropriate functions for it. Of the functions allotted to it, some would obviously be designed to provide oversight of other Community institutions (reporting, appointing, and dismissing). A noticeable absence, however, is oversight of the Council of Ministers.

Initially Parliament was little more than a figleaf of democracy for the technocratic drive towards the creation of a Common Market. With time as later Treaty revisions have added other goals to the original economic ones, greater emphasis has been placed on the democratic quality of Community institutional activity. Thus, democratic accountability, responsiveness/accessibility, transparency and freedom of information have become central contemporary concerns.

With each revision of the Treaty of Rome more scope is found for Parliament. Particularly, its role in the legislative process has evolved, as will be seen, to now take in a multitude of areas. While Parliament still cannot initiate and enact legislation on its own (unlike most parliaments), it is now an equal player with the Council in the expanded co-decision procedure for enacting legislation, a procedure which is examined later and which represents an important contemporary focus for the institutional balance of the Community.

If and when Parliament acquires truly independent legislative functions, and that day still seems far away, the days of a nominated Commission as it now stands will probably be numbered. It will not then be desirable to continue allotting important functions to a technocratic body without an increased democratic accountability.

For the present debate concerning the wider topic of institutional reform within the Community is focused on the need to streamline the institutions and the decision-making procedures to prepare for enlargement. In that context it is hard to see how further complexity in both structures and procedures can be avoided.

Institutional Autonomy and Co-operation

Institutional autonomy is the corollary of institutional balance of power. This means that. within the limits of their powers and functions, Community institutions are expected to guard and use their respective powers and privileges. Each institution has been given the power to use Community courts to restrain the others from trespassing on its powers.

> In *Parliament v. Council*,[2] the former alleged that the Council had not properly re-consulted it after making changes to a Commission proposal dealing with visas after Parliament had expressed an opinion on it. The Court of Justice stated:
>
> > due consultation of the Parliament in the cases provided for by the Treaty constitutes an essential formal requirement breach of which renders the measures concerned void. Effective participation of the Parliament in the legislative process laid down by the Treaty represents an essential factor in the institutional balance intended by the Treaty. This function reflects the fundamental democratic principle that the people should take part in the exercise of power through the intermediary of a representative assembly.

Community institutions can also use the Community courts to force each other to discharge their Treaty obligations. On another occasion Parliament succeeded in obtaining a court ruling that the Council had failed to fulfil its Treaty obligations regarding the creation of a common transport policy, an issue of considerable importance to tourism.[3]

Generally Community institutions are obliged under the Rome Treaty to cooperate with each other to help achieve Treaty objectives. While this is made

---

[2] *European Parliament v. Council* [1997] E.C.R. I–3213.
[3] See p. 183.

explicit in some cases, as with the co-decision procedure for making Community laws,[4] it has a general application to all inter-institutional behaviour and explains the willingness of one institution to respond to requests from another. An example of this relevant to tourism arises when the Commission investigates petitions passed to it for investigation by the Parliament's Committee of Petitions.[5]

TYPES OF COMMUNITY LAWS

When the Treaty of Rome was drafted in the 1950s it was understood that the creation of a Common Market (and the replacement of national standards with 'harmonised' Community standards) would require new mechanisms for moving towards new Community standards which, if they were to be accepted, would have to be legally binding. It was also recognised that a means for providing a formal legal basis for formally recording the many decisions of Community institutions would have to be established. Both requirements meant the creation of a new Community legal order, one whose relationship with current legal norms within the Member States would also have to be addressed.

Thus, the Treaty as interpreted, created an entirely new and separate legal order and system, one which is presided over by a single court – the Court of Justice – which provides definitive rulings but solely on issues of Community law. As will be seen, the Court has played a significant role in tourism matters in ensuring the Community lives up to the objectives set out in the Treaty.

The Community legal system is also unique in terms of state organisations whose acts or measures nearly always depend on the consent of states before they are binding. What is different about Community legal norms is that while Member States may have a say, as we will see, in the creation of individual legal rules, once made, they are binding on governments.

The legal measures which institutions can adopt to advance the Community's objectives are set out in Article 249.

> In order to carry out their task and in accordance with the provisions of this Treaty, the European Parliament acting jointly with the Council, the Council and the Commission shall make regulations and issue directives, take decisions, make recommendations or deliver opinions.

The two principal measures for promulgating new laws are the regulation and the directive. Before explaining these measures, a brief note about the presentation and referencing of Community legal texts.

---

[4] See p. 130.
[5] See p. 92.

Referencing Community Legal Measures

Article 253 of the Treaty of Rome states that the:

> Regulations, directives and decisions adopted jointly by the European
> Parliament and the Council, and acts adopted by the Council or the
> Commission, shall state the reasons on which they are based and shall
> refer to any proposals or opinions which are required to be obtained
> pursuant to this Treaty.

Following this, under the Council's Rules of Procedure[6] the actual text of a
regulation, directive, decision or recommendation must be proceeded by:

- the names(s) of the institutions adopting the measure,
- a reference to the provisions under which the measures is adopted – 'Having
  regard to',
- a citation of the proposals submitted, opinions obtained and consultations
  held,
- a statement of the reasons on which the measure is adopted – 'Whereas'.

These recitals of the legal basis and facts justifying a measure, which is found
in all Community texts, is needed both to clarify the appropriateness of the
legal basis of a measure in the Treaty or any enabling legislation and also to
permit judicial review of the measure and its effects. Clear identification of the
Treaty legal basis is needed because, according to the Treaty, different legislative
procedures must be used depending on what the law deals with. Further,[7] the
choice of Treaty legal basis can determine whether unanimity is required within
the Council of Ministers before it can adopt a proposal, or whether a proposal
must follow, say, the co-decision legislative procedure. If the wrong legal basis
is adopted this may leave the measure vulnerable to attack in the Court of Justice.

When formally adopted, most Community legal measures must be published
in the Community's Official Journal. Under Article 254 of the Treaty most
regulations, directives and decisions

> shall be published in the Official Journal of the European Communities.
> … Other directives, and decisions, shall be notified to those to whom they
> are addressed and shall take effect upon such notification.

When a Commission or Council decision – such as a regional policy decision

---

6 Council Decision 682/02, OJ L 230/25, 28.2.02.
7 See p. 41.

approving an operational programme with a tourism element, or a competition decision determining whether a merger, say, between two airlines or hotel groups can go ahead – is notified to an individual person or Member State, the text is not usually published in the Official Journal, unless the relevant law requires publication, and it is referenced by a reference system particular to the Commission department which issues the decision.

Regulations

> A regulation shall have general application. It shall be binding in its entirety and directly applicable all Member States – Article 249.

This most innovative category of law created by the Treaty is based on the need for truly independent Community rules made without recourse to national law makers. Once validly made a regulation possess direct legal effect even on individual persons. However the use of such a far reaching type of law is restricted by the terms of the Treaty, that is, regulations can only be made for topics allowed by the Treaty. While it sometimes explicit about their use, the Treaty is also sometimes not explicit at all and in theory allows a choice as between a regulation and a directive. However, there is an in-built bias in the Treaty against regulations and in favour of directives. This derives from the subsidiarity principle and Protocol 30, para 6/7 of the Treaty of Rome which states that:

> Other things being equal, directives should be preferred to regulations and framework directives to detailed measures. ... Where appropriate and subject to the need for proper enforcement, Community measures should provide Member States with alternative ways to achieve the objectives of the measures.

The choice essentially depends on the degree of discretion the Community wishes to offer the Member States on the policy issue in question. If the achievement of the policy objective requires precision without any scope for local discretion then a regulation remains the appropriate measure.

An example of a regulation affecting tourism which shows how the referencing requirements mentioned above are meet is:

COUNCIL REGULATION (EEC) No 2409/92
of 23 July 1992
on Air Fares and Rates for Air Services

The Council of the European Communities,

Having regard to the Treaty establishing the European Economic Community, and in particular Article 84 (2) thereof,
Having regard to the proposal from the Commission, (1)
Having regard to the opinion of the European Parliament,(2)
Having regard to the opinion of the Economic and Social Committee,(3)

Whereas it is important to establish an air transport policy for the internal market. …
Whereas the internal market shall comprise an area without internal frontiers in which the free movement of goods, persons, services and capital is ensured. …
Whereas air fares should normally be determined freely by market forces;
Whereas it is appropriate to deal with all matters of pricing in the same Regulation. …

has adopted this Regulation: …

(1) OJ No C 258, 4.10.1991, p.2.
(2) OJ No C 125, 18.5.1992, p.150.
(3) OJ No C 169, 6.7.1992, p.15.

The text of regulations, directives etc. are set out in articles. When interpreting the articles of any Community legal measure, use can be made of the measure's preamble and even the Commission proposal on which it is based and also opinions produced during its making in order to clarify its meaning.[8]

Directives

A more utilitarian type of law, the directive, was also established by the Treaty, but its legal effect is generally only felt when filtered through Member States law-making procedures. Article 249 of the Treaty provides that:

A directive shall be binding, as to the result to be achieved, upon each

---

[8] See p. 82.

Member State to which it is addressed, but shall leave to the national authorities the choice of form and methods.

This is generally considered to mean that transposing (implementing) national legal measures must be taken. Thereafter two laws will exist – the Community directive and the national law.

The Commission monitors whether Member States enact implementing measures both by the date stipulated in the directive and substantively, that is to make sure they do not alter or leave out directive requirements. A tourism example of a directive title is as follows:

**COUNCIL DIRECTIVE
OF 13 JUNE 1990
on Package Travel, Package Holidays and Package Tours
(90/314/EEC)**

The Preamble following the title of a Directive (the part after 'Having ...' and before the start of Article 1) is configured in the same manner as a regulation.

Experience has shown that Member States sometimes fail either to implement a directive on time or to do so properly. Such failures are taken seriously by the Commission both because it means a state is not honouring its commitments and also the measure may have been intended to protect individuals and the failure may deprive the individual of that protection. However, the Court of Justice has held that in certain circumstances, individuals who suffer loss through State failure to implement directives properly or at all can claim compensation against the state. These circumstances broadly concern whether the directive is sufficiently clear that it can be seen to be intended to confer enforceable right on individuals for their protection. This has been of benefit to tourists.

In *Dillenkofer v. Germany*[9] when Germany failed to implement an important tourist protection – the part of Package Travel Directive protecting tourists against insolvent tour operators – within the prescribed time period, a German tourist who was subsequently forced to pay his own way home when his German tour operator became insolvent, claimed damages against the state. Unsure of the law, the local court referred the issue to the Court of Justice. In ruling that the claim was admissible, the Court stated:[10]

---

[9] [1996] E.C.R. I–4845. See also p. 304.
[10] *Ibid.*, p.4880.

> failure to take any measure to transpose a directive in order to achieve the result it prescribes within the period laid down for that purpose constitutes per se a serious breach of Community law and consequently gives rise to a right of reparation for individuals suffering injury if the result prescribed by the directive entails the grant to individuals of rights whose content is identifiable and a casual link exists between the breach of the State's obligation and the loss and damage suffered.

Decisions

A third and more focused Community legal measure is a Decision which is 'binding in its entirety upon those to whom it is addressed' – Article 249(2), Rome Treaty. In other words acts of Community institutions which are intended to have legal force only in relation to named specific parties (states, individuals, companies) are promulgated as Decisions. Three areas relevant to tourism where decisions are frequently taken concern a Commission review of a:

- proposed merger or takeover, say between two hotel groups or airlines,
- State aid scheme beneficial to tourism SMEs,
- an operational programme agreed under the Community Structural Funds.

An example of the title of the latter involved Community approval of an earlier operational programme for tourism in Ireland which was titled as follows:

> ### COMMISION DECISION
> ### C(94) 1972
> ### of 29 July 1994
>
> concerning the granting of assistance from the European Regional Development Fund (ERDF), and the European Social Fund (ESF), to an operational programme for Tourism under Objective 1 Community Support Framework for structural assistance for Ireland.

Whether Decisions are published in the Community Official Journal depends on the legislation under which the decision is taken. If the legislation requires publication then it is published in the Official Journal. Thus, when making decisions affecting notified mergers etc. Article 20(1) of Council Regulation 4064/89[11] on the Control of Undertakings provides that:

---

[11] OJ L 395, 30.12.89 as amended. See p. 376.

The Commission shall publish the decisions which it takes pursuant to Article 8(2) to (5) in the Official Journal of the European Communities.

The publication shall state the names of the parties and the main content of the decisions; it shall have regard to the legitimate interest of undertakings in the protection of their business secrets.

In a takeover case involving two hotel chains,[12] the title of the decision was as follows:

Non-Opposition to a Notified Concentration
(Case No IV/M1133– BASS plc/Saison Holdings BV)
(98/C 156/09)

On 23 March 1998, the Commission decided not to oppose the above notified concentration. ... The full text of the decision is only available in English and will be made public after it is cleared of any business secrets it may contain.

If publication in the Official Journal is not required, then the Commission secretariat general responsible for the decision references it under it under a C reference, as in the case of the Decision above. The decision can still, however, become public because it is say placed on the Community website or the named person to whom it is addressed is a public entity within the Member State.

Recommendations

"Recommendations shall have no binding force" – Article 249. A tourism example of a recommendation is Council Recommendation 86/666 on Fire Safety in Existing Hotels,[13] the Preamble of which states:

THE COUNCIL OF THE EUROPEAN COMMUITIES:
Having regard to the Treaty establishing the European Economic Community, and in particular Article 235 thereof,
Having regard to the proposal from the Commission ...
Whereas, with the rapid expansion of tourism and business travel, more and more people need to stay in hotels in Member States other than their

---

[12] OJ C 156/11, 21.5.98.
[13] OJ L 384/60, 31.12.86.

country of origin; whereas such persons are entitled to adequate protection in the host country and to be informed of the nature and extent of that protection. ...
HEREBY RECOMMENDS MEMBER STATES. ...

The fact that recommendations can be ignored without fear of sanction indicates they are not a significant means for furthering Treaty objectives either in tourism or other areas. Indeed, the idea of a recommendation, which can only be agreed with Member State approval, yet the same Member States cannot be compelled to implement it, may seem curious. However, it is possible that a recommendation may precede a more binding Community act, such as a directive, if hoped-for voluntary compliance with the recommendation is not forthcoming.

In deciding whether to adopt a measure as either a regulation, directive or recommendation, the latter appears appropriate for issues on which the Community wishes to pronounce a position but cannot agree either on the details or whether it should be binding or the subject matter does not easily lend itself to a binding format.

There was some discussion regarding the appropriate legal form for the hotel fire safety Recommendation. When Parliament first called on the Commission to produce a proposal on the issue it wished the matter dealt with by means of a regulation.[14] The Commission however explained its choice of a recommendation as follows:[15]

> Technically and materially, the harmonisation of such a vast collection of laws and regulations [of Member States fire safety rules] is an extremely time consuming task and specific regulations for existing hotels must be found much more quickly. [Yet it] is essential to find a system that can be flexibly adapted to practical situations without losing sight of the primary aim: to protect human life.

> There is also a great diversity in the enforcement and application, generally on a very decentralised basis, of this type of regulation, precisely to allow the necessary flexibility for a case-by-case assessment of the situation.

---

[14] EP, Report of the Committee on the Environment, Public Health and Consumer Protection on Fire Safety Regulations in Hotels in the European Community, Working Documents 1978 – 1979, 95/78, p. 6.

[15] Commission, Proposal for a Council Recommendation on Fire Safety in Existing Hotels, COM(83) 751 final, 11.1.84, p. 7.

The Economic and Social Committee also commented on the choice of measure.[16]

> Another type of instrument, such as a Regulation or Directive, would be impeded by the inherent difficulties pertaining to such instruments, by the sheer duration of the harmonisation process, by a lack of flexibility in applying safety regulations in special cases and by political difficulties.

> Although it would have preferred a more binding legal instrument, the Committee acknowledges that ... the choice of 'recommendation' is justified by the fact that at present some national laws are either inadequate or complex to enforce. Although the recommendation will not be mandatory, the Committee would urge that the Member States, once they have taken ton a political commitment by endorsing it in the Council of Ministers ... should endeavour to see that it is applied. ...

Resolutions

A resolution is a formally adopted statement of a Community institution's will or preferences in a policy area. In making the statement the institution may be trying to give guidance to or influence others on an issue. It is not a legal measure mentioned in the Treaty of Rome and as such it has no binding legal effect. However, it is an important and widely used instrument in the continuous dialogue which takes place among and between Community institutions, the Member States, industry, unions and civil society.

By highlighting an issue and signalling the need for more decisive action, a resolution can be used to send a signal to the Commission on the need for a legislative proposal in an area. The Preamble to the Council Directive 95/57 on the collection of statistical information on tourism[17] referred to two resolutions passed by Parliament.

A resolution can also be used, not to promote the need for legislation, but when developments or debate surrounding an issue reaches a certain point where political guidance is needed to help map out future approaches. An example of this is the Council Resolution on the future of European tourism[18] which traced the course of the preceding debate, stressed the importance of tourism in the

---

[16] ESC, Opinion on the proposal for a Council Recommendation on Fire Safety in Existing Hotels, OJ C 248/4, 17.9.84.

[17] OJ L 295/32, 4.12.9.

[18] OJ C 135/1, 6.2.02. A more wide-ranging Parliament resolution is the resolution responding to a Commission Communication on working together for the future of European tourism, P5 TA(2002)0222, 14.5.02.

European economy, and merely identified the methodological themes or aims (consultation, networking, research, information gathering and dissemination) of future action.

OUTLINE OF COMMUNITY INSTITUTIONS

Besides the five institutions of the European Community recognised by the Treaty of Rome (Parliament, Council, Commission, Court of Justice and Court of Auditors) other bodies are also mentioned in the Treaty – particularly, the Economic and Social Committee and the Committee of the Regions. While these latter bodies are consultative only, they have figured prominently in the debates regarding Community involvement in tourism and are also examined.

European Parliament

The most general statement of the functions of the European Parliament is set out in Article 192 of the Treaty of Rome which states that:

> the European Parliament should participate in the process leading up to the adoption of Community acts by exercising its powers under the procedures laid down in Articles 251 and 252 and by giving its assent or delivering advisory opinions.

The legislative procedures referred to in Articles 251 and 252[19] indicate that, while Parliament cannot initiate and enact laws on its own, it has a co-decision function with the Council of Ministers in some cases and a lesser consultative function in others. Other articles in the Treaty provide for further procedures and in fact the current position regarding parliamentary involvement in Community decision-making is quite complex and reflects the evolving relationship between Parliament and Council.

Treaty provisions concerned with the European Parliament typically deal with issues such as numbers and elections of members, rules of procedure, the holding of meetings etc. Information on these and other matters such as Parliament's sessions, can be found on Parliament's extensive web site:

http://www.europarl.eu.int

The General-Secretariat of Parliament, which is divided into Directorates-General, assists Parliament in performing its tasks. Directorate E of D–G 2

---

[19] See p. 131.

(Common Policies) provides specific back-up to the parliamentary committee dealing with tourism.

Remaining discussion in this part will focus on Parliament's committees and the ways Parliament facilitates complaints from Union citizens about Community laws and institutions since these have particular relevance to tourism.

While Parliament must await a formal proposal from the Commission which kick starts the legislative procedure, it can influence the areas which the Commission produces proposal on. In Article 192 Parliament, acting by a majority of its members, can

> request the Commission to submit any appropriate proposal on matters on which it considers that a Community act is required for the purpose of implementing this Treaty.

This provides Parliament with the opportunity to influence the choice of areas made by the Commission for future initiatives or actions. Acting under the duty of cooperation with other Community institutions to secure the Treaty's objectives, the Commission is unlikely to ignore such a request.

Parliamentary committees

Because of the range and complexity of issues Parliament must deal with and also because of the large number of its members, Parliament conducts a significant part of its business through committees, and in some cases sub-committees, of its members, each committee dealing with a range of allotted areas.

Parliament's Rules of Procedure[20] set out the duties and procedures of committees. Rule 150 states in part that: Parliament shall set up standing committees whose powers shall be defined in an annex to the Rules of Procedure. Annex VI establishes 17 standing committees, one of which is the Committee on Regional Policy, Transport and Tourism, and another of which is a Committee of Petitions. The function of standing committees under Rule 154 is to "examine questions referred to them by Parliament".

In terms of legislative procedures, committees play a vital role in enabling Parliament carry out its legislative functions. Under Rule 60 Proposals from the Commission and other documents of a legislative nature shall be referred by the President to the committee responsible for consideration.

The Committee on Regional Policy, Transport and Tourism "is responsible

---

[20] 14th edition, OJ L 202/1, 2.8.99. A revised set of Rules is due to come into force in 2004.

for matters relating to Community regional policy … a common transport policy … [and] tourism". However, many issues indirectly affect tourism and are dealt with by other committees. Sometimes Parliament will entrust a multi-dimensional issue to the committee most centrally concerned and then authorise other committees to feed opinions into the report which will be produced by the lead committee.

A tourism example of this arose in 1996 when the Commission proposal for a multi-annual programme to assist European tourism 'Philoxenia' came before Parliament.

At the sitting of July 3, 1996 the President of Parliament announced that he had referred the proposal to the Committee on Transport and Tourism as the committee responsible and to the Committee on Budgets, the Committee on Regional Policy and the Committee on Culture, Youth, Education and the Media for their opinions.[21] Attached to the final Report were the Opinions of the other committees.

The website of the Committee on Regional Policy, Transport and Tourism is at:

http://www.europarl.eu.int/committees/rett_home.htm

and should be consulted for information about its members, meetings, hearings and reports.

Parliament and the citizens of the Union

Two specific mechanisms – the petition and the Ombudsman – are provided in the Treaty of Rome to enable Parliament to respond to complaints and grievances from Union citizens about Community activities. A number of petitions and complaints to the Ombudsman have concerned tourism issues.

Petitions to the Committee on Petitions

Article 21 of the Rome Treaty declares that:

Every citizen of the Union shall have the right to petition the European Parliament in accordance with Article 194.

Article 194 in turn declares that Union citizens, and natural/legal persons residing in the Community:

---

[21] EP, Session Document, Report on the Proposal for a Council Decision on a First Multi–annual Programme to assist European Tourism, A4–0298/96, 3.10.96.

shall have the right to address ... a petition to the European Parliament on matters which come within the Community's fields of activity and which affects him, her or it directly.

Petition has been defined by Parliament as:

all complaints, requests for an opinion, demands for action, reactions to Parliament resolutions or decisions by other Community institutions or bodies forwarded to it by individuals and associations.[22]

The right to petition Parliament (without paying a fee) has been increasingly used over the years. In 1987 a specific committee of Parliament, the Committee on Petitions, was established to deal with petitions. Parliament's current Rules of Procedure define its responsibilities as encompassing:

1. petitions (Article 21 of the EC Treaty), consideration thereof and action to be taken in connection therewith, and relations with the Ombudsman;

2. the monitoring accompanying the implementation of current expenditure for which it has responsibility, on the basis of periodic reports provided by the Commission.

The website of the Petitions Committee is at:

http://www.europarl.eu.int/committees/peti_home.htm

and should be consulted for information about its members, meetings, hearings and reports. Among the reports available on the Committee's web site are its informative annual reports which provides details of petitions that have been investigated.

Part of the reason for the increasing popularity of the petition right is that the Treaty of Rome does not give a right of direct access to the Court of Justice for citizens to complain about violations of Community law. The right of petition carries no costs for the individual, but the Committee cannot award damages either.

The main attraction of the petition is that it must and will be acted upon, both by Parliament – because of its Treaty basis – and by the Commission, to whom

---

[22] EP, Report on the deliberations of the Committee on Petitions for the parliamentary year 1996–1997, A4–0190/97, 28.5.97, p. 9.

petitions are frequently passed for information/action, because of the Commission's Treaty responsibility to monitor and enforce observation of Community law and also because the Commission must under Article 197 reply to questions put by Parliament's members.

The procedure when the Committee receives a petitions (for which no formal format is prescribed and can be done by mere letter without using a lawyer) is that the Committee examines it to see that:

- it is admissible,

- it is brought by a Community citizen,

- it relates to a matter of Community law, the activities of Community institutions and bodies or a project all/partly funded by Community funds.

Tourism Examples of closed (finished) Petitions

A British petitioner wanted to travel to Bruges on the Eurostar, but was detained in Brussels by the Belgian authorities on the grounds that her passport had been forged (photograph replaced). Deported from Belgium, the petitioner complained that she had been deprived of the right to freedom of movement within the European Union. ... The British passport office conceded that faulty material might have been used to attach the photograph in the passport, and reimbursed the petitioner the cost of her trip to Belgium.[23]

A British petitioner complained that as a qualified European Mountain Leader, who brought English clients on walking holidays in the Val d'Aosta region of Italy, he was charged under regional Italian law with offences connected with offering services for which he was unqualified. The Commission took the view that the case was similar to a number of tour guide cases where national laws were held to be in breach of the Treaty. After initiating infringement proceedings against Italy in late 1997, the Italian authorities announced that Directive 92/51/EEC had been incorporated into Italian law with regard to the profession in question.[24]

The Chairman of the 'British Spear fishing Association' complained that the Greek authorities refused to issue skin-diving permits to members of his association, although they were issued to Greek citizens. The Commission decided to initiate infringement proceedings against Greece

---

[23] EP, Report on the deliberations of the Committee on Petitions for the parliamentary year 1998–1999, A4–0117/99, p.7.

[24] *Supra*.

> for violation of Articles 12 and 49 of the Treaty (freedom to provide services and discrimination on the basis of nationality). Ass a result, the Greek authorities adopted new rules in compliance with Community legislation. Non-Greek EU citizens can now apply for permits on the same basis as Greek nationals.[25]

Complaints to the Ombudsman

The second Treaty mechanism designed to enable Parliament respond to citizen grievances, this time about how Community institutions and bodies carry out their administrative activities, is set out in Articles 21 and 195 (1) of the Treaty. Article 21 declares:

> Every citizen of the Union may apply to the Ombudsman established in accordance with Article 195.

Article 195 in turn obliges Parliament to appoint an Ombudsman to

> receive complaints from any citizen of the Union or any natural or legal person ... concerning instances of mal-administration in the activities of the Community institutions or bodies. ...[26]

Maladministration is not defined in the Treaty, but the working definition used by the Ombudsman is as follows:

> Maladministration occurs when a public body fails to act in accordance with a rule or principle which is binding upon it.[27]

The Ombudsman's functions relate only to investigating allegations of failure by Community institutions to act in accordance with principles of good administration, not to complaints about national institutions, although a single complaint can often involve interchanges between the two since national institutions often act on behalf of Community ones. The Ombudsman also cannot investigate cases which have been or are the subject of proceedings before courts.

---

[25] EP, Committee on Petitions, Petition 70/96. For further examples of successful petitions involving restrictions on tourist free movement, see p. 37.

[26] See also Article 43 of the Charter of Fundamental Rights of the European Union.

[27] European Ombudsman, Annual Report for 1999, p.17. The Code of Good Administrative behaviour, adopted by European Parliament resolution on the Annual Report on the Activities of the European Ombudsman, C5–0302/2001 – 2001/2043(COS), point 7 and available at http://www.euro–ombudsman.eu.int/code/pdf/en/code_en.pdf is an attempt to clarify the principle of good administration.

Despite occasional opposition from Community institutions, the Ombudsman does investigate instances of alleged failure by Community institutions to act in conformity with Community law and this can lead the Ombudsman to adopting legal interpretations of measures which might be contested by other institutions.

The Ombudsman is declared by Article 195(3) to be "completely independent in the performance of his duties". His only power however under 195(1) is to "conduct enquiries for which he finds grounds". If those enquiries establish a case of maladministration, he must inform the institution concerned, which then has three months to "inform him of its views". Thereafter the Ombudsman must forward a report to the institution concerned and to Parliament. He must also inform the complainant of the outcome of his enquiries.

The Ombudsman's website is at:

http://www.euro-ombudsman.eu.int/home/en/default.htm

and should be consulted for information regarding, among other things, activities, how to make a complaint and previous decisions.

Instances of maladministration can range from the minor (failure to acknowledge receipt of a complaint/letter) to the more serious (irregular management of Community funds). Among the Annual Reports of the Ombudsman to Parliament are complaints related to a range of tourism issues, such as:

- failure to give adequate reasons for not renewing funding for a Dutch film festival,[28]

- failure by Commission to deal properly with a complaint concerning the way which the UK implemented the Package Holiday Directive,[29]

- failure by Commission to properly examine the alleged contradictory use of Community funds in Spain to enlarge a commercial harbour which was in the immediate vicinity of a beach, the regeneration of which was also benefiting from Community funding,[30]

- failings in Commission investigations of Belgian and UK restrictions on the freedom of movement of football supporters,[31]

- alleged Commission mishandling of financial aspects of a rural regeneration through sustainable tourism project in Bulgaria,[32]

- the alleged improper award of a Blue Flag to a beach in Portugal.[33]

---

[28] European Ombudsman, Annual Report for 1998, p.230.
[29] *Ibid.*, p.118.
[30] European Ombudsman, Annual Report for 1999, p.140.
[31] European Ombudsman, Annual Report for 1997, p.59.
[32] European Ombudsman, Annual Report for 1999, p.180.
[33] European Ombudsman, Annual Report for 1996, p.48.

Tourism Examples

A complaint concerned a near two-year delay by the Commission in responding to/disposing of a complaint about the legality of Italian state charges for the issuing of Italian passports. The Ombudsman rejected the complaint, finding no maladministration, the delay being explained by the complexity of the query which had necessitated the conduct of a survey of other Member States practise in this area. The Commission's response to the original complaint is worth noting because it deals with whether a passport can be seen as a barrier to the Treaty guarantee of free movement for citizens. According to the Ombudsman the Commission stated:

> Community law requires Member States to issue a passport or an identity card to their citizens. The fact that Italy imposes an annual tax on the passport is compatible with Community law, because 'the costs of the passport and the procedure of issuing it fall within the competence of the member States. (The Commission did not consider that) the system of issue of passports impedes the free movement of persons in the light of Community law.[34]

A complaint was made by ETEN (European Tourism Education Network) that the Commission had failed to pay the outstanding 40% of an agreed subvention for two tourism projects – establishment of an international tourism students association and publication of a thesaurus and dictionary of tourism terminology. ETEN also complained that the Commission had failed to respond to its letters. When the Commission (DG XXIII) admitted and apologised for the failure to respond to the letters and indicated that internal procedures were being reviewed, the Ombudsman concluded that 'no further remark' seemed necessary.[35]

As regards the Commission failure to pay the outstanding sums, and a counter-claim by the Commission for repayment of part, both justified by the Commission on the basis that ETEN had not fulfilled the contract conditions, the Ombudsman decided that since the Commission had genuine doubts over the fulfilment of the contract conditions by ETEN, there was no maladministration involved.

A complaint was made alleging maladministration following the exclusion of a contractor who claimed unrivalled experience from a tender list for TACIS funding for tourist industry projects in Russia.

---

[34] European Ombudsman, Annual Report for 1997, p.151.
[35] European Ombudsman, Annual Report for 1997, p.90.

> In his decision, the Ombudsman stated that the Commission enjoys a large degree of discretion in deciding to award a contract following an invitation to tender. That discretion cannot justify, however, manifest errors in the selection procedure. In using its discretion, the institutions must base its decision on some objective criteria which can be reviewed. … In this case, the Commission based its assessment on a number of prima facie objective criteria which were reflected in the tables of comparative assessment of the merits of participants. Even though the complainant's consortium showed expertise and competence in the field of this particular project, there was no evidence that the Commission used its discretion in an arbitrary or discriminatory way.[36]

A complaint was made alleging failure by the Commission to take account of the effects of unemployment in dealing with an application for an exemption from competition rules for an airline alliance.[37] The Commission contended that the Ombudsman was not competent to determine whether unemployment was an issue which as a matter of law could be taken into account. The complaint also alleged that the Commission did not acknowledge or reply to submissions it had invited.

> The Ombudsman observed that the applicable Regulation contained no such obligation [to respond to submissions]. However, by inviting third parties to submit observations, intended to assist it in its analysis, the Commission had placed itself in a situation where the citizens could reasonably expect a reaction from it; all the more so in this case, as the [complainant] had an interest in the decision by virtue of they fact that its members were possibly affected by it. The Commission's failure to give a reaction … had been, therefore, an instance of maladministration.

Regarding the non-competence issue –

> In this case, however, a fundamental misunderstanding should be corrected. The service responsible for drafting the Commission's replies to the Ombudsman … appeared to have assumed that 'wrong application of the law' cannot be 'maladministration'. In fact, the opposite is true; it can never be good administration to fail to act in accordance with the law. The first and most essential task of the Ombudsman when conducting inquiries into possible maladministration in the activities of a Community institution or body is to establish whether the institution concerned has acted lawfully.

---

[36] European Ombudsman, Annual Report for 1997, p.146.

Council of the European Union

Article 7 of the Treaty of Rome declares that, among other bodies, the tasks of the Community shall be carried out by a ... Council. Article 203 provides:

> the Council shall consist of a representative of each Member State at ministerial level, authorised to commit the government of that Member State.

The Council of Ministers, which is presided over by the minister from whatever state holds the presidency of the Union at that particular time, is different from the "European Council"[38] which is the title given by the Treaty on European Union to meetings of the prime ministers of the Member States of the Union. While this body has certain important general functions, they are not sufficiently closely connected with tourism issues to be of further interest in this account.

Formally, there is only body called the Council of Ministers. It deals with many different areas and the composition and Member State representatives vary accordingly. Because the number of areas and meetings are potentially great, Article 2 of the Council's Rules of Procedure[39] provides that:

> The Council may meet in different configurations according to the subject matter dealt with. The Council in its General Affairs and External Affairs configuration ... shall fix the list of these configurations, which is set out in Annex 1.

Annex 1 lists nine configurations, with tourism coming under the Competitiveness (Internal Market, Industry and Research) Council. Under the previous sixteen configurations tourism was part of the Internal Market, Consumer Affairs and Tourism Council.[40] Before this specific tourism Councils were authorised and meet mainly in the late 1980s and early to mid 1990s.[41] The homepage of the Council's website is at:

http://ue.eu.int/en/info/main.htm

and should be consulted for information on, among other things, the Council's

---

[37] European Ombudsman, Annual Report for 1998, p.46.

[38] And also different from the Council of Europe which is a completely separate international organisation. See p. 5.

[39] Council Decision 2002/682 adopting the Council's Rules of Procedure, OJ L 230/8, 28.8.02.

[40] OJ C174/2, 23.6.00.

[41] For some press releases of previous Tourism Council meetings, see Press Release Brussels 13.5.96, Press 129, Nr. 7072/96; Press Release Brussels, 26.11.97, press 358, Nr. 12664.

functions, activities, composition, working methods, presidency and Secretariat. An example of a meeting involving tourism ministers is:[42]

Report of the Internal Market, Consumer Affairs and Tourism Council to the Goteborg Council

1. Introduction

> This is the Internal market, Consumer Affairs and Tourism Council (IMCT) response to the request by the Helsinki European Council to submit a strategy for the integration of environmental protection and sustainable development into internal market policy to the Goteborg Council, in June 2001. ...

While different articles in the Rome Treaty confer various functions on the Council of Ministers, the most generally expressed statement of the Council's functions is set out in Article 202 which provides that in order to attain the objectives set out in the Treaty, the Council shall:

– ensure co-ordination of the general economic policies of the Member States;

– have power to take decisions;

– confer on the Commission, in the acts which the Council adopts, powers for the implementation of the rules which the Council lays down.

In addition to this, the Council is specifically bound or empowered by many other articles, particularly those relating to the creation of the internal market (which obviously includes the tourism internal market) to adopt or participate in adopting Community laws and measures.

In legislative and policy terms, the Council is thus the lead Community institution and since it is representative of Member States interests is able, or at least has been able, to determine what the Community does and how quickly or slowly it moves towards its objectives. Voting within the Council is critical in deciding whether Commission proposals are accepted, rejected or altered.[43] If the Council does not reach the necessary agreement on a Commission proposal, the proposal has no chance of succeeding.

Yet, the Council does not have compete discretion as to what is does or, more to the point, does not do. If a Treaty provision is sufficiently precise then it can impose an obligation on the Council to act. In a case[44] which had

---

[42] Press Release Brussels, 19.5.01, Nr. 8970/01, p.1.
[43] See p. 126.
[44] *European Parliament v. Council* [1985] E.C.R. 1513. See also p. 183.

considerable implications for opening up transport markets and thus facilitating tourist movement, the Court of Justice held that the Council had failed to comply with a sufficiently precise Treaty obligation to ensure that Common Market freedom to provide services operated in the transport area.

Further, as part of the balance of power between Community institutions, the Rome Treaty imposes a significant limitation on the Council's powers. The Council is not allowed undertake legislative or policy initiatives on its own. In most cases it is only allowed act on receipt of a proposal from the Commission. If none is proposed, the Council cannot act on its own. The Council can, however, indicate its priorities and wishes to the Commission regarding areas of possible action by using the power conferred on it by Article 208 to:

> request the Commission to undertake any studies the Council considers desirable for the attainment off the common objectives, and to submit to it appropriate proposals.

The Council is assisted in performing its functions by two bodies:

- The Committee of the Permanent Representatives of the Member States (known by its French acronym COREPER).
- A General Secretariat.

Under Article 207(1) of the Rome Treaty COREPER is "responsible for preparing the work of the Council and for carrying out the tasks assigned to it by the Council". Article 19 (1) of the Council's Rules of Procedure[45] supplements this by requiring COREPER to see to it that in the Council's acts:

> the following rules and principles are observed … the principles of legality, subsidiarity, proportionality and providing reasons for acts …

Rule 19(3) of the Council's Rules of Procedure also provides:

> Committees or working parties may be set up by, or with the approval of, Coreper with a view to carrying out certain preparatory work or studies defined in advance.

COREPER has established a wide range of working parties to prepare reports to feed into the deliberations of the Council. These parties fall into two types – roughly 100 regular sectoral working parties and a variable number of ad-hoc working parties set up to deal only with a particular dossier, in total approximately

---

[45] OJ L 230/15, 28.8.02.

250. It is the function of the Presidency under Article 21 of the Council's Rules of Procedure to "organise the meetings of the various committees and working parties so that their reports are available before the Coreper meetings at which they are to be examined".

While there are currently a number of committees whose activities can indirectly affect tourism, such as the Committee on Cultural Affairs, there is currently no committee dealing specifically for tourism. The last working party which dealt with tourism was the Working Party on Economic Questions "Tourism" which met a number of times under the Austrian Presidency in the latter half of 1998. The purpose of the Group, which reported to COREPER was to agree a draft compromise text of the Presidency on a proposal for a Council Decision on a first multi-annual programme, provisionally titled "Philoxenia" to assist European tourism.[46]

As regards the Council's General Secretariat, Article 207 (2) of the Rome Treaty provides that:

> The Council shall be assisted by a General Secretariat … The Council shall decide on the organisation of the General Secretariat.

Article 23 (3) of the Council's Rules of Procedure declares that The General Secretariat shall be closely and continually involved in organising, coordinating and ensuring the coherence of the Council's work and implementation of its work programme.

The Secretariat is thus responsible for facilitating the work of the Council and COREPER and the various working parties. The General Secretariat is divided into Directorates General which in turn are divided into Directorates. Directorate I of Directorate General C of the Council Secretariat deals with tourism. Within the Council's Legal Service, Team I deals with tourism matters.

Commission of the European Community

The Commission is one of the Community institutions established under Article 7 of the Rome Treaty. Its pre-eminent functions are outlined in Article 211 as follows:

> In order to ensure the proper functioning and development of the Common Market, the Commission shall:
>
> - ensure that the provisions of this Treaty and the measures taken by the institutions pursuant thereto are applied;

---

[46] See also p. 69.

- formulate recommendations or deliver opinions on matters dealt with in this Treaty, if it expressly so provides or if the Commission considers it necessary;
- have its own power of decision and participate in the shaping of measures taken by the Council and by the European Parliament in the manner provided for in this Treaty, and;
- exercise the powers conferred on it by the Council for the implementation of the rules laid down by the latter.

Although this passage indicates that the Commission's functions are to be exercised solely to ensure the proper functioning and development of the Common Market, in fact other provisions of the Treaty confer specific functions on the Commission which are much broader in scope than the Common Market. The functions listed in Article 211 broadly correspond with:

- ensuring the administrative and legal enforcement of Community policies and laws,
- a general advisory role for the benefit of the Community,
- a general participatory role in the Community, and
- a legislative role.

The Commission maintains an extensive website at:

http://www./europa.eu.int/comm

from which access can be gained to information on the Community's activities in all the areas of Commission responsibility and also, among other things, information about the appointment, identify, responsibilities and removal of Commission members and the Commission President. The remainder of this part focuses only on those aspects of Commission activities of direct relevance to tourism. But firstly a note regarding the organisation of the Commission's services and tourism.

Commission Departments

The Treaty of Rome assumes the Commission will establish the departments to help it discharge its responsibilities. Article 218(2) provides that:

The Commission shall adopt its Rules of Procedure so as to ensure that both it and its departments operate in accordance with the provisions of this Treaty.

Article 19 of the Commission's Rules of Procedure[47] states that:

> A number of Directorates-General and equivalent departments forming a single administrative service shall assist the Commission in the performance of its tasks

The Directorates-General and equivalent departments shall normally be divided into directorates and directorates into units.

Commission members when first appointed are allocated the areas which they will have responsibility for in preparing the Commission's business and implementing its decisions. The relevant department dealing with that area will come under the control and responsibility of that Commission member. Thus, a Commission member can have responsibilities which straddle a range of different departments.

The current structure of Commission departments was reorganised on the accession of a new Commission and Commission President in 1999.[48] Tourism was transferred from the previous Directorate-General 23 to the Enterprise Directorate-General[49] and, in what was a downgrading of its scale, is now dealt with in one Unit, Unit 3 under Directorate D which is titled Services, Commerce, Tourism, e-business and IDA.

Locating the Unit within the Enterprise Directorate has naturally focused the Units outlook onto issues like competitiveness, innovation and employment. This suggests a somewhat lop sided approach to the wide range of issues involved in tourism, although the language of issues like competitiveness and employment can be used elastically to cover a surprisingly wider range of tourism topics.

Before 1999 an entire directorate, Directorate D within DG 23,[50] with three constituent Units, was devoted to tourism:

- Unit 1 dealt with development of tourism policy and relations with the industry, third party countries and international organisations.
- Unit 2 dealt with stimulation of competition in tourism.
- Unit 3 dealt with promotion of tourist interests and quality.

The Commission is assisted in its tourism tasks by an advisory committee on

---

[47] OJ L 308/26, 8.12.00.

[48] Commission, Memorandum from the Vice–President for Administrative Reform in agreement with the President, Reorganisation of the Commission Administrative Structure, SEC (1999) 1494/3.

[49] Commission, PERS (1999) 163/4 and (1999) 191/4.

[50] The Tourism Directorate within DG 23 had a chequered history, a former head and other staff being dismissed and the group itself being subjected to a number of audits and investigations, some details of which are set out in two special reports of the Court of Auditors.

tourism established by Decision 664/86[51] and comprised of representative of Member States governments and industry representatives.[52] This body appears to play an increasing role as a forum for broad ranging consultation by the Commission. The current website of the Enterprise Directorate General on tourism is at:

http://europa.eu.int/enterprise/services/tourism/index_en.htm

Among other things, it provides information about Community involvement in tourism, relevant Community legislation, tourism statistics and services of benefit to European tourism.

Enforcement and monitoring role of Commission

Article 226 of the Rome Treaty lays down a specific procedure to be followed by the Commission where it considers a Member State has failed to fulfil an obligation under the Treaty. Once the Commission has formed an initial non-compliance view,

> it shall deliver a reasoned opinion on the matter after giving the state concerned the opportunity to submit its observations. If the state concerned does not comply with the opinion within the period laid down by the Commission, the latter may bring the matter before the Court of Justice.

Thus the stages under an Article 226 investigation are:
• Commission investigation leading to formation of non-compliance view,
• communication of view to Member-State,
• Member-State submits its observations,
• Commission delivers reasoned opinion,
• continuing Member-State non-compliance with opinion within deadline, and
• Commission initiates legal proceedings before Court of Justice.

Often the threat of legal proceedings before the Court of Justice of default by a Member-State is enough to secure compliance. However, in many cases its necessary to institute proceedings and occasionally, under Article 228, the

---

[51] OJ L 384/52, 31.12.86. See also p. 47.

[52] For a recent account of the role and functions of this committee in relation to promoting tourism strategies at Community level, see Commission, Communication on working together for the future of European tourism, COM(2001) 665 final, 13.11.01.

Commission seeks fines against states for failure to comply with a court judgement, since if the Court finds non-compliance "it may impose a lump sum or penalty payment on the State" – Article 228(2).

> Article [228] proceedings against France (transposal of Article 5 in relation to several species of birds) have been referred to the Court for a second time … for failure, seventeen years after the Directive entered into force and ten years after the ruling, to implement the Directive properly and in full. When referring the case to the Court the Commission also proposed that France should be required to pay a daily fine of ECU 105 000 from the dote of the second judgement. … The Commission had also decided to refer the matter of the opening and closing dates of the hunting season for migratory birds in France to the Court for non-compliance with Article 7(4); it had received numerous complaints on the subject; and Parliament had received numerous petitions, some supporting and some opposing the French system of open and closed seasons to which the Commission took objection.[53]

Among the ways in which the Commission monitors and enforces Community laws and policies are:

- receiving/investigating complaints from Union citizens directly or through petitions referred to it by Parliament about the spending of Community funds,
- investigating allegations of anti-competitive behaviour, and
- monitoring Member States implementation of directives.

Tourism Examples

The World-wide Fund for Nature UK lodged a complaint with the Commission over plans announced in 1991 by the Irish authorities to build a visitor's centre in a national park in the west of Ireland using Community Structural Funds. The Commission subsequently opened an investigation into the project, including the alleged infringement of environmental law and the eligibility of the project for structural funds.

> On October 7, 1992 the Commission announced that it did not intend to initiate infringement proceedings against Ireland since it had found that the project did not infringe community environmental law.[54]

---

[53] Second Annual Survey of the implementation and enforcement of Community environmental law, January 1988–December 1999, p.85.

[54] *WWW UK v. Commission* [1997] 2 C.M.L.R. 55, 62.

Following a complaint by British Midland airline, the Commission held in 1992that Aer Lingus, an Irish airline, had abused its dominant position on the Dublin-London route, in breach of Article 82 (then 86) of the Treaty of Rome by terminating its interlining agreement with British Midland. A fine of 750,000 ECU was imposed on Aer Lingus and it was ordered to resume interlining with British Midland, but only for a period which was objectively necessary for a competitor to become established on the market. This was set at two years, subject to review.[55]

General role of the Commission in the Community's activities

The way the Commission plays a general role in the life of the Community is by proposing measures and initiatives aimed at furthering the Community's goals as set out in the Treaty. This role should be evident in the many examples provided in these pages.

The Commission's direct participatory role in tourism is, not surprisingly, somewhat narrow given the limited direct reference to tourism in the Treaty.[56] The web-site of the previous Commission Directorate General responsible for tourism described that role as follows:[57]

> One of the main roles of DG XXIII's Tourism Directorate is to play a co-ordinating role within the European Commission, aiming to ensure that the interests of tourism are fully taken into account in the preparation of legislation and in the operation of programmes and policies which are not themselves conceived in terms of tourism objectives. In practice very many programmes and policies now either include a tourism dimension or have a significant impact on tourism-related activities.

The need for this role was emphasised by the Court Auditors in a special report on tourism.

> Given the dispersal of the various measures having an impact on tourism among the various DGs, sound co-ordination is absolutely essential.[58]

However, during the 1990s this role was not always carried out satisfactorily.

---

[55] Commission, Community Competition Laws in the Transport Sector Recent Landmarks 1991–1997, p.13.

[56] See p. 24.

[57] www.europa.eu.int/en/comm/dg23/tourisme; no longer in operation.

[58] Court of Auditors, Special Report 3/96 on a tourist policy and the promotion of tourism, OJ C 17/10, 16.1.97.

Among the failings found by the Court of Auditors were:

- lack of systematic consultations with other departments, and
- non-consultation by other departments of the tourism unit.[59]

A significant part of the participatory activities carried out by the current tourism unit concerns the generation (through commissioned studies, surveys) and distribution (meetings, events, publications) of specialised information of relevance to European tourism. Two significant elements in this are:

- periodic reports on Community measures affecting tourism.[60]
- an internet guide to EU support for tourism enterprises and tourist destinations.[61]

The tourism unit has also been laudably pro-active in contributing efforts to tackle child sex tourism.

Legislative role of the Commission

The principal basis for the Commission's authority to enact legislation is contained in Article 202 of the Rome Treaty which states that:

> To ensure that the objectives set out in this Treaty are attained the Council shall … confer on the Commission, in the acts which the Council adopts, powers for the implementation of the rules which the Council lays down.

The Commission uses this power regularly. A tourism example of such a delegation of law-making power is:

COMMISSION REGULATION (EC) NO 2121/98
of 2 October 1998

laying down detailed rules for the application of Council Regulations (EEC) No 684/92 and (EC) No 12/98 as regards documents for the carriage of passengers by coach and bus.

As a supplement to its enforcement and legislative roles, the Commission also issue guidance notices or guidelines outlining its approach to enforcing

---

[59] *Ibid.*, p.11.
[60] See p. 17.
[61] Text available at http://europa.eu.int/comm/enterprise/services/tourism/policy–areas/ eu_schemes.htm.

legislation. This is most evident in those areas where Commission approval is required, as for instance in areas relevant to tourism, the approval of Community support frameworks under regional policy or the approval of state aids under competition law. Examples of these guidelines are contained in the respective chapters on regional policy and competition policy.

The Court of Justice

The Treaty of Rome established a specific court – the oddly titled (for an originally predominantly economic Community) Court of Justice, (not to be confused with the European Court of Human Rights[62] established under a human rights convention of the Council of Europe, a separate mainly European inter-governmental body) – to provide final and authoritative rulings on issues of law arising under the Treaty of Rome.

The Treaty also provides for the establishment of a second court, the Court of First Instance, which "shall have jurisdiction to hear and determine at first instance ... certain actions or proceedings" dealing among other things with reviewing the legality of laws made under co-decision, compensation claims against the Community and staff claims – Article 225. This Court which was first established in 1988 therefore operates under the rubric of the Court of Justice, but at the same time is separate from it. No other judicial courts are provided for under the Treaty, thus there is no system of Community courts operating in Member States akin to federal courts operating alongside state courts in the United States. Consistent with this, access to both Community courts is severely restricted by the Treaty and thus ordinary citizens cannot generally bring proceedings in the Court of Justice.

It was entirely logical for the Treaty to establish a new court which would be responsible for its interpretation and for the interpretation of laws made under the Treaty, since without it there would not have been a way of ensuring the consistent interpretation of Community law across Member States. Without such harmony it is doubtful if the Community could have evolved as it has. Not would there be a conclusive means for determining disputes concerning the employment of Community officials since this too is a responsibility of the Court of Justice. The Court of Justice has its own web-site at:

www.curia.eu.int/en/index.htm.

This should be consulted for information regarding the courts composition, activities, division into chambers, statute, rules of procedure and activities,

---

[62] See http://www.echr.coe.int/.

numbers of judges/advocates-general, appointment, term of office, removal etc. The texts of recent judgements are also available through this web site. Otherwise the Court judgements are available from its annual publication, the European Court Reports. In the remainder of this section, only those aspects of the Court that can be illustrated through tourism examples will be looked at.

An Advocate-General is an independent official who assists the Court in the task of legal reasoning. Under Article 222:

> It shall be the duty of the Advocate-General, acting with complete impartiality and independence to make in open court, reasoned submissions on cases which .... require his involvement.

The main Treaty statement of the functions of the Court of Justice is contained in Article 220 which provides:

> The Court of Justice and the Court of First Instance, each within its jurisdiction, shall ensure that in the interpretation and application of this Treaty the law is observed.

Although the Treaty does not define what it means by the word 'law', it is clear it includes the provisions of the Treaty itself, the secondary laws (regulations, directives, and decisions) made under the Treaty and certain principles developed by the Court itself.[63] The interpretation of national laws to see if they infringe Community laws is not, as such, a function of the Court of Justice and the Court is careful to say it does not do this. What happens in infringement cases brought by the Commission against a Member State is that the Court interprets Community measures relative to national ones, and declares whether the state has failed to comply with its obligations.

The task of interpreting the Treaty is not a simple one of seeing whether something is expressly mentioned in the Treaty or not. Rather, interpreting involves looking not only at the actual words used in the text, but also at the ideas behind individual Treaty provisions and also at the grander scheme envisaged when reading a range of Treaty provisions together. Similar considerations apply when interpreting regulations and directives which, as was seen earlier,[64] contain lengthy preambles which recite the legal basis, reasons and facts on which the law is based. Thus the process of interpretation by the two Community courts can be a creative and also an uncertain one.

---

[63] See p. 25.
[64] See also p. 82.

Types of legal proceedings

Under the Treaty of Rome the principal types of legal proceedings which the Court of Justice/Court of First Instance can hear are:

- proceedings against Member-States for failure to fulfil Community law obligations,
- proceedings seeking the annulment of Community legalisation or Community institution decisions,
- proceedings against a Community institution for failure to act under Community law,
- appeals to the Court of Justice from decisions of the Court of First Instance,
- proceedings based on requests from courts of Member States seeking preliminary rulings from the Court of Justice on points of Community law.

The following tourism examples illustrate a number of these proceedings.

Proceedings against Member States

Under Article 226 of the Rome Treaty the Commission is empowered, after delivering a reasoned opinion on the matter, to seek judgment in the Court of Justice against a Member States it considers to have failed to fulfil an obligation to implement legislation.

The following extract comes from a proceeding taken by the Commission against Greece before the Court of Justice[65] for failing to implement a directive.

JUDGMENT OF THE COURT (Fifth Chamber)

26 June 1997

(Failure to fulfil obligations — Failure to transpose Directive 92/43/ EEC)

In Case C–329/96,

Commission of the European Communities, represented by Maria Condo Durande, of its Legal Service, acting as Agent, with an address for service in Luxembourg at the office of Carlos Gómez de la Cruz, of its Legal Service, Wagner Centre, Kirchberg,

applicant,

---

[65] [1997] E.C.R. I–3799.

Hellenic Republic, represented by Evi Skandalou, Legal Assistant, First Class, in the Special European Community Legal Service of the Ministry of Foreign Affairs, assisted by Nana Daphniou, Legal Assistant, Second Class, in the same Service, acting as Agents, with an address for service in Luxembourg at the Greek Embassy, 117 Val Sainte-Croix,

.....

having regard to the report of the Judge-Rapporteur,

after hearing the Opinion of the Advocate General at the sitting on 24 April 1997,

gives the following

Judgment

By application lodged at the Court Registry on 8 October 1996, the Commission of the European Communities brought an action under Article 169 of the EC Treaty for a declaration that, by failing, within the prescribed period, to adopt and/or notify to it the laws, regulations and administrative provisions necessary to comply with Council Directive 92/43/EEC of 21 May 1992 on the conservation of natural habitats and of wild fauna and flora (OJ 1992 L 206, p.7, hereinafter 'the Directive'), the Hellenic Republic has failed to fulfil its obligations under the EC Treaty and that directive.

1. Member States were required under Article 23 of the Directive to bring into force the laws, regulations and administrative provisions necessary to comply with it within two years of its notification and forthwith to inform the Commission thereof. Since the Directive was notified to the Greek authorities on 5 June 1992, the period laid down for its implementation expired on 5 June 1994.

2. Noting that this period had expired, and not having been informed of the measures for transposing the Directive into Greek law, the Commission initiated proceedings for a declaration of failure to fulfil obligations under Article 169 of the Treaty. By letter of 9 August 1994 it put the Greek Government on formal notice to submit to it its observations within two months.

Since the Greek Government did not reply to that letter, the Commission sent to it, on 21 June 1995, a reasoned opinion requesting it to adopt the measures necessary for compliance within two months of notification.

In the absence of any notification of transposition measures by the Hellenic Republic, the Commission brought the present action.

3. In its defence the Greek Government does not deny that the Directive was not transposed within the prescribed period. It merely points out that the delay in transposing the Directive has been attributable to technical legislative problems.

4. Since the Directive was not transposed within the period which it prescribed, the action brought by the Commission must be held to be well founded.

5. It must accordingly be held that, by failing to adopt within the prescribed period the laws, regulations and administrative provisions necessary to comply with the Directive, the Hellenic Republic has failed to fulfil its obligations under Article 23 thereof.

Costs

6. Under Article 69(2) of the Rules of Procedure, the unsuccessful party is to be ordered to pay the costs. Since the Hellenic Republic has been unsuccessful, it must be ordered to pay the costs.

On those grounds,

THE COURT (Fifth Chamber)

hereby:

Declares that, by failing to adopt within the prescribed period the laws, regulations and administrative provisions necessary to comply with Council Directive 92/43/EEC of 21 May 1992 on the conservation of natural habitats and of wild fauna and flora, the Hellenic Republic has failed to fulfil its obligations under Article 23 thereof;

Orders the Hellenic Republic to pay the costs.

Proceedings seeking annulment of Commission Decision

Under Article 230 of the Treaty of Rome, the Court of Justice/Court of First Instance has jurisdiction to hear cases "on grounds of lack of competence, infringement of essential procedural requirement, infringement of the Treaty or of any rule of law pertaining to its application, or misuse of powers".

In *Italy v. Commission*,[66] Italy sought annulment of a Commission decision prohibiting it from implementing an Italian law dealing with the transfer of air passenger traffic from one Milan airport to another. The Commission decision was taken under powers conferred on the Commission by a regulation dealing with the freedom of air carriers to access routes within the Community. The Italian challenge was based on the alleged wrongful application of Community law by the Commission, but failed because the Court of Justice agreed with the Commission's view of the law.

Appeals to Court of Justice against decisions of Court of First Instance

Under Article 225(1) of the Treaty of Rome a right of appeal lies against a decision of the Court of First Instance to the Court of Justice "on points of law only and in accordance with the conditions laid down by the [Court's] Statute".

In *IPK-Munchen v. Commission* the Court of Justice[67] dealt with an appeal from the Court of First Instance,[68] which had dismissed an action by IPK, seeking the annulment of a Commission decision refusing to pay the outstanding balance of Community funding due in respect of an information network established by IPK on ecological tourism projects in Europe. The Commission refusal was based on the belief that the project as completed was not what had been promised. IPK alleged that interference by Commission officials had prevented it from smoothly progressing the project. The Court of First Instance held that, despite proving some interference from Commission officials, IPK had not shown that this inhibited the smooth operation of the project, whereas the Court of Justice differed and held, given the type of interference, it:

> was likely to have had an impact on the smooth running of the project. … In circumstances such as those, it was for the Commission to show that, notwithstanding the interference in question, the applicant continued to be able to, manage the project in a satisfactory manner. … It follows that the Court of First Instance erred in law by requiring the applicant to furnish proof that the Commission officials' actions made it impossible for it to engage in proper cooperation with its partners in the project.

---

[66] [2001] E.C.R. I–385. For further details of this case, see p. 40.
[67] [1999] E.C.R. I–6814.
[68] [1997] E.C.R. II–1665.

Proceedings based on a request from a court of a Member State seeking preliminary rulings from the Court of Justice on points of Community law

This important type of case arises under Article 234 of the Treaty of Rome according to which a court or tribunal in a Member State when hearing a case which raises an issue of interpreting the Treaty, assessing the acts of Community institutions, or interpreting the statutes of bodies established by act of the Council, can request the Court of Justice to give a preliminary ruling on the issue in question. Any level of national judicial body can use this procedure and consequently it is the most widely used means of bringing cases before the Court of Justice

   The request for the preliminary ruling takes the form of carefully worded questions prepared by the national body as to the meaning of Community law. One such request came from Finland:

> In *AFS Finland*[68] the Supreme Administrative Court in Finland asked the Court of Justice for a preliminary ruling (under the predecessor of Article 234) as to whether a non-profit association in Finland which co-ordinated international student exchanges was within the scope of the Package Holiday Directive. The case arose following an order by the Finnish consumer protection agency to AFS to suspend its business over AFS's refusal to register with the agency on the basis that its activities amounted to a package travel business within the meaning of the Directive. The request for the preliminary ruling on the meaning of the Directive arose when AFS appealed to the administrative court. In ruling that the student exchanges were not within the package holiday directive, the Court of Justice concluded:[70]
>
>> The answer to the first part of the first question must therefore be that the Directive does not apply to travel:
>>   – comprising students exchanges of about six month's or a year's duration;
>>   – the purpose of which is attendance by the student at an educational establishment in the host country in order to familiarise himself with its people and culture; and
>>   – during which the student stays with a host family as if he were a member thereof free of charge.
>
> In view of the foregoing, there is no need to reply to the other questions put by the national court. ... The costs incurred by the Finnish

---

[69] [1999] E.C.R. I–825.
[70] At p. 852.

> Government, the United Kingdom Government and the Commission, which have submitted observations to the Court, are not recoverable. Since these proceedings are, for the parties to the main proceedings, a step in the proceedings pending before the national court, the decision on costs is a matter for that court.

Court of Auditors

The Court of Auditors (oddly titled since it is not a court in the usual legal sense) was not one of the original institutions of the Community. It was established only in 1975 and started its work in 1977. The principal reason for the creation of this body was that the cumulative increases in the collection and spending of Community monies made it necessary to create a newer more independent financial oversight body with its own resources. The website of the Court is at:

http://www.eca.eu.int/EN/left.htm.

It describes the functions and powers of the Court, how it conducts its audit, provides details of the court's members, appointment removal, and reports and opinions. The main function of the Court is curtly expressed in Article 246 of the Treaty of Rome, which states that:

The Court of Auditors shall carry out the audit.

As part of the audit, under Article 248(1) the Court must provide Parliament and the Council with:

a statement of assurance as to the reliability of the accounts and the legality and regularity of the underlying transactions.

Other provisions of the Treaty also develop the meaning of audit. Under Article 248 the Court must "examine the accounts of all revenue and expenditure" of the Community and its bodies. The qualitative aspect of the audit relates to the provisions of Article 248(2) which states that:

the Court of Auditors shall examine whether all revenue has been received and all expenditure incurred in a lawful and regular manner and whether the financial management has been sound. In doing so, it shall report in particular on any cases of irregularity.

As to how the audit is to be carried out Article 248(3) provides that:

The audit shall be based on records and, if necessary, performed on the spot in the other institutions of the Community, on the premises of any body which manages revenue or expenditure on behalf of the Community and in the Member States, including on the premises of any natural or legal person in receipt of payments from the budget.

In addition these bodies are obliged to forward any document or information to the Court of Auditors. Among additional powers and duties imposed on the Court are:

- the drawing up of an annual report,
- to submit observations, particularly in the form of special reports, on specific questions and deliver opinions at the request of one of the other institutions of the Community, and
- to assist the Parliament and the Council in exercising their powers of control over the implementation of the budget.

From an examination of the Courts various reports, it is clear that two of the main objects of the Court in carrying out its audits are:

- The promotion of sound methods for financial management in all its aspects (pre-calls for tenders/bids, construction/implementation of selection criteria, on-going monitoring of aid contract performance, ensuring adequate flow of on-going and termination of project information, submission of interim and final reports, all to be carried out in accordance with pre-determined criteria).
- The uncovering and pursuit of fraud and irregularities.

Reports and opinions of the Court of Auditors do not possess any intrinsic legal effect. No one is compelled merely because of a criticism or a recommendation in a Court report to alter a practise or undertake a course of action. However, the standing of the Court's views results from the fact that it is an independent body charged with concern for objective and proper financial standards in the operation of the Community's budget. Further, the other Community institutions must consider any views it expresses due to the general requirements of co-operation and respect which all Community institutions are subject to. In any event, the Court of Auditors is obliged to publish in its annual report the replies of other Community institutions to its observations (Article 248(4)). This forces the other institutions to consider carefully and respond to any criticisms the Court may make.

Special reports on tourism

The Court of Auditors has so far produced two special reports in the area of tourism:

- Special Report 4/92 of the European Court of Auditors on expenditure relating to the European Year of Tourism.[71]
- Special Report 3/96 on tourist policy and the promotion of tourism, together with the Commissions replies.[72]

The first Special Report uncovered serious shortcomings in the management of expenditure by the Community's institutions related to a Community initiative in 1990 – the European Year of Tourism (EYT), which was intended to exploit the integrative role of tourism and to stress its economic and social importance. After this:

> In 1994 the Court carried out a horizontal audit of tourist policy and the promotion of tourism. [During] its first-on-the-spot audit at the Commission, the Court found that there had been serious irregularities, leading to the suspension of two members of DG XXIII's staff, and that the Commission had not released any information on this matter. The Court found that the irregularities in question were related to the serious shortcomings reported in its 19922 Report on the European Year of Tourism...[73]

Arising from this:

> the Court decided to present a Special Report immediately as a way of contributing to the clarification of the current situation of the measures in favour of tourism, by pointing out the inadequacies in the management and control systems.[74]

The *Second Special Report* of the Court of Auditors on tourism looked at expenditure on tourism in relation to:

- the follow up to EYT,
- direct measures under the tourism action plan 1993–96, and
- co-ordination between tourism and other Community policies.

---

[71] 30.9.92.
[72] OJ C 17/1, 16.1.97.
[73] *Ibid.*, p.3.
[74] *Supra.*

Follow-up to EYT investigations

The Court's audit found a wide variety of shortcomings by all bodies, (national co-ordinating committees, their implementing agents, DG XXIII) in the financial management of expenditure/revenue in the national implementation of co-financed projects, including:[75]

- failure of the French committee's operational agent to follow national budgetary procedures or control procedures,
- insufficient recording of documents to enable reconstruction of declared expenditure and revenue,
- failure of French implementing agent to inform Commission of disappearance of invoices and accounting documents,
- DG XXIII failure to insist on report and financial statement deadlines being met,
- failure to point out conflict of interest in role of DG XXIII employee as member of a working party of a national committee, secretary of a tourism national federation and Commission employee, and
- Other failures related to attempts to recover monies arising from mis-spendings during EYT.

Direct measures under tourism action plan

Among the failings found during the audit of the tourism action plan were:[76]

- Slowness in establishing selection and financing procedures and standard contract clauses,
- management of important files by temporary/external staff,
- authorising officers making to a contract before gaining the approval of the financial controller and after submission of incorrect proposals,
- inadequacies in selection of project bids such as requesting some candidates to provide further information while rejecting other bids for insufficient information,
- failure of annual report to comply with terms of Decision authorising action plan by describing instead of evaluating Commission tourism activities,
- failure by the Commission to obtain detailed statement of expenditure from contractor before making payments,

---

[75] *Ibid.*, p.6.
[76] *Ibid.*, p.8.

- late notification by the Commission of contractor of unacceptable low quality of work, and
- Commission payment for non-eligible expenditure.

Other tourism audits

In 1995 the Court of Auditors made on-the-spot checks in four Member States of the OPs (operational programmes under the Structural Funds) specifically intended to support the development of tourism in the Community's regions.[77] Financial management failings were found in each state.

In Italy, six of the seven projects checked within the framework of the tourism OP has received Community funding... even though they were the subjects of legal proceedings [in Italy which neither the Commission nor the national monitoring committee were aware of].

In the United Kingdom, a declaration of expenditure concerning the tourism OP had to be submitted four times because of inconsistencies with the previous implementation report.[78]

In Ireland, in one series of projects the feasibility studies overestimated the likely volume of visitors and revenue. ... In the case of the construction of an amusement park, subsidies were granted against the advice of the independent assessors, who have to be consulted in accordance with the guidelines for granting assistance. In view of the problems which the project faces – specifically too few visitors and under-capitalisation – there is a risk that the investment will be lost.[79]

In Greece the renovation of holiday bungalows belonging to the national tourism organisation was included in the public investments part of the OP when it was only eligible as a private investment measure. Further,

> The work actually carried out did not correspond to the technical plans, which were submitted for signature. ... Two luxury VIP bungalows have been put at the disposition of the State.

European Economic and Social Committee

As was seen in Chapter 2 the Economic and Social Committee of the European Community has played an important part in the Community dialogue on the role of tourism in the Community. It is appropriate now to look more closely at

---

[77] *Ibid.*, p.12.
[78] *Supra.*
[79] *Ibid.*, p.13.

this Committee. Firstly, however, note should be taken of the Committee's comprehensive and informative website at:

www.esc.eu.int

This should be consulted for information regarding the Committee's composition, organisation and procedural details, activities and publications. Under Article 257 of the Rome Treaty:

An Economic and Social Committee is hereby established. It shall have advisory status.

The Committee shall consist of representatives of the various economic and social components of organised civil society and, in particular representatives of producers, farmers, carriers, workers, dealers, craftsmen, professional occupations, consumers and the general interest.

According to this website:[80]

The Economic and Social Committee is the European consultative body which represents the various categories of economic and social activities. It offers them a forum for debate and reflection both at European level and in the Member States.

The ESC is made up of 222 members, drawn from organisations representing employers, workers, farmers, SMEs, commerce, crafts, co-operatives, mutual benefit societies, the professions, consumers, environmentalists, families, "social" NGOs etc.

In other words, the ESC is the European-level forum for reflection of civil society organisations and associations.

The reference to civil society is significant. Usually a parliament represents a people and not organised groups advocating particular economic and social interests within society. However, since the Community was and still in large measure is concerned with economic matters, it is perhaps not surprising that the Treaty-makers wanted a means of ensuring specific business, worker and other vested interest group inputs into its decision making procedures and provided for the Economic and Social Committee.

---

[80] www.esc.eu.int/pages/en/org/memo.htm.

The members of the Committee, who are appointed by the Council on the nomination of the Member States, are obliged under Article 27(1) of the Committee's Rules of Procedure[81] to "form three Groups representing employers, employees and the various other economic and social components of organised civil society" (such as environmental and consumer organisations, farmers, craftworkers, disabled etc).

Under Article 261 the Economic and Social Committee can perform its advisory role on three possible occasions:

- when the Treaty requires consultation (which is often),

- when Parliament, the Council or the Commission consider it appropriate to consult the Committee, and

- when the Committee "issues an opinion on its own initiative in cases in which it considers such action appropriate".

Consultation means awaiting the opinion of the Committee and its specialised sections together with a record of the proceedings and then taking account of the contents. It does not mean accepting the opinion. The value of the Committee's opinions resides in how well they articulate the economic and social perspectives of the organisations from which the members are drawn[82] and how cogently they argue those perspectives.[83]

As required by Article 261 of the Treaty the Committee has created "specialised sections for the principal fields covered" by the Treaty. None of the current sections has tourism in its title and different sections deal separately with environmental, transport and cohesion issues. However, the section headed "Section for the Single Market, Production and Consumption" includes tourism within its remit under the sub heading "Services".

Sections can contain up to 80 members. Their work is usually facilitated by the earlier operation of Study Groups, acting under Rule 17 of the Rules of Procedure, of Committee members (aided by consultants and others) who are often able to progress an opinion to the point where it is presented in draft form to the Section. Committee opinions are adopted at full sessions of the Committee, called plenary sessions.

---

[81] OJ C 268/1, 4.10.02.

[82] Though the ESC members do not as such represent the groups from which they are drawn because Article 258 of the Treaty provides that: "The members of the Committee may not be bound by any mandatory instructions. They shall be completely independent in the performance of their duties, in the general interest of the Community".

[83] According to the Committee web site: "An impact study carried out by the ESC secretariat comparing Committee proposals and texts adopted by the Council also indicates that two–thirds of ESC proposals find their way into final provisions".

The Economic and Social Committee has historically been active in the tourism area,[84] supporting Commission efforts (so far unsuccessful) to develop a more coherent and integrated tourism policy. Some impression of how the Committee operates procedurally can be gleaned from the following extract from a Committee text on tourism.[85]

On 26 January 1999 the Economic and Social Committee, acting under the second paragraph of Rule 23 of its rules of Procedure, decided to draw up an Opinion on European Tourism Policy (Own-initiative opinion).

The Section for the Single Market, Production and Consumption, adopted it opinion on 12 March 1999. The rapporteur was Mr. Lustenhouwer.

At its 362nd plenary session (meeting of 24 March 1999) the Economic and Social Committee adopted the following opinion by 80 votes to three, with six abstentions …

The work of the Economic and Social Committee is facilitated by its own Secretariat General which is divided into directorates. Directorate A – Consultative Work is divided into three secretariats, of which Section INT – Single Market, Production and Consumption – deals with tourism issues.

Committee of the Regions

Another Community body which has played a noticeable role in attempting to ensure a higher profile for tourism within the Community is the Committee of the Regions. Not one of the original Treaty bodies, it was created in 1992 (becoming operational in 1994) to ensure an enhanced representation of regional interests at Community level.

Regional issues are pervasive throughout the Treaty, though they have their greatest focus in Article 2, which cites economic and social cohesion as among the basic Community objectives. This is amplified in Title XVII, and also in

---

[84] Among previous opinions relevant to tourism are: ESC, Opinion on the Initial Guidelines for a Community Policy on tourism, CES (84) 4, 26.10.83; OJ C 358/52, 31.12.83; ESC, Opinion on Tourism and Regional Development, CES 1063/90, 20.9.90; ESC, own initiative Opinion on Tourism, CES (94) 1021, 15.9.94; CES (94) 453; OJ C 393/168, 31.12.94; ESC, own initiative Opinion on European Tourism Policy, CES (99) 323, 24.3.99; Opinion on the Commission Communication on working together for the future of European tourism, CES (2002)1009, 18.9.02.

[85] ESC, Own initiative Opinion on European Tourism Policy, CES (99) 323/2, 24.3.99.

Title XV dealing with trans-European networks. Since tourism is still seen as offering significant opportunities for regional development, it was to be expected that the Committee would devote attention to it and this has been the case.[86]

The representative and functional nature of the Committee of the Regions is set out in Article 263 of the Rome Treaty which states:

> A Committee, hereinafter refereed to as 'the Committee of the Regions', consisting of representatives of regional and local bodies who either hold a regional or local authority mandate or are politically accountable to an elected assembly, is hereby established with advisory status.

Although representative, Committee members may not, also under Article 263,

> be bound by any mandatory instructions. They shall be completely independent in the performance of their duties, in the general interest of the Community.

The Committee of the Regions maintains its own website at:

www.cor.eu.int

This should be consulted for information regarding the Committee's organisation and membership, its functions, activities, rules of procedure and publications. The Committee of the Regions performs its advisory function by issuing opinions where, under Article 265;

- The Treaty requires consultation,
- "in all other cases, in particular those which concern cross-border cooperation, [where either the Council or Commission] consider it appropriate",
- after the Economic and Social Committee is consulted, the Committee of the Regions "considers that specific regional interests are involved",
- where on its own initiative the Committee considers such action appropriate, and
- where it is consulted by Parliament.

---

[86] Among the Committee's publications relating to tourism are: COR, Opinion on the Commission's Green paper, COR 376 (95), 6.9.95; COR, Opinion on the Proposal for a Council Decision on a first multi-annual programme to assist tourism – Philoxenia (1997–2000), COR 302/96, 6.12.96; COR, Opinion on the role of local and regional authorities in tourism development and the impact of European Union measures in the sphere of tourism, COR 157/98, 13.7.99; COR, Opinion on enhancing tourism potential for employment, COR 291/99 fin, 14.5.00; COR, Opinion on rural tourism in the text of Agenda 21, COR 254/2000 fin, 14.12.00.

The range of occasions on which it is entitled to issue an opinion (internal market and freedoms, transport, environment, regional policy, trans-European networks etc.) is now sufficiently broad that the Committee's remit covers most issues potentially impacting on tourism.

Procedurally, the Committee of the Regions operates by means of (confusingly named) commissions which are dealt within Chapter 4 of the Committee's Rules of Procedure.[87] Under Rule 44:

> At the beginning of each four-year term, the plenary assembly shall set up commissions to prepare its work ... Members of the Committee must belong to at least one commission ....

The functions of a commission are defined in Rule 46:

> The Commission shall in particular draw up the draft versions of opinions and resolutions. These drafts shall be submitted to the plenary Assembly for adoption..

Presently the Committee has established 9 Commissions. The Commission for Territorial Cohesion Policy deals with a range of topics including tourism. According to a former web page of this Commission:[88]

> Committee of the Regions' opinions on Tourism – guided by the work of Commission 5 – make recommendations on topics such as rural tourism, business tourism. They stress how tourism can become an effective tool in reducing unemployment in many cities and regions. Closely linked to this are the issues of training and professional development and the exchange of know-how and experiences between regions.

The following extract from an opinion of the Committee of the Regions on tourism[87] illustrates the procedures it follows in arriving at an opinion.

---

[87] OJ L 18/22, 22.1.00.

[88] www.cor.eu.int/corz105.htm, 31.10.01.

[89] COR, Opinion on the Proposal for a Council Decision on a first multi–annual programme to assist tourism – Philoxenia (1997–2000), p.1. The reference to Subcommision 2 refers to a type of sub group authorised under the Committee's previous Rules of Procedure, and not under the current rules, which instead in Rule 53 allows the establishment of working groups.

The Committee of the Regions

HAVING REGARD TO   the proposal for a Council Decision on a First Multi-annual Programme to assist European Tourism ...

HAVING REGARD TO   the decision taken by the Council ... to consult the Committee of the Regions on the matter.

HAVING REGARD TO   its decision on 8 March 1996 to direct Sub-commission 2 'Tourism and Rural Areas' to draw up the relevant Opinion.

HAVING REGARD TO   the Draft Opinion ... adopted by Subcommission 2 on 9 October 1996 (Rapporteurs: Mrs Segerston-Larson and Mr Lafay).

adopted the following Opinion at its 15th Plenary Session on 13–14 November 1996 ...

The work of the Committee of the Regions is assisted, under Rule 59 of the Committee's Rules of Procedure, by a Secretariat-General. Within this Secretariat the Directorate for Consultative Works, Unit B–1 services the commission which deals with tourism.

COMMUNITY DECISION-MAKING PROCEDURES

There are two basic questions regarding the decision-making procedures that the institutions of the European Community must follow:

• How are decisions reached within the different Community institutions?
• How are decisions reached between the different Community institutions?

Decision-Making within Community Institutions

Within the Council of Ministers

The general principle governing decision-making in the Council of Ministers is set out in Article 205(1) of the Treaty which states that:

> Save as otherwise provided in this Treaty, the Council shall act by a majority of its members.

Elsewhere in the Treaty different articles provide for decision-making within the Council to be on the basis of either:

- unanimity,
- common accord,
- qualified (weighted) majority voting,
- simple majority voting.

Among the areas of relevance to tourism for which unanimity within the Council is required under the Treaty of Rome are the right of movement and residence, state aid, culture and certain environmental provisions. Once the Treaty of Nice is ratified a significant number of areas will move from requiring unanimity to qualified majority voting.

The procedure for decision making by qualified majority voting is described in Article 205 which allots numbers of votes to the different Member States, with larger Member States (Germany, France, Italy, United Kingdom) having 10 votes each and the other states having a range of votes from the eight to five to three and two. For their adoption, acts of the Council shall require at least:

- 62 votes in favour where this Treaty requires them to be adopted on a proposal from the Commission, and
- 62 votes in favour, cast by at least 10 members, in other cases.

Qualified majority voting within the Council is required in various tourism-related areas, such as the right of establishment, services, internal market, consumer protection, transport, vocational training, and environment.

The enlargement of the Community will, in the interest of effective decision-making, require some alterations to the weighting and significance of Member State voting under the qualified majority system. While this is a matter of great importance for the Community and the entire enlargement project, it is beyond the scope of this book.

Within the Commission

According to Article 219 The Commission shall act by a majority of the number of Members provided for in Article 215. In turn Article 5 of the Commission's Rules of Procedure provides that Commission decisions shall be adopted if a majority of Members specified in the Treaty vote in favour.

Within Parliament

Save as otherwise provided in this Treaty, the European Parliament shall act by an absolute majority of its Members. The Rules of Procedure shall declare the quorum – Article 198.

An instance where an ordinary majority of members is sufficient arises under Article 192 concerning a request to the Commission to submit to Parliament a proposal to implement some Treaty provision.

Under Parliament's Rules of Procedure much parliamentary business is passed onto committees of members, who generally act either by majority vote or where the Rules provide for automatic adoption of a document, by the absence of a stipulated number of members objecting. Thereafter, the Rules provide that when the matter comes before Parliament in plenary session (all members acting together or under quorum) matters can be deemed passed in the absence of specified objections or by the necessary usually absolute majority.

Parliament's internal legislative procedures

Parliament's Rules of Procedure (Rules 53–73) divide the occasions on which Parliament deals with legislative proposals from the Commission into Readings. Two Readings are currently provided for (a third was abolished by Treaty of Amsterdam). Each of these is divided into a committee stage Reading and a plenary stage Reading:

• First Reading committee stage involves the relevant parliamentary committee examining and reporting on a proposal from the Commission.

• First Reading plenary stage involves Parliament as a whole considering the Commission proposal on the basis of the committee report and passing a resolution expressing its opinion on the proposal.

Provision is also made for delaying final adoption of the Second Reading resolution to allow for the Commission express a view on amendments to the proposal proposed by Parliament.

If the Council accepts Parliament's position then the proposal is adopted and that is the end of the legislative procedure. If the Council does not accept all/any of Parliament's amendments to the Commission's proposal, it must formulate what the Treaty in Article 251(2) calls a 'common position' and essentially refer the proposal back to Parliament. Then Parliament embarks on its Second Reading:

• Second Reading committee stage involves the relevant parliament committee considering the common position and making a recommendation to Parliament.

• Second Reading plenary stage involves Parliament as a whole considering the common position on the basis of the committees report and approving, rejecting, or accepting with amendments the common position that is then communicated to the Council.

The remaining steps in the legislative procedure are further described below.

Decision-Making between Community Institutions

The Treaty of Rome provides for a variety of procedures to be followed, involving the different Community institutions before various decisions can be reached.

The range and complexity of these procedures reflects the power balances both between the Member States and the Community and between the institutions themselves. The different decision-making procedures provided by the Treaty concern:

- the making of legislation,
- the adoption of the Community budget,
- the making of international agreements, and
- a miscellaneous group of other procedures.

Further discussion will be confined to legislative procedures.

Legislative Procedures

There are three stages to Community law-making:

- The preparation of proposals within the Commission and the exercise by the Commission of its right of initiative (exclusive competence to initiate proposal for Community laws) by forwarding a proposal to the Parliament and Council.
- Formal proceedings between and within Parliament and Council, with the Commission entitlement to halt the process at any time by withdrawing its proposal.
- Implementation of measures (directives in 90% of cases) by the Member States

Before examining the law-making procedures a brief note about the current emphasis on improved quality of Community law-making. Poorly drafted, excessively complex and impactful laws can reduce public acceptability of Community laws and damage the Community's image. While a variety of factors can contribute to difficult legislation, such as the nature of the subject or political compromise, amendments made by Parliament or the Council, or the way a Member State transposes a directive, the Commission has been keen to improve the acceptability of legislation by improving the preparation of its proposals. Along with improved consultation, systematic integrated assessment of impacts (business, environmental, social, health, consumer etc) of major proposals is a key means for doing this. To this end the Commission has prepared guidelines[90] for itself which are based around clearly identifying:

---

[90] Commission, Enterprise Working Paper, Business Impact Assessment pilot Project, Final

the problem, the policy objective, the alternative policy options, the costs and benefits of the impacts of each option assessed according to an appropriate analysis, the appropriate Community measures or mix of measures.

Impact assessment of legislative proposals is, however, only a methodological tool, an aid to decision-making, not a substitute for political judgement.[91]

The different legislative procedures provided for in the Treaty of Rome, together with the reference used in official Community documentation to identify them, are as follows:

1. The Council acting without consultation of the European Parliament.

2. The Council acting with consultation of the European Parliament – CNS.

3. The Council acting in co-operation with Parliament – SYN.

4. The Council acting in co-decision with Parliament – COD.

5. The Council acting after obtaining Parliament's assent – AVC.

6. The Council acting by common accord with Parliament and the Commission.

Further discussion will be confined to the co-decision procedure since it is increasingly the most likely procedure to be used for Community measures affecting tourism.

Co-Decision between Parliament and Council

The co-decision procedure for making directives involving Council and Parliament, with the participation of the Commission, is now the most widely used legislative procedure.[92] This is because many areas that used to be subject to the co-operation/consultation procedure in Article 252 of the Rome Treaty were transferred to co-decision by the Amsterdam Treaty. This change reflects the desire to give a greater role in Community law making to the Community's only truly democratic institution, Parliament. The Council maintains a co-decision website at:

http://ue.eu.int/codec/en/index.htm

Report– Lessons learned and the way forward, March 2002; Commission, Communication on simplifying and improving the regulatory environment, COM(2002) 726 final, 5.12.01.

[91] Commission, Communication on Impact Assessment, COM(2002) 276 final, 5.6.02, p.10.

[92] See generally Council website http://ue.eu.int/codec/en/index.htm.

which explains how the procedure operates. Parliament maintains a website at

> http://wwwdb.europarl.eu.int/dors/oeil/en/observ.htm

which allows the procedure used for current and previous measures to be traced. Currently measures in the following areas relevant to tourism[93] must be put through co-decision:

- citizenship, ban on nationality discrimination,
- free movement for workers/services/establishment/ harmonisation measures concerning the internal market,
- transport, trans-European networks,
- consumer protection, culture,
- ERDF, and
- environmental action programmes.

Details of co-decision

Article 251 of the Treaty of Rome sets out in lengthy terms the intricate procedures to be followed when the Treaty requires use of the co-decision procedure. These procedures can only start with a proposal from the Commission and they require close co-operation between all three institutions in order to work effectively.[94] They can be lengthy involving three readings each by Parliament and Council (not in all cases) and the use of a conciliation committee to resolve outstanding differences. With all their different permutations, the procedures are too lengthy to be described here.

   Since co-decision is seen at its fullest where Council and Parliament disagree on a proposal, it may be useful to briefly outline the procedure used then.

- *First Reading* – after the Commission prepares and sends a proposal to the Council and Parliament, the latter at first reading adopts a position and informs the Council. If at its first reading the Council does not agree with Parliament's opinion, the Council must adopt a **common position** in which it sets out its reasons and which it then sends to the Parliament. The Commission must also tell Parliament what it thinks of the Council's common position.

- *Second Reading* – Parliament considers the common position during its

---

[93] See Annex 1 for a list of the areas.

[94] A common approach was agreed by the three institutions in a joint declaration on practical arrangement for co–decision, OJ C 148/1, 28.5.99.

second reading. If a majority of Parliament's members reject the Council's position the proposal falls and can only be resurrected by a new proposal from the Commission. If however, and again by an absolute majority, Parliament during its second reading proposes changes to the common position, the text then goes to the Council for a second reading and to the Commission which must express an opinion on Parliament's amendments.

- *Conciliation Committee* – if the Council does not approve all of Parliament's changes then the President of the Council and the President of the European Parliament must call a meeting of what the Treaty calls the 'conciliation committee' within six weeks.

This Committee, which maintains its own informative web site at:

http://www.europarl.eu.int/code/default_en.htm

is composed of equal numbers from Council and Parliament, has the job of reaching agreement between both institutions on a joint text. It works on the basis of addressing the common position through the changes proposed by the Parliament. The Commission must take part in conciliation committee proceedings and is obliged to take all necessary initiatives to try and reconcile the positions of Parliament and Council.

The conciliation committee has six weeks to do its work and if it does not approve a joint text within that time the proposal falls.

- *Third Reading* – if the committee approves a joint text it is sent for adoption/approval by Parliament and Council during third readings in both institutions. If both agree to it, the measure is adopted. If either fails to approve it, it is deemed to have fallen.

In reflecting on this elaborate procedure, it is important to note that while the Commission is not a legislative partner in the process (it will ultimately be a Parliament and Council measure) it can influence the eventual outcome in a number of ways. Firstly it formulates the initial proposal and can withdraw it at any time before final adoption and introduce an amended proposal. Further, while the Council generally acts by qualified majority voting under the co-decision procedure, if it wishes to amend a Commission proposal, it must, except when inside the Conciliation Committee, act unanimously – Article 250(2).

To illustrate co-decision, the stages involved in the enactment of Regulation 899/2002 dealing with air carrier liability[95] in the event of an accident are set

---

[95] OJ L 140/2, 30.5.02. Taken from
http://wwwdb.europarl.eu.int/oeil/oeil_ViewDNL.ProcedureView?lang=2&procid=4232.

out below. It will be noted that the procedure required obtaining the opinion of the Economic and Social Committee, and that the Commission introduced an amended proposal after Parliament amended its original proposal. Further, there was no third reading because Parliament agreed with the Council's common position adopted at its first reading.

Co-decision Procedure: Air Carrier Liability

Stages in the procedure

Events	Documents: references	Dates of publication	
	Source reference	*Equivalent references* *of document*	*in Official Journal*
Journal			
Initial proposal	CE	COM(2000)0340	
	C5–0294/2000	06/06/2000	C337 28–NOV–00 068(E)
Opinion of ESC	CES	CES0046/2001	
	25/01/2001	C123 25–APR–01 047	
Report tabled	PE	A5–0093/2001	
	PE286.622	20/03/2001	
EP opinion 1st reading	PE	T5–0192/2001	
	05/04/2001		C021 24–JAN–02 256 312(E)
Modified proposal	CE	COM(2001)0273	
	C5–0210/2001	21/05/2001	C213 31–JUL–01 298(E)
Council common position	CSL	10794/1/2001	
	C5–0641/2001	19/12/2001	C058 05–MAR–02 008(E)
Commission assessment	CE	SEC(2001)1946	
		10/01/2002	
Recommendation for			
2nd reading tabled	PE	A5–0052/2002	
	PE301.845	21/02/2002	
EP decision			
(second reading)	PE	T5–0093/2002	
		12/03/2002	
Final act	LEX	2002R0889	
		13/05/2002	L140 30–MAY–02 002

CHAPTER CONCLUSION

The detail provided in this chapter on the institutions, laws and decision-making procedures of the European Community testify to a carefully and elaborately structured body which is constantly juggling with a range of power balances. While all the institutions are subject to a Treaty based duty of cooperation, each, as it should do, maintains its own perspectives, procedures and secretariat to help it do this. Looked at from a distance one can talk of a Community view or approach to an issue, but from close up, with a greater awareness of the roles and perspectives of the different institutions and the procedures and laws which draw them together, the picture is far more complex.

STUDENT TASKS

Undergraduate questions:

1. Describe the co-decision procedure between Parliament and Council.

2. What does maintaining the institutional balance within the Community mean? How important is it?

3. Describe the principal types of law which can be made under the Treaty of Rome and provide examples relevant to tourism.

4. What is COREPER? Describe its role.

5. Describe in general terms the array of tasks entrusted to the Commission under the Treaty of Rome.

Post-graduate questions:

1. If you had to construct a set of institutions to carry out the objectives of the European Community under the Treaty of Rome, consider the various factors which you would have to take into account.

2. Consider the involvement of the Petitions Committee and the Ombudsman in tourism matters.

3. Do you think that the increased scope of the co-decision procedure between Parliament and the Council of Ministers is a positive contribution towards tourism in the Community?

4. Consider the enforcement powers of the Commission in relation to measures affecting tourism.

CHAPTER 4

FREE MOVEMENT AND TOURISM[1]

INTRODUCTION

Tourism in the European Community depends on free movement. Free movement means the ability of tourists, tourism workers and tourism service providers to participate in the tourism common market by crossing the Community's external and internal borders/remaining in other Member States without being unjustifiably hindered by national laws and practices. It refers principally to entry and stay controls, though by covering nationality discrimination, it also indirectly deals with equality of treatment of tourists and citizens.[2] Such national controls can concern:

- the requirements of documentation as a condition of entry to a Member State.
- the conduct of checks at borders and other matters.
- nationality discrimination.
- public policy/security/health obstacles.

The Treaty establishing the European Community (Treaty of Rome) deals with free movement issues and tourism not from a tourism perspective, but in the context of Community citizenship, common market or illegal immigration matters. The position would probably be different if the Treaty allowed for a more direct Community role in tourism.

Community law and policy on tourism free movement treats Union citizens (tourists) and non-Union citizens (third country tourists) differently. Tourists benefit from Community laws and policies designed to facilitate the operation of the common market and promote Union citizenship.

Third country tourists who represent a major part of the tourism market must clearly be able to enter, travel between and stay within any Member State for the duration of their holiday. They are, however, subject to greater controls

---

[1] Marc McDonald.

[2] International human rights texts generally guarantee equal treatment between citizens and foreign visitors, though this right depends on the foreign visitor being legally present in the host State. Illegal entrants would not enjoy the same equality guarantee.

by Community and national laws. Indeed as will be seen, there is no single legal framework at Community level which deals comprehensively with third country tourists. Current controls, as will also be seen, are not related to tourism but to issues of combating illegal entry into the Community. While there is little direct Community law in this area so far, a transition is taking place which, as will be seen, should lead to greater clarity regarding short stay rights of non-Union citizen as tourists. Thus, the following players and issues arise in relation to free movement and Community tourism:

- tourists – Union and non-Union citizens.
- tourism workers – Union and non-union citizens.
- external and internal entry to Community/Member States.
- length of stay – short/long stays and residence.
- frontier checks – operation of external and abolition of internal.
- tourism service providers.
- residual member public policy State controls.

The linkages between the various issues can be seen as follows.

Free Movement and Tourism

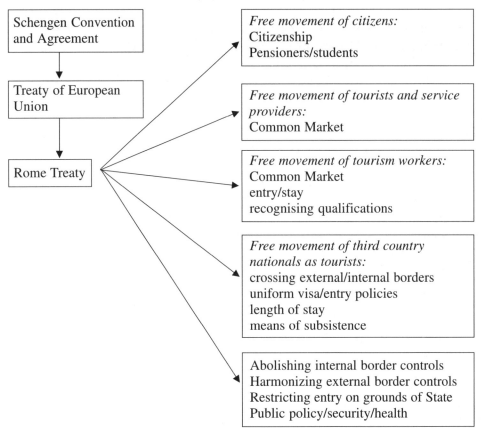

| Schengen Convention and Agreement | *Free movement of citizens:* Citizenship Pensioners/students |

Rome Treaty leads to:

Free movement of citizens:
Citizenship
Pensioners/students

Free movement of tourists and service providers:
Common Market

Free movement of tourism workers:
Common Market
entry/stay
recognising qualifications

Free movement of third country nationals as tourists:
crossing external/internal borders
uniform visa/entry policies
length of stay
means of subsistence

Abolishing internal border controls
Harmonizing external border controls
Restricting entry on grounds of State
Public policy/security/health

Learning Outcomes

After reading this chapter, the student should:

- appreciate the free movement dimension to European Community tourism,
- understand the range of issues involved in attaining free movement,
- appreciate the human rights dimension to free movement issues,
- understand how Union citizens and non-Union citizens are treated differently,
- appreciate the difficulties the Community faces in removing internal controls fully.

These learning objectives will be addressed through the following headings:

The Treaty, Free Movement and Tourism.
Beneficiaries of Free Movement.
Conduct of Frontier Controls.
Permitted Restrictions on Free Movement of Tourists and Tourism Workers.
Tourism Service Providers.

THE TREATY, FREE MOVEMENT AND TOURISM

Historically, Community law has not adapted a global approach to the range of tourism-related persons who can benefit from the Treaty guarantees of free movement. Initially and for reasons to be explained, only tourism workers and service providers benefited, then tourists were apparently included, later movement rights were extended to pensioners and students, and finally the notion of Community citizenship was established, offering potential for a global Community approach to free movement questions, but still restricted to Union-citizens. Only recently, as will be seen, are there signs of a serious Community engagement with the remaining major gap in Community law in this area – a harmonised framework for dealing with the vital matter of free movement rights for third country nationals, principally as tourists.

Discussion on how the Treaty of Rome deals with free movement and tourism begins with Treaty references to the internal market. Article 3(1)(c) presently lists as one of the Community's activities the creation of:

an internal market characterised by the abolition, as between Member States, of obstacles to the free movement of goods, persons, services and capital.

This locates free movement at the heart of the internal market and explains the Community's pre-occupation with national laws and practices which hinder free movement.

The meaning of Article 3(1)(c) is expanded in Article 39 for workers, Article 49 for service providers and Article 43 for the freedom of establishing a business in another State. Article 39 has survived the various Treaty revisions largely intact and provides:

Freedom of movement for workers shall be secured within the Community.

Article 39(3) goes on to spell out what this means. Subject to residual State rights to impose limitations on various grounds, it means workers have rights to:

- accept offers of employment,
- move freely within other Members States,
- stay in the Member State, and
- remain there after being employed.

The exclusive emphasis on the free movement of workers, as opposed to other travellers such as tourists, in the initial version of the Treaty of Rome reflected the early primarily economic focus of the European Economic Community. Later amendments to the Treaty of Rome have widened the scope of the European project to include a focus on a union of Member States (as opposed to an economic community) and the idea of citizenship, with much attention devoted to the idea of free movement of citizens and persons independently of the internal market.

Within that context Article 18(1) of the Treaty of Rome, as amended by the Maastricht Treaty in 1992, after declaring that all citizens of the Member States are citizens of the Union, now provides:

> Every citizen of the Union shall have the right to move and reside freely within the territory of the Member States, subject to the limitations and conditions laid down in this Treaty and by the measures adopted to give it effect.

> The Council may adopt provisions with a view to facilitating the exercise of the rights referred to in paragraph 1; save as otherwise provided in this Treaty, the Council shall act in accordance with the procedure referred to in Article 251. The Council shall act unanimously throughout this procedure.

Thus, a new (and additional Treaty) basis for free movement rights was created, Community citizenship, and obviously benefits Union citizens as tourists. However, so far it cannot be directly relied on by citizens in litigation to assert movement rights beyond what Community law otherwise provides. This is because the Article 18(1) right is made subject "to the limitations and conditions laid down in this Treaty and by the measure adopted to give it effect." Title IV envisages a number of flanking measures related to strengthened external border controls and these have not yet been agreed.[3]

The citizens free movement right has echoes of the human right to free

---

[3] See p. 150.

movement, which all Member States treat as a fundamental right and is regarded highly in the European Convention on Human Rights and Fundamental Freedoms.

The Commission stated recently, in the context of steps Member States might take under Community law to control the flow of persons, that all this now means:

> that any application of the notions of public policy or public security by the Member States will not only be subject to strict scrutiny so that their scope cannot be determined unilaterally by each Member State ... but also that such Community law scrutiny will be inspired by the basic human rights as enshrined in the Convention ... Moreover, because of this common background ... any recourse to the right of refusal of entry or of expulsion is unlikely to place the citizen of the Union concerned in jeopardy as to the enjoyment of his basic rights in another Member State. Furthermore, the measures adopted for the protection of public policy, public security or public health must be applied in accordance with the principle of proportionality... Proportionality requires justified grounds for a measure, justified balance between the measure and the objective, and justified balance of interests of the individual and the State concerned.[4]

The entitlement to the free movement right is, however as indicated earlier, restricted to Union citizen tourists and does not include third country tourists. The current version of the Treaty of Rome does however contain framework provisions for dealing with the entry and stay of third country nationals in the Community. While this framework in Title IV is called "Visas, Asylum, Immigration and other Policies related to Free Movement of Persons" and is intended to provide a means for resolving at Community level some difficult entry/stay problems regarding controls over immigrants, asylum seekers and criminals, it will also ultimately produce a common Community law regulating entry and stay condition for third country tourists in the Community. The specific tourist issues involved in this are explored later.

---

[4] Commission, Communication to the Council and the European Parliament on the Special Measures concerning the Movement and Residence of Citizens of the Union which are justified on grounds of Public Policy, Pubic Security or Public Health, COM (1999) 372 final, p.7.

BENEFICIARIES OF FREE MOVEMENT

Tourism Workers

This section briefly outlines two of the free movement issues relating to the free movement of Union citizens as tourism workers.[5]

Entry

The implementing legislation for the Treaty guarantee for Member State tourism workers to work in other Member States is Council Directive 68/360[6] on the abolition of restrictions on movement and residence within the Community for workers of Member States and their families. Article 3 states that:

1. Member States shall allow the persons referred to in Article 1 (Member State nationals and their families within Regulation 1612/68, OJ No L 257/13, 19.10.68) to enter their territory simply on production of a valid identity card or passport.

2. No entry visa or equivalent document may be demanded save from members of the family who are not nationals of a Member State.

Article 10 of Regulation 1612/68 lists the members of a tourism workers family entitled to enter and remain with the worker. They are the spouse and descendants under 21 or dependants and also dependant relatives in the ascending line of the worker and his/her spouse.

Further, tourism workers enjoy a right to a residence permit (where this is required by local law) in the host Member State simply by virtue of their visa/passport and confirmation of engagement by the employer, while members of their family are given a right to a residence permit simply on production of their visa/passport and official documentary proof establishing their relationship with the worker.

These key provisions constitute the basic legal entitlement of tourism workers to move within the Community. However, as will be seen, family members who are not nationals of a Member State only benefit from the right of movement while in the company of the worker, although there are proposals to remove this restriction.

Consideration of the grounds of public policy, security or health (in Article 4(3) which allows entry to be refused to tourism workers) is contained in a later section.

---

[5] For a fuller account see Commission, Communication on Free Movement of Workers – achieving the full benefits and potential, COM (2002) 694 final, 11.12.02.

[6] OJ L 257/13, 19.10.68.

Reporting requirements

Member States have however reserved to themselves the power to require Union workers to report their presence to the competent national authority. So long as the period for doing so is not unreasonable or the punishment for not doing so is not excessive, Community law is not infringed.[7]

Recognition of tourism worker qualifications

Tourism in the Community depends on workers qualified in tourism professions in one Member State being free to work in another Member State where entry to that profession is regulated, and have their qualifications assessed and possibly recognized so that they can gainfully use them. In some Member States there is very little regulation of tourism occupations, while in others there is and difficulties can arise over the non-recognition of migrants qualifications.

The issue is dealt with by a number of Community laws, which because of the importance of the matter for the operation of the common market, require Member State authorities to give consideration to qualifications obtained in other Member States and to assess their compatibility with host state require-ments. Under Council Directive 89/48[8] on a general system for the recognition of higher education diplomas awarded on completion of professional education and training of at least three years duration, a Member State government cannot simply refuse to recognise qualification obtained elsewhere, but must instead assess/examine the qualification to determine compatibility. According to the Court of Justice:

> That examination procedure must enable the authorities of the host Member State to assure themselves, on an objective basis, that the foreign diploma certifies that its holder has knowledge and qualifications which are, if not identical, at least equivalent to those certified by the national diploma. That assessment of the equivalence of the foreign diploma must be carried out exclusively in the light of the level of knowledge and qualifications which its holder can be assumed to possess in the light of that diploma, having regard to the nature and duration of the studies and practical training to which the diploma relates.[9]

Whether Member States complied with this requirement arose in a number of tour guide cases in the early 1990's and a number of Member States were held

---

[7] *Watson* [1976] E.C.R. II–1185, 1199.
[8] OJ L 19/16, 24.1.89.
[9] *Tourist Guides, Re* [1994] E.C.R. I–923.

to be in breach of Community law over their failure to establish systems for assessing non-national tour guide qualifications compatibility with local laws and crediting such qualifications.

In *Commission v. Spain*[10] Spain was held to be in breach of its Treaty obligations because of a law which regulated the profession of tourist guide and limited access to it in a number of ways, including allowing only holders of a diploma issued after sitting a Spanish national exam to conduct tour guiding. The Court of Justice stated that:[11]

> The Commission claims that ... Spain has failed ... to enable the diploma issued by that other Member State to be recognised, or the person holding the diploma to be tested solely on the matters not studied, if his or her training is judged in accordance with the Spanish criteria to be incomplete.
>
> In that respect, it should be recalled that the Court has consistently held that a Member State which receives a request to admit a person to a profession to which access, under national law, depends upon the possession of a diploma or a professional qualification must take into consideration the diplomas, certificates and other evidence of qualifications which the person concerned has acquired in order to exercise the same profession in another Member State, by making a comparison between the specialised knowledge and abilities certified by those diplomas and the knowledge and qualifications required the national rules.

The issue of recognising foreign tourism qualifications has also arisen regarding ski instructors.

In *Ski Instructors in France*[12] complaints were made that France refused to recognise ski instructor qualifications from other Member States. After intervention by the Commission, France was granted a short term derogation from Directive 89/48 allowing it, before recognising a foreign qualification, to impose an aptitude test rather than allow the normal choice between an adaptation period and an aptitude test.

---

[10] [1994] E.C.R. I–923.

[11] At p.940. See also Commission, Community Actions affecting Tourism, COM (97) 1419, 11.7.97, p.42 note of complaint of alleged a breach of Directive 68/366 by Greece concerning the recognition by the Greek authorities of hotel management qualifications obtained outside Greece.

[12] Press Release IP/97/99, 7.2.97.

> However, the aptitude test could only be imposed if the foreign qualification was not equivalent to the French one, the aptitude test was not disproportionate and was justified by particular safety risks to those receiving tuition.

Tourists

In this section it is proposed to trace the piecemeal development of Community free movement rights of Union-citizen tourists, and to outline the consolidating proposals currently being considered within the Community.

Entry of tourists

The right of entry of Member State tourists into other Member States is also based, perhaps surprisingly, on the guarantee to workers just described for the following reason. When a Member State national presents at an internal frontier, he cannot as a matter of systematic policy of the host State, be questioned about the purpose of the visit, the length of stay or even whether he/she has sufficient financial means of support. If the national possesses the necessary documents, entry must be allowed and any queries as to whether he/she is actually entitled to the benefit of the free movement guarantee postponed until if and when he applies for a residence permit.

> In *Commission v. Netherlands*[13] a German national was asked questions at the Dutch border by border officials under Dutch aliens legislation about the purpose and duration of his visit and how much cash he had with him. He was then refused entry. The Court of Justice upheld the Commission complaint that the Netherlands acted in breach of Directive 68/360. Relying on both Article 3 of the Directive and case law, the Court stated:[14]
>
> > More generally, the obligation to answer questions put by frontier officials cannot be a precondition for the entry of a national of one Member State into the territory of another.

Thus, although the basis of the tourist right of entry is the status of a worker who cannot be questioned, and not the status of tourist, the fact that border officials are prevented as a general rule, subject to security etc considerations

---

[13] [1991] E.C.R. I–2637.
[14] At p.2655.

dealt with below, from asking questions about the nature and purpose of visits means that a Member State national with the intention of acting as a tourist gains the protection of Article 3.

Where a Union citizen tourist who is not a national of the host state does not possess a valid passport or identity card, for example where it has expired, it is lawful to refuse entry and turn the person back at the border check. If a tourist is a national of the Member State in question, it is also permissible to make non-possession of the necessary passport/identity card subject to sanction so long as the sanction is not disproportionate. Imprisonment might well be disproportionate.

In *Wijsenbeck*[15] a Dutch national failed to produce his passport in Rotterdam airport after a scheduled flight from Strasbourg. He was fined in a lower Dutch court and on appeal the case was referred to the Court of Justice regarding whether the Dutch law which required production of the passport was compatible with the citizen's right of free movement under Article 18. The Court held that the citizen's right could not be relied on in this way pending the enactment of measures under Title IV of the Treaty (which would strengthen external border controls and make it possible to remove internal border controls such as passport checks) and these had not been enacted. Reference was also made to the clear requirement under Article 3(1) of Directive 68/360, discussed earlier, that entry to another Member States as conditional on production of a passport or identity card, as the case may be. The Court noted that any penalty imposed by the Dutch court had to be proportionate.

Entry over whole territory

The Court of Justice has declared,[16] in the context of the worker's right of entry into another Member State under Directive 68/360 that:

> Right of entry into the territory of Member States and the right to stay there and to move freely within it is defined in the Treaty by reference to the whole territory of these States and not by reference to internal subdivisions.

---

[15] [1999] E.C.R. I–6207.
[16] *Rutili v. Minister for the Interior* [1975] E.C.R. II–1219, 1234.

Residence and Tourism

Workers and tourists

For short term tourism workers and tourists, Council Directive 68/360, Article 8 confers a right of residency of up to three months, subject to, in the case of employees, possession of a document from their employer regarding the duration of their employment and also subject to the host state being competent if it wishes to require the worker to 'report his presence in the territory.'

For long-term tourism workers, free movement would be meaningless if it did not also include an entitlement to reside in the host State in order to work or to seek work. Similarly, in the case of longer stay tourists, the right of entry needs to be supplemented by a right of residence in the host state. There is some legislation on both matters.

Article 4 of Directive 68/360 links entry and residence for all workers, including tourism workers, by providing that:

> Member States shall grant the right of residence in their territory (to Member State nationals and their families) ... who are able to produce ... the document with which they entered their territory (and) a confirmation of engagement from the employer or a certificate of employment.

Supplementary provisions are also made for the families of workers.

Member States cannot impose any other formalities to secure the residence permit and cannot take it back because the person is no longer working. Under Article 7(1):

> A valid residence permit may not be withdrawn from a worker solely on the grounds that he is no longer in employment. ...

Non-possession of a residence permit is not a matter of great legal significance. While Member States remained entitled to declare by their laws that non-possession is a legal wrong, the consequences cannot be severe.

In *R. v. Pieck*[17] a UK court asked the Court of Justice for a ruling on the application of Community law in a criminal prosecution against a Dutch national for overstaying the period stamped on his passport. The Court of Justice considered:

> whether the failure on the part of a national of a Member State of the Community, to whom the rules on freedom of movement for workers

---

[17] [1980] E.C.R. II–2171, 2186.

apply, to obtain the special residence permit prescribed in Article 4 of Directive No 68/360 may be punished by measures which include imprisonment or a recommendation for deportation.

Among the penalties attaching to a failure to comply with the formalities required as proof of the right of residence of a worker enjoying the protection of Community law, deportation is certainly incompatible with the provisions of the Treaty since, as the Court has already confirmed in other cases, such a measure negates the very right conferred and guaranteed by the Treaty ... As regards other penalties such as fines and imprisonment, whilst the national authorities are entitled to impose penalties in respect of failure to comply with the terms of the provisions relating to residence permits which are comparable to those attaching to minor offences by nationals, they are not justified in imposing a penalty so disproportionate to the gravity of the infringement that it becomes an obstacle to the free movement of persons. This would be especially so if that penalty included imprisonment.

Pensioners and students

The right of residence conferred by secondary Community law has been extended beyond workers who have worked outside their own Member's State to other categories of person on the basis that completion of the internal market and its guarantee of free movement permits this. Workers who have not worked outside their own State are thus entitled to retire and reside in other Member States. Directive 90/365[18] states in the Preamble that:

it is desirable that this right of residence also be granted to persons who have ceased their occupational activity even if they have not exercised their right to freedom of movement during their working life.

And goes on to provide in Article 1:

Member States shall grant the right of residence to nationals of Member States who do not enjoy this right under other provisions of Community law and to members of their families as defined ... provided that they themselves and the members of their families are covered by sickness insurance in respect of all risks in the host Member State and have sufficient resources to avoid becoming a burden on the social assistance system of the host ... State during their period of residence.

---

[18] OJ L180/28, 13.7.90.

Students pursuing courses of vocational training are also granted a right of residence[19] in a host state on the basis that, regardless of nationality, students must be guaranteed access to vocational training and an accompanying right of residence needed to facilitate this access.

2001 Consolidating Proposals

The piecemeal approach to free movement issues described above, was driven by the absence of a legal basis in the Rome Treaty for a global approach to free movement issues. As already indicated this was changed by the creation of Union citizenship in 1992. However, it has taken until 2001 for the Commission to produce proposals[20] which exploit this basis and seek to provide a comprehensive treatment of free movement and residency issues for Union citizens and their families. These proposals recognise that the introduction of Union citizenship:

> generalised, for the benefit of all citizens, the right to enter, the right to reside and the right remain in the territory of another Member State.[21]

However:

> the sector-by sector, piecemeal approach to the right of free movement and residence [in current Community law dealing with workers, establishment and provision of services, pensioners and students] needs to reviewed in order to facilitate the exercise of this right.[22]

While much of its content is related to residency questions, particularly for non-Union citizens who are family members of Union citizens, the proposed directive principally seeks to consolidate the existing legal provisions relating to short term stays in other Member States which are more likely to be tourist in nature. Under the proposal the capacity of a Union citizen to act as a tourist is, in the first instance, dependant on being free to leave one's own State. While this and the issuing of passports or identity cards, would previously have been subject to national law, Article 5(1) of the proposed directive treats it as an issue of Community law and states that:

---

[19] Council Directive 93/96/EEC, OJ L 317, 18.12.93.

[20] Proposal for a European Parliament and Council Directive on the Right of Citizens of the Union and their Family Members to Move and Reside Freely within the Territory of the Member States, COM (2001) 257 final, 23.5.01.

[21] At p. 2.

[22] At p. 21.

All Union citizens shall have the right to leave their territory to travel to another Member State with a valid identity card or passport.

For family members who are not nationals of a Member State, this right shall be the same as for the Union citizens they accompany or join.

The right to leave is dependant on possession of a passport or identity card, thus Article 5(3) proposes:

Member States shall issue to their own nationals, and renew, an identity card or passport stating their nationality.

The remainder of the proposed directive deals separately with:
* entry and residence for up to six months,
* residence for more than six months,
* permanent residence, and
* restrictions on entry and residence on grounds of public policy, public security or public health.

The main tourism interest here concerns entry and residence for up to 6 months since this covers the vast majority of tourists. Article 6 of the proposed directive declares the general right of entry which will benefit Union citizens acting as tourists:

Member States shall grant Union citizens and their family members, irrespective of nationality, leave to enter their territory with a valid identity card or passport. No entry visa or equivalent formality may be imposed on Union citizens. ... The right of Union citizens [and their third country family members] to enter the territory of a Member State shall include the right to reside there for a period of no more than six months with a valid identity card or passport. The Member State may only require the person concerned to report their presence on the territory within a time limit, which may be not less than fifteen days. Failure to comply with this requirement may make the person liable to penalties, which shall be proportionate and non-discriminatory.

The basic right of entry, incidentally, also covers Union citizens and family members wishing to stay longer than 6 months, but the right of residency is made subject to some additional requirements, which can include a compulsory registration obligation. The residence right only extends to Union citizens who:

(a) are engaged in gainful activity in an employed or self-employed capacity; or

(b) have sufficient resources for themselves and for their family members without recourse to welfare funds in the host Member State during their stay
and that they have sickness insurance covering all risks in the host Member
State; or

(c) are students admitted to a courses of vocational training; or

(d) are a family member of a Union citizen who satisfies [the above conditions]
– Article 7(1).

Third-Country Tourists

This section deals with current and proposed rules which affect nationals from
countries outside the Community acting as tourists within the Community (third
country tourists).

As yet there is no Community legislation granting a right of entry and free
movement to third country tourists regardless of whether they reside inside or
outside the Community.[23] Some Member States have in effect agreed to forego
the right to operate checks at internal frontiers on all types of third country
tourists under the provisions of the Schengen Agreement and Convention
(discussed later) on the basis of the establishment and consistency of compensatory external frontier controls. Other Member States retain the right to control
the entry of third country tourists into their territory at their external and internal
borders. This legal position will however change. Title IV of the Treaty of
Rome declares in Articles 61 and 62 that within five years of the Amsterdam
Treaty coming into force (1 May 2004) the Council must adopt measures aimed
at addressing a number of free movement issues affecting third country nationals.
These issues concern:

- the absence of controls when crossing internal frontiers,

- the operation of external border controls, and

- the conditions under which third country nationals can enter and move freely
within the Community for up to three months.

---

[23] A special legal regime applies to Switzerland – Agreement between the European Community
and its Member States, of the one part, and the Swiss Confederation, of the other, on the free
movement of persons, OJ L 114/6, 30.4.02 – which regulates questions of free movements
for work and other matters between the Community and Switzerland. Tourists, as recipients
of tourism services, benefit under Article 5(3) which provides that "Nationals [of the
Community and Switzerland] entering [each other's territory] solely to receive services shall
have the right of entry and residence". Article 1 of Annex 1 provides the same entry conditions
as apply inside the Community to tourist travel between the Community and Switzerland. It
requires both parties to the Agreement to allow each other's nationals and members of their
families [as defined] to enter their territory simply on production of a valid identity card or
passport.

The legal justification for these measures will be the common market. Article 61(a) directly and expressly links the adoption of measures under Title IV with Article 14 of the Treaty – 'in accordance with Article 14'. Article 14, it will be recalled, establishes the internal market, thus making it clear that the purpose of action under Article 61 and 62 in providing for third country nationals entering and moving within the Community is the operation of the common market. Demand for tourism services inside the Community from third country tourists clearly affects the operation of the common market.

Note should be taken of how Article 14(2) refers to "the free movement of ... persons". Elsewhere in the Treaty the term "citizen" is used in relation to the Union, thus possibly implying that "persons" in Article 14 includes non-Union citizens as well. However, the end words of Article 14(2) indicate that non-Union citizens can only comprise the internal market where they are lawfully present in the Community in accordance with Title IV. So, the lawfulness of entry determines the ability of non-Union nationals to act as tourists within the internal market and equally measures adopted under Title IV hold the key to whether entry is lawful or not.

The following discussion of travel issues and third country tourists – focusing on external border controls, visas, internal border controls and Schengen acquis – centres around three sets of Commission proposals in 1993, 1995 and 2001.

External border controls

The rationale for having a Community policy on the entry of third country nationals into Member States for short stays comes, not from the desire to facilitate tourist movement, but from the desire to abolish controls at internal borders. However, Member States are only prepared to agree to the abolition of internal controls if they have confidence in the consistency and uniformity of strict Community-wide controls on the entry of third country nationals in whatever Member State they chose to enter the Community through.

The legal basis for any proposals under Title IV is thus, not the creation of a genuine internal tourism market operating in an area without internal frontiers, but the creation of an area of 'freedom, security and justice,' a treaty euphemism for the control and prevention of illegal immigration etc, as now set out in Article 61 of the Treaty of Rome.[24]

In 1993 the Commission published a proposal for a decision by the Council on the drawing up of a Convention on the crossing of the external borders of the Member States.[25]

---

[24] Previously dealt with under Title VI of the Treaty on European Union, Maastricht 1993.

[25] OJ C 11/6, 15.1.94. At that time before the insertion of the present Title IV into the Treaty

The proposed Convention would have applied to two categories of short-stay third country nationals – those who resided in the Community and those who did not. The former (such as a Tunisian tourist, lawfully resident in France, returning from Tunisia to Italy for a short holiday before returning to France) would have been entitled under Article 8 to cross external frontiers and enter other Member States without a visa so long as they held a residence permit, valid travel documents, documentation "justifying the purpose and conditions of the intended stay" and sufficient means of subsistence both for the stay and return/onward journey.

The second category of visitor which the proposed Convention would have covered, the third-country tourist who did not lawfully reside in the Community, would have been authorised under Article 7 to cross the external frontier for a short stay on possession of the same documentation as the resident and additionally, a valid visa. Other elements of a common external frontier policy proposed in the convention involved:

- creating a joint list of persons who must be refused entry on grounds of public policy or national security.
- computerised exchange information about persons on the joint list.
- uniform policy on departure or expulsion of third country nationals no longer entitled to stay.
- reimbursement of Member States for financing expulsions.

In an attempt to forestall the arrival of persons not entitled to cross the Community's external frontiers, Article 14(2) of the proposed Convention would have required Member States to impose legally binding responsibilities on carriers (airlines, ferries and international bus carriers):

> to oblige the carrier to take all necessary measures to ensure that persons coming from third countries are in possession of valid travel documents and of the necessary visas.

And if the third country national was refused entry into Community territory:

> to oblige the carrier, where required by the control authorities, to assume responsibility without delay (this may include covering the cost of accommodation until departure) and to return to the state from which he was transported or to the State which issued his passport or to any state to which he is certain to be admitted.

---

any Commission proposal for harmonizing law in this area had to take the legal form of a convention (because the issue was outside the Rome Treaty) which required all States to agree to it.

While this proposed convention was never adopted, its core elements are likely to be found in any eventual law. Progress has been made with one aspect of a common external frontier policy – the issuing of visas, although a Community visa still does not exist.

Visas and third country tourists

A visa is a specific entry permission which a State historically speaking may or may not require of visitors from another State depending of the closeness of ties between the two and other reasons. If Member States of the Community remain independent in deciding which tourists from which States require a visa before entering, the resulting variations in practice could render the entry and movement of third country tourists in the Community difficult.

In Regulation 539/01[26] the Community agreed on two lists of States – those whose nationals must hold a visa to enter any Member State (Annex I) and those whose nationals do not (Annex II). Both lists are exhaustive in the sense that Member States "will be precluded from unilaterally determining the visa rules for any third country at all".[27] Visa is defined in Article 2 as:

> an authorization issued by a Member State or a decision taken by such state which is required with a view to:
> – entry for an intended stay ... of no more than three months in total
> – entry for transit through the territory of that Member State or several Member States except for transit at an airport.[28]

A uniform format for a common visa was laid down in Council Regulation 1683/95[29] in order to ensure high technical standards:

> notably as regards safeguards against counterfeiting and falsification.

---

[26] OJ L 81/1, 21.3.01.

[27] Commission, Proposal for a Council Regulation listing the third countries, COM(2000) 27 final, 26.1.00, p.3.

[28] Under Annex 9 of the Chicago Convention on International Civil Aviation, persons who remain in the international air transit section of an airport are exempt from the need to obtain a visa, though duly notified exceptions to this are permitted. In fact, based on the possibility of passengers present in transit in the international sections of airports illegally leaving the airport to take up illegal residence in the country, the Council of the European Union has adopted a Joint Action – 96/197/JHA, OJ L 63/8, 13.3.96 – in which Member States are obliged to require an air transit visa of nationals of third countries included on the joint list annexed hereto who do not already hold an entry or transit visa – Article 3.

[29] OJ L 164/1, 14.7.95.

However, this does not create a binding Community visa (mutually recognizable by the Member States). It is intended only to prevent easy falsification of visas issued under a Community format.

Among the states in Annex II whose nationals do not need a visa to enter the Community are: Australia, Brazil, Japan, Mexico and the United States. Among the States in Annex I whose nationals do need a visa are: Algeria, China, Egypt, India, Russia, Nigeria, South Africa and Turkey.[30]

For tourists from Annex II states, dispensing with the need for a visa greatly facilitates free movement and thus the common market in tourism.

For a tourist from an Annex I state already in the Community who wishes to enter another Member State, the position is more complex. Whether the tourist needs to get a visa from the second state depends on which state the tourist first enters the Community through and the other state to be visited.

For example, a tourist from third country Z (included in Annex II) lawfully holidaying in France under a short stay visa issued by France buys a package coach tour which takes in Member States B and C. If B and C is Ireland and the UK separate visas for and from each of these states will be required to continue with the tour. If B and C is Belgium and the Netherlands no further visas will be required. The reason why no further visa will be required is that Belgium and the Netherlands and indeed all the other Community states have agreed on the mutual recognition of visas issued under the *Schengen Acquis* (a parallel legal framework explained later), while Ireland and the UK have not. The reason why the UK refuses to agree the mutual recognition of visas issued by other Member States appears to involve sharp concerns over illegal migration, trafficking and security. In the case of Ireland its approach is dictated by the desire to avoid having to reintroduce border checks on movement to and from Northern Ireland which would be necessary since Northern Ireland would be outside the Schengen area.

As is evident from this, there is so far no Community law which guarantees the automatic and mutual recognition of visas by Member States. Until this happens the common market in tourism will remain incomplete.

Internal border controls

Controls at land border crossings and also at air and sea ports on travel between Member States (internal border controls) which check the movement of tourists, both Union citizens and third country nationals, impede the operation of the tourism common market by making entry more cumbersome. Both citizen tourists and third-country tourists alike can be required to show entry

---

[30] For the full lists, see www.europa.eu.int/eur–lex/en/consleg/pdf/en_2001R539_do_001.pdf.

documentation, while the third country tourist may also have to prove additional matters.

Community efforts to support the common market in tourism by securing the removal of internal border controls and the parallel creation of a uniform travel right (based on Community law) for third country tourists to enter and move freely within the Community have so far been unsuccessful.

The legal case for removing internal border controls was articulated by the Commission as far back as 1993:

> As the Commission has stated on numerous occasions … the completion of the internal market, an area without internal frontiers, presupposes also the abolition of all controls at internal frontiers, wherever their form and whatever their justification.[31]

Among the consequences of not removing these controls, the Commission has listed:

- the travel progress of the third-country nationals not resident in the Community is impeded by the need to secure in advance different visas from different states,
- third-country family members of Union citizens who reside within the Community and who travel on their own within the Union can, depending on national laws, be required to also obtain visas in advance before visiting other Member States, and
- providers of services within the Community cannot send an employee who is a third-country national lawfully resident in one Member State to another in connection with their business without overcoming the obstacle of obtaining a visa in advance.

The Commission directly linked the operation of internal border controls with difficulties faced by third country nationals lawfully resident in one Member State travelling as tourists to another:[32]

> As a direct consequence of the disparity between national laws and the lack of coordination between them, some planned intra-Community trips are not made. The formalities, the need to go to an embassy or a consulate which may be a fair distance from one's home, the need in some cases to go in person, the expense and time involved, or quite simply the withholding

---

[31] Proposal for a Council Directive on the Right of Third–country Nationals to Travel in the Community. Explanatory Memorandum COM(95)346 final, p.4, 12.7.95.

[32] *Ibid.*, p.7.

of the visa, are so many reasons why intra-Community trips are not made. This applies in particular to brief visas to neighbouring Member States.

Thus, one of the objectives of the internal market, namely that consumers should be able to obtain goods … from wherever the terms seem to them to be the most favourable … has therefore not been achieved.

The same applies, perhaps with even greater force, to the provisions of services in the Community. Tourism is an example which springs immediately to mind: as it is often easier for a third-country national who lives in a Member State to visit his home country rather than another Member State, the tourism industry undoubtedly suffers as a result. By and large, the difficulties third-country nationals encounter when going to another Member State are an obstacle to the freedom of service providers established in that Member State to provide their services.

Some States disputed the legal argument that the operation of the internal market meant the removal of internal controls over all persons. They claimed it only meant removal of controls over Union citizens and controls could still remain over third country nationals.[33]

The free movement of persons is one of the four fundamental freedoms upon which the EU is founded. Despite the entry into force of the internal market on 1 January 1993, this freedom has not been fully established in the EU. The concept of one market without internal frontiers is elaborated in Article 7a TEU but after a time it became apparent that different States had diverging interpretations of the provision: while the Commission and the majority of Member States understood Article 7a (formerly Article 8a EC Treaty, now Article 14) to mean the abolition of all border controls for EC citizens as well as third country nationals, other Members, in particular the UK, held that Article 7a only applied to EC citizens and allowed for maintaining controls on third country nationals. Under these circumstances, the States which have interpreted Article 7a in a wider sense have joined the Schengen Convention.

Article 7a of the TEU states:

The Internal market shall comprise an area without internal frontiers

---

[33] Keane A, *The Third Pillar of the Treaty on European Union Co–operation in the Fields of Justice and Home Affairs*, EP, Directorate General for Research. Working Papers, People's Europe Series W–8, 1996, p.25.

in which the free movement of goods, persons, and services and capital is ensured in accordance with the provisions of the Treaty.

There is however much contention as to whether free movement is to apply only to Community nationals and not to the broader term of 'persons' to include non-Union citizens. The Commission in its interpretation stated 'any interpretation of Article 8a (now 7a) that confined its effects to Community nationals only would deprive that article of any practical effectiveness.

Schengen Acquis

The slowness of Community institutions to agree to the abolition of controls at internal frontiers led a number of Member States to reach agreement among themselves to abolish such controls in advance of Community-wide agreement. Thus, in 1985 a number of States signed an Agreement in the Luxembourg village of Schengen declaring their desire to remove internal border controls on all persons whatever their origin through a two stage procedure, the second stage being the making of the Schengen Convention in 1990 and its on-going implementation through a wide number of initiatives and legal measures, collectively known as the *Schengen Acquis*.

The belief of the Schengen signatories that they were actually trying to achieve an objective of the Treaty of Rome is clear from the Preamble to the Convention:

Having decided to implement the intention expressed ... of bringing about the abolition of checks at their common borders on the movement of persons and facilitating the transport and movement of goods,

Whereas the Treaty establishing the European Communities, supplemented by the Single European Act, provides that the internal market shall comprise an area without internal frontiers,

Whereas the aim pursued by the Contracting parties coincides with that objective. ...

Additional provisions in the Convention reinforce the Community ethos of the Convention – the Convention is only open to Community Member States (though Norway and Iceland also operate it) and is also subject to any provisions of Community law. Since the Amsterdam Treaty in 1999, the Schengen acquis has been brought within the ambit of the Treaty of Rome and Community actions. Protocol B to the Treaty of Amsterdam formally affirms the Community ethos of Schengen and replaces the Schengen executive Committee with the Council of the European Union as the responsible Schengen institution. After authorising the closer co-operation envisaged in the Schengen acquis, Article 1 of the Protocol goes on to provide that:

> This co-operation shall be conducted within the institutional and legal framework of the European Union and with respect for the relevant provisions of the European Union and of the Treaty establishing the European Community.

As and when the Community gets around to making its own laws in this area, they will replace the Schengen ones. The key provision of the Schengen acquis is Article 2(1) of the Convention which pithily states that:

> Internal borders may be crossed at any point without any checks on persons being carried out.

Related provisions allow for the temporary restoration of controls for reasons of national security/policy and also for the continuation of normal police powers of control applicable to the general population.

   To compensate for the removal of internal border controls and the risks of illegal migration and trafficking involving third country nationals, the Convention provides for an enhanced uniform external border policy.

> Cross-border movement at external borders shall be subject to checks. ... Checks shall be made in accordance with uniform principles – Article 6(1).

Among the uniform principles are:

> Checks on person shall include not only the verification of travel documents and of other conditions governing entry ... but also checks to detect and prevent threats to the national security and public policy of the Contracting Parties – Article 6(2)(a).

> Additionally third country nationals can be asked to substantiate the purpose and conditions of their planed visit and have sufficient means of support or be in a position to legally acquire such means – Article 5(1).

The wide range of supporting measures necessary to operate a common external border policy (including refusing entry to a person put on a list by any other State, greater co-operation between security forces covering the exchange of data through a European Information System) has lead to the creation of large body of legal measures which lie beyond the tourism focus of this work.[34]

Another part of the Schengen common external border policy connected to removing internal border controls is the adoption of uniform rules of when a visa is or is not required and the mutual recognition of visas so that once lawfully entered, a third country tourist can enter and travel over the entire Schengen area.

The mutual recognition of visas is dealt with by the creation of a Schengen visa. Article 10 of the Schengen Convention states that:

> A uniform visa for the entire territory of the Contracting Parties [all Community States except Ireland and the UK] shall be introduced. This visa ... may be issued for periods not exceeding three months.

A Schengen visa is:

> valid for one or more entries (across external borders), provided that neither the length of a continuous visit not the total length of successive visits may exceed three months in any half year as from the date of first entry.

The free movement of third country tourists is made explicit in Article 19(1) which states that:

> Aliens [all third country nationals] holding a uniform visa who have legally entered the territory of a Contracting Party may move freely within the territories of all the Contracting parties throughout the period of validity of their visa provided they fulfil the conditions of entry. ...

Thus, a South African tourist arriving in Paris with a French issued Schengen visa is free, after being subject to an external frontier check at the airport, to catch a connecting flight to Frankfurt without obtaining another visa and without further official document check.

The Schengen process has proved so popular that by 2002 Austria, Belgium, Denmark, Finland, France, Germany, Greece, Iceland, Italy, Luxembourg, the Netherlands, Norway, Portugal, Spain and Sweden had abolished internal border checks on travel between them. Only two Member States, Ireland and the United Kingdom had not agreed to the removal of internal border controls and the recognition of the uniform visa – though they have participated in some aspects of the process and nationals of both states when crossing internal frontiers

---

[34] For a list of Community measures supporting standardisation of external borders controls see, www.europa.eu.int/eur–lex/en/lif/reg/en_register_191020.html.

between the Schengen states benefit from the abolition of internal border checks by the Convention. However, Article 6 of the Convention makes clear that Irish and UK nationals must be subject to Schengen external border checks when entering the Schengen area from their own state, but only for the passport check provided for under Community law and not any other.

The implementation of the Schengen Convention in so many Member States removed much of the practical urgency for the European Community to itself enact legislation removing internal border controls. Indeed, the Community closely followed the Schengen experience with a view to learning from it as and when it is able to secure agreement among Member States on the passage of corresponding Community legislation.

1995 proposals

To return to the history of efforts to enact Community legislation facilitating free movement, in 1995 the Commission tried unsuccessfully to make progress at Community level on the issue of free movement for tourists, among others, by publishing two complimentary proposals for directives, one dealing with the rights of third-country nationals to travel in the Community[35] and the other dealing with the abolition of internal border controls.[36] The content of these need only be briefly noted since they reproduce the core ideas found in the Commission's 1993 proposals and the Schengen acquis.

As might be expected, the legal justification for both proposals was the creation of an internal market comprising an area without internal frontiers in which the free movement of persons would be ensured.

The rationale for the proposed Directive[37] on eliminating internal border controls was the need for clarity and legal certainty in a legally complex area and also to:

> ensure that the crossing of an internal frontier in the internal market is treated in the same way as the crossing of a boundary between provinces, counties, regions. ...

According to the Commission:[38]

---

[35] Commission, Proposal for a Council Directive on the Right of Third Country Nationals to Travel in the Community, COM(95) 346 final, 12.7.95.

[36] Proposal for a Council Directive on the Elimination of Controls on Person Crossing Internal Frontiers. Explanatory memorandum COM (95) 347 final, 12.7.95.

[37] Proposal for a Council Directive on the Elimination of Controls on Person Crossing Internal Frontiers. Explanatory memorandum COM (95) 347 final, p.6.

[38] *Ibid.*, p.5.

There can be no escaping the fact that, alone among the different freedoms of movement referred to in Article 7a (now Article 14), the free movement of persons has not so far been achieved. ... This is because the accompanying measures essential to the elimination of controls either have been adopted but have not yet been put into effect ... or are still under discussion.

The core idea in the proposed directive was set out in Article 1, which stated that:

All persons, whatever their nationality, shall be able to cross Member States frontiers within the Community at any point, without being subject to any frontier control or formality.

Frontier was defined as common land frontier, airports for intra-Community flights, sea ports for intra-Community sea crossings and also rail or road terminals for links by bridge or tunnel.

Member States would have been permitted to restore frontier controls in the event of a serious threat to public policy or security through specific procedures. Moreover, Member States would still have been able to carry out normal law enforcement procedures on visitors and would have been entitled to require visitors to possess any necessary documents (identity cards, residence permit) under law – only frontier control would have been banned, not other controls which would, however, have to have been exercised without discrimination between local and cross-border traffic. Care would need to have been taken over the location of controls near the frontier.

For example, a check on identity papers or travel documents [lawfully performed by police] a few miles inland of the internal frontier, at a point on a motorway where there were no entrance or exit roads between it and the frontier, would thus be discriminatory and would have to be regarded as a frontier control in disguise.[39]

This proposed directive was not adopted.

The key freedom in the proposed directive on the travel rights of third country nationals was set out in Article 1, which stated:

Member States shall grant third-country nationals who are lawfully in a Member State the right to travel in the territories of the other Member States in accordance with this Directive.

---

[39] *Ibid.*, p.7.

Three categories of third country national would have benefited – those living outside the Union who do not need a visa to enter the Union who could stay up to three months, those who do need a visa could stay for a period defined in the visa, and those who reside lawfully within the Community who could also stay up to three months.

2001 proposals

More recently the altered constitutional and political climate operating in the Community since the transfer of issues of emigration and related matters from Title VI of the Maastricht Treaty to Title IV of the Rome Treaty, and particularly the recasting of a timetable for action to be taken in this area, has made it likely that new legislation will be adopted in the near future.

In 2001 the Commission issued another proposal for a directive to deal with internal travel rights for third country nationals.[40] Two broad categories of traveller would be dealt with – those travelling up to three months and those travelling up to six months. While it is obvious that tourists can fall into either category, only the former will be looked at. The legal basis for the proposal is Article 62(3) of the Treaty which requires the Council to adopt by May 1, 2004:

> measures setting out the conditions under which nationals of third countries shall have the freedom to travel within the territory of the Member States during a period of no more than three months.

Three types of third country national are provided for:
- travellers who need a visa,
- travellers who do not need a visa,
- travellers who hold residence permits from one of the Member States.

For third-country nationals who need and hold a uniform visa the key article is Article 5 which in effect proposes that they be allowed travel freely in the territory of all Member States throughout the period of validity of the visa if they:
- hold a valid passport,
- are not considered a security threat,
- have sufficient means of subsistence, both for the period of the intended stay and for the return to their country of origin or transit into a third state. ...

---

[40] Commission, Proposal for a Council Directive relating to the conditions in which third–country nationals shall have the freedom to travel in the territory of the Member States for periods not exceeding three months, COM (2001) 388 final, 10.7.01.

Where the third country traveller does not need a visa, then under Article 6 the same bulleted requirements would apply

Third country travellers holding a residence permit from one of the Member States would enjoy a similar freedom under Article 7 and would also be subject to the bulleted requirements above. A valid residence permit would in effect operate as a substitute for a visa. No travel right would be conferred on those illegally present in a Member State.

CONDUCT OF BORDER CONTROLS

Leaving aside whether internal border controls are compatible with the tourism common market, once such controls are in operation, under national or Community law, certain rules govern their conduct. For convenience Union citizens and third country tourists will be treated separately.

Checks on Union Citizens at Internal Border Controls

The basic Treaty provisions granting free movement for Union citizens based on citizenship and on the common market set the context for how checks at internal border controls can be conducted.

The citizenship implications for how border checks can be conducted have not so far been dealt with by the Court of Justice. However, there is considerable guidance available on the common market implications for border checks. Directive 68/360 on the abolition of restrictions on movement of workers, as already indicated, requires only the production by tourists who are Union citizens of a valid passport or identity card to gain entry to another Member State. Both the Commission and the Court of Justice have had to remind Member States of the implications of this.

> In the Commissions view, the mere fact of stamping a passport with an entry or exit stamp is contrary to Community law and all the old Member States have been prevailed upon to abolish the practise. After they joined the Community, the Commission drew the attention of Greece, Spain and Portugal to its unlawfulness by sending them a letter of formal notice. Spain and Portugal have just informed the Commission that they have issued instructions to the effect that the stamping of Community nationals passports must cease. The Commission has therefore terminated the infringement proceedings against these two countries.[41]

---

[41] IP (88) 350.

The name on the passport must in principle be accepted.

> On February 7, 1988, Mr Labhras Ó Murchu, an Irish citizen and chairman
> of the association of Irish traditional musicians, was stopped at Leeds airport
> in England by passport control officials who demanded that he 'translate'
> his own name, which appears in Gaelic on his passport, into English. ...
> The Commission is now able to inform ... that it has contacted the United
> Kingdom authorities who have in turn informed it that the Home Office has
> taken steps to ensure that incidents similar to the one described in the ...
> question do not occur in future ... the Home Office has instructed that an
> officer must in principle accept the name given on a passport... [42]

The most definitive statements of the legal position as to how frontier controls
may be operated are to be found in Court of Justice pronouncements:

> the only restriction which Article 48 of the Treaty (now Article 39) lays
> down concerning freedom of movement in the territory of Member States
> is that of limitations justified on grounds of public policy, public security
> or public health. This restriction must be regarded not as a condition
> precedent to the acquisition of the right of entry and residence but as pro-
> viding the possibility, in individual cases where there is sufficient justifica-
> tion, of imposing restrictions on the exercise of a right derived directly
> from the Treaty. It does not therefore justify administrative measures
> requiring in a general way formalities at the frontier other than simply the
> production of a valid identity card or a passport. [43]

And also:

> That condition (production of a valid identity document or passport), which
> is the only one laid down by Article 3 of the two directives (68/360 and
> 73/148), cannot be supplemented by the requirement of proving inclusion
> in one of the classes of persons mentioned in those directives. ... More
> generally, the obligation to answer questions put by frontier officials cannot
> be a precondition for the entry of a national of one Member State into the
> territory of another. ... The United Kingdom, however, insists that it is
> necessary to ask questions in order to verify the validity of the identity
> documents produced. In that connection, it need merely be observed that
> the lawfulness of controls as to the validity of the document produced

---

[42] EP Written Question No 138/88; QXWO138/88EN.
[43] *R. v. Pieck* [1980] E.C.R. II–2171, 2185.

derives from the requirement laid down in Article 3 of both directives that the identity card or passport should be 'valid'.[44]

Besides checking the validity of passports or identity cards, where justified, checks on Union citizens at internal frontiers can also only be carried out where they do not affect the right of entry and where their frequency etc are not such as to impede the free movement of workers.

In *Commission v. Belgium* the Commission complained to the Court of Justice about a Belgium practise of border-checking returning Community nationals resident in Belgian to see if they were carrying their residence permit (as Belgium law required – Belgium citizens were subject to a similar obligation). The Commission alleged that this infringed the right of free entry guaranteed by Directive 68/360, although persons found without the card were still allowed enter. The Court disagreed:[45]

> The Commission disputes the compatibility with Community law of the controls at issue in so far as they are carried out at the time of entry into Belgian territory and are thus added to the requirement of production of a valid identity card or passport.
>
> It must be stated in the first place that provided that the controls criticised by the Commission are not a condition of entry into Belgian territory, they are not prohibited by the wording of the provisions of the directives relied upon by the Commission. ... However, the carrying out of such controls upon entry ... may, depending on the circumstances, constitute a barrier to the free movement of persons within the Community, a fundamental principle of the EEC Treaty to which the aforementioned directives are intended to give full effect. That would be the case in particular if it were found that the controls in question were carried out in a systematic, arbitrary or unnecessarily restrictive manner. ... It is not disputed in the present case that the controls at issue are carried out sporadically and unsystematically.

Checks on Third Country Tourists

The nature and extent of checks on third country tourists depends on whether the checks are conducted under national or Community law or the *Schengen Acquis*. If and when the Commission proposal for a directive on the travel rights

---

[44] *Commission v. Netherlands* [1991] E.C.R. I–2637, 2655.
[45] *Commission v. Belgium* [1989] E.C.R. I–997, 1010.

of third country nationals becomes law, that will determine the matters to be checked. The removal of internal border controls in most Member States under Schengen obviously means that the travel documentation of third country tourists is not checked at internal frontiers. Any systematic checks on them conducted near the frontier runs the risk of being regarded as a control in disguise and contrary to at least the spirit of Schengen. Presumably Schengen states can conduct random checks on third country tourists anywhere on their territory and if the necessary entry/stay conditions are not satisfied to act accordingly.

PERMITTED RESTRICTIONS ON FREE MOVEMENT OF TOURISTS AND TOURISM WORKERS

The rights of entry and stay/residence of citizen tourists/tourism workers are not unlimited. Different Treaty provisions impose similar restrictions. Under Article 18(1) of the Treaty of Rome the right of Union citizens whether acting as tourists or not to move freely within the Union is:

> subject to the limitations and conditions laid down in this Treaty and by the measures adopted to give it effect.[46]

Within the context of workers' freedom of movement, Article 39(3) of the Treaty of Rome provides that it is:

> subject to limitations justified on grounds of public policy, public security, or public health.

Similar restrictions are permitted on the self-employed person's right of establishment under Article 46(1) and the service provider's right to provide services under Article 55. Equally, Community laws which harmonise exemptions from customs and other duties and taxes on crossing Community boundaries for travellers carrying goods of a non-commercial nature also permit national restrictions based on these grounds.[47]

---

[46] In *R. v. Adams* [1995] All E.R. (EC) 177 an English court refused to refer to the Court of Justice the question whether Article 18(1) permitted a Member State to rely on national security reasons to justify refusal of entry to a Union citizen of a Member State travelling to a different part of the same Member State. Perhaps surprisingly the Court took it on itself to declare at p.90: "In addition we hold that if Article 18(1) is given a broad interpretation, it is, in any event, subject to an implied derogation in respect of the interests of security of Member States". Uncertainty of this type usually justifies a referral to the Court of Justice.

[47] *Heinonen* [1999] E.C.R. I–3599.

Thus, in a variety of contexts the tourist/tourism worker's entitlement to move freely in the Community can be legitimately restricted by Member States on grounds of public policy, security, or health.

Both implementing legislation and a significant volume of case law have elaborated the meaning of these grounds of restriction and their application. The Commissions 2001 proposal dealing with free movement issues for Union citizens and their families, mentioned earlier, proposes consolidating the existing measures and also incorporates case law.

Council Directive 64/221[48] on the co-ordination of special measures concerning the movement and residence of workers on grounds of public policy, security and health is the principal implementing measure in the case of workers/tourists and deals with entry, residence permits and expulsions.

> The objective of the Directive is to offer to its beneficiaries specified safeguards and guarantees when the Member States resort to measures on grounds of public policy, public security or public health, as these grounds are derogations from the fundamental freedoms provided for by the Treaty and should therefore be interpreted strictly. ...[49]

Under Article 1, Directive 64/221 applies:

> to any national of a Member State who resides in or travels to another Member State of the Community, either in order to pursue an activity as an employed or self-employed person, or as a recipient of services [and] also to the spouse and to members of the family who come within the provisions of the regulations and directives adopted in this field. ...

Since tourists are classified as recipients of services,[50] the Directive's provisions also apply to them. A number of clear statements in the Directive limit the justification which Member States can use for these restrictions.

> Such grounds shall not be invoked to serve economic grounds – Article 2(2).

> Measures taken on grounds of public policy or of public security shall be based exclusively on the personal conduct of the individual concerned – Article 3(1).

---

[48] OJ L 850/64, 4.4.64.

[49] Commission, Communication on the Special Measures concerning the Movement and Residence of Citizens of the Union which are justified on grounds of Public Policy, Public Security or Public Health COM (1999) 372 final, p.3.

[50] *Luisi and Carbone v. Ministero del Tresoro Public* [1984] E.C.R. 378.

> Previous criminal convictions shall not in themselves constitute grounds for the taking of such measures – Article 3(2).

> Expiry of the identity card or passport used by the person concerned to enter the host country and to obtain a residence permit shall not justify expulsions from the territory – Article 3(3).

> The only diseases or disabilities justifying refusal of entry into a territory or refusal to issue a first residence permit shall be those listed in the Annex – Article 4(1).

Thus, in relation to public health, according to the Commission:

> Member States may not set any general requirement that before entry into the country citizens of another Member State need to provide proof that they are not suffering from any illness mentioned in the Annex.[51]

though before granting a first residence permit Member States may require provision of a medical certificate to establish the person is not suffering from any of the Annex diseases.

Among the diseases listed in the Annex are developing/active tuberculosis, syphilis and certain other infectious diseases. In fact, however, according to the Commission:

> The public health grounds are somewhat outdated given the current level of integration of the European Union and the development of new means to handle public health problems.

The Annex also specifies that:

> drug addiction and mental illnesses might threaten public policy or public security, but not public health.

Interpretation of the Restrictions on Free Movement

Member States have made significant use of these permitted restrictions to justify limits on the free movement of Union citizens. While Community law cannot limit states' discretion in this area as to what constitutes public security etc, it is empowered to examine the legality of measures taken to ensure a harmonious approach to the interpretation of the grounds of restriction. Any such measures, according to the Commission:

---

[51] *Supra* p. 12.

should be interpreted strictly and in the light of all the provisions of the Treaty.[52]

In *Calfa*[53] a Greek court sought a preliminary ruling from the Court of Justice under Article 234 (formerly Article 177) concerning a Greek law which required a court to impose a mandatory punishment of life expulsion from Greece on an Italian tourist found guilty of possession and use of prohibited drugs in Crete. After firstly emphasising the fundamental principle that tourists have the freedom to visit other States as recipients of services and that expulsion was 'the very negation of that freedom', the Court of Justice considered whether expulsion could be justified under the public policy exception.[54]

> Under the Court's case-law … it must be accepted that a Member State may consider that the use of drugs constitutes a danger for society such as to justify special measures against foreign nationals who contravene its laws on drugs, in order to maintain public order.
>
> However, as the Court has repeatedly stated, the public policy exception, like all derogations from a fundamental principle of the Treaty, must be interpreted restrictively.

After reciting the salient points of Article 3 of Directive 64/221, the Court continued:[55]

> It follow that an expulsion order could be made against a Community national such as Ms Calfa only if, besides her having committed an offence under drugs laws, her personal conduct created a genuine and sufficiently serious threat affecting on the of the fundamental interests of society. … In the present case … expulsion for life automatically follows a criminal conviction, without any account being taken of the personal conduct of the offender or of the danger which that person represents for the requirements of public policy. … It follows that the conditions for the application of the public policy exception provided for in Directive 64/221 … are not fulfilled and that the public policy exception cannot be successfully relied upon to justify a restriction on the freedom to provide services …

---

[52] *Supra* p. 3.
[53] [1999] E.C.R. I–11. See also *R. v. Adams supra.*
[54] At p.30.
[55] *Supra.*

Drawing on cases such as this, the Commission's 2001 proposed Directive contains new provisions limiting the reasons Member States can rely on along the following lines:[56]

- the personal conduct of the individual concerned must represent a present and sufficiently serious threat, affecting one of the fundamental interests of society. Justifications that are removed from the particulars of the case or that rely on considerations of general prevention shall not be accepted – proposed Article 25.

- before taking an expulsion decision on grounds of public policy or public security, the host Member State shall take account of considerations such as how long the individual concerned has resided on it territory, his/her age, state of health, family and economic situation, social and cultural integration into the host country and the extent of his/her links with the country of origin – proposed Article 26.

- the only diseases or disabilities justifying refusal of leave to enter or leave to reside on the territory of a Member State shall be the diseases subject to quarantine listed in International Health Regulation No 2 of the World Health Organisation of 25 May 1951 and other infectious diseases or contagious parasitic diseases if they are the subject of protection provisions applying to nationals of the host country – Article 27.

TOURISM SERVICES AND FREE MOVEMENT

The freedom to travel to another Member State to either temporarily or permanently provide a tourism service there is another free movement right of importance to European tourism. The former freedom is guaranteed under Article 49 of the Treaty of Rome and the latter under Article 43. At different times tour operators, travel agents, airlines, ferry and cruise companies use either freedom. Travel fairs are probably based on the Article 49 freedom.

The Treaty, however, also permits Member States to restrict the exercise of these freedoms where the restriction is a proportionate expression of legitimate Member State public policy, public health or public security. This is commonly done in the Member States often by means of a licence/permit requirement in order to control tour operators, travel agents, airlines and accommodation providers. The degree of control tends to be greater in States where tourism is economically particularly important and where, additionally tour guides and

---

[56] Commission, Proposal for a European Parliament and Council Directive on the right of citizens of the Union and their family members to move and reside freely within the territory of the Member States, COM (2001) 257 final, 23.5.01, pp.41,42.

sports institutions, including ski instructors, can be made subject to a licence requirement. The justification for such controls is equally a mix of the development of the tourism sector and the protection of tourists.

> In a series of near identical cases in the early 1990s[57] against **France, Italy** and **Greece** the Court of Justice considered the compatibility with the services freedom of national restrictions which required tour operators bringing a tour party to another State to use tour guides which held a national qualification or licence in the host State. The Member States sought to justify these restrictions on grounds of national policy, the policy being the proper appreciation of the culture and heritage of the host State. As a matter of law the Court of Justice accepted that this could be a legitimate basis for restricting Community free movement.
>
> > The general interests in the proper appreciation of places and things of historical interest and the widest possible dissemination of knowledge of the artistic cultural heritage of a country can constitute an overriding reason justifying a restriction on the freedom to provide services.[58]
>
> However, the principle of proportionality in Community law required that the specific means used by Member States to achiever this policy – the imposition of the need to obtain a qualification from the State authorities – went no further than was necessary and that no less restrictive means was available. This is where the Member State laws were incompatible with Article 49. In *Commission v. France*, the Court stated:[59]
>
> > the requirement in question in the French legislation goes beyond what is necessary to ensure the safeguarding of that interest inasmuch as it makes the activities of a tourist guide accompanying groups of tourists from another Member State subject to possession of a licence.
>
> The reason why the French restriction was unduly restrictive was that a less restrictive means was available – the tour operator's self interest.
>
> > the profitable operation of such group tours depends on the commercial reputation of the operator, who faces competitive pressures from other tour companies; the need to maintain the reputation and the competitive pressure themselves compel companies to be selective in employing tourist guides and exercise some control over the quality of their

---

[57] *Commission v. France* [1991] E.C.R. I–659; *Commission v. Italy* [1991] E.C.R. I–709; *Commission v. Greece* [1991] E.C.R. I–727.
[58] *Commission v. France* [1991] E.C.R. I–659, 687.
[59] *Ibid.*, p 687.

> services. Depending of the specific expectations of the groups of tourists in question, that factor is likely to contribute to the proper appreciation of laces and things of historical interests and to the widest possible dissemination of knowledge relating to the artistic and cultural heritage.[60]

State restrictions have also affected air transport services. The Commission has taken successful proceedings against States over discriminatory airport landing charges and discriminatory bilateral air transport agreements with non-Member States. In the former cases the unjustified discrimination was between intra-Community and internal flights[61] and in the latter cases it concerned nationality clauses.

> In *Commission v. UK*[62] in 2002 the UK sought to defend the ability to revoke an airline's operating authorisation under a bilateral air transport agreement with the US on US/UK flights on grounds of the airline's owner's/controller's nationality. It cited grounds of public policy, the possible danger of having to allow any carrier fly such routes, as justification. The Court of Justice disagreed. It firstly stated the guiding principle on State public policy as being the need for the UK to show:
>
>> a direct link between [a sufficiently serious threat affecting one of the fundamental interests of society] which, must, moreover, be current and the discriminatory measure adopted to deal with it.[63]
>
> After holding that the agreement did not limit the revocation grounds to this, the Court further saw no link between the threat and the range of those potentially within the revocation power.
>
>> In any event, there is no direct link between such threat to the public policy of the United Kingdom ... and generalised discrimination against Community airlines.[64]

CHAPTER CONCLUSION

The survey in this chapter of how the European Community has dealt with free

---

[60] *Ibid.*, p. 687.
[61] See further p.197.
[62] Case 466/98, 5.11.02.
[63] *Ibid.*, para.57.
[64] *Ibid.*, para.59.

movement and tourism indicates that a fully functioning common market in tourism still does not exist. There are proposals to deal with the remaining areas affecting free movement which have traditionally been under exclusive Member State control. It is, nonetheless, surprising nearly half a century since the Rome Treaty came into force that there is no Community law removing internal border checks for tourists within the Community, nor is there a law governing the entry and stay conditions for third country nationals as tourists. Fortunately the Schengen initiatives have removed much of the sting of this failure. Also on the positive side Member States have responded to Community initiatives to ensure nationality restrictions do not impede free movement for citizen-tourists and, as is clear from the last section of the chapter, are recognising that the logical working out of free movement principles means accepting significant limits on Member State's ability to reimpose movement restrictions on citizen tourists.

STUDENT TASKS

Undergraduate questions:

1. Outline the range of component freedoms, which make up the Community freedom of movement.

2. Trace the evolution of Community legal protection from free movement for workers to free movement for Union citizens.

3. Explain when a tourism worker may need to obtain a residence permit and outline the permitted consequences for failing to obtain it.

4. Describe the issues, which remain to be tackled at Community level before the Community can replace the *Schengen Acquis* with its own provisions.

5. Describe the types of question, which officials at internal frontiers may lawfully ask of Union citizens entering the territory.

Post-graduate questions:

1. Consider why it has proved so difficult to secure agreement among Member States for the removal of checks at internal frontiers.

2. Discuss the scope available to Member States to lawfully refuse permission to Union citizens to enter or remain on their territory for health reasons

3. Consider the Commission's proposals for facilitating short-stay travel within the Community for third country nationals.

CHAPTER 5

COMMUNITY TRANSPORT POLICY AND TOURISM[1]

INTRODUCTION

The European Community has consistently recognised the relationship between transport and tourism. According to the European Commission as far back as 1982:

> Since tourism is an activity in which mobility plays the key role, developments in transport are a matter of fundamental concern to the tourist.[2]

The mobility theme was reiterated by the Commission in 1994:[3]

> Mobility is the characteristic of out times. This is the age of mass travel, encouraged by rising personal affluence and steadily increasing leisure time. Cross-border holiday travel has boomed, leading to a great expansion of air services, and also to large increases in the volume of long-distance car journeys. And personal mobility is still on the rise, not just for holiday travel, but also for many social and economic reasons.

More recently, the Commission noted how tourist travel had become a key factor in transport demand generally:[4]

> The links between transport and tourism indicate the importance for both subjects of their points in common. With the constant increase in disposable income in the EU, one of the key drivers of the demand for transport on

---

[1] Marc Mc Donald, Willem Buijs, Jan-Willem Proper, Dennis Ketel.
[2] OJ C 115/17, 30.4.84.
[3] Commission, The Trans–European Transport Network, 1994, Office for Official Publications of the EC, ISBN 92–826–9299–X, p.11.
[4] Commission, Report on Community Measures Affecting Tourism (1997/99) COM(2001) 171 final, 28.3.01, p.18.

many EU air and land transport routes is now tourist traffic. However, there is also a strong influence from transport services: the quality of transport has had and will have a major impact on the continued success of the tourist industry in many regions. In this context, over the past years, increasing congestion of the European air space with considerable delays and other inconveniences resulting from it were recorded.

The types of transport used by tourists vary across the Member States. According to a Eurobarometer survey:[5]

European holiday makers use their own car (58%), the plane (31%) (whether charter or scheduled flights) or the train (10%) to reach their holiday destination. On the spot, their privileged means of transport are still their own car, but then followed by walk and tourist coach. Unsurprisingly, the Greeks use boats (undoubtedly the most adequate means to reach their numerous islands) in similar proportions to their own car (respectively 43% and 48%). The French (74%), the Italians (63%) and the Spanish (61%) use their own cars in proportions significantly higher than the European Union average (58%). The Swedes (31%), the British (28%), the Irish (26%), the Danes (25%), the Austrians (24%) make above average (16%) use of charter flights. The Irish, the Luxembourg and the British make above average use of scheduled flights (respectively 33%, 33% and 23% against the European Union average 15%). Cars are means of transport used mainly by the middle age categories (25-39 and 40-54), tourist coaches by the eldest (55+).

Tourist destination flows within the Community are also varied. According to the same study, other Member States of the European Union are the preferred destination of citizen tourists. This is particularly true for Luxembourg (91% of responses designate another European Union country), Belgium (74%) and Germany (73%). The average European travels thus mostly on an intra-regional basis.

The table below shows the tourist flows between the Member States on an incoming and outgoing basis.

---

5   Commission, Facts and Figures on the Europeans on Holidays 1997–1998, A Eurobarometer survey 117, Report 3/98 Executive Summary, p.8. Available at http://europa.eu.int/comm/public_opinion/archives/eb/ebs_117_en.pdf.

Table 5.1: Tourist Flows in Europe[6]

Originating Member State	Number 1 Destination	Number 2 Destination	Another EU country	A country outside EU
B	France (24%)	Spain (21%)	74%	13%
DK	France (10%)	Greece (9%)	59%	9%
D	Spain (17%)	Italy (15%)	73%	9%
GR	Germany (2%)	France (2%)	8%	1%
E	France (2%)	Portugal (2%)	10%	4%
F	Spain (7%)	UK (2%)	22%	8%
IRE	Spain (19%)	UK (18%)	58%	14%
II	France (8%)	Spain (4%)	25%	5%
L	France (23%)	Spain (19%)	91%	10%
NL	France (20%)	Spain (9%)	67%	9%
A	Italy (19%)	Greece (13%)	65%	14%
P	Spain (9%)	France (4%)	19%	2%
FIN	Spain (8%)	Sweden (6%)	32%	6%
S	Spain (12%)	Greece (10%)	53%	8%
UK	Spain (18%)	France (9%)	52%	16%
EU15	France (19%)	Spain (19%)	44%	9%

Tourist transport demand is of course not the same as general passenger transport demand, but it the major part of it and justifies the focus in this chapter on a range of general transport issues within Community transport policy. How large a part tourism and leisure transport demand play in overall passenger demand is clear from the following:

> Holiday related trips and other leisure trips by Europeans counted for about 80 % in 2000, with business trips having generated the remaining 20 %. Comparing the year 2000 with 1999, a strong movement towards holidays involving no pre-bookings was registered, reaching nearly one-quarter of the total volume. Non-paid accommodation is estimated for more than 20 % of the accommodation used in all outbound trips during 2000.[7]

---

[6] *Ibid.*, p.5. Footnotes omitted. The column 'Another EU country' includes the total number of responses designating any State in the EU. Percentages are rounded up or down depending whether the figure is above or below .5%.

[7] Commission, Report on Community Measures affecting tourism (2000), SEC (2002) 300 final, 15.3.02, p.5.

Growth in Transport Demand

The major phenomenon in transport over the last decades has been the uninterrupted growth in demand. The Commission stated in a Transport White Paper in 1992:[8]

> Transport is a growth industry. Its development depends on the development of the economy as a whole. Despite regional variations and different developments in the various transport modes, demand has experienced virtually uninterrupted growth since the 1970s.

> In general transport demand, for both goods and passengers, runs in parallel to growth in GDP, although there are indications that a lower GDP growth may result in a disproportionately smaller, and higher, GDP growth rates in disproportionately higher growth of transport activity…

> The following main factors have been identified as contributing to this growth:

> - … locational shifts from urban to new industrial sites and a dispersal of economic activities; these changes have been amplified by the continuing process of economic integration within the Community …
> - the rising share of the service industry and its multi-sites business have caused rapidly growing professional mobility over short, medium and long distances.
> - the increase of net disposable income and demographic changes have led to higher rates of car ownership and increased holiday and leisure time travelling.

General data on rising transport demand are disturbing and the Commission has declared its policy now is to break the link between rising GDP and rising transport demand.[9] The following tables[10] indicate significantly increasing use

---

[8] Commission, Communication on a global approach to the construction of a Community framework for sustainable mobility, COM (92) 494 final, 2.12.92.

[9] Commission, White Paper European transport policy for 2010: time to decide, COM (2001) final, 12.9.01, p.10.

[10] Taken from DG Energy and Transport website at www.europa.eu.int/comm/energy_transport/ etif/transport_passenger_a/performance_by_mode.pkm.html. See also Commission, EU Energy and Transport in Figures, Statistical Pocketbook 2001, p.161. pkm denotes one person transported a distance of one kilometre and can comprise two dimension of transport performance – 30 people drive 10 kilometres producing a 300 pkm or 2 people drive 150 kilometres also producing a 300 pkm. "mio pkm" means million passenger kilometres.

of air and car, continued annual increases in air travel and almost continuous decline in both rail and coach travel as means of transport. The car remains by far the most used means of transport (see Table 5.2 on p. 179 below).

There seems little doubt that tourism has played a significant role in increased transport demand, both generally and in relation to air travel and along various land routes at particular times of the year.

The growth in transport demand produces negative consequences when demand outstrips the capacity of the infrastructure and the environment to cope. Sustainable transport is a particular concept which has emerged in response to this and looms large in future Community transport planning. A significant focus of the remainder of this chapter concerns:

- the pressures which increased transport demand place on the environment and infrastructure, and
- the principles underlying the wide range of Community responses to this pressure.

Two additional themes of Community transport policy which will be explored in this chapter concern the on-going liberalisation of transport markets and the promotion of safety in passenger transport.

Within the European Commission responsibility for the common transport policy rests with the Directorate General Energy and Transport, formerly DG VII. Of the seven directorates within this DG four deal with transport matters – Directorate B deals with trans-European networks, E deals with inland transport, F deals with air transport and G deals with maritime transport. Comprehensive information about the Commission's activities regarding transport are available from its website at:

http://www.europa.eu.int/comm/transport/index_en.html.

Access to the texts of transport legislation and policy documents can be obtained from either this website or from the Community law website at:

www.europa.eu.int/eur-lex.

The linkages between the various issues dealt with in this chapter can be seen as follows (see p. 180 below):

Table 5.2: Passenger Transport in the EU

1000 mio pkm

	Passenger cars	Buses & Coaches	Tram + Metro	Railway	Air	Total
1970	1 582	269	39	219	33	**2 142**
1980	2 295	348	41	248	74	**3 006**
1990	3 199	369	48	268	157	**4 041**
1991	3 257	378	48	276	166	**4 126**
1995	3 506	382	47	274	202	**4 410**
1996	3 558	391	48	282	209	**4 488**
1997	3 622	393	49	285	222	**4 571**
1998	3 702	402	50	287	241	**4 682**
1999	3 788	406	51	295	260	**4 801**
2000	3 789	413	53	303	281	**4 839**
1991-00	**+ 16 %**	**+ 9 %**	**+ 10 %**	**+ 10 %**	**+ 70 %**	**+ 17 %**

Source : tables 3.5.4, 3.5.6, 3.5.7, 3.5.8, 3.5.11

Average annual change
% per year

	Passenger cars	Buses & Coaches	Tram + Metro	Railway	Air	Total
1970-80	+3.8	+2.6	+0.4	+1.2	+8.4	**+3.4**
1980-90	+3.4	+0.6	+1.7	+0.8	+7.8	**+3.0**
1991-00	+1.7	+1.0	+1.0	+1.1	+6.0	**+1.8**
2000	+0.0	+1.6	+3.8	+2.6	+8.1	**+0.8**

Modal split
%

	Passenger cars	Buses & Coaches	Tram + Metro	Railway	Air
1970	73.8	12.6	1.8	10.2	1.5
1980	76.4	11.6	1.4	8.2	2.5
1990	79.2	9.1	1.2	6.6	3.9
1991	79.0	9.2	1.2	6.7	4.0
1995	79.5	8.7	1.1	6.2	4.6
1996	79.3	8.7	1.1	6.3	4.6
1997	79.2	8.6	1.1	6.2	4.9
1998	79.1	8.6	1.1	6.1	5.1
1999	78.9	8.5	1.1	6.1	5.4
2000	78.3	8.5	1.1	6.3	5.8

Transport and Tourism

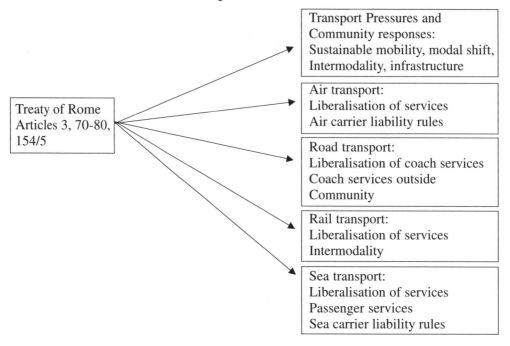

Learning Outcomes:

After reading this chapter, the student should:

- have an understanding of the impact of Community involvement in transport on tourism,
- appreciate the significance of concepts like sustainable mobility, modal shift and intermodality, and how they relate to Community transport and tourism,
- understand the importance of trans-European networks,
- have an awareness of the ways Community transport policy seeks to promote greater access to transport markets and greater safety in passenger transport.

These learning outcomes will be addressed through the following headings:

The Treaty and Transport.
Transport Pressures and Community Responses.

Air Transport and Tourism.
Road Transport and Tourism.
Rail Transport and Tourism.
Sea Transport and Tourism.

THE TREATY AND TRANSPORT

Article 3 of the Treaty establishing the European Community (Treaty of Rome) includes among the activities of the Community:

a common transport policy.

Title V of the Treaty headed *Transport,* covers Articles 70 to 80, including Article 70 which states that:

The objectives of this Treaty shall, in matters governed by this Title, be pursued by Member States within the framework of a common transport policy.

This means that the Treaty's general provisions and specifically those relating to the common market apply:

to the transport sector except in so far as it specifically provides otherwise. The specific provisions on transport, far from setting aside fundamental Treaty rules such as those concerning the establishment of a common market, have as their object to give effect to and complement them by common actions.[11]

The types of transport covered by the common transport policy, under Article 80, are rail, road and inland waterway. Sea and air transport can be brought within the Title's provisions, under Article 80(2), to the extent that Member States agree. As will be seen this has happened many times on a topic-by-topic basis.

The potential content of the common transport policy is indicated by Article 71 which states:

1. For the purpose of implementing Article 70, and taking into account the distinctive features of transport, the Council shall, acting in accordance

---

[11] Commission, Communication on a global approach to the construction of a Community framework for sustainable mobility, COM (92) 494 final, 2.12.92, p.18.

with the procedure referred to in Article 251 and after consulting the Economic and Social Committee and the Committee of the Regions, lay down:

(a) common rules applicable to international transport to or from the territory of a Member State or passing across the territory of one or more Member States;

(b) the conditions under which non-resident carriers may operate transport services within a Member State;

(c) measures to improve transport safety;

(d) any other appropriate provisions.

This list of topics does not cover all issues of transport concern. One area not mentioned in Title V but nevertheless within its scope concerns freedom to provide transport services. This is because Article 51(1), which contains the part of the Treaty dealing with freedom to provide services, states:

> Freedom to provide services in the field of transport shall be governed by the provisions of the Title relating to transport.

The freedom to establish a business in another Member State under Article 43 is also relevant to transport even though not mentioned in Title V:

> Article [43] of the Treaty is in particular properly applicable to airline companies established in a Member State which supply air transport services between a Member State and a non-member country. All companies established in a Member State within the meaning of Article [43] ... are covered by that provision, even if their business in that State consists of services directed to non-member countries.[12]

Competition is another significant area of Community involvement with transport, although not listed explicitly in Title V. As can be seen in Chapter 8 on competition policy and tourism, transport issues are regularly dealt with under the Community's competition jurisdiction.

Articles 72 to 77 develop the meaning of Articles 70 and 71. They create a legal framework for dealing with public or private discrimination between different carriers, the giving of state aid or support/protection to carriers and other matters. Under Article 76 Member States cannot support or protect certain transport operations by means of taxation, unless it has the explicit permission of the Commission. These conditions contribute to the development of the single market.

---

[12] *Commission v. Belgium*, Case C–471/98, para. 133. Judgment delivered 5.11.02.

Other provisions in the Treaty of transport and tourism relevance are contained in Title XV dealing with trans-European networks and are dealt with separately in this chapter.

Little use was made of the Treaty provisions dealing with the common transport policy up to the mid 1980's in the key area of creating a common market in transport services through liberalising transport markets A large number of Commission proposals were held up in the Council because of disagreements among the Member States.

> In *Parliament v. Council* in 1985[13] Parliament sought a ruling from the Court of Justice that the Council had failed in its Treaty obligations to implement the common transport policy. The Council argued that the Court could not say it had failed to fulfil its obligations because, although there were many transport measures it had failed to enact, the Treaty did not really fix what the common transport policy should consist of, and so there was no way of judging if the Council had not done what it was allegedly supposed to do. The Court agreed with this in some respects, but also pointed to the Treaty emphasis on the freedom to provide transport services and held that this was one significant dimension of the common transport policy which the Treaty was explicit about and which the Council had manifestly failed to act on.

After this matters changed and the rush to complete the internal market by 1992 added a significant impetus to Community action based on the transport provisions of the Treaty. 1992 was the key year. According to the Commission:[14]

> The end of 1992 will mark the beginning of a new departure for the Community's common transport policy (CTP). ... For many years progress towards the realisation of the CTP was slow, especially when measured against the importance of transport in the Community economy. ... The Court of Justice had to intervene several times on basic questions of interpretation of the Transport provisions of the Treaty of Rome in order to make progress possible. This process reached its climax in 1985 when the Court declared that the inland transport of goods and passengers should be open to all Community firms. ... The 1985 landmark judgement of the Court coincided with the Commission's White Paper on the completion of the internal market. ... The Commission then placed transport in the

---

[13] *European Parliament v. Council* [1985] E.C.R. 1513.

[14] Commission, Communication on a global approach to the construction of a Community framework for sustainable mobility, COM (92) 494 final, 2.12.92, p.4.

forefront of the moves towards the completion of the internal market. ... Since then the CTP has developed rapidly, encompassing a wide range of measures, actions and initiatives aiming at bringing about a single market for transport services. ... Other important components of this emerging reality are improved competitiveness, financial performance and efficiency of transport undertakings and improvements in the functioning and quality of transport systems, including safety, reliability and passenger comfort. ... Measures have also been taken for the protection of the environment. ... The implementation of the Treaty on European Union agreed at Maastricht will at once confirm and give a new impulsion to the evolution of the CTP. ... The provisions on trans-European networks and economic and social cohesion provide a new basis for the Community to contribute to the establishment and development of transport infrastructure. The new title on industry underlines the need for ... competitiveness of Community enterprises. At the same time the Union Treaty emphasises that in accordance with the principle of subsidiarity, the CTP must consist of actions which cannot be realised adequately by the Member States individually. ...

Therefore, 1992 marks an important turning point in the evolution of the CTP from a policy which aimed essentially at the completion of the internal market ... towards a more comprehensive policy designed to ensure the proper functioning of the Community's transport systems. ...

TRANSPORT PRESSURES AND COMMUNITY RESPONSES

Transport pressure results both from increased demand and the overuse of some modes of transport, particularly the car. As indicated earlier, demand has continued to increase and has even shifted from rail to air, while passenger car use, already at a high level as far back as 1970, has continued its upward trend.

The pressures associated with increased transport demand can be broadly grouped into infrastructure and environmental pressures.

Pressure on Infrastructure

When the infrastructure cannot cope with increased demand, wasteful congestion follows.

During the 1990s Europe began to suffer from congestion in certain areas and on certain routes. The problem is now beginning to threaten economic competitiveness. ... This was the serious warning made in the 1993 White paper on Growth, Competitiveness and Employment: 'Traffic jams are not only exasperating, they also cost European dear in terms of productivity. Bottlenecks and missing links in the infrastructure fabric; lack of interoperability between modes and systems. Networks are the arteries of the single market. They are the life blood of competitiveness, and their malfunction is reflected in lost opportunities to create new markets and hence in a level of job creation that falls short of our potential ... the trans-European network itself suffers increasingly from congestion: some ... 10% of the road network is affected daily by traffic jams. And 16 000km of railways, 20% of the network, are classed as bottlenecks. Sixteen of the Union's main airports recorded delays of more than a quarter of an hour on more than 30% of their flights. Altogether these delays result in consumption of an extra 1.9 billion litres of fuel, which is some 6% of annual consumption.[15]

Pressure on the Environment

The growth in transport demand not only leads to pressures on capacity. It also contributes to broader environmental problems. The effects of economic and technological developments over the last decade have exacerbated the areas of conflict between transport and environment. These now include:

- pollution–
    in 1998 energy consumption in the transport sector was to blame for 28% of emission of CO_2, the leading greenhouse gas. According to the latest estimates, if nothing is done to reverse the traffic growth trend, CO_2 emissions from transport can be expected to increase by around 50% to reach 1,113 billion tones in 2010, compared with the 739 million tones recorded in 1990. Once again road transport is the main culprit since it alone accounts for 84% of the CO_2 emissions attributable to transport.[16]

- operational pollution – transport also contributes to water and soil pollution and is a source of noise and vibrations,

- land-intrusion – transport infrastructure causes land-intrusion with permanent and often irreversible impact on the landscape and the urban environment,

- congestion – transportation is also increasingly the cause of congestion. The volume of private car ownership and use is growing and has an impact on travel speed and economic use of the infrastructure.

---

[15] Commission, White Paper European transport policy for 2010: time to decide, COM (2001) final, 12.9.01, p.7.
[16] Commission, White Paper, p.10.

In addition to the above, transport activity is also the cause of physical damage to persons and property including fatal accidents. The resulting economic costs are very difficult to quantify but they remain a substantial burden, financial and otherwise, to be borne by society as a whole.

COMMUNITY RESPONSES

The Commission does not believe that the European Community has the legal capacity to attempt to solve all the problems besetting European transport.

> A simplistic solution [to the increasing growth in transport demand] would be to order a reduction in the mobility of persons and goods and impose a redistribution between modes. But this is unrealistic as the Community has neither the power nor the means to set limits on traffic in cities or on the roads. ...[17]

Within the confines of the Treaty and especially the principle of subsidiarity, while the Community has full competence in certain areas, such as the internal market, it must still respect the principle of proportionality which significantly limits what can be done. In other areas, where the Community shares competence with the Member States, subsidiarity imposes additional constraints. Thus, under the current legal regime, the Community's response to ever increasing transport demand will be limited.

Current Community policy as articulated by the Commission in the 2001 White Paper pursues the following objectives:

– under the heading "Improving Efficiency and Competitiveness":
  • furthering cohesion,
  • improving market access,
  • integrating transport systems,
  • ensuring fair pricing.
– under the heading of "Improving Quality":
  • ensuring environmental sustainability,
  • ensuring safe transport systems,
  • ensuring a fair deal for the transport user, the consumer.

Without attempting to catalogue the range of possible actions and rationale related to each policy objective, which in any case is adequately set out in the White Paper, it is enough for present purposes to identify four key related

---

[17] Commission, White Paper, p.11.

concepts which underpin and drive present Community approaches. These concepts reflect the concern that present transport patterns cannot continue into the longer term and must be addressed. Each has a clear application to tourist transport. The four concepts concern:

- Sustainable mobility.
- Modal shift.
- Intermodality.
- Transport infrastructure.

Their relationship to tourism can be seen from the following diagram.

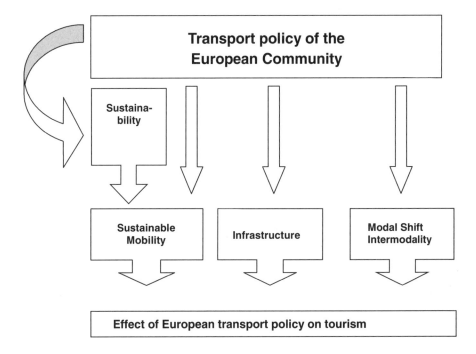

Sustainable Mobility

Sustainable mobility is the larger concept within Community policy and embraces many issues. It arises from the need to bring into balance the demands for passenger transport and the capacity of transport systems to move that demand in a safe, environmentally sustainable and economically viable manner. It seems clear that developing a sustainable transport network can be an outstanding basis for further developing sustainable tourism.

Modal Shift

Modal shift is a requirement of sustainable mobility and derives from the excessive use of car and airplane over other forms of transport. It refers to the need to relieve pressure on these means of transport which have excessive environmental impacts by encouraging greater use of more environmentally friendly means of transport, such as rail or sea transport.

Intermodality

Intermodality refers to a Community policy of pursuing strategies which encourage greater use of different modes of transport in a single journey so that the congestion associated with one mode of transport, usually road or air, is reduced. In tourism terms it primarily involves greater use of rail in connection with air travel.

> Intermodality with rail must produce significant capacity gains by transforming competition between rail and air into complementary between the two modes, with high-speed train connections between cities. We can no longer think of maintaining air links to destinations for where there is a competitive high-speed rail alternative. In this way, capacity could be transferred to routes where no high-speed rail service exists. ... For example, there are plans for the new Turin-Milan high speed link to include a connection to Maplpensa airport.[18]

An example of air/rail intermodality is the TGV terminal at Paris Charles de Gaulle Airport which directly links TGV trains with a number of regional and other destinations.

Much remains to be done to make intermodality a practical reality. In terms of its impact on travellers, ticketing, baggage handling and journey continuity are important issues.

> *Intermodality for people*
> In passenger transport, there is considerable scope for improvements to make travelling conditions easier and facilitate modal transfers, which are still highly problematic. Far too often passengers are put off using different modes of transport for a single journey. They have problems obtaining information and ordering tickets where the journey involves several transport companies or different means of transport, and transferring from one mode to another can be complicated by inadequate infrastructure. ...

---

[18] Commission, White Paper, p.38.

The principle of subsidiarity notwithstanding, priority should be given in the short term to at least three fields of action:

1. Integrated ticketing

To facilitate transfer from one network or mode to another, encouragement needs to be given to the introduction of ticketing systems which are integrated (and thus ensure transparency of fares) between rail companies or between modes of transport (air-coach-ferry-public transport – car parks) ... Some railway companies, as in the Netherlands, are already offering an integrated 'train & taxi' service in a single ticket. ...

2. Baggage handling

Intermodality also means providing related services, especially baggage handling. While it is currently possible to check in for a flight at a station, passengers have to look after their baggage themselves and hold on to it during transfers. ...

Air rail: a combination that works

An innovative way of promoting intermodality for travellers has been developed in Germany ... Lufthansa has concluded an agreement with Deutsche Bahn to offer trips combining a rail journey between Stuttgart and Frankfurt with flight connections in Frankfurt to or from anywhere in the world. Passengers can book a single rail/air ticket in a single transaction. They can check their baggage when arriving at the station and in the event of a problem enjoy the sane rights as ordinary air passengers, regardless of whether they are dealing with Deutsche Bahn or Lufthansa... Should this service, which is currently at the test stage, prove a success, the two companies could conclude similar agreements for other connections where the trains journey is under two hours. Estimates point to 10% of Lufthansa's short and medium haul domestic flights eventually transferring to rail. The capacity this creates would be to the benefit of medium and long haul flights ...

3. Continuity of Journeys

Journeys have to be thought of as continuous, which means land-use and town planning policies will play a vital role. The main metro, train and bus stations and car parks should be geared towards exchanges between the car and public transport and should offer related services (e.g. shops).[19]
...

---

[19] *Ibid*, p.80.

Transport Infrastructure

Infrastructure as used by the Commission in the 2001 White Paper on transport refers to direct targeted financial support by the Community to different types of transport infrastructure in order to combat congestion and bottlenecks and reduce environmental impacts. For Community action to be justified under the principle of subsidiarity there must be a clear trans-European benefit and thus "added-value" at Community level. While Member State investment has often been supported from the Structural and other Funds, this has not served Community needs.

> Europe is equipped with roads, railways, waterways, ports and airports which do not function and relate to each other according to the needs of a continental-sized economy and society ... too fragmented and lacking interconnections, they are about as complete as a pack of cards with aces missing. Nor are they good enough to deliver a wining hand.[20]

The Commission recognised the importance of Community investment in transport infrastructure for tourism at an early stage. In 1982 it stated that:[21]

> The importance of transport infrastructure for tourist traffic is a point that scarcely needs emphasis: it is via the roads and motorways that the great majority of tourists reach their holiday destinations in the mountains or by the sea. Hence they can be the means of relieving the pressure on some of the tourist centres and holiday resorts and give access to other places and regions in the Community.

> A number of Community financial instruments already contribute to the financing of transport infrastructures: European Regional Development Fund, the New Community Instrument (NCI), the interest subsidies available to certain countries participating in the European Monetary System, and above all the European Investment Bank which alone has co-financed over 1 600 kilometres of motorway in the Community. Nevertheless, the special criteria governing the use of these instruments sometimes prevent their being used for the benefit of transport infrastructures, especially in the more developed regions of the Community, through which the great flood of Community tourist traffic passes.

---

[20] Commission, The Trans–European Transport Network Office for Official Publications of the EC, Luxembourg 1994, p.2.
[21] Commission, Initial Guidelines for A Community policy on Tourism, OJ C 115/19, 30.4.84.

It was for this reason that the Commission, in its communication of November 1979 on the development of transport infrastructures, suggested that an instrument should be introduced to deal specifically with transport infrastructures, i.e. to provide support tailored to the exact requirements of each project of Community interest adopted. This specific financial instrument is the cornerstone of the policy on transport infrastructures recommended by the Commission.

In infrastructure terms the common transport policy initiative which has a significant capacity to affect tourist travel is the trans-European transport network. This is because of its potential to contribute to a better distribution of tourism traffic.

TRANS-EUROPEAN TRANSPORT NETWORKS

The idea of trans-European transport networks (TEN-T) emerged in the 1980s in conjunction with the proposed Single Market. In a Commission publication in 1994[22] three reasons were identified for creating such networks:

- existing networks have been fashioned according to national needs and priorities
- the single market needs transport infrastructures tailored for a single European economic space and capable of meeting significant increase in transport demand
- the poorer regions at the periphery need much better transport links with the central parts of the Union.

Although tourism is not one of the objectives of the trans European transport network it will clearly benefit from the development of the transport network. According to the Commission in 1982:[23]

> After the completion of the Trans-European Transport Network, numerous tourism possibilities will emerge for the exploitation of high-speed rail. It will offer safe and fast transport throughout the European Community. It will be more attractive for tourists to choose railway connections instead of the polluting coach and air connections.

---

[22] Commission, The Trans–European Transport Network, Office for Official Publications of the EC, Luxembourg 1994, p.2.

[23] Commission, Community Policy on Tourism, Initial Guidelines, OJ C 115/18, 30.8.84.

And in 1997:[24]

> the development of the trans-European network ... [and] the inter-operability of the trans-European high-speed rail system ... will contribute to and facilitate the movement of tourists in the EU.

The Community website dealing with trans–European networks is:

> http://www.europa.eu.int/comm/transport/themes/network/english/hp-en/aatransen.htm

Three Articles in the Treaty of Rome were devised to deal with trans-European networks. Article 154 states that:

> To help achieve the objectives referred to in Articles 14 and 158 and to enable citizens of the Union, economic operators and regional and local communities to derive full benefit from the setting-up of an area without internal frontiers, the Community shall contribute to the establishment and development of trans-European networks in the areas of transport, telecommunications and energy infrastructures.

Under Article 154(2):

> action by the Community shall aim at promoting the interconnection and interoperability of national networks as well as access to such networks. It shall take account in particular of their need to link island, landlocked and peripheral regions with the central regions of the Community.

Article 155 mandates the drawing up of a series of guidelines covering the objectives, priorities and broad themes of trans-European networks. Two pieces of Community legislation articulate TEN objectives:

- Decision 1692/96[25] laying down Community guidelines for the development of the trans-European network in transport,

- Regulation 2236/95 laying down general rules for the granting of financial aid in the field of trans-European networks.[26]

---

[24] Commission Staff Working Paper, Community Actions affecting Tourism, SEC(97) 1419, 11.7.97 at p. 71.

[25] OJ L 228/1, 9.9.96 amended by Decision 1346/01, OJ 185/1, 6.7.01.

[26] OJ L 228/1, 23.9.95 amended by Regulation 1655/99, OJ L 197/1, 29.7.99. Consolidated text available at http://europa.eu.int/eur–lex/en/consleg/pdf/1995/en_1995R2236_do_001.pdf.

The objectives for this transport network are set out in Article 2 of Decision 1692/96:

1. The trans-European transport network shall be established gradually by 2010 by integrating land, sea and air transport infrastructure networks throughout the Community in accordance with the outline plans indicated on the maps in Annex I and/or the specifications in Annex II [annexes omitted].

2. The network must:
   (a) ensure the sustainable mobility of persons and goods within an area without internal frontiers under the best possible social and safety conditions, while helping to achieve the Community's objectives, particularly in regard to the environment and competition, and contribute to strengthening economic and social cohesion;
   (b) offer users high-quality infrastructure on acceptable economic terms;
   (c) include all modes of transport, taking account of their comparative advantages;
   (d) allow the optimal use of existing capacities;
   (e) be, insofar as possible, interoperable within modes of transport and encourage intermodality between the different modes of transport;
   (f) be, insofar as possible, economically viable;
   (g) cover the whole territory of the Member States of the Community so as to facilitate access in general, link island, landlocked and peripheral regions to the central regions and interlink without bottlenecks the major conurbations and regions of the Community;
   (h) be capable of being connected to the networks of the European Free Trade Association (EFTA) States, the countries of Central and Eastern Europe and the Mediterranean countries, while at the same time promoting interoperability and access to these networks, insofar as this proves to be in the Community's interest.

14 Priority Projects

Annex III of Decision 1692/96 lists 14 priority transport projects within the TEN-T. Through these priority projects the EU aims for an optimum combination and integration of the various modes of transport and gradual achievement of interoperability of network components These projects are due to be finished by the year 2010. They are:

1. High-speed train/combined transport north-south: Nuremberg-Erfurt-Halle/Leipzig-Berlin, Brenner axis: Verona-Munich.

2. High-speed train (Paris-Brussels-Cologne-Amsterdam-London): Belgium: F/B border – Brussels – Liège – B/D border; Brussels – B/NL border; United Kingdom: London – Channel Tunnel access; Netherlands: B/NL border – Rotterdam – Amsterdam; Germany: (Aachen) G27 Cologne – Rhine/Main.

3. High-speed train south: Madrid-Barcelona-Perpignan-Montpelier, Madrid-Vitoria-Dax.

4. High-speed train east: Paris-Metz-Strasbourg-Appenweier-(Karlsruhe) with junctions to Metz-Saarbrücken-Mannheim and Metz-Luxembourg.

5. Conventional rail/combined transport: Betuwe line: Rotterdam – NL/D border – (Rhine/Ruhr).

6. High-speed train/combined transport: France-Italy: Lyon-Turin-Milan-Venice-Trieste.

7. Greek motorways: Pathe: Rio Antirio, Patras-Athens-Thessaloniki-Promahon (Greek/Bulgarian border) and Via Egnatia: Igoumenitsa-Thessaloniki-Alexandroupolis-Ormenio (Greek/Bulgarian border)-Kipi (Greek/Turkish border).

8. Motorway: Lisbon-Valladolid.

9. Conventional rail link: Cork-Dublin-Belfast-Larne-Stranraer.

10. Malpensa Airport (Milan).

11. Fixed rail/road link between Denmark and Sweden (Øresund fixed link) including access routes for road, rail and air.

12. Nordic triangle (rail/road).

13. Ireland/United Kingdom/Benelux Road link.

14. West Coast main line (rail).

Detailed maps of the network are available in Annex I of Decision 1692/96.

Progress in completing these projects has been slow. According to the Commission in 2001:[27]

> It is apparent today that the development of the trans-European network is not only far from uniform but also very slow. Scarcely 20% of the infrastructure planned in the 1996 decision has been finished. It is debateable whether it can be completed by the planned deadline of 2010. ... These delays are due to local opposition to the building of new infrastructure, the lack of an integrated approach during the planning, evaluation and funding of cross-border infrastructure, and also reduced

---

[27] Commission, White Paper, p.50. Emphases omitted.

public funding as a result of a general slowdown of investment in transport infrastructure. … Nevertheless, whatever the delay to certain projects, support should continue to be given to the trans-European network, which is an important factor in European competitiveness and improves the links between the European Union's outlying regions and its central markets.

The Commission then proposed a two stage revision of the network guidelines, which besides adding some new projects, such as the trains Pyrenean high capacity rail route, will also propose alterations to the funding rules.

To guarantee successful development of the trans-European network, a parallel proposal will be made to amend the funding rules to allow the Community to make a maximum contribution – up to 20% of the total cost – to cross-border railway projects crossing natural barriers but offering a meagre return yet demonstrable trans-European added value, such as the Lyon-Turin line already approved as a priority project. …[28]

Decision 1692/96 is not the only legislation on which the establishment of the TEN-T is based. Council Directive 48/96[29] obliges Member States to work on the interoperability of the high-speed rail system. Under Article 2 interoperability means the ability of the trans-European high-speed rail system to allow the safe and uninterrupted movement of high-speed trains that accomplish the specified levels of performance. This ability rests on all the regulatory, technical and operational conditions, which must be met in order to satisfy essential requirements.

AIR TRANSPORT AND TOURISM

Community involvement in air transport is extensive largely because air transport is an activity which uniquely fits the Community's functions regarding the common market.

Discussion of Community activity in this section will focus of three issues with the most impact on tourists:

• liberalising the provision of passenger air transport services,

• managing problems of capacity and congestion,

• attempting to ensure passenger safety.

---

[28] *Supra.*
[29] OJ L 235/6, 17.9.96.

Liberalisation

In 1984 the Commission recognised the impact of air travel costs on tourism:[30]

> In its memorandum of 4 July 1979 on the European Community's contribution to the development of air transport services, the Commission noted that the general level of tariffs among the regular airlines was too high, and that private passengers did not have enough alternatives. Although charter transport had gained a strong foothold in air travel within Europe and had brought about price competition between the charter companies, this had done nothing to stimulate competition between the companies providing scheduled flights in Europe. Those companies still geared their tariff policy primarily to business travel, an area in which tariffs were not necessarily a decisive factor, whereas a cut in prices would probably attract other passengers and fill the aircraft.
>
> To improve air transport services in the Community and meet user requirements, the Commission recommended the establishment of an efficient European network which would not be hindered by national barriers and would offer the various categories the lowest possible fares. With this in view, the memorandum proposed changes in the tariff structure of regular services to provide more attractive fares for the tourist market and for inter-regional transport.

Concerns like these lead to a major Community focus on dismantling State controls over passenger air services within Europe during the 1980s and 1990s and lead, finally, by the end of 1992, to the Council enacting three major pieces of legislation, the so-called 'Third Package,' forcing deregulation of air services on the Member States. These are:

- Regulation 2408/92[31] guaranteeing free access to Community air routes – "Community air carriers shall be permitted by the Member States concerned to exercise traffic rights on routes within the Community" – Article 3(1).

- Regulation 2409/92[32] prohibiting Member States from setting air fares in most cases – "Fares shall be set by free agreement between the parties to the contract" – Article 4.

- Regulation 2407/92[33] requiring Community airlines to obtain an operating

---

[30] Commission, Initial Guidelines on a Community Policy on Tourism, OJ C 115/18, 30.4.84.
[31] OJ L 240/8, 24.8.92. Text available at http://europa.eu.int/eur–lex/en/consleg/pdf/1992/en_1992R2408_do_001.pdf.
[32] OJ L 240/15, 24.8.92.
[33] OJ L 240/1, 24.8.92.

licence and requiring Community airlines to be kept within majority Community control.

Regulation 2408/92 is a key measure since it is intended to secure the basic freedom for Community air carriers to provide services in the air passenger transport sector within the Community without State interference[34] and clearly has particular relevance to tourism. The Commission has been vigilant in trying to ensure that Member States do not create indirect hindrances to the exercise of this freedom.

Airport Charges

One area which has been subject to some scrutiny by the Commission concerns the imposition of airport landing charges, airport or passenger taxes and similar charges. While such charges in themselves do not appear to constitute lack of conformity with Community law – assuming they reflect a proportionate and legitimate public policy – any differentials in how such charges are structured are closely examined by the Commission to see whether they impede the services freedom or, in some cases, constitute an abuse of a dominant position in the marketplace.

In *Commission v. Portugal*[35] the Commission claimed that Portugal had failed to respect the Article 49 guarantee of freedom to provide services (and its application to air transport via Regulation 2408/92) when it passed legislation imposing higher departure/security taxes on intra-Community flights (Member State to Member State) than on internal Portuguese ones. The Court of Justice firstly held that the Portuguese law did restrict the services freedom because the taxes would impact on airline and passengers costs. Secondly, the Court rejected the view that just because differential tax rates did not cause nationality discrimination, did not mean they were permitted.

What the Commission actually complains of is the fact that ... the

---

[34] Some transitional provisions have expired. For a case dealing with the effect of transitional provisions on other parts of the Regulation, see Court of Justice decision in *Flightline v. Secretario de Estado dos Transportes*, C–181/00, 9.7.02.

[35] [2001] E.C.R. I–4845, para. 26. See also *Commission v. Italy* [2001] E.C.R. I–5203 and *Styianskis v. Greece* C–92/01, 6.2.03 where Italian and Greek laws respectively, which similarly imposed differential airport departure taxes as between domestic and intra–Community flights were held not to comply with Reguation 2408/92. For a series of Commission decisions in which the Commission held that airport authorities abused their dominant position by imposing discriminatory landing charges, see p. 373.

> Portuguese Republic made the provision of air transport services
> between Members States more difficult than the provision of domestic
> air transport services within a Member State ... Article [49] precludes
> the application of any national legislation that, without objective
> justification, restricts the freedom of a service provider to provide
> services, and in the perspective of the single market, that application
> of any national legislation which has the effect of making the provision
> of services ... more difficult.
>
> Portugal also sought to defend the differentials on the basis of seeking to
> promote air links with regional airports and the need for regional
> development. The Court accepted that under the Regulation (see below)
> this is permitted, but on closer examination, it could not find any basis on
> which the differentials were actually related to this. Thus, since the Court
> could not find any objective justification for the differences in tax rates, it
> decided that Portugal had infringed Article 49.

Public Service Obligations and Contracts

Article 4 of Regulation 2408/92 contains an important inroad or derogation
from the general freedom to provide air services and has a particular relevance
to tourism. It allows Member States, after following a defined procedure, to
impose defined controls – a public service obligation (PSO) followed by a public
service contract– over access to air routes for listed reasons and even allows
state aid for the operation of such routes.

The justification is as follows. A Member State may, after various
consultations including informing the Commission,

> impose a public service obligation in respect of scheduled air services to
> an airport serving a peripheral or development region in its territory ...
> any such route being considered vital for the economic development of
> the region in which the airport is located, to the extent necessary to ensure
> on that route the adequate provision of scheduled air services satisfying
> fixed standards ... which standards air carries would not assume if they
> were solely considering their commercial interest – Article 4(1)(a).

Where other forms of transport cannot ensure an adequate and uninterrupted
service, the PSO can include a requirement that the carrier guarantee to operate
the route for a defined period – Article 4(1)(c).

If no carrier chooses to operate a route subject to a PSO, and subject to
review by the Commission (and also if other forms of transport cannot ensure
an adequate and uninterrupted capacity exceeding 30,000 seats per year), a

Member State:

> may limit access to that route to only one carrier for a period of up to three years – Article 4(1)(d).

To encourage a carrier to bid for what is effectively a route monopoly, a Member State:

> may reimburse an air carrier … for satisfying standards required by a public service obligation … such reimbursement shall take into account the costs and revenue generated by the service – Article 4 (1)(h).

Thus, by using what is in effect a public service contract, a State can still control a route, remove all competition and subsidise the operator.

Public service obligations have been used on a hundred routes in France, Sweden, the United Kingdom, Portugal, Ireland and Norway.[36] With such a large number of PSOs, it is not surprising that the Commission has emphasised the need for careful monitoring to ensure they do not become a disguised means of restricting the market.[37] How vital a route may be to the promotion of economic development in a peripheral/development region can in some cases be difficult to assess.

In Ireland where the state has imposed a number of such obligations[38] the air routes in question mainly serve regions along the west coast which are important tourism areas but which suffer from peripherality in development terms.

In the proceeding against Portugal mentioned earlier, Portugal sought to defend the different rates of departure tax partly by claiming that they were needed to support peripheral/development regions like the Azores and Madeira. In rejecting this excuse, the Court of Justice held that under the Regulation:

> Those obligations must be defined beforehand and any financial quid pro quo must be capable of being identified as specific compensation for the obligation in question.

Portugal had not done this, nor had it claimed that it had imposed such an obligation. Besides, the Court noted that other not so disadvantaged Portuguese regions would also benefit from the support.

---

[36] Commission, Impact of the Third Package of Air Transport Liberalization Measures, COM(96) 514 final, 22.10.96, p.i.

[37] *Supra* p.v.

[38] For details of the routes, see OJ C 265/4, 15.9.00.

Impact of the Third Package

The impact of the liberalising forces unleashed by the Third Package has been mixed. In a three-year review in 1996 the Commission noted how the package had both improved and failed to improve competition among carriers:

> the liberalization process is producing a significant number of positive results without the instability that some may have feared. Market access possibilities are being used. New routes and services are being created. On some of the most heavily travelled routes, new entrants are bringing competitive pressure to bear on traditional duopolies. ... The market share of the dominant so-called flag carriers has also fallen noticeably. ... On the other hand, as yet, many routes continue to be serviced by monopolies or duopolies and in those circumstances significant consumer benefits have not appeared ... the process is far from complete.[39]

Regarding fares:

> An impressive number of promotional fares has developed and the share of passengers travelling on scheduled flights with reduced prices has passed from 60.5% in 1985 to 70.9% in 1995. ... However, these tickets are often accompanied by restrictions with regard to schedules flexibility and are available only for a limited number of seats.
>
> In contrast to the promotional fares most of the fully flexible fares have continued to increase. On certain routes these fares can be described as excessive. ... The Commission could in certain cases examine potential abuses of dominant position under Article 86 of the Treaty.[40]

Liberalisation has particularly contributed to the emergence of low cost no-frills carriers who skilfully exploit the freedom to provide air services wherever they wish and at whatever prices they wish. These carriers fly mostly to regional airports since this is less costly (moderate landing fees, airport taxes). In so doing they contribute to the opening up of regional destinations and contribute to a better seasonal spread of tourist flows.

Low cost carriers and the other factors noted at the start of this chapter have lead to a huge increase in air passenger traffic:

> Of all the different modes, air transport has shown by far the largest increase

---

[39] Commission, Impact of the Third Package of Air Transport Liberalization Measures, COM (96) 514 final, 22.10.96, p.1.

[40] *Supra*, p.ii.

over the last twenty years. Expressed in passenger/kilometres, air traffic has increased by 7.4% a year on average since 1980, while the traffic handled by the airports of the Fifteen has shown a five-fold increase since 1970.[41]

According to the Commission in 1999 the increase will continue:

world-wide demand for air travel will continue to grow strongly in the next two decades, at a rate of about 5% per year. However, this forecast should be adjusted to take into account major events that cannot be anticipated.[42]

The increased air traffic flows have brought problems.

During the past 10 years EU policy successfully opened up national markets and made it possible for new carriers to provide innovative services. This in turn has had an impact on the quality of air services in peak times, and the number of delays due to air traffic problems has risen considerably.[43]

Every day, more than 25 000 aircraft fly over the skies of Europe, and judging by growth trends the figure can be expected to double every ten to fifteen years. Though the skies are vast, this traffic density poses some real problems. The increasing number of delays is a clear sign of saturation … Yet airlines expect air traffic to double by 2010. To sustain such growth, air traffic management will need to be reformed and sufficient airport capacity guaranteed in the enlarged European Union.[44]

The Commission White Paper should be consulted for further detail on the possible solutions to these problems.

Airports

The accessibility and efficiency of Community airports is a matter of importance for both tourist service providers and tourists. Access to airport of choice is

---

[41] Commission, White Paper, p.35.

[42] Commission, The European Airline Industry: From Single Market to.World – Wide Challenges, COM (1999) 182 final, 20.5.99, p.6.

[43] Report from the Commission, Community Measures affecting tourism, COM(2001) 171 final, 28.3.01, p.19.

[44] Commission, White Paper, p.35.

influenced by a variety of factors including congestion, slot availability,[45] cost of infrastructure improvements and landing charges.

> In its 1994 Communication 'The way forward for civil aviation in Europe' the Commission identified scarcity and cost of infrastructure as a main cause of the high costs incurred by European air travellers.[46]

The Commission White Paper published in 2001 suggested a range of remedies, including the more efficient use of airports, aircraft and air space, most of which are beyond the concerns of this text.

The provision of new airport capacity, while a goal of the common transport policy, must respect all Community laws, including competition laws.

In *Italian Traffic Distribution Rules*[47] non-Italian carriers complained to the European Commission that Italian rules which required them to move from the older Milan airport, Linate, to the newer more distant, Malpensa (one of the priority projects of the trans-European transport network) before proper transport links with the city were operational, would place them at a competitive disadvantage to the Italian carriers who remained at the better linked older airport. The complaints were based on Article 8 of Regulation 2408/92 which, while allowing Member States move traffic within an airport system (listed in one of the Regulations Annexes) to relieve congestion, also requires that there should be no discrimination on grounds on nationality or carrier identity and that the means adopted respects the principle of proportionality. The Commission agreed that the traffic distribution rules operated in a discriminatory manner and ruled that Italy could not apply them.[48]

---

[45] With a view to stimulating competition on Community air routes and easing capacity at congested airports, Regulation 95/93 – OJ L 14/1, 22.1.93 – on the allocation of slots (a slot is the period when an airplane can land/take off) at Community airports, tries to ensure that unused slots are made available to new route entrants. Commission amended proposal on common rules for the allocation of slots, COM (02) 623 final,7.11.02 proposes the repeal of Regulation 95/93 and the creation of a more structured, uniform and transparent process for the allocation of slots at Community airports. Community website at http://www.europa.eu.int/comm/transport/themes/air/english/at_5_en.html.

[46] Commission, Communication on the European Airline Industry: From single market to world–wide challenges, COM(1999) 182 final, 20.5.99, p.12.

[47] OJ L 337/42, 12.12.98.

[48] An attempt by Italy to have the Commission decision annulled in the Court of Justice on a variety of grounds including a misapplication of the principle of proportionality failed – *Italy v. Commission* [2001] E.C.R. I–375.

Air Carrier Liability Rules

The aspect of air passenger safety of most immediate relevance to tourists which the Community has recently focused on concerns airline liability to pay passenger compensation in the event of an accident – "the inevitable link between safety and the issues of liability cannot be denied."[49]

Community interest in this area was triggered by the failure until recently of the international civil aviation community to reform and update the relevant world convention – the Warsaw Convention[50] – which established universal rules governing with airline liability for passenger death, injury and property loss. To understand the manner in which this issue has been dealt with at Community level, it is necessary to briefly outline what the Warsaw Convention attempts, and in recent times, has failed to do.

> The Warsaw Convention of 1929 was a significant landmark in international aviation. Essentially it represented a deal between the airlines and the travelling public (represented by national governments) in the case of accidents occurring during international carriage by air. Normally the burden of proving fault lies with the claimant. The Warsaw Convention reverses this procedure. The airlines accept fault unless they can prove that they had taken all necessary measures to avoid damage. To balance this reversal of the normal burden of proof, airline liability was limited unless the claimant could prove 'wilful misconduct'. ...

> The Warsaw Convention and subsequent related agreements have been a success. However, increasingly, problems have arisen. In particular, with the passage of time the limits on liability have become unacceptably low, despite attempts to raise them. This has led to several countries replacing the Warsaw limits, thereby removing one of the principal benefits of the Warsaw Convention, its near universal applicability. It has been evident for sometime that radical change would be needed if the whole system was not to collapse.[51]

The Community has been to the fore in promoting radical change. Its approach

---

[49] Commission, Proposal for a Council Regulation on air carrier liability in case of accidents, COM(95) 724 final, 20.12.95, p.3.

[50] Convention for the Unification of Certain Rules relating to International Carriage by Air, 12.10.29.

[51] ESC, Opinion on the Proposal for a Council Regulation on air carrier liability in case of air accidents, OJ C 212/38, 22.7.96. The general liability limit under Warsaw was approximately $10,000.

has been tailored by the Rome Treaty focus on maintaining the common market, and promoting safety and consumer protection.

> Given ... that Member States have variously taken steps to increase the Warsaw limit ... leading therefore to different terms and conditions of carriage and given also that differences subsist between the liability rules for domestic and international transport, it is obvious that the situation risks fragmenting the internal aviation market so far achieved.
>
> In addition, one of the most important factors in all modes of transport and thus in aviation is the question of safety and quality of service. ... The original low limit set by the Warsaw Convention was in part a protection for an infant industry whose risk factors were largely unknown and therefore considered high. In such a climate the interest was to reduce as far as possible the financial liability of the carrier even to the detriment of the passenger. Today, the situation is totally different; it is perceived to be one of the safest modes of transport. This image of a safe and high-quality service is at odds with a system whereby the passenger is still treated as taking a risk, which justifies a lower level of compensation in the event of death or injury... The objective of the internal aviation market is also to take account of the needs of the air transport user. The low limits are, as stated above, largely inadequate and unsatisfactory for the passenger victim. ... Moreover, the fact that the passenger has to prove wilful misconduct on the part of the carrier in order to recover compensation above the limits ... makes settlements less predictable, more expensive and time-consuming.[52]

The key elements of the Community legal response which eventually emerged – Council Regulation 2027/97[53] on air carrier liability in the event of accidents – reflected these concerns. It also reflected a desire to dovetail with the broad structure of the recently agreed replacement for the Warsaw Convention – the not yet in force Montreal Convention[54] – and thereby maintain a universal legal framework for international passenger air travel. It is clear that international civil aviation and tourist movement benefits from an internationally accepted liability framework. The key elements of the liability regime created by

---

[52] Commission, Proposal for a Council Regulation on air carrier liability in case of accidents, COM(95) 724 final, 20.12.95, p.3.

[53] OJ L 285/1, 17.10.97 as amended by Regulation 889/2002, OJ L 140/2, 30.5.02.

[54] Convention for the Unification of Certain Rules relating to International Carriage by Air, 29.6.99. Text available in Annex A, COM (2000) 446 final, 14.7.00. The Community approved the Montreal Convention in Council Decision 2001/539, OJ L 194/38, 18.7.01.

Regulation 2027/97 are:

- airlines are prohibited from imposing any limits on the amount of compensation they may have to pay in the event of an accident,
- no defence of taking all necessary measures will be available to an airline for claims up to 100,000 SDRs (approx €146,000), but a defence of reasonable care will be available for claims in excess of this,
- Community airlines are obliged to make early uncontested payments to meet immediate economic needs on a basis proportionate to the hardship suffered and a sum of at least 16,000 SDRs per passenger in the event of death.

> It is intolerable that victims or their relatives should have to wait for the results of lengthy litigation. Air accidents normally are of a serious nature with dramatic consequences and involve in most instances a significant number of passengers far away from home. Therefore it is reasonable to .. ensure the payment of a lump sun to take care of immediate financial implications.[55]

- Community airlines must make available to passengers at all points of sale a summary of the rules set out in an Annex to the Regulation and any time-limits on making claims for compensation,
- passengers will be able to sue an airline in the country of their domicile, rather than having to take proceedings where the airline is based or the flight originated or the ticket sold.

ROAD TRANSPORT AND TOURISM

Inside the Community

Tourism within the Community has benefited from Community liberalisation of national markets for bus and coach services and also from minimizing the formalities attached to coach and bus travel. According to the Commission in 1982:[56]

> Free access to the market for passenger transport by road is an objective of the transport policy of the Community. As long ago as July 1966, Regulation ... 117/66 on the introduction of common rules for the international carriage of passengers by coach and bus provided that occasional coach and bus

---

[55] *Supra* p.7.
[56] Commission, Community Policy on Tourism, OJ C 115/17, 30.4.84.

services should be exempt from the requirement of authorisation by any Member State except by the one where the vehicle is registered. Since occasional services are pre-eminently tourist services, Regulation ... 117/66 has played a vital role in the development of tourism within the Community.

The current Community law governing use of coach services of relevance to tourism is Regulation 684/92[57] on common rules for the international carriage of passengers by coach or bus. Article 3(1) continues the liberalisation of passenger coach and bus services across internal Community boundaries[58] for different categories of bus transport and coach transport by providing that:

> Any carrier for hire or required referred to in Article 1 shall be permitted to carry out the transport services defined in Article 2 without discrimination on ground of nationality or place of establishment. ...

However, Article 3(1) also lays down certain conditions. The carrier:

- [must be] authorised in the State of establishment to undertake carriage by coach and bus;
- satisfy the conditions laid down in accordance with Community rules on admission to the occupation of road passenger transport operator;
- meet legal requirement on road safety as far as the standards for drivers and vehicles are concerned.[59]

While the Regulation elsewhere distinguishes between regular, occasional and other types of international coach and bus services, it is clear that the operation of occasional coach and bus services comes within Article 3(1). Since occasional services are mainly used by tourists, tourism benefits from this liberalisation.

Occasional services are defined negatively as services other than regular services by Article 2(3)(1).[60] Coach tours for tourists can sometimes operate quite regularly and questions of degree can determine when a service ceases being occasional. The coach operator has a practical interest in remaining

---

[57] OJ L 74/1, 20.3.92 as amended. Consolidated text available at http://europa.eu.int/eur–lex/en/consleg/pdf/1992/en_1992R0684_do_001.pdf.

[58] By virtue of their membership of the European Economic Area Norway, Iceland and Liechtenstein are also covered by this Regulation.

[59] Commission, Report on the application of Council Regulation 684/92 on common rules for the international carriage of passengers by coach and bus, COM(96) 190 final, 10.5.96, p.2.

[60] The original pre–amendment version of Article 2(3)(1) contained a lengthy list of the different types of occasional services which were exempt from the authorisation requirement and very clearly covered most types of tourist coach services.

occasional because once regular any timetable changes, even minor ones, can require a new application for national authorisation which may take some time to obtain because consultation with authorities in the relevant other states is required.

Of further benefit to tourism is the minimisation of formalities involved in operating an occasional international coach or bus service. Traditionally when services where operated to another state a separate authorisation to provide the service was required from that state. However, according to Article 4(1): "Occasional services ... shall not require authorisation". This means that a coach tour provider for an international occasional service, while already subject to the need to obtain an authorisation from its state of establishment, does not need to obtain an authorisation from any of the other Member State which will be visited during the coach tour. Thus, an occasional coach tour from Germany to Italy does not require an authorisation from the Italian authorities to enter Italy and continue to its point of destination in Italy, though it will need a domestic authorisation from the German authorities. The provider only requires a journey form.[61]

Whether a coach or bus has to cross a state outside the Community during its trip from one Member State to another with the same tour party makes no difference.

> The Commission departments also interpreted Regulation 684/92 as meaning that passenger transport services between two Member States which involve transit on a closed door basis through a third-country, i.e. with no scope for picking up or setting down passengers, are to be considered as intra-Community transport and hence subject to the provisions of Regulation 684/92.[62]

Thus, a coach travelling from Germany to Italy through Switzerland which does not set down or pick up passengers in Switzerland, also does not need an authorisation from the Italian authorities and is treated the same as the coach tour travelling directly from Germany to Italy.

Further, once in Italy the coach tour can provide local excursions for its tour party without authorisation from the Italian authorities. Under Article 12 of Regulation 684/92:

> Within the framework of an international occasional service, a carrier may carry out occasional services (local excursions) in a Member State other than that in which it is established.

---

[61] Details on this form are set out in Article 11.
[62] *Ibid.*, p.5.

However, to ensure that only the original tour party is carried in the coach, Article 12 goes on to provide that:

> Such services shall be intended for non-resident passengers previously carried by the same carrier on one of the international services … and must be carried out with the same vehicle or another vehicle from the same carrier.

Outside the Community

The movement of tourists originating in the Community by coach and bus to destinations in central and eastern Europe has been facilitated by an international agreement made in 2001 – the Interbus Agreement on the international occasional carriage of passengers by coach and bus.[63] Tourist travel by occasional coach service to from and across Switzerland is covered by a separate agreement but involves similar basic ideas.[64] The object of the Interbus Agreement is to harmonise rules on market access, fiscal, social and technical requirements not only for traffic between the Community and non-Member States, but also for traffic between these States.

From a tourism perspective the part of the Interbus Agreement of most direct relevance concerns the reduction in formalities affecting occasional services, that is the removal of the need for the coach operator to obtain an authorization from the state of destination in order to bring the coach tour into the state. Since tourists are significant users of occasional coach services, the removal of the need for an authorization facilitates tourism. Article 6 of the Interbus Agreement states that:

> The following occasional services shall be exempt from authorization on the territory of any Contracting Party other than that in which the transport operator is established:
>
> > Closed-door tours, that is to say services whereby the same bus or coach is used to carry the same group of passengers throughout the journey and to bring them back to the place of departure. The place of departure is in the territory of the Contracting Party in which the transport operator is established.

---

[63] See COM (2001) 540 final/2, 12.10.01. The previous Agreement on the International Carriage of Passengers by Road by means of Occasional Coach and Bus Services (ASOR), OJ L 230/39, 5.8.82, was not flexible enough to enable new States to join and many of its signatories have joined the Community.

[64] Agreement between the European Community and the Swiss Confederation on the Carriage of Goods and Passengers by Rail ad Road, OJ L 114/91, 10.4.02.

The coach operator must, however, under Article 10 bring a prescribed control document with him/her issued by the competent authority in the State where the operator is established.

Other Community measures dealing with transport which indirectly have a bearing on tourism deal with safe road transport of passengers and recognition of qualifications. As regards safety of passenger transport, Regulation 3820/85 harmonises conditions of competition and the improvement of working conditions and road safety which, among other things benefits tourist safety.

In *Re Hume*[65] the Court of Justice was asked to clarify the meaning of the Regulation dealing with postponed rest periods for drivers. Hume was a coach driver who was prosecuted in the UK for failing to take sufficient rest period within the defined time. Hume availed of the facility of postponing a rest period but disputed that he had to take it in conjunction with other compulsory rest periods. The issue was purely one of the interpretation of the wording and was reasoned deductively by the Court.[66]

> Clearly the objective of improving working conditions and road safety can best be attained by interpreting Article 8(5) of the Regulation as requiring the postponed weekly rest period to be taken together with the weekly rest period for the second week. Such an interpretation guarantees drivers; by way of compensation for a rest not taken by them, a longer and uninterrupted rest period, thus enabling then to take a proper rest. Moreover, it is apparent from the context of Article 8(6), that the intention of the legislature was to provide generally for the reduction of a rest period to be compensated by the extension of another rest period.

RAIL TRANSPORT AND TOURISM

After an early misplaced optimism about the contribution of international rail transportation to tourism:[67]

> The European railways networks are making a steady and intensive effort to improve their international passenger transport facilities by increasing commercial speed, improving passenger service and comfort, stepping up train frequencies and establishing direct connections ...

---

[65] [2000] E.C.R. I–7809, 7831.
[66] At p.4.
[67] Commission, Community Policy on Tourism, Initial Guidelines, OJ C 115/18, 30.4.84.

by the mid-1990s the declining role of rail transport was causing concern.[68]

> railways should play a much greater role in tackling the transport challenges facing the Community, as we move towards the new century. Urgent action is required to revitalise the sector, so that it performs better and more fully satisfies the demands of our society. For this, Europe needs a new kind of railway.

The 2001 Transport White Paper linked revitalization with liberalisation of the rail sector:[69]

> Rail transport is literally the strategic sector, on which the success of the efforts to shift the balance [from flying] will depend. ... Revitalising this sector means competition between the railway companies themselves. ... The priority is to open the markets, not only for international services ... but also for cabotage on the national markets and for international passenger service.

While technical difficulties, infrastructure weaknesses and in particular interoperability also prevent the rail network realising its potential,[70] it is clear that other more market-driven factors also hinder the rail networks ability to play an appropriate role in the international transport of tourists. A recent report[71] highlighted the current undeveloped state of international passenger rail transport in the Community and the numerous marketing and organizational difficulties which hinder its ability to offer an attractive alternative to air transport. Among the problems noted are:

- the average daily number of international trains is about 2650, while the number of flights is about 24,000 to 26,0000 daily, 60% of these being over distances of less than 730 km,

- fewer travel agencies sell train tickets than sell air tickets,

- excessively complex and expensive fares structures – "the basic principle of fares definition is based on the distance and speed of the train". The longer

---

[68] Commission White Paper, A Strategy for revitalising the Community's Railways, COM(96) 421 final, 30.7.96.

[69] Commission, White Paper European Transport Policy for 2010: time to decide, COM(2001) 370 final, 13.9.01, p.13.

[70] *Ibid.*,p.29. Recent developments to address these deficits include the "infrastructure package (OJ L 75, 15.3.01) and proposals for a second package of operational measures" – see http://www.europa.eu.int/comm/transport/rail/newpack/np_en.htm.

[71] Commission, Developing EU (International) Rail Passenger Transport, February 2002. Text available at http://www.europa.eu.int/comm/transport/rail/library/ogm–report.pdf.

the trip, the more expensive it is (this is not a principle for air flights, where the price paid is more a reflection of the level of competition),[72]

- lack of comprehensive information about train services and delays, poor customer communication and little support when trains are delayed, limited on-board information,
- poor prioritisation for international trains on lines, and
- often poor levels of comfort on international services, overloaded trains, unnecessary retention of passports by train staff.

Other structural problems also affect the provision of international services, particularly:

- the predominance of co-operating traditional State owned undertakings in international rail transport – "these arrangements mean that there has, as yet, been no effective competition in the provision of [international rail passenger] services",[73] and
- the difficulty of newcomers breaking into the market – "there is a serious lack of transparency concerning conditions for the operation of new international services. The procedures for getting a licence and the authorisation needed to operate and to get the slots, in order to run an international service, seem to be "invented" as and when such a request is presented to those responsible".[74]

Essentially "any competitive advantage international train services have [over flights] may be erased by poor customer care and a lack of a commercial attitude in many cases".[75]

Tour operators are sceptical about the use of international trains for tourism. They:

> tend to consider international trains as a marginal mode of transport (10% max of the market for trips of max 700km, seasonal ski-trains, and night trains) with a limited capacity to compete with the airline industry in the present conditions due to too high consumer prices, the absence of transfer services at the destination, too difficult baggage handling in particular where there are connections, and a very complex price system.[76]

---

[72] *Ibid.*, p.13.
[73] Commission, Consultation Paper on International Rail Passengers Rights and Obligations, Brussels, October 2002, p.4. Text available from http://www.europa.eu.int/comm/transport/rail/library/cd_en.pdf.
[74] *Ibid.*, p.26.
[75] *Ibid.*, p.10.
[76] *Ibid.*, p.22.

To make international rail travel more attractive, tour operators believe that the rail industry:

> should offer a co-ordinated management system, integrating all networks, in order to have fewer points of negotiation, a contract for charter trains and standardized procedures ... tour operators demand:
>
> • a 'one-shop' system including 'final trip segment' service,
>
> • easier access to information and tickets,
>
> • luggage handling services for their clients (currently, where they are available on long-distance national services, they are not available for international services).[77]

Following this the Commission intends launching a variety of initiatives,[78] including a proposal for a regulation, designed to remove passenger related obstacles which prevent international passenger rail transport from realising its potential. The need for a regulation results from the unique nature of international rail travel, the weak bargaining power of consumers and the fact that the standard international rail travel contract is not subject to the Unfair Terms Directive.[79] While both policy (monitoring, quality standards) and legislative approaches are under consideration, it is certain the legislative approach will be extensive.

Many legal issues relating to international rail passenger travel are already subject to international agreement. COTIF/CIV[80] deals, among other things, with liability rules for passenger injury and loss, while rail companies offer a standard contract for international rail travel.[81] The proposed regulation is likely to address a variety of issues, including the following:

• improved provision of information – covering rail and intermodal timetables, fares and ticketing, contract terms, sales outlets –

> Information and reservation systems should offer both air and (high speed) train services between two places. There should also be information on

---

[77] *Ibid.*, p.27.

[78] Commission, Consultation Paper on International Rail Passengers Rights and Obligations, Brussels, October 2002.

[79] See p. 330.

[80] COTIF – Convention Concerning International Carriage by Rail.1985. CIV is an annex to COTIF which establishes Uniform Rules concerning the Contract for International Carriage of Passengers and Luggage by Rail. Both operate under the auspices of OTIF, the Intergovernmental Organisation for International Carriage by Rail. Website at http://www.otif.org The 1999 Vilnius Protocol to CIV will update many provisions of CIV but is not yet in force.

[81] Developed under the auspices of CIT, a trade body of rail and maritime transport operators.

urban transport systems. It is strange that air passengers are provided during their trip with extensive information on what car rental company they could use on arrival, whereas information on rail links between airports ands the city centre is hardly provided, let alone the possibility to purchase a ticket for this service.[82]

- interoperability of ticketing and baggage handling systems.
- rail carrier liability rules – the Vilnius Protocol changes to CIV are not yet in force and passenger claims are subject to outdated liability limits. Also different limits currently apply in different Member States. The new air carrier liability rules and probable changes to sea carrier liability rules raise question whether a similar rules structure should apply to rail passengers death/personal injures, that is strict liability up to a defined limit and fault liability with/without limits beyond that.
- rail delay – possible approaches are improved delay information, specifying delay rights such as withdrawal, re-routing, assistance, compensation, money back. High speed and non-high speed services should be treated differently. On average compensation levels for high speed could be twice those for non-high speed, e.g. for a rail trip lasting more than 2 hours and delayed at least 30 minutes, compensation could be 50% ticket cost and 100% for a delay of 60 minutes. While not exactly comparable with the delay proposal for air delays, they are more severe on carriers because more of the factors causing rail delay are controllable.

SEA TRANSPORT AND TOURISM

Community legal involvement in sea transport with specific relevance to tourism centres on:
- completing the internal market in maritime passenger services,
- improving ferry/cruise ship safety for passengers, and
- creating Community-wide sea carrier liability rules.

Regarding completing the internal market, two basic regulations apply, one dealing with passenger transport services between Member States (intra-Community) and the other dealing with passenger transport services within Member States (maritime cabotage).

---

[82] Commission, Consultation Paper, p.20.

Intra-Community Services

For maritime passenger services between Member States, Article 1(1) of Regulation 4055/86[83] provides that:

> Freedom to provide maritime transport services between Member States and between Member States and third countries shall apply in respect of nationals of Member States who are established in a Member State other than that of the person for whom the service is intended.

This covers both intra-Community passenger services and also the carriage of passengers by sea between Member States and third countries. Any national restrictions on this freedom must be based on legitimate public policy and respect the proportionality principle. In case law before the Court of Justice, it has been held that:

- the operation of different tariff rates for the same compulsory piloting services under Italian law between a ferry company which operated between Genoa, Italy and Corsica, France and shipping traffic between two Italian ports, was declared incompatible with Community law. The Court viewed the higher tariffs payable by the ferry as impacting on the cost of providing ferry services and placing the ferry company at a disadvantage with those who benefited from the lower tariffs.[84]

- the payment under French law of higher charges when passengers arrive from or embark for ports situated in another Member State than when they travel to a port situated on its national territory amounted to a failure by France to apply the principle of freedom to provide maritime services under Article 1(1) above. The Court stated:[85]

> Where national legislation, though applicable without discrimination to all vessels ... operates a distinction according to whether vessels are engaged in internal transport or in intra-Community transport, thus securing a special advantage for the domestic market and the internal transport services of the Member State in question, that legislation must be deemed to constitute a restriction on the freedom to provide maritime services contrary to Regulation No 4055/86.

- the imposition of higher harbour dues on boats taking tourists for day trips

---

[83] OJ L 378/1, 31.12.86 as amended. Consolidated text available at http://europa.eu.int/eur–lex/en/consleg/pdf/1986/en_1986R4055_do_001.pdf.

[84] *Corsica Ferries v. CPPG* [1993] E.C.R. I–1783.

[85] *Commission v. France* [1993] E.C.R. I–5161, 5170.

from Rhodes in Greece to Turkey than dues payable for domestic or intra-Community transport was prohibited under Article 1 unless the different rates were objectively justified.[86]

Maritime Cabotage

For the provision of maritime services within Member States (maritime cabotage) Article 1 of Regulation 3577/92[87] states that:

> As from 1 January 1993, freedom to provide maritime transport services within a Member State (maritime cabotage) shall apply to Community ship owners who have their ships registered in, and flying the flag of a Member State, provided that these ships comply with all conditions for carrying out cabotage in that Member State. ...

Among the maritime transport services liberalized by this Article are passenger services between ports on the mainland of the same Member State and also of particular relevance to tourism:

> island cabotage: the carriage of passengers or goods by sea between:
> - ports situated on the mainland and on one or more of the islands of one and the same Member State,
> - ports situated on the islands of one and the same Member State. ...

All the derogations originally allowed under the Regulation have expired, except in the case of Greece where a derogation for island cabotage for regular passenger and ferry services in vessels under 650gt continues until January 1, 2004.[88]

In an familiar inroad to liberalization, the Regulation also allows Member States to support ferry services which would otherwise not be commercially viable in two ways – public service contracts and public service obligations (PSOs). Under Article 4:

> A Member State may conclude public service contracts with or impose public service obligations as a condition for the provision of cabotage services, on shipping companies participating in regular services to, from

---

[86] *Naftiliaki v. Greece* C–435/00, 14.11.02.

[87] OJ L 72/36, 25.3.93.

[88] Though the Greek government has signalled its intention not to avail of this derogation after November 2002 – Commission, Report on the implementation of Council Regulation 3575/92 applying the principle of freedom to provide services to maritime cabotage (1999–2000), COM(2002) 203 final, 24.4.02, p.6.

and between islands. Whenever a Member State [does this] it shall do so on a non-discriminatory basis in respect of all Community shipowners.

In imposing public service obligations, Member States shall be limited to requirements concerning ports to be served, regularity, continuity, frequency, capacity to provide the service, rates to be charged and manning of the vessel. Where applicable, any compensation for public service obligations must be available to all Community shipowners.

The only permitted reason for imposing a PSO is similar to that for an air PSO and is to ensure that:

scheduled services to ports serving peripheral regions of the Community or thinly served routes [where the service is] considered vital for the economic development of that region, [and] where the operation of market forces would not ensure a sufficient service level.[89]

Compensation is the key issue in attracting an operator onto a route with a PSO and should relate only to the

reimbursement of operating loses incurred as a direct result of fulfilling certain public service obligations.[90]

Certain further conditions must also be satisfied. There should generally be a public tender for the contract, preceded by adequate publicity with adequate information and the contact should generally be awarded to the lowest bid and should be limited to a reasonable and not overlong period, normally five years.

State aid compensation to regular passenger ferry services to islands is not, however, exempt from the need to be notified to the Commission and assessed for compatibility with the Treaty. The reason for this is to avoid anti-competitive cross-subsidisation.

In its assessment of compatibility with the Treaty, the Commission will verify whether or not aid may divert significant volumes of traffic or involve overcompensation, which could allow the selected carrier to cross subsidise operations on which other Community carriers compete.[91]

---

[89] Commission, Community Guidelines on State Aid to Maritime Transport, OJ C 205/12, 5.7.97.

[90] *Supra.*

[91] *Supra.*

All but four Member States have imposed public service obligations on sea routes.[92] The routes include routes frequented by tourists such as Marseilles/Toulon/Nice – Corsica, 19 Italian mainland routes to Sicily/Sardinia, Spanish mainland – Canaries/Baleares, Scottish mainland – Shetlands/Orkney, Portuguese mainland – Madeira/Azores.

The way the PSO is structured must also respect Treaty freedoms and any national restrictions must act proportionally and be based on real public policy considerations.

> In *Analir v. AGE*[93] a Spanish decree imposed a public service requirement for sea passenger transport to its islands by means of a prior authorisation linked to tax compliance. A shipping company wishing to operate a service had to apply for authorisation and would only get it if its tax affairs were in order. According to the Court of Justice the prior authorisation requirement was a restriction of the Treaty services freedom.
>
>> It is settled case-law that freedom to provide services requires not only the elimination of all discrimination on grounds of nationality ... but also the abolition of any restriction, even if it applies without distinction to national providers of services and to those of other Member States, which is liable to prohibit, impede or render less attractive the activities of a provider of services established in another Member State. ... It is clear that national legislation [such as the Spanish law] which makes the provision of those services subject to prior authorisation is liable to impede or render less attractive the provision of those services and therefore constitutes a restriction on the freedom to provide them. ...
>
> Spain then argued that its scheme constituted a legitimate exception to the principle of freedom of services on the basis of an overriding public interest. The Court agreed that such an exception was possible, but declared that whether it actually arose in this case was a matter for the national court to decide in accordance with the proportionality principle. But it stressed:
>
>> so as to circumscribe the exercise of the national authorities' discretion, so that it is not used arbitrarily [that] the nature and scope of the public service obligations to be imposed by means of a prior authorisation scheme must be specified in advance. ... Furthermore, all persons

---

[92] Commission, Report, p.7 and Annex 2.
[93] [2002] E.C.R. I–1271.

> affected by a restrictive measure based on such a derogation must have a legal remedy available to them.[94]
>
> On the second issue whether the Spanish law allowing refusal of the permit because of arrears of tax payments conformed with the Regulation, the Court held that since 'capacity to provide' the service is a listed matter in the Regulation, arrears of taxes etc are relevant to the solvency of an undertaking and thus to 'capacity to provide' and in that way only was permitted.[95]

Sea Passenger Safety

A series of major ferry disasters involving heavy loss of life resulting from the sinking of the Herald of Free Enterprise and the Estonia passenger ferries have lead to a number of Community measures designed to prevent such occurrences and where they occur, deal with the aftermath.

- Council Directive 35/99[96] deals with a system of mandatory surveys for the safe operation of regular ro-ro ferries and high speed passenger craft services. Ro-ro ferry means a sea-going passenger vessel carrying more than 12 passengers with facilities to enable road or rail vehicles to roll on and roll off the ship. The Directive covers regular international services to or from Community ports and obliges Member State to conduct various verifications of necessary documents relating to passenger safety both before the start of a new service and existing services and thereafter to make regular checks. Under Article 10(1):

> A host State shall prevent the operation of a ro-ro ferry or high-speed passenger craft on a regular services ... whenever deficiencies are found during the surveys ... which pose an immediate danger to life, the ferry or craft, its crew and passengers.

---

[94] In another recent case on the effect of Regulation 3577/92, *Commission v. France* [2000] E.C.R. I – 6137, France was held to have infringed Community law by reserving the right to provide transport services including passenger transport services between French ports to French registered ships.

[95] The final issue concerned whether the Spanish law could use both the public service contract and the imposition of public service obligations for the same sea route. The Court held this could be done but only if the overall requirement of the Regulation was observed and also, taken in conjunction, both ways of ensuring the service is provided do not have disproportionate effects in limiting the freedom of other service providers.

[96] OJ L 138/1, 1.6.99. A related safety measure is Council Directive 18/98 on safety rules and standards for passenger ships, OJ L 144/1, 15.5.98.

- Council Directive 98/18[97] sets general safety rules and standards for passenger ships operating between ports in the same Member State.

- a proposed Directive on the enhanced safety of passenger ships will extend to the whole Community higher stability requirements introduced in northern States for ro-ro ships to resist capsize when a defined amount of wave water enters the vehicle deck.[98]

> The stability of passenger vessels following a collision is of key importance for the safety of ro-ro passenger ships. The longer a ship remains afloat in the case of serious damage, the more efficient will be the evacuation of passengers and crew and search and rescue operations be. This consideration becomes even more important in view of the escalating size of ro-ro ships serving Community ports and the increasing number of passengers and crew they carry. Indubitably, one of the major dangers for a ro-ro ship with an enclosed deck is the effect of a "build-up of significant amounts of water on that deck".

- Directive 41/98[99] deals with identification of passengers on board a ferry in the event of an accident. The preamble recites that:

> Information must be complied on passenger and crew in order to facilitate search and rescue and the efficient handling of the aftermath of an accident, i.e. identifying the person involved, providing clearer information … such information would prevent unnecessary anxiety on the part of relatives and other persons regarding persons on board passenger ships involved in maritime accidents.

Under Article 4(1):

> All persons on board any passenger ship which departs from a port located in a Member State shall be counted before the passenger ship departs.

Under Article 5(1):

> The following information shall be recorded regarding every passenger ship that departs from a port located in a Member State to undertake a voyage of more than twenty miles …

---

[97] OJ L 144/11, 15.5.98. Similar rules for ships operating between different Member States currently exist under the International Maritime Organisation.

[98] Commission, Communication on the enhanced safety of passenger ships in the Community, COM(2002) 158 final, 25.3.02, p.3. See also Amended Proposal, COM (2002) 721 final, 4.12.02.

[99] OJ L 188/35, 2.7.98.

- the family names,
- their forenames or initials,
- their sex,
- an indication of the category of age ... to which each person belongs, or the age, or the year of birth,
- when volunteered by a passenger, information concerning the need for special care or assistance in emergency situations.

Sea Carrier Liability Rules

Recently the Commission has turned its attention to the question of the legal rules which fix the liability of ferry and cruise operators to pay compensation to passengers who suffer personal/property injury or loss while on board.[100] Three reasons have contributed to this interest (though it coincided with activity at IMO level to harmonize the prevailing international law in this area, see below):

- the increasing risk of injury with bigger ships and greater number of holiday makers using them,
- variations in Member State laws, and
- the existence of a Community liability regime for air passengers.

Current international law is based on the Athens Convention,[101] which operates in some but not all the Member States. It uses fault rather than strict liability to determine compensation, that is the passenger must prove that carelessness by the carrier caused or contributed to the accident in order to secure an entitlement to compensation. This can be difficult when the cause of an accident is unclear. The burden of proving carrier fault is, however, eased for ship-type accidents, that is accidents related to collision, explosion, fire, defect in the ship. In such cases, the Athens Convention presumes carrier fault, which means the onus is shifted onto the carrier to prove reasonable care was taken to prevent the accident. Loss to cabin luggage is treated in the same way as personal injury, that is the rule varies depending on whether it was a ship-type accident or not. Passenger vehicles, however, are treated better than cabin luggage in that carrier fault is presumed (so the burden shifts to the carrier) regardless of whether it is a ship-type accident. Of great significance is the fact that an overall liability limit applies to all types of personal and property loss under the Athens Convention.

---

[100] Commission, Communication on the enhanced safety of passenger ships in the Community, COM(2002) 158 final, 25.3.02.

[101] International Maritime Organisation, Athens Convention relating to the Carriage of Passengers and their Luggage by Sea 1974; Protocol to the Athens Convention 1990, not yet in force.

Passengers cannot recover more than Euro approx. 46,000 for personal injury or death and a lower limit for property loss, except in the rare case where it can be shown the a carrier acted intentionally or recklessly (extreme carelessness) and with knowledge that damage would probably result.

> The Commission is of the firm opinion that the liability regime which applies for passengers carried by sea needs to be updated and strengthened in favour of passengers. Many features of the Athens Convention as it stands are outdated and fail to meet the expectations of citizens travelling on passengers ships in Community waters and beyond.[102]

Whether the much more favourable liability regime for air passengers should be applied to sea passengers is a different matter. Different liability regimes:

> between the two mode of transport has been justified by reference to the contrasts between the roles of a passenger on board a passenger ship or a cruise ship and an air passenger. While the latter normally is expected to remain seated for the main part of the voyage, the passenger on board a ship, in particular a cruise ship, is considerably more mobile and active and has more time and opportunities to engage in acts of contributory negligence. A cruise ship passenger may often be more comparable to a customer in a restaurant, discotheque. ... Since none of these service providers is normally subject to strict liability, it has been considered unfair to place such a burden on the carrier of passengers by sea.[103]

Any Community law, according to the Commission, should be based on the following policy choices:

- a distinction should be made between shipping incidents (collision, ship defect, fire, explosion etc) and other incidents (trips, falls etc unrelated to shipping where the passenger has more control over the circumstances which cause the injury),
- shipping incident loss should be subject to a strict liability regime up to euro 250,000; for claims in excess of this the carrier should be able to avoid liability if it shows it acted carefully,
- non-shipping incident loss should be subject to normal fault liability rules, that is the onus should be on the injured passenger to prove lack of care before being entitled to compensation,

---

[102] *Ibid.*, p.10.
[103] *Ibid.*, p.11.

- an overall liability limit should apply to all sea passenger claims regardless of the type of incident, but the limit should be sufficiently high 'to fully cover foreseeable looses.'
- passenger claims should be allowable directly against the carrier's insurers.

The Commission has not indicated its thinking about claims for property loss, an important issue for tourists, given the large numbers who bring cars and caravans etc. full of holiday luggage on to ferries.

CHAPTER CONCLUSION

Tourist demand is a large part of transport demand. Along with the environment, transport is one of the areas where the Treaty of Rome ill-equips the Community to manage sustainable growth. The Community focus on completing the common market is itself a cause of increased demand, and contributes in part to the congestion issues which are so prevalent in road and air transport. Community efforts to promote sustainable mobility and in particular to promote a shift in use from plane and car to rail and sea transport are laudable objectives, but are unlikely to produce significant results for some time. With some self interest, the Community has undertaken an ambitious task in the trans-European transport networks In the meantime the pressures of unremitting transport demand mean that safety and compensation issues grow in importance.

STUDENT TASKS

Undergraduate questions:

1. Explain the pressure which tourist movements place on the European transport network.

2. Consider the legal basis of the trans-European network – transport and assess the network's importance for tourism.

4. Assess the particular impact of Community competition policy on airport operations.

5. Take any one mode of transport and highlight how Community measures have had an impact on tourism.

Postgraduate questions:

1. Explain the concept of intermodality and consider its relevance to Community tourism.

2. Explore the concept of public service obligations in regional air or maritime passenger transport and, in relation to a chosen region, assess its importance for tourism.

3. Explain how Community measures have sought to facilitate tourist movement in the Community by rail and, in relation to a chosen intra-Community rail route, assess how this has impacted on tourist use of that route.

4. The Commission White Paper in 2001 does not propose major initiatives to reduce increasing transport demand. Explain why this is so and develop an argument against this view.

CHAPTER 6

COMMUNITY COHESION POLICY AND TOURISM[1]

INTRODUCTION

From the beginning of the European integration process, in the preparatory meetings among the original six Member States, the idea of a cohesion policy pursued through regional development and promoted at European level was present. Along with the creation of a common market, the need to invest in poorer areas to enable them to adjust to the common market was recognised. It was accepted that the common market held the potential to concentrate wealth in the more central and developed regions and actually accentuate regional differences.

Regional differences are just one aspect of a wider lack of cohesion among the Member States of the Community. As will be seen, the Treaty identifies the strengthening of economic and social cohesion as the larger objective of which targeted regional actions form part. But since the pursuit of cohesion through regional development has the greater impact on tourism, it alone will be dealt with.

Community policy towards regional development operates primarily by giving Community funds to public and private bodies in less prosperous regions for productive investment in an attempt to redress their competitive disadvantages. Such funding is provided in the context of an agreed regional development plan between the Community and a Member State which involves spending both Community and state and sometimes private sector funds. While public funding, especially to private companies, risks distorting competition in the common market, it is considered justified by the greater need to reduce regional disparities. Among the general types of project supported are:

- transport, water and sewage infrastructure.
- aid to enterprises for both capital and operational expenditure, including improving technology research and development, business innovation.

---

[1] Ariane Portegies, Marc McDonald.

• modernising administrative structures.

Cohesion policy is firstly set out in the Treaty establishing the European Community (Treaty of Rome) and then developed within different funding instruments also identified in the Treaty and detailed in secondary legislation. While much of the detail of these instruments deals with monitoring the effective use of funds, they also identify the policy objectives to be pursued.

The amounts of money involved in Community funding for regional development are enormous. For the period 2000–2006 €260 billion (at 1999 prices, indexed at a rate of 2% per annum) has been allocated to spending on regional development in the European Union. €213 billion has been committed to the fifteen Member States: €195 billion to Structural Funds programmes[2] and €18 billion to the Cohesion Fund. The remaining €47 billion has been earmarked for the central and eastern European states seeking to join the Community, through a programme called the Instrument for Structural Policies for Pre–accession (ISPA), to help them prepare for membership. In most instances Member States are obliged by Community funding rules to provide matching funding of their own, thereby bringing global regional spending in the Community to a much higher figure.

The Community spends its money on regional development through a series of legal measures called financial instruments. The principal group of financial instruments, devoted to removing structural weaknesses, that is economic factors general to a region which inhibit economic growth, are called the Structural Funds and consist of:

• The European Regional Development Fund (ERDF).

• The European Agricultural Guidance and Guarantee Fund (EAGGF).

• The European Social Fund (ESF).

Only the first two will be examined in this chapter along with the following funds, also of relevance to tourism:

• Leader.

• Interreg.

• The Cohesion Fund.

• ISPA.

The general approach to the spending of Community funding through the

---

[2] Commission, Structural Actions 2000–2006, Commentary and Regulations, February 2000, ISBN 92–828–7767–1. Available at http://www.europa.eu.int/comm/regional_policy/sources/docgener/guides/compare/refo_en.pdf.

Structural Funds is that the broad framework of spending programmes for different regions is agreed at Community level with Member States. Private/ public body applications are then made to national approval bodies. Decisions on funding applications are made according to compatibility with the general and specific funding criteria and Community law.[3]

The spending of so much Community money on regional development raises important legal issues regarding the proper and effective use of the funds. Legal instruments are extensively used to provide a framework within which funds are authorized, objectives and priorities set and the administration of the funds supervised and evaluated. The Community has developed an extensive range of programming, oversight, monitoring, reporting and evaluation obligations in an attempt to ensure honest and effective use of funds and minimise legal challenges based on bias or improper use. Compliance with this framework at all levels helps ensure that legal claims concerning misspending of funds do not often come before Community courts. Discussion of this framework forms a significant part of this chapter.

Detailed information about these legal instruments and about regional policy in general is available at the Commission website:

http://www.europa.eu.int/comm/regional_policy/index_en.htm

TOURISM IN COHESION POLICY

Community sources have consistently articulated a positive role for tourism in Community regional development. In 1993 a commissioned report for the European Parliament[4] stated that:

> Tourism has considerable potential for boosting the economies of less– developed regions. Many of the under–developed regions of the Community are relatively well endowed with natural tourist attractions, and already attract a disproportionate share of tourism expenditure. Allied to this tourism potential are features already mentioned – the expected rapid growth of the sector, its labour intensity and ability to generate a rapid and highly visible impact on incomes and employment by injecting new expenditure from external sources. The multiplier effects of these expenditures can generate additional benefits while tourism operations may also provide market expansion opportunities for local investors.

[3] The Structural Funds process is further described at p. 238.
[4] EP Directorate General for Research Working Papers, The Role of the EC in regard to Tourism and Regional Development, Regional Policy Series, E–1 External Study, October 1993, p.107.

More recently the Commission stated in the context of the Structural Funds,[5] which as will be seen are the primary mechanism for Community support for regional development.

> The job creation potential of tourism makes it a sector with particular importance in regional development terms, whereas it can also contribute to the diversification of regional activity (particularly in rural areas and areas in industrial decline). There is also a considerable positive indirect impact of tourist expenditure on the expansion of other businesses. Regions 'lagging behind' in their development tend to have a good potential for tourism development. For these reasons, tourism has progressively become a major element for Community support through the Structural Funds.

The Commission concluded:

> Tourism is recognised as representing an important economic asset for many regions, rural communities and cities. Balanced and sustainable tourism development will therefore be supported through the modernisation of infrastructures, upgrading professional skills and improving integration within the industry.

The amounts spent on tourism have varied with the programming period, the changes in objectives and the amounts available. Easy comparisons are not possible. The following figures provide some indication of the amounts spent:

- in the 1975–1985 period 1.2% of the total ERDF resources were directed to tourism–related projects,[6]

- in the 1989–1993 period approximately ECU 2.149 billion were allocated to tourism from the Structural Funds,[7] and

- in the 1994 –1999 period approximately EUR 4.2 billion were allocated to tourism projects by the ERDF[8] and an earlier report[9] estimated that almost

---

[5] Report from the Community on Community Measures affecting Tourism (1997/1999), COM(2001) 171 final, 28.3.01, p.16. See also Court of Auditors Special Report 3/96 on Tourism Policy and the Promotion of Tourism OJ C 17/11, 16.1.97.

[6] EP, Session Documents, Opinion in the form of a co–report of the Committee on Regional Policy and Regional Planning on Tourism and Regional Development in: Report of the Committee on Transport and Tourism on a Community Policy, A3–0155/91/Part B, 30.5.91.

[7] Commission, Report on Community Measures Affecting Tourism, COM(94) 74 final, 6.4.94, p.61.

[8] Report from the Community on Community Measures Affecting Tourism (1997/1999), COM(2001) 171 final, 28.3.01, p.16.

[9] Commission, Community Measures Affecting Tourism, SEC(97) 1419, 11.7.97, p.60.

6% of all appropriations from the Structural Funds were allocated to the tourism sector for the same period.

Among the types of tourism projects aided by Community funds under regional development programmes are ones which improve/revitalize/create:

- new visitor attractions such as museums, galleries, historic buildings, monu-ments, heritage sites, gardens,
- cultural interpretative centres,
- health, sport and marine facilities,
- walkways, trails,
- urban amenity through regeneration,
- tourism business networks.

Tourism Examples of Aided Projects

Piedmont, Italy – "Tourism development supported by the Structural Funds in Piedmont focused on four strategic zones with a high tourism potential – Lake Maggiore, the Val di Susa skiing district, the city of Turin and the Canavese castle circuit. The tourism development projects adopted an integrated approach by financing a mix of infrastructure improving local attractiveness, aid schemes to small and medium–sized tourism business and tourism promotion programmes. Value was added both by the good partnership between local and regional administrations, and the greater impact achieved through concentration of activities in limited areas".[10]

Saarland, Germany[11] – "An historical landmark on the edge of ruin was saved at the last minute when funding was provided to turn it into a modern ecological centre. … The estate at Imsbach has a long history. In 1811, Napoleon Bonaparte gave it to Colonel Lapointe, whose family maintained the property until 1929. This marked the beginning of difficult times for the Imsbach estate. … In 1987 it was finally decided to renovate the estate, and to convert it into a regional centre for information and activities on ecology. … The restoration works on the main building were designed to turn it into a conference centre hosting seminars on a variety of environmental issues.

---

[10] Commission Guidelines for Regional Development Programmes 2000–2006, p.6. Available at http://europa.eu.int/comm/regional_policy/sources/docgener/informat/irgu_en.pdf .

[11] Taken from (uncritically presented) examples on Commission web site titled 'Success Stories – Profiles of Projects in Europe' at http://www.europa.eu.int/comm/regional_policy/projects/stories/index_en.cfm.

The renewable energy systems used in the buildings serve as demonstration projects and as subject matter for conferences and workshops. Other themes covered are agriculture, energy, tourism and nature conservation. Participants and visitors may then dine in the on–site restaurant which uses only organically grown produce, and employs the latest energy–saving techniques in the kitchen. … Among the actions undertaken, restoration work on the main building cost a total of DM 4,150,000, of which the European Union contributed 40%, or nearly DM 1,660,000 in the context of rural development aid. The Community is also supporting another project to create a small eco–hotel."

Powys, Wales[12] – "In 1990, a number of people [in a rural community in Wales decided] that their ancestral culture might provide the key to new economic growth. They decided to mobilise the population of 35 hamlets in South Pembrokeshire (Wales, United Kingdom), initially in order to take stock of the situation. A thousand people took part in these surveys, confirming the initial premise: that the region's main assets are its culture and natural heritage. These served as the basis for launching new ventures, centred mainly on tourism".

The first step was to define a 'product' in terms of local identity: it was called the 'Landsker Borderlands'. The first project involved laying out five thematic trails along paths, towpaths and other dirt tracks. Together they form an 80 km network of walks, linking all the villages. … As well as being a tourist attraction, these trails embody a desire to maintain the countryside and encourage people to value their natural heritage. This change in attitude has injected these areas with new energy, with villagers starting to maintain traditional furniture, buildings and old farming equipment. … Several fine monuments are benefiting from this: Llangollen Medieval Hospice, an old local brewery, etc. An annual cultural festival features performances of Welsh works and an association is actively engaged in protecting the Welsh language to serve as an instrument of historical research. Tourism–related training courses, including one on welcoming and accommodating visitors, are organised by the Welsh Tourist Board … "In 1990 the standard of living in South Pembrokeshire was well below the Community average but now some 300 small projects are contributing to the economic development of the area, involving around 3,000 people, at a total cost of ECU 3.6 million. 20% of the investment has been funded by the EU under the Leader programme".

---

[12] *Supra.*

Noteworthy in a number of these stories is the local development perspective, emphasising the importance of local factors and characteristics to develop initiatives.

These promotional stories make a good starting point for further investigation by students of the impact or importance of Community regional development for tourism.

Regional Development and Tourism

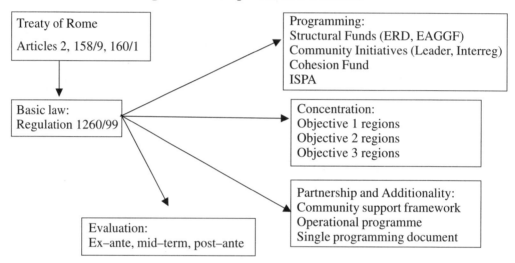

Learning Outcomes:

After reading this chapter, the student should:

- appreciate the scope of cohesion policy in the European Community,
- understand why tourism plays a central role in regional development,
- be able to identify the main principles and the instruments of the Structural Funds,
- appreciate in particular the importance of programming and evaluation in regional policy.

These learning outcomes will be addressed through the following headings:

The Treaty, Economic and Social Cohesion and Regional Development.
Community Perspectives on the role of Tourism in Regional Development.
Principles and Instruments of the Structural and Other Funds.

THE TREATY, ECONOMIC AND SOCIAL COHESION AND REGIONAL DEVELOPMENT

The Rome Treaty does not as such establish a Community regional policy. However, Article 2 which sets out the most basic statement of the Community's objectives, obliges the Community

> to promote throughout the Community a harmonious, balanced and sustainable development of economic activities, a high level of employment and of social protection ... a high degree of competitiveness and convergence of economic performance ... and economic and social cohesion and solidarity among Member States.

Economic and social cohesion are the key words. Cohesion in particular is taken to mandate Community measures aimed at reducing disparities between regions since disparities weaken Community cohesion. This theme is taken up in Title XVIII of the Treaty headed *Economic and Social Cohesion* and particularly in Articles 158 and 159 which flesh out some of the means by which cohesion is to be attained.

Article 158 sets economic and social cohesion as the overall objective. Its first sentence requires the Community to develop and pursue its actions leading to strengthened cohesion within a context of "overall harmonious development". The second sentence of Article 158 then locates regional actions within this context.

> In particular, the Community shall aim at reducing disparities between levels of development of the various regions and backwardness of the least favoured regions or islands, including rural areas.

Article 159 identifies three approaches by which regional cohesion objectives must be attained:
- Member States implementing their own regional policies.
- Community implementation of the internal market.
- a range of dedicated Community funds.

It is the last one of these which is of most importance for present purposes. Article 159 goes on to provide that:

> The Community shall also support the achievement of these objectives by actions it takes through the Structural Funds (European Agricultural Guidance and Guarantee Section; European Social Fund; European

Regional Development Fund), the European Investment Bank and the other existing financial instruments.

Other Treaty provisions dealing with these funds are dealt with later in this chapter.

Community funding for regional development, as would be expected, is intended to benefit regions within the Community. However, a recently established Community fund described in more detail later– the Instrument for Structural Policies for Pre–accession (ISPA) – also provides funds for regional development outside the Community, that is in states who have not yet joined the Community but are scheduled to do so. This instrument will assist the applicant countries in the run–up to accession in particular by supporting the development of transport and environmental protection measures and thus indirectly benefiting tourism.[13]

COMMUNITY PERSPECTIVES ON THE ROLE OF TOURISM IN REGIONAL DEVELOPMENT

With so much Community money available to support regional development projects including tourism projects, it is not surprising that Community institutions have a lot to say on the topic. Community dialogue has tended to focus on:

- the potential of tourism in fostering regional cohesion and a perceived continuing failure to capitalize on this potential,

- the relationship between tourism expenditure under the Structural Funds and wider Community involvement in tourism,

- the role of the Commission,

- the ways in which Member States propose projects for Community funding, and

- the role of regional authorities in forging policies affecting tourism.

In this section it is proposed to give only a flavour of this dialogue.

---

[13] Two other Community programmes of relevance to the applicant states – PHARE and SAPARD – can be briefly noted. PHARE's objectives are consolidation of the countries' institutions, their participation in Community programmes, regional and social development, industrial restructuring and development of SMEs. SAPARD's aims are to modernise agriculture and to promote rural development. For a list of tourism related development projects financed under PHARE, see Commission, Community Actions Affecting Tourism, SEC(97) 1419, 11.7.97, Annex 7.

Infrastructure and Product Quality

In 1991 Parliament commented extensively on the relationship between regional development and tourism. It bemoaned the fact that:

> the intervention of the European Regional Development Fund in regard to tourism has hitherto been circumstantial and not based on an integrated sectoral perspective, and predominantly directed to infrastructure rather than the creation of productive economic activities and is therefore not contributing to endogenous regional development as fully as it should[14]

and further considered that tourism:

> continues to offer prospects for a healthy and sound economic and social development of the Community's less–favoured regions and that these prospects are not being fully exploited even though in many cases they afford the main realistic basis for increased economic activity.[15]

After requesting the Commission:

> to re–examine its role in regard to tourism and to the application of the ERDF to related economic initiatives and to act more decisively and creatively in this field. ...[16]

Parliament called on the Commission

> in the context of economic and social cohesion, and in view of the higher unemployment in the least–developed regions, to devote a greater volume of Structural Fund resources to the training and further training of employed and unemployed persons in the tourist industry'.[17]

Many of these views are more fully developed in the explanatory statement accompanying the report[18] and merit closer study.

The Council Decision in 1992 approving a Community Action Plan to assist tourism[19] agreed that:

---

[14] EP, Resolution on a Community Tourism Policy, OJ C 183/77, 15.7.91.
[15] *Ibid.*, p.80.
[16] *Ibid.*, p.81.
[17] *Ibid.*, p.86.
[18] EP, Report of the Committee on Transport and Tourism on a Community Tourism Policy, Part B: Opinions, A3–0155/91/Part B.
[19] OJ L 231/26, 13.8.92.

tourism can make an effective contribution to achieving economic and social cohesion in the Community.

Among the categories of tourism for which measures were approved for funding in the Decision Annex were cultural tourism, tourism and the environment and rural tourism. No mention is made however of the integration of these measures in the Community's actual cohesion policy.

Doubts persisted over the effectiveness of the 1992 Plan. According to research commissioned by the European Parliament on the role of the Community in regard to tourism and regional development:[20]

> The Action Plan's specific priorities – strengthening the horizontal approach to tourism in both Community and national policies, and supporting specific measures to assist tourism, its quality and competitiveness – are laudable but the constraints under which direct EC tourism policy operates suggest the Plan will not have a significant impact on the Community's tourism industry.

The Court of Auditors carried out a special audit in 1996 of Community spending in tourism, covering a number of initiatives, including the Action Plan and tourism spending under the Structural Funds.[21] In addition to uncovering various weaknesses in the Commission's management of the 1992 Plan, the audit noted that the first two annual reports on the Action Plan[22] did not:

> include any evaluation of those of the Community's activities that have an impact on tourism, but merely describes them.

And the second was only:

> in the Commission's own words, an 'attempt at evaluating' the impact of the indirect measures for tourism.

Establishing the Committee of the Regions

The establishment of the Committee of the Regions (COR) by the Treaty of

---

[20] EP, Directorate General for Research, Regional Policy Series, Working Papers, The Role of the EC in regard to Tourism and Regional Development, E–1, External Study, 10–1993, Executive Summary, p.xii.

[21] Special Report 3/96 on tourist policy and the promotion of tourism, together with the Commission's replies OJ C 17/1, 16.1.97.

[22] *Ibid.*, p.9.

Maastricht in 1992 marked an important step in the evolution of Community interest in regional development. Functioning as a consultative body in which a regional perspective would always be articulated, the Committee published two important opinions in 1995 relevant to regional policy and tourism.

In the introduction to its Opinion on the Commission Green Paper on the role of the Union in the field of tourism,[23] the Committee pointed out that:

> tourism can help foster economic and social cohesion and reduce territorial and regional imbalances within the Union, and that many local and regional authorities exercise powers in the area of tourism.

Not surprisingly the Committee emphasised the fact that local authorities and even local bodies have primary responsibility for developing tourism and it also stressed the importance of coordination of action between Commission DGs. Concerning the Structural Funds:

> The COR stresses the need to put tourist undertakings on an equal footing with other businesses for the purpose of Structural Fund aid. It points out that regional and local authorities can secure coordinated application of Structural Fund and national resources for promoting tourism.

> It is also important, as far as possible, to forge links between the Community's general objectives for tourism and Structural Fund aid for tourism. However, local and regional needs and priorities must constantly be at the root of projects supported by the Community at local and regional level.

Reflecting the belief that tourism was still not benefiting as it should from Community regional funding, the Committee's conclusion emphasised the importance of establishing

> a basis to ensure that the Union takes greater account of the specific interests in the area of tourism in connection with planning and implementation of other Community policies.

The second Opinion issued in 1995 on policy for the development of rural tourism in the regions of the European Union[24] advocated a strengthening of rural tourism as an important and complementary element of rural development strategy. If this were done it would

---

[23] COR 376 (95), 6.9.95.
[24] COR 19 (95), 1.2.95.

help offset the problems of disadvantaged regions, and correct distortions and inequalities, as well as being a source of additional revenue and new job ... helping to fight exclusion as well.

The Committee was clear that the needs of Community regional development were not being met.

Openings for Community or sectoral intervention (Objectives 5a, 5b, 1, funding of pilot projects etc) already exist in many areas of interest. Obviously these are still too fragmentary and underfunded when seen in relation to the potential scope for global development generated by promotion of tourism. At the same time a number of tasks or requirements are undoubtedly overlooked by this plethora of instruments for action.

On the broader question of how best to advance overall Community interest in tourism, the Committee emphasised that:

the European Union has no competence in the field of tourism policy and that Community measures to develop rural tourism can only be taken within the framework of other Community policies and the Structural Funds.

In 1999 the Committee of the Regions produced an Opinion on the role of local and regional authorities in tourism development[25] and advocated more:

consideration to the needs of the tourist sector when formulating Community policies which also have an effect on tourism... as well as a more active involvement of local and regional authorities in forging and implementing policies affecting the tourism sector.

Despite the large amounts of money being spent under the Structural Funds and other financial instruments in furtherance of Treaty objectives, the Committee still found:

that it is difficult to ascertain more precisely the impact of these measures. It is very difficult to evaluate accurately the effects of the structural policies. ... Evaluating the way measures affect tourism is even more difficult, since tourism embraces a broad range of economic activities of varying scope.

As a means of ensuring a better impact of regional spending, the Committee suggested that:

---

[25] COR 157 (98), 13.7.99.

Member States earmark a proportion of Structural Fund aid for tourism under the relevant development plans and programmes, in order to strengthen (a) direct EU cooperation with local and regional authorities and (b) interregional, trans–national and cross–border cooperation on the further development of tourism.

Useful summaries of how regional policy initiatives impact on tourism are contained in periodic reports from the Commission on Community measures affecting tourism.[26] However, these reports contain little analysis of regional policy and tourism and contribute little towards a debate on the matter. The reports and opinions of the Court of Auditors and the Committee of Regions, do not seem to have lead to a stronger role of tourism in the discussions on Community policy towards regional development.

The role to date of the Committee of the Regions has added a new perspective to the discussion at European level on regional development and regional policy issues. A voice has been given to the regions themselves for issues that concern them, and tourism is clearly one of these issues. The actions taken as a result of this remain to be seen.

PRINCIPLES AND INSTRUMENTS OF THE STRUCTURAL AND OTHER FUNDS

The principles and instruments of Community policy towards regional development have been constantly reformed and refined. After each period of funding reforms have attempted to improve the policy's effectiveness by simplifying procedures and catering for new Member States.

The current policy principles of regional development for the period 2000–2006 are set out in Regulation 1260/99 laying down general provisions on the Structural Funds[27] and will be explained over the following pages. The relevant headings are:

- Concentration.
- Programming.
- Additionality.

---

[26] For a list of these, see p. 17.

[27] OJ L 161/1, 26.6.99. See also Commission, Communication concerning the Structural Funds and their coordination with the Cohesion Fund – Guidelines for programmers in the period 2000–2006, OJ C 267/99, 22.9.99; Commission, Structural Actions 2000–2006 – Commentary and Regulations, February 2000, Part I. Text available at http://europa.eu.int/comm/regional_policy/sources/docgener/guides/compare/refo_en.pdf.

- Partnership.
- Evaluation.

Before this in order to form an impression of how the overall system works, the steps involved in allocating and spending Community funds for regional development under the Structural Funds will be outlined:[28]

Stages in the Structural Funds Process ...

- Preparation by the Member State and/or regional authority of a Regional Development Plan for an eligible region or area ...
- Submission of a Regional Development Plan by a Member State for a particular region(s), its prior appraisal by the Commission services in accordance with the current requirements in the Objectives specified in the Structural Funds regulations;
- Negotiation on the development strategy and funding priorities between the Member State and/or regional authorities and the Commission;
- The drawing up of an agreed programming document [either a single programming document or a community support framework with supporting operational programmes] setting out the budgetary envelop aims, objectives, priorities, eligible measures, monitoring and evaluation procedures and general implementation requirements;
- Programme implementation – project selection and approval, ongoing monitoring and evaluation against prior agreed indicators;
- Ex–post evaluation of the achievements of the programme as measured by prior agreed economic and physical indicators.

Programme implementation is the responsibility of the Member States and/or regional authorities and is achieved through the establishment of a monitoring Committee composed of Member State representatives, the Commission, economic and social partners and other partners as appropriate. The Monitoring Committee is responsible for the overall co–ordination of the financial and physical progress of the programme. The Monitoring Committee sets the ground rules for project selection, financing and monitoring against agreed financial and physical indicators.

---

[28] Commission, A Handbook on Environmental Assessment of Regional Development Plans ad EU Structural Funds Programmes, September 1999, p.7.

Concentration

The principle of concentration requires that Community aid should be focused on a limited number of problems. Therefore a set of priority objectives for Community funding is determined. The nature and number of these has varied over the different programming periods:

- 1–5 in the 1989–1993 programme.
- 1–6 in the 1994–1999 programme.
- 1–3 in the 2000–2006 programme

Table 6.1 below lists the set of objectives agreed upon for the 1994–1999 programme, taking into account the accession of Sweden and Finland. Regions in Europe that complied with the criteria of these objectives were eligible for structural and/or cohesion funding.

Table 6.1: Priority objectives of the Structural funds (1994–1999)

Objective	Aim
1	Economic adjustment of regions whose development is lagging behind.
2	Economic conversion of declining industrial regions.
3	Combating long–term unemployment, integrating people into working life.
4	Facilitating the adaptation of workers to changes in the industry/ preventing unemployment.
5a	Facilitating the adaptation of the structures in the sector of agriculture and fisheries to CAP.
5b	Economic diversification of fragile rural areas.
6	Meeting specific problems of thinly populated regions in the Nordic countries.

Priority Objectives 1, 2, 5b and 6 were strictly region oriented, that is if a defined geographic area complied with the set criteria, it became eligible for funding. Objectives 3, 4 and 5a were meant to combat specific problems that could be found anywhere in the Community.

The Structural Funds programme for 2000–2006 reduced the number of priority objectives. There are now three:

Table 6.2: Priority objectives of the European Structural Funds (2000–2006)

Objective	Aim
1	Economic adjustment of regions whose development is lagging behind
2	Supporting the economic and social conversion of areas facing structural difficulties.
3	Supporting the adaptation and modernisation of policies and systems of education, training and employment.

Defining the regions that meet these priority objectives involves two issues – identifying the geographical size or limits of a region and determining the criteria for eligibility of the region for priority objective status. Eligibility criteria vary according to the objectives and are set out below. The geographic issue is dealt with under Article 13 of Regulation 1260/99[29] laying down general provisions on the Structural Funds. This establishes a common methodology for fixing the extent of a region for Objective status.

> Plans submitted under Objective 1 shall be drawn up at the geographical level deemed by the Member State concerned to be most appropriate but shall, as a general rule, cover a single region at NUTS Level II.[30]

As can be seen in the map below, large areas of the Community qualify under either Objective 1 or 2.

Article 7 of Regualtion1260/99 requires that the €195 billion available for the 2000–2006 period be split among the different objectives as follows:

- Objective I   – 67.9%
- Objective II   – 11.5%
- Objective III   – 12.3%

The remaining amounts are made up of:

- Community Initiatives – 5.3%
- Others – 1.3%

---

[29] OJ L 161/1, 26.6.99.

[30] NUTS stands for Nomenclature of Territorial Statistical Units. It is a common system of classification of the regions established by the Statistical Office of the European Communities in cooperation with the national institutes for statistics.

Map 1: Objective 1and 2 Regions of the Structural Funds (2000–2006)[31]

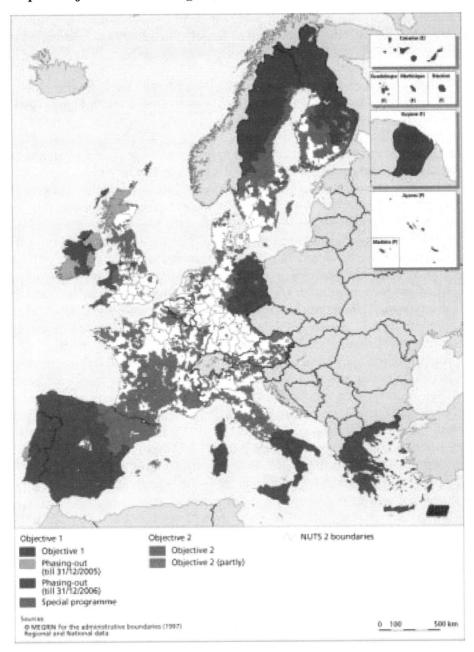

Objective 1
- Objective 1
- Phasing-out (till 31/12/2005)
- Phasing-out (till 31/12/2006)
- Special programme

Objective 2
- Objective 2
- Objective 2 (partly)

NUTS 2 boundaries

Sources
© MEGRIN for the administrative boundaries (1997)
Regional and National data

0 100   500 km

---

[31] Taken from http://www.europa.eu.int/comm/regional_policy/funds/prord/guide/euro2000–2006_en.htm. Original in colour.

Objective 1 regions

These are regions that are considered to lag behind the rest of the Community in economic terms. They are defined in Regulation 1260/99 as regions where *per capita* GDP is less than 75% of the Community average:

> measured in purchasing power parities and calculated on the basis of Community figures for the last three years available on 26 March 1999 – Article 3(1).

This figure is the same as in previous programmes. Using these criteria the Commission fixed the list of Objective 1 regions in 1999.[32]

Objective 1 now also includes the former Objective 6 areas. These were areas identified under the 1994 – 1999 programme as having an extremely low population density (less than 8 people per sq. km.). This objective was created by the Act of Accession of Austria, Finland and Sweden and allowed Community funding to be spent on regions in Sweden and Finland with a very low population density. For the amounts spent under this heading, see Table 3 below on contributions to tourism under Objectives 1 and 6. Objective 1 now also includes the most remote Community regions (French overseas departments, the Canary Islands, the Azores, Madeira). Objective 1 will affect 22.2% of the Community population, while under the 1994–1999 programme it affected 26.6%.

As the map above indicates, some areas which previously qualified for Objective 1 status under the 1994–1999 programme because they were below the 75% figure no longer do so. These regions are the success stories of regional policy in that they have succeeded in increasing their income above the qualifying thresholds. The regions are: East Berlin, Hainaut, Cantabria, Corsica, Valenciennes, Douai and Avesnes, Molise, southern and eastern Ireland, Flevoland, Lisbon and the Tagus Valley, Northern Ireland and the Scottish Highlands and Islands. However, the 2000–2006 programme still allocates degressive transitional assistance to these regions.

Community contributions to tourism under Objectives 1 and 6 for the 1994–1999 period can be seen from the following table:

---

[32] Commission, Decision 1999/502 drawing up the list of regions covered by Objective 1 of the Structural Funds for the period 2000 to 2006, OJ L 194/53, 27.7.99.

Table 6.3: Contributions to tourism through Objectives 1 and 6 from the Structural Funds (1994–1999)[33]

Member State	Objective 1/6 (MECU) 1994/1999
Belgium	37
Denmark	not eligible
Germany	800
Greece	733
Spain	1099
France	106
Ireland	466
Italy	1725
Luxembourg	not eligible
Netherlands	6
Austria	39
Portugal	657
Finland	12
Sweden	20
UK	154
Total	**5854**

For the period 2000–2006, it remains to be seen what proportion of the funds are allocated to tourism development, although the Commission has published an indicative list of the percentage amounts each state will receive under Objective 1.[34] The newly introduced evaluation and compulsory mid–term review procedures may make closer investigation of tourism expenditure possible.

---

[33] Adapted from the Commission, Community Actions affecting Tourism, SEC(97) 1419, 11.7.97, p.62.

[34] Commission, Decision 1999/501 fixing an indicative allocation by Member State of the commitment appropriations for Objective 1 of the Structural Funds for the period 2000 to 2006, OJ L 194/49, 27.7.99.

Tourism examples of priority actions in Objective 1 programmes[35] for the 2000–2006 period

---

Crete, Greece – *Priority 2:* Safeguarding the environment and narrowing the disparities between regions:

There are many intra–regional disparities between coastal and interior areas. Crete has a wild natural interior beauty which is ignored by the most of the tourists of coastal areas. The programme will help the diversification and improvement of the tourist product by increasing in value and promoting mountain activities, cultural assets, and the touristic infrastructure of its mountains with the improvement of the existing infrastructure and the creation of conditions for lasting development by taking environmental problems more into consideration.[36]

Andalusia, Spain – *Priority 1:* Improvement of competitiveness and employment, and development of production structures:

A wide variety of aid is proposed to industrial, commercial and service businesses. This may involve material or non–material investment, funding the transition towards clean technologies, creating or adapting areas and services to businesses, improving their capacity for organisation (organisation, management, infrastructures, establishing networks, control of quality and procedures), aid for internationalisation and external promotion, or improving the conditions whereby they are financed. Farming businesses may receive aid to improve the processing and commercialisation of their products; the food industry will receive investment in order to establish logistics centres, to modernise its equipment, etc. Tourist businesses may claim aid and services in order to develop their products. Co–ordination between local bodies in charge of tourism with be strengthened and the quality of the information material will be improved. Lastly, social economy businesses will receive support for their activities insofar as they create new jobs.[37]

---

[35] http://www.europa.eu.int/comm/regional_policy/country/prordn/index_en.cfm?gv_pay=ALL&gv_reg=ALL&gv_obj=ALL&gv_the=9.
[36] Objective 1 Programme for Crete, *supra*.
[37] Objective 1 Programme for Andalusia, *supra*.

Objective 2 regions

These are areas experiencing structural difficulties, usually though not always reflected in very high unemployment. They also include regions which qualified under Objective 5b under the 1994–1999 programme. According to Article 4 (1) of Regulation 1260/99:

> The regions covered by Objective 2 shall be those with structural problems whose socio-economic conversion is to be supported ... and whose population or area is sufficiently substantial. They shall include in particular areas undergoing socio–economic change in the industrial and service sectors, declining rural areas, urban areas in difficulty and depressed areas dependant on fisheries. Article 4 also spells out the more specific requirements for each of these areas.

Regions undergoing socio-economic change in the industrial/service sector

Under Article 4(5) regions undergoing socio-economic change must represent all or part of a NUTS III area and, starting from a higher industrial employment base than the Community average, have an unemployment rate above the Community average for the last three years and an observable fall in industrial employment calculated according to defined criteria.

Rural Areas

Under Article 4(6) an eligible rural area must have either:
- a population density of less than 100 people per km^2,
- at least twice the percentage Community average employed in agriculture,
- average unemployment rate over last three years above Community average, or
- decline in population since 1985.

Areas dependant on fisheries

Under Article 4(8) these are areas where fishing related employment is a significant percentage of total employment and:

> which are facing structural socio–economic problems relating to the restructuring of the fisheries sector which result in a significant reduction in the number of jobs.

Urban areas in difficulty

Under Article 4(7) the types of difficulty must include at least one of the following:

• higher long term employment than the Community average.

• a high level of poverty.

• particularly damaged environment.

• high crime and delinquency rates,

• low educational levels among the population.

Among other areas which may also qualify for Objective 2 funding, under Article 4(9), are areas adjacent to those listed above and rural areas suffering a decline of the working agricultural population.

Regulation 1260/99 also stipulates that no more than 18% of the Community population should be eligible for Objective 2 funding and provides the means for calculating a ceiling from which this percentage can be worked out for each Member State. Using these the Commission has fixed a population ceiling for each of the Member States.[38] The present figure is an increase from the 1994 – 1999 figure of 16.3%.

---

[38] Commission, Decision 1999/503 establishing a population ceiling for each Member State under Objective 2 of the Structural Funds for the period 2000 to 2006, OJ L 194/58, 27.7.99.

Table 6.4: Contributions to tourism through Objective 2 from the Structural Funds for 1994–1999[39]

Member State	Objective 2 (MECU) 1994/1999
Belgium	10
Denmark	11
Germany	15
Greece	not eligible
Spain	–
France	150
Ireland	not eligible
Italy	71
Luxembourg	–
Netherlands	42
Austria	8 (*)
Portugal	not eligible
Finland	5 (*)
Sweden	15 (*)
UK	288
Total	**615**

The planned expenditures on tourism development, ECU 587 million in the 12 Member States for 1994–1999, was supplemented with a further ECU 28 million for tourism–related measures in the new Member States for 1995–1999.

---

[39] *Supra.* For equivalent figures for the 1989–1993 period, see Commission, Community measures affecting tourism, COM(94) 74 final, 6.4.94, p.60.

**Tourism examples of priority actions in Objective 2 programmes for the
2000–2006 period**

Rheinland/Pfalz, Germany – *Priority 2*: *Tourism, Leisure and Quality of
Life*:

> Investing in projects in the tourism and leisure sector is the main aim
> of this priority. Young entrepreneurs in or starting–up companies in the
> tourism sector will be given support as will measures related to
> information and communication technology investments. Special
> emphasis will also be put on infrastructure investments for cultural
> and environmental projects and for measures aimed at preventing natural
> disasters.[40]

Salzburg, Austria – *Priority 1*: *Tourism and Leisure*:

> In order to develop the tourism and leisure industries measures under
> this priority aim at improving general tourism infrastructure with an
> important emphasis on winter tourism. Furthermore, cooperation
> between enterprises will be promoted and counselling services
> enhanced.[41]

In the current 2000–2006 Structural Fund programme, rural development can
be found in all Objective 3 areas, as well as being an important pillar in the
Common Agricultural Policy.

Programming

According to Community law, Community funding for regional development
must be channelled through a programme. Article 9 of Council Regulation 1260/
1999[42] laying down general provisions on the Structural Funds defines
programming as:

> the organising, decision–making and financing process carried out in a
> number of stages to implement on a multi–annual basis the joint action of

---

[40] Objective 2 programme for Tirol 2000–2006, accessible from http://www.europa.eu.int/comm/
regional_policy/country/prordn/index_en.cfm?gv_pay=ALL&gv_reg=ALL&gv_
obj=ALL&gv_the=9.
[41] Objective 2 Programme for Salzburg, *supra*.
[42] OJ L 161/1, 26.6.99.

the Community and the Member States to attain the Objectives referred to in Article 1.

In effect a programme represents the procedural framework for using Treaty financial instruments, such as the Structural Funds, to attain Treaty ends, such as targeting the weaker regions, that is, the Objective 1 and 2 regions.

There are two dimensions to programming – financial and organizational. The former will be looked at first.[43]

Financial aspects of programming

As already indicated, Community cohesion policy operates, under Article 159 of the Treaty, through several financial instruments:

- the Structural Funds.
- the European Investment Bank (EIB).
- "other existing financial instruments" – Article 159.
- the Cohesion Fund.
- instrument for structural policies for pre–accession states.

The Structural Funds represent the largest funding instrument in the Community's cohesion policy and is also the most important instrument in terms of funds for tourism in Europe. As previously indicated the Structural Funds consist of:

- European Regional Development Fund (ERDF).
- European Agricultural Guidance and Guarantee Fund, Guidance Section (EAGGF).
- European Social Fund (ESF).

Among the other existing financial instruments are Interreg and Leader+, both of which, as will be seen, are of great importance to tourism. A further fund devised for the current applicant countries – the instrument for structural policies for pre-accession (ISPA) also has potential relevance to tourism

Further examination is confined to the ERDF, EAGGF, EIB, Leader, Interreg, the Cohesion Fund and ISPA.

---

[43] For organisational aspects including procedures for making plans and programmes on a country and regional basis, see p. 266.

European regional development fund

The basic function of the ERDF is set out in Article 160 of the Rome Treaty.

> The European Regional Development Fund is intended to help redress the main regional imbalances in the Community through participation in the development and structural adjustment of regions whose development is lagging behind and in the conversion of declining industrial regions.

Under Article 2(1) of Regulation 1783/99[44] the ERDF is obliged to contribute funding towards three broad categories of project:

- productive investment.
- infrastructure.
- the development of endogenous potential.

In attempting to meet these criteria, Article 2(2) lists tourism among the current tasks of the ERDF:

> In application of paragraph 1, the financial contribution of the ERDF shall support ... (d) the development of tourism and cultural investment, including the protection of cultural and natural heritage provided that they are creating sustainable jobs.[45]

Within the Structural Funds the ERDF is by far the greatest fund and together with the EAGGF the most importance source of funding for tourism in the Community. In the 1989–1993 period it contributed 86% of Structural Funds[46] aid for tourism, while the figure for 1993–1999 was 72%.[47]

---

[44] OJ L 213/1, 13.8.99.

[45] Tourism was not directly mentioned in the earlier ERDF regulations detailing the scope and forms of assistance of the ERDF, although Regulation 2083/93, OJ L 193/34, 31.7.93, did provide in Article 2(5) that "When submitting applications to the ERDF, Member States shall ensure that a sufficient proportion is allocated to investment in industry, craft industry and services, [...]".

[46] Commission, Community measures affecting tourism, COM(94) 74, 6.4.94, p.60.

[47] See also Table 6.5 at p. 251.

Table 6.5: ERDF Contributions to Tourism[48]

Member State	ERDF Contrib. MECU	Share of Total Structural Funds
Belgium	51,5	89,5%
Denmark	17,5	68,0%
Germany	59,3	6,7%
Greece	683	93,1%
Spain	575,5	50,3%
France	476,9	91,4%
Ireland	354,0	76,0%
Italy	932,7	48,7%
Luxembourg	0,9	90,0%
Netherlands	54,2	82,5%
Austria	94,1	88,9%
Portugal	571,0	86,9%
Suomi/Finland	17,2	72,3%
Sweden	45,7	91,8%
United Kingdom	496,1	24,8%
TOTAL	**4 429,6**	**70,0%**

Information about Objective 1 regional programmes for the 2000–2006 period is available at Commission web site:

http://www.europa.eu.int/comm/regional_policy/country/prordn/search.cfm?gv_pay=ALL&gv_reg=ALL&gv_obj=1&gv_the=9&LAN=EN

---

[48] Adapted from the Commission staff working paper on Community actions affecting tourism, SEC(97) 1419, 11.7.97, p.63, the figures relate mainly to 1994–1999 period.

Tourism related examples of past ERDF assisted projects

Sicily, Italy –

In the north-western part of Sicily the ERDF contributed under the multi-fund regional programme for Sicily to the excavation of the city of Segesta. The assistance of 3 MECU by the ERDF financed considerable parts of the whole scheme, including the uncovering of the Agora, the old city wall, as well as remains of an old Arabic city and a later Norman settlement. The complex attracts many tourists at all seasons and gives an example of the Structural Funds' contribution towards strengthening non–seasonal tourism and permanent culture related employment. Moreover, in spring and summer various cultural events (theatre, concerts) in the old Greek theatre enhance local attractiveness.[49]

Basilicata, Italy – Within the Community Support Framework for Italy 1989 to 1993 the ERDF contributed to the restoration of the Castle of Lagopesole in Avigliano (region of Basilicata in Italy).The project was an example of the combination of preserving cultural heritage:

with commercial use, cultural research as well as environmental protection. [It was anticipated that firstly] the refurbished castle will accommodate the Frederician Institute of the National Council for Research, charged with the restoration and re–utilisation of historic monuments in the Mezzogiorno as well as environmental monitoring. Secondly, the building will house the national centre for the safeguarding of forests. Thirdly, the co–operative of the castle based in the renovated building organises guided tours, conferences, exhibitions, music and theatre events. A restaurant for visitors is managed by the same co–operative.[50]

EAGGF guidance section

This inelegantly titled Fund is more specifically aimed at speeding up the adjustment of agricultural structures with a view to the reform of the common agricultural policy. It attempts to re-establish a balance between agricultural production and market capacity. In other words, to encourage a reduction in

---

[49] Commission, Communication on Cohesion Policy and Culture – A Contribution to Employment, COM(96) 512 final, 20.11.96, p.11.

[50] *Ibid.*, p.7.

quantities produced by farmers, by for example diversifying their activities for alternative incomes. Rural areas are focused on.

Tourism was one of the areas identified in the now repealed Council Regulation 4256/88[51] laying down provisions for implementation of the EAGGF Guidance Section. With the object of the development and structural adjustment of the less-developed regions, Article 5 provided that:

> Financial assistance by the Fund may relate to the following ... encourage-ment for tourist and craft investments, including the improvement of living accommodation on agricultural holdings.

The current Regulation 1257/99[52] on support for rural development from the EAGGF further develops the provisions of the earlier regulations and permits funding for "diversification of activities with the aim of complementary or alternative activities – Article 2 – and more specifically encouragement for tourist and craft activities – Article 33".

Table 6.6: EAGGF Contributions to Tourism (1994–1999)[53]

Member State	EAGGF Contrib.	Share of Total Structural Funds
Belgium	1,0	
Denmark	6,5	
Germany	38,7	4,3%
Spain	7,7	
France	35,0	6,7%
Italy	26,8	
Luxembourg	0,1	
Netherlands	1,4	
Austria	9,7	
Suomi/Finland	6,6	
Sweden	5,1	
United Kingdom	20,0	
TOTAL	**158,2**	**2,2%**

---

[51] OJ L 374/25, 31.12.88.

[52] OJ L 160/80, 26.6.99.

[53] Adapted from the Commission staff working paper on Community actions affecting tourism, SEC(97) 1419, 11.7.97.

European Investment Bank

The Treaty of Rome establishes and defines the functions of the European Investment Bank (EIB).[54] Article 267 indicates that the bank's function is to support the "balanced and steady development of the common market." This it does by granting loans and giving guarantees:

> which facilitate the financing of ...
>
> (a) projects for developing less–developed regions;
> (b) projects for modernising or converting undertakings for fresh activities
>   ... where the size or nature is such that they cannot be entirely financed
>   by the various means available in the individual Member States;
> (c) projects of common interests to several Member States which are of
>   such a size or nature that they cannot ...
>
> In carrying out its task, the Bank shall facilitate the financing of investment programmes in conjunction with assistance from the Structural Funds and other Community instruments.

Thus, a significant function of the EIB is to support regional development investment. In reviewing the period 1990–1994, the Commission reported on the activities of the EIB in the field of tourism.[55]

> As part of its task of providing long–term finance for investments contributing to the implementation of Community policies, the ... EIB assists tourism in various ways.
>
> Most of the EIB's activities are concerned with reducing regional disparities. ... Accordingly, action to strengthen tourism facilities is restricted almost exclusively to regions in receipt of Community Structural Funds: more than three–quarters of the finance granted between 1990 and 1994 fell under this heading. ...
>
> The assistance given to these regions is mainly to small or medium-sized hotels (nearly 1 200 projects received ECU 632 million between 1990 and 1994) ... and is financed by global loans concluded with banks ... which are in close touch with local conditions. ... The hotel projects are concerned to a great extent with business tourism, which throughout the year supports the economic expansion of regions less immediately attractive to tourists.

---

[54] The Bank's website is at http://www.eib.eu.int.
[55] Commission, Community Measures Affecting Tourism, COM(96) 29 final, 5.2.96, p.66.

> ... Most of the other investments covered very diverse establishments and served to reinforce the tourist appeal of the regions concerned: camp sites, ski lifts, leisure areas and also, patricianly in Italy, buildings and sites of a cultural or architectural interest. ... In addition ... the EIB financed an exceptionally large–scale project contributing to the Community's tourist appeal, i.e. the Euro Disney park in the Paris area.

In 1995:

> loans for projects in the 15 Member States amounted to ECU 18 603 million, of which 68% was assistance to projects contributing to the development of the less favoured regions [...] industry and services received ECU 4 617.1 million, of which ECU 137.1 million was specifically for tourism, leisure and health.[56]

Research utilising the banks website will further detail the bank's involvement in tourism.

Other existing financial instruments – community initiatives

Community Initiatives are a further set of Community spending programmes within the Structural Funds which the Commission alone is authorized to initiate to help address specific kinds of development problems in European regions not accorded priority status under the Structural Funds. While the Commission initiates these programmes, the appropriate authorities in the Member States implement them.

The Preamble to Regulation 1260/1999[57] laying down general provisions on the Structural Funds recites:

> there should be provision for operations of Community interest carried out at the initiative of the Commission to supplement those implemented under the priority objectives.

This is developed in Article 20, which states that:

> The Community initiatives shall cover the following fields:
>
> (a) cross-border, trans-national and inter-regional co-operation intended

---

[56] Commission, Staff Working Paper on Community Actions Affecting Tourism, SEC(97) 1419, 11.7.97, p.69.

[57] OJ L 161/20, 21.6.99.

to encourage the harmonious, balanced and sustainable development of the whole of the Community area ('Interreg');

(b) economic and social regeneration of cities and of urban neighbourhoods in crisis, with a view to promoting sustainable urban development ('URBAN');

(c) rural development ('Leader');

(d) trans–national co-operation to promote new means of combating all forms of discrimination and inequalities in connection with the labour market ('EQUAL').

The number of Community initiatives has been reduced from 14 under the 1994–1999 programme to 4 under the 2000–2006 programme. The Structural Funds budget available for these initiatives has also been reduced from 9% to 5.3% of the total budget – Article 7(6).

Article 21(1) requires the Commission to lay down guidelines for each initiative describing the aims, scope and appropriate method of implementation. Such guidelines have been made in the case of Leader+ and Interreg, both of which are of special relevance to tourism and will be looked at more closely.

Leader+

Leader+[58] is a follow–up to Leader I and Leader II which belonged to earlier periods. The hallmark of the Leader+ initiative is that it supports locally based initiatives that try to address the pressures that rural areas in the Community are facing. These pressures arise from the reform of the Common Agricultural Policy as well as changes in patterns of international trade, growing demands to conserve the natural environment, and other changes in economic life. While measures under the other programmes also address these pressures, though from different perspectives, Leader+ is based on the idea of empowering local people to use their resources to ensure the long term sustainability of their communities. It does this by piloting new means of regeneration, or in the Commission's own words, by acting as

a laboratory which aims to encourage the emergence and testing of new approaches.[59]

---

[58] See generally Commission Notice laying down guidelines for the Community initiative for rural development, OJ C 139/5, 18.5.00. Although Article 20 of Regulation 1260/99 uses the term Leader, Article 1 of the Commission Notice uses the term Leader+.

[59] *Ibid.*, p.6.

Thus, the objective of Leader+ is to find innovative solutions to problems facing rural communities that can serve as models for developing rural areas elsewhere. Local people, with their special knowledge of the economic, social and cultural situation are asked to put together development strategies referred to as a Business Plan. They are subsequently expected to play a major role in putting the development strategies into effect. The Commission guidelines set out general selection criteria under three action headings:

- integrated territorial rural development strategies of a pilot nature.
- support for co-operation between rural territories.
- networking.

However, responsibility for devising procedures and more specific selection criteria is devolved to the Member States. These must then be submitted to the Commission for approval. The actions must advance the following three themes:

- enhancing the natural and cultural heritage.
- reinforcing the economic environment.
- improving the organizational abilities of their community.

The amounts of funding available under Leader+ are significant.

> The total EU contribution to LEADER+ in the period 2000–2006 will be EUR 2020 million, financed under the EAGGF-Guidance Section. The Community typically co-finances measures up to a maximum of 75 % of the total cost in Objective 1 regions, and at up to 50 % in all other areas.[60]

Much of this will find its way into tourism related projects. Looking back to Leader II:

> Initial indications from the 1994–1999 period are that the tourism sector was the sector which received the highest share of financial support under Leaser II. More than half of the financial allocations under some programmes were allocated to projects for development of rural tourism activities.[61]

As to the type of tourism project assisted:

> The tourism projects assisted were typically of a small size such as creating

---

[60] Commission, Report on Community Measures affecting Tourism (2000), COM(2002) 300, 15.3.02, p.39.
[61] *Ibid.*, p.38, n.103.

accommodation in rural areas (rural gites, bed & breakfast), or concerned development of recreational tourism in rural areas such as development of nature tourism, outdoor pursuits (canoeing, horse riding, mountain biking, walking holidays etc.), craft activities for tourists etc.. Some LAGs financed projects with the aim of improving the attractiveness of their villages in the interests of both local residents and tourists e.g. restoring traditional buildings or financing projects concerned with reinvigorating local cultural traditions and heritage.[62]

Tourism examples of past Leader+ programmes[63]

Arca Umbria, Italy – the objective was to benefit from the region's natural environment in terms of its agricultural produce, tourism potential and local craft services. Means to achieve these objectives were a.o. the development of farm holidays, agri–tourism and country sports.

Parque cultural de los Molinos in Teruel, Spain – the objective was to bring benefits to the local people and avoid random exploitation which would destroy the natural heritage, by developments to cater for visitors, centered on the park: accommodation and restaurants for visitors, historical and nature conservation, and crafts.

Pays Cathare, France – the objective was to promote economic development, and to raise the number of tourists from 640 000 to 1 million from 1991 to 1995. The promotion of local produce was an integral part of the programme.

Interreg

As previously noted, the power to create a Community initiative for trans-European cooperation (Interreg) was created by Article 20 of Regulation 1260/99. The Commission formally established the initiative and published appropriate guidelines in 2000.[64] Under paragraph 3(1) of these guidelines, the Commission stated that:

---

[62] *Ibid.,* p.39.

[63] Publication CEC, DG XVI, 1998.

[64] Commission, Communication laying down guidelines for a Community Initiative concerning trans–European cooperation intended to encourage harmonious and balanced development of the European territory – Interreg III, OJ C 143/6, 23.5.00.

> The overall aim of the Interreg initiatives has been, and remains, that national borders should not be a barrier to the balanced development and integration of the European territory … the presence of borders cuts off border communities from each other … [and] border areas have been neglected under national policy.

Thus, Interreg focuses on different types of border areas, that is ones which suffer from national isolation, being far from the centres of economic activity and political decision-making or on the periphery of Europe. Interreg projects must be jointly selected and implemented by the parties in different states and involve not only institutional bodies but also economic and social partners and non-governmental bodies.

Because Interreg focuses on border regions, care must be taken when putting forward projects to ensure that the needs of a cross border area reflect a local perspective and not a national one. With a history of looking towards national centres, this can be difficult.

> In many cases, the actual cross-border nature of INTEREG has not emerged very clearly. … All too often border programmes were developed in parallel and in accordance with a national perspective and were then presented to the European Commission jointly with a neighbouring country.[65]

The current Interreg guidelines identify three strands of activity as suitable for financial support:

- cross border cooperation – strand A.[66]
- trans–national cooperation – strand B.
- interregional cooperation. – strand C.

Annex II to the guidelines provides an indicative list of priority tasks and eligible measures under the different strands. These include in relation to urban, rural and coastal areas.

> Cross–border rural development, principally through the marketing and promotion of activity products, the encouragement of tourist and craft activities … and development of village and preservation of the rural heritage.

---

[65] Commission, Community initiative INTERREG II 1994–1999:An initial evaluation, January 1999, p.3. Text available at http://europa.eu.int/comm/regional_policy/sources/docgener/informat/interreg_en.pdf.

[66] The list of eligible areas under strand A is set out in Annex I to the Guidelines. These include border areas separated by sea, as well as adjoining land areas.

In the context of SMEs, tourism and local development the guidelines prioritise:

> Development of quality and environmentally friendly tourism, (including farm tourism) through projects for investment, design and introduction of new tourism products (cultural tourism, environmental tourism) which create sustainable jobs ... promotional measures, market studies and establishment of shared reservations systems.

Interreg regions are diverse and tend to fall into 2 categories:

- less prosperous regions where the focus is on communications and infrastructure projects. 75% of the budgets were used for these measures;
- regions nearer to the "centre" of the Community where the focus is more on cooperation between social and economic groups and know–how projects.

Information about regional development programmes funded under Interreg during the 2000–2006 period is available via:

> http://www.europa.eu.int/comm/regional_policy/country/prordn/
> index_en.cfm?gv_pay=ALL&gv_reg=ALL&gv_obj=13&gv_the=9

Tourism examples of past and current Interreg projects

Karelia, Finland/Russia[67] –

> The aim of this project is to develop and strengthen cooperation between the authorities responsible for the Oulanka National Park, situated in the Kussamo upland area of Finland, and the Paanajärvi National Park, situated in the north–west corner of the Russian Karelia. The parks' authorities are seeking to address certain issues which will increase the tourist potential of the parks. For example, while the two parks share a common border, there is no through route allowing visitors to go from one park to another without making a detour. Other key actions will include developing the services provided for visitors. Principally, the idea is to increase the number of international visitors to the area.

---

[67] Taken from http://www.europa.eu.int/comm/regional_policy/interreg3/doc/pdf/fi–russ_en.pdf.

Celtic Sea Cruise Consortium, Ireland/Wales[68] –

The port authorities of Dublin, Dun Laoghaire and Holyhead [Wales] have been awarded £146,000 of Interreg grant to develop a joint marketing campaign to attract new cruise ship business to the regions. Independently the ports have achieved some success in promoting themselves to cruise liner companies, however, with the impetus of EU funding, a joint coherent strategy can be developed. A number of partners from both regions are assisting in the development of the strategy which involves raising awareness of the Celtic Ports – the common history and heritage that unite them and co-ordinating specific tourism and marketing information from the region. Underpinning the marketing initiative will be development of a unifying image for the Celtic Sea Ports. As well as marketing the tourism aspects of the regions, the partners will develop enhanced standards and procedures including the provision of high quality technical information on the ports and related facilities.

Cohesion fund

Reflecting the priority in Article 2 of the Rome Treaty that economic and social cohesion is a prime Community objective, Article 161 of the Treaty provides that:

A Cohesion Fund … shall provide a financial contribution in the fields of environment and trans-European networks in the area of transport infrastructure.

However, under a Protocol to the Treaty, a state can only qualify for assistance from the Fund if two conditions are met – it has a per capita GNP of less than 90% of the Community average and it operates an economic convergence programme. Effectively, the Fund only benefits environmental and trans–European transport network projects in Greece, Spain Ireland and Portugal.

The Fund was established by Regulation 1164/94[69] and makes €18 billion available for the 2000 – 2006 programming period. Indicative allocations set out in Annex I of the Regulation suggest the eligible states will receive the following allocations:

- Spain between 61% and 63.5%.

---

[68] Taken from http://www.interreg.ie.
[69] OJ L 130/1, 25.5.94.

- Greece between 16% and 18%.
- Portugal between 16% and 18%.
- Ireland between 2% and 6%.

Eligibility will be re–examined midway, i.e. before the end of 2003, in light of updated GNP levels.

While the rate of Community assistance under the Fund must generally be between 80% and 85% of public expenditure, this can be reduced in proportion to the revenue generated by projects, such as toll roads and the polluter–pays principle.[70] Applications for project funding are submitted by the States and are:

> adopted by the Commission in agreement with the beneficiary Member State – Article 10(1).

> Projects must be of a sufficient scale to have a significant impact ... – Article 10(3).

While it is clear that assistance from the Cohesion Fund cannot be spent directly on tourism, projects financed under it can have an impact on tourism activity, especially as tourism is an important economic activity in all the countries eligible for finance by the Cohesion Fund.

In guidelines published in 1999[71] addressed to the cohesion states to help them prepare programming strategies for the Structural Funds and their links with the Cohesion Fund, the Commission identified the problems to be tackled: disparities in terms of regional income, infrastructure, human capital endowments and the competitiveness of enterprises. The basic factors determining regional competitiveness were identified: transport, energy, telecommunications, and infrastructure for a high quality environment. Furthermore, the Commission mentioned aspects of key importance for employment creation by competitive enterprise, i.e.:

> support for enterprises, business support services and areas with particular potential: environment, tourism and culture ...

Regarding tourism and culture, the 1999 guidelines briefly refer to the advantages of funding for local development, namely sustainable quality tourism, made possible by the modernization of infrastructure, upgrading of skills and the encouragement of partnerships between enterprises.

---

[70] *Ibid.*, Article 7.
[71] The Structural Funds and their coordination with the Cohesion Fund: Guidelines for programmes in the period 2000–2006, European Commission, 1999.

Information about the transport and infrastructure projects aided by the Cohesion Fund for the 1993–1999 period are available via:

http://www.europa.eu.int/comm/regional_policy/funds/procf/cf_en.htm

ISPA

The meaning and object of ISPA (Instrument for Structural Policies for Pre–accession) is evident from Article 1(1) of Regulation 1267/99[72] which states that:

Definition and Objective

The Instrument for Structural Policies for Pre–accession ... [ISPA] is hereby established.

ISPA shall provide assistance to contribute to the preparation for accession to the European Union of the following applicant countries: Bulgaria, Czech Republic, Estonia, Hungary, Latvia, Lithuania, Poland, Romania, Slovakia and Slovenia [...] in the area of economic and social cohesion, concerning environment and transport policies in accordance with the provisions of this Regulation.

The Community assistance granted under ISPA shall contribute to the objectives laid down in the Accession Partnership for each beneficiary country and to corresponding national programmes for the improvement of the environment and of transport infrastructure networks.

Thus, ISPA which has an annual budget of €1.04 billion and which can contribute up to 75% of the local expenditure figure, is similar to the Cohesion Fund with its focus on environment and transport, but is different in that it is spent outside the Community in the Central and Eastern European States and as part of their accession process leading to full membership of the Community. Two other Community instruments similarly assist the applicant states – Sapard (€520 million per year) which focuses on agriculture and rural development and Phare (€1.56 billion per year) which focus on preparing the administrative capacity of applicant States as well as industrial restructuring.

Since the focus of ISPA funding is on enabling applicant states to comply with investment–heavy environment directives, like dealing with waste and with transport projects which enable national networks to link with trans

---

[72] OJ L 161/77, 26.6.99. The Commission website for ISPA is at http://www.europa.eu.int/comm/regional_policy/funds/ispa/ispa_en.htm.

European transport networks, tourism is only indirectly affected by ISPA. Among project approved so far are the reconstruction and extension of Sofia Airport in Bulgaria.

In 2000 a committee of the European Parliament[73] emphasized the importance of tourism in relation to enlargement and the role of Community funding channelled through the importance of ISPA and Interreg.

> Tourism has so far not played any role in relation to enlargement. In the applicant countries there is some cultural and city tourism. This situation is due firstly to the problem of the inadequate infra structure ... and to the extremely bad marketing. The applicant countries should therefore be urged to target effectively the funds made available to them under the aid programmes (ISPA, INTERREG), for example to develop infrastructure, cultural projects, etc. The governments authorities on the one hand and the regional and local authorities on the other hand should be encouraged to attach greater importance to tourism aid ...

Additionality

Article 11(1) of Regulation 1260/99 laying down general provision on the Structural Funds explains:

> In order to achieve a genuine economic impact, the appropriations of the Funds may not replace public or other equivalent structural expenditure by the Member State.

In other words, Member States must spend their own funds alongside Community funds. Article 11(2) provides a formula for working out the mandatory level of expenditure by Member States.

> As a general rule, the level of expenditure ... shall be at least equal to the amount of average annual expenditure in real terms achieved in the previous programming period ...

Article 11(3) also requires the Commission to verify at three different times whether a Member State is complying with this additionality requirement. These are before approval of any programming documents by the Commission, mid–term and no later than end of 2005.[74]

---

[73] EP, Report on the enlargement of the European Union, PE 285.644/fin/Part 2, 19.9.00, p.104.
[74] Guidance on how additionality can be verified is set out in Commission, The Verification of

The principle of additionality reflects a cautious approach by the Community towards the danger of states replacing their own expenditure with Community funding. However, in the past some States might not have sought Community funds which might have benefited tourism projects because they was unable to commit the necessary own funds. According to a Parliament report in 1991.[75] Community contributions for the period 1989–1991 for tourism under Objective 1 CSFs in the most tourism dependant States of Greece, Spain and Portugal was 3.1%, 2.4% and 3.5% respectively (of total Community aid for Community Support Frameworks).[76] These figures were much lower than those for the less tourism dependant states and prompted the following remark:

> Perhaps the most important conclusion which may be drawn from the tables annexed is that those Member States ... which are currently the most dependant on tourism ... are the least inclined to devote public resources to developing the industry. ... Since the regions concerned frequently lack alternative sectors of economic activity which might replace tourism as a source of employment, the unwillingness to devote more resources ... in such regions seems most regrettable.

Under Article 11(3) of Regulation 1260/99 responsibility for the verification procedures lies with the Commission and Member States are obliged to furnish it with the necessary information.

Partnership

Under Community Structural Funds policy the principle of partnership implies close cooperation between the European Commission, and the competent authorities in each Member State at national, regional, local or other level. According to Article 8(1) of Regulation 1260/99, the basic law on structural funds:

> Community actions shall compliment or contribute to corresponding national operations. They shall be drawn up in close consultation,

---

Additionality for Objective 1, Working Paper 5. Text available at http://www.europa.eu.int/comm/regional_policy/sources/docoffic/working/doc/additionality_en.pdf.

[75] EP, Session Documents, Opinion in the form of a co–report of the Committee on Regional Policy and Regional Planning on Tourism and Regional Development in: Report of the Committee on Transport and Tourism on a Community Policy, A3–0155/91/Part B, 30.5.91, p.11.

[76] *Ibid.*, p.15. For an explanation of CSF, see p. 267.

> hereinafter referred to as the 'partnership', between the Commission and
> the Member State, together with … the regional and local authorities …
> the economic and social partners … any other relevant competent bodies
> within this framework.

To reinforce the point that partnership must involve consultation at all stages, Article 8(1) goes on to spell out:

> Partnership shall cover the preparation, financing, monitoring and
> evaluation of assistance. Member States shall ensure the association of
> the relevant parties at the different stage of programming, taking account
> of the time limit for each stage.

In effect, this means that Member States consult their national partners (trade unions, employers, farmers etc) on the development plans drawn up for submission to the Commission, and then specify in the plans the provision made for consultation of the partners.

Thus, this part will review the planning procedures which reflect both the principle of partnership and the principle of programming discussed earlier. Unlike the earlier part, the focus will be on the organisational aspect of programming.

Community funding for regional development programmes can originate in two ways: through programmes initiated at national level and/or at Community level. Before a programme can be approved at Community level Member State authorities are generally required to also pledge funding of their own.

Inherent in the partnership and programming process is the preparation of a series of documents which help set the context or framework within which the spending and its underlying justification occur. Much of the reasoning for these documents derives from the Community's desire to ensure sound financial management of its funds. Regulation 1260/99[77] identifies three such documents:

- Community Support Frameworks (CSF).
- Operational Programmes (OP).
- Single Programming Documents (SPD).

Under Article 14(1):

> Each plan, Community support framework, operational programme and
> single programming document shall cover a period of seven years. … The
> programming period shall begin on 1 January 2000.

---

[77] OJ L 161/1, 26.6.99.

Each of these documents will now be explained and their relevance to tourism highlighted.

Community support frameworks

According to Article 9 of Regulation 1260/99 Community support framework means:

> the document approved by the Commission, in agreement with the Member State concerned, following appraisal of the plan submitted by a Member State and containing the strategy and priorities for action of the Funds and the Member State, their specific objectives, the contribution of the Funds and the other financial resources. The document shall be divided into priorities and implemented by means of one or more operational programmes.

A Community Support Framework therefore reflects an agreement which identifies the development problems of an area and lists priorities for tackling them under the different Objectives of the Structural Funds. While a CSF can cover a multitude of problems and actions, tourism obviously plays a significant part in many CSFs, most often as a means for economic regeneration of a depressed region. Operational programmes are described in further detail below.

Tourism examples of Community Support Frameworks

Corsica, France – The French CSF[78] for 1989–93 concerning Corsica contained many references to tourism. Corsica's development problems were highlighted– high unemployment, inadequate level of vocational qualification and skill and low GDP *per capita*, heavy external trade deficit. Tourism was identified as an economic strength of the island and the advantages of developing it were outlined:

> Dependent upstream on transport infrastructures, tourism determines in its turn the growth potential of other sectors (agriculture, distributive trades and market services). Although hit in the early 1980s by a relative recession, it still offers considerable potential for the island's economic development... Corsica's attractions are linked to its geography and

---

[78] Community Support Frameworks 1989–93, FRANCE, Pamphlet/Brochure produced by the Commission of the European Communities.

history. The preservation and exploitation of places of interest would consequently help to enhance the island's tourist appeal and improve the local quality of life.

The CSF identified the relevant aims of tourism actions as follows:

The measures to be implemented in the area of tourism aim, on the one hand, to achieve a wider dispersion of tourism–related activities over the island's territory, making more tourists visit the interior and developing cultural tourism (through the exploitation of the island's historical heritage) and, on the other hand, to support the creation of facilities likely to extend the summer peak season (water–sports centres, combined activities, business tourism, etc.).

The CSF also divided the priorities for Community action between infrastructure and productive activities. The infrastructure focus was on ports and airports supplemented by internal communication networks, and water availability –

an increase in receipts from tourism, presupposes the removal of internal obstacles through the modernization of the road network.

On tourism as a productive activity:

the category of tourists traditionally visiting the island militates for spreading seasonal peak over time, e.g. by promoting 'business tourism', and to other areas of the island by exploiting the beauties of its interior. This approach would help to overcome the disadvantages linked to the seasonal pattern of activities, whereby the workforce employed in the hotel and catering trade tends to be imported, and provide new opportunities for developing the island's interior.

The CSF also identified aims supporting agricultural and rural development which could relate to tourism –

In order to satisfy needs linked to tourism, diversification will include market garden and fodder crops … synergy will also be established between measures to promote traditional products and the development of complementary activities, in particular tourism and rural craft industries.

The Netherlands – the Dutch CSF for the period 1989–1991[79] aimed at reviving regions affected by industrial decline and listed tourism as offering potential for regional development. Among the conversion objectives for the area, the text mentions:

Promotion of quality improvement

The Kwaliteitscentrum Noord–Nederland is providing assistance, primarily to small and medium–sized firms, with the setting up of quality assurance systems. Quality improvement offers considerable opportunities for industry, the transport sector and tourism.

Priority 2 deals with the role of tourism in the region's development priorities.

Further development of tourism potential

In view of the opportunities for tourism in the region, assistance will be granted for the expansion of tourism infrastructure, particularly for boating, the main centres of attraction and longer–stay tourism. Since these investments will have a substantial effect on regional development only if they are combined with an intensive image boosting and promotional campaign, measures of that nature will be given priority in the granting of assistance ... The ESF will finance tourism–related training measures concerned with upgrading and diversifying the region's tourist appeal and improving the qualifications of people employed in the tourist industry, the aim being to exploit the opportunities and strengths which exist in this field ... The following training measures may be envisaged: in the hotel industry: improving the skills of staff (matching supply to demand); in the provision of tourist services: vocational training (guides, cultural and sports monitors, reception staff, craft workers);rural tourism: training in reception, management and the organization of activities.

Operational programmes

Under Article 9 of Regulation 1260/99[80] an operational programme is defined as:

The document approved by the Commission to implement a Community support framework and comprising a consistent set of priorities comprising

---

[79] Community Support Frameworks 1989–91, NETHERLANDS, Pamphlet/Brochure produced by the Commission of the European Communities, pp.15–20.

[80] OJ L 161/12, 26.6.99.

multi–annual measures and which may be implemented through recourse to one or more Funds, to one of more existing financial instruments and to the EIB. An integrated operational programme means an operational programme financed by more than one Fund.

Thus, an operational programme is based on and is intended to implement a Community Support Framework. It is approved by the Commission, not the Council or the Member State, and lasts over a number of years.

Funding for tourism has been part of many operational programmes. While operational programmes generally cover a multitude of supports and actions over a range of industries, it is also possible to have an entire operational programme devoted to tourism funding. Such was the case with Ireland in 1992. The preamble to the relevant Commission Decision[81] stated:

> Whereas the aims of the operational programme are to maximise Ireland's tourist potential by increasing tourism revenue and thereby creating employment and so contribute to the priorities laid down for measures under the Community Support Framework for Ireland in question

Single programming documents (SPDs)

According to Article 9 of Regulation 1260/99 single programming document means:

> a single document approved by the Commission and containing the same information to be found in a Community support framework and operational programme.

An SPD thus combines two documents in one, the advantage being that the Commission needs to take only a "single decision" to make the funding system operational.

> A SPD contains the development strategy and details the actions to be funded; a CSF contains the development strategy but the actions to be funded are detailed in separate OPs.[82]

Allocation of funding to tourism can also arise under SPDs.

---

[81] Commission Decision C (94) 1972, 29.7.94. For information on other specifically tourism operational programmes for the 1993–1999 period, see Commission, Staff working paper, Community actions affecting tourism, SEC (97) 1419, 11.7.97, p.61.

[82] Commission, A Handbook on Environmental Assessment of Regional Development Plans and EU Structural Funds Programmes, August 1998, p.7.

Tourism Examples of OPs and SPDs

Regional Operational Programme for Calabria, Italy:[83] –

> The European Commission will actively participate in the development of Italy's Mezzogiorno by part-financing the Objective 1 programme for the Calabria region in 2000–2006. The programme is instrumental in implementing the Community Support Framework for Italy's Objective 1 regions. The contribution from the Structural Funds amounts to EUR 1 194 million out of an overall budget of EUR 5,863 million. Final approval date: August 8, 2000 Priority 4: Local development systems (EU contribution: about EUR 653,66 million) Promoting local production systems (in particular industrial districts and export systems) and new businesses, supporting demand for high-quality services and improving tourism supply.

Border, Midland and Western Operational Programme, Ireland[84] – Priority 2:

> Local enterprise development (EU contribution: about EUR 104,93 million) Measures under this priority will seek to tap into the entrepreneurial skills at the local level and to target projects where market failure has been demonstrated. Access to risk capital and in–company training will be particularly important. Tourism will be targeted in the less visited regions, commercial forestry will be encouraged to foster employment and environmental benefits, and infrastructure investments are planned in the fisheries and aquaculture sectors.

Flevoland, Netherlands SPD –

> There are four broad areas of activity or priorities in the single programming document which was approved: development of urban areas (€39.1 million), development of rural areas (€23.7 million), strengthening of production structures (€39.5 million) and social cohesion and the labour market (€20.2 million).
>
> The programme for Flevoland aims to promote investment in business or business, support activities with high growth potential in

---

[83] Commission, Community Measures Affecting Tourism (2000), SEC(2002) 300, 15.3.02, p.34.

[84] *Supra.*

some areas. Small and medium-sized enterprises will get special attention through support for research and development, development of e-commerce and the inter-nationalisation of their activities. An interesting aspect of the programme is the development of city outskirts through the stimulation of tourism and recreation activities.

The contribution of the EAGGF Guidance Section amounts to €10 million. This programme concerns the continuation of an active renewal policy in Flevoland. Coherent activities will be supported which will strengthen the rural area. Survival of the agricultural activity is vital for the provincial economy, as is the preservation of the rural landscape. Recreation and tourism are becoming more and more important in the transition of the urban area to the rural area, the city outskirts. Another aim is to improve the viability and nature values of the rural area.[85]

Evaluation

Evaluations of Structural Funds programmes have been an intrinsic part of the funding process almost from the beginning. Throughout the reforms of the regional policy, the evaluation and monitoring procedures have been strengthened and further elaborated. Presently Regulation 1260/99 provides for a variety of mechanisms for ensuring the propriety and effectiveness of spending under the various Funds. Title IV is headed *Effectiveness of Assistance from Funds* and imposes a series of oversight obligations on various parties, located within each Member State, including:

- monitoring by a managing authority and a monitoring committee,
- monitoring indicators,
- annual and final implementation reports,
- various financial controls,
- evaluation.

The Commission itself is also subject to a reporting obligation under Article 45 of the Regulation 1260/99 under which it is obliged to produce yearly and three yearly reports for debate by the various Community institutions dealing, in the former case with the activities of each Fund and related matters, and in the latter case with the progress made towards economic and social cohesion.[86]

---

[85] Commission, Twelfth Annual Report on the Structural Funds (2000), COM(2001) 539 final, October 3, 2001, p.46.

[86] For on–line versions of these annual reports, see http://www.europa.eu.int/comm/regional_policy/sources/docoffic/official/repor_en.htm.

Evaluation of programme performance is particularly important. Article 40 provides that:

> In order to gauge its effectiveness, Community structural assistance shall be the subject of ex-ante, mid-term and ex-post evaluation designed to appraise its impact with respect to the objectives set out in Articles 158 and 160 of the Treaty of Rome and to analyse its effects on specific structural problems

Ex-ante Evaluation

The purpose of ex-ante evaluation "shall be to provide a basis of preparing the development plans, assistance and programming complement of which it shall form part. Ex-ante evaluation shall be the responsibility of the authorities responsible for preparing the plans assistance and programme complement" – Article 41(1).

> The concept of the ex-ante evaluation includes the process through which it is undertaken, as much as the contents of the evaluation report. The Structural Fund regulation makes clear that the evaluation forms part of the programming document. The Commission's guide to the ex-ante evaluation suggests that the evaluation should be an interactive process between the evaluator and those responsible for the preparation of the plans, with the evaluators providing expert input and engaging in constructive dialogue with the planners. The ex-ante evaluation is therefore not only the content of the evaluation report, but also the process through which the evaluators interacted with the planners. The ultimate objective is to enhance the quality of the programming documents and thereby enhance the effectiveness and impact of the assistance supported by the Structural Funds.[87]

Mid–term Evaluation

Mid-term evaluation "shall examine, in the light of the *ex-ante* evaluation, the initial results of the assistance, their relevance and the extent to which the targets have been attained. It shall also assess the use made of financial resources and the operation of monitoring and implementation" – Article 42.

Mid-term evaluations of Structural Funds programmes were introduced in

---

[87] Commission, Twelfth Annual Report on the Structural Funds (2000), COM(2001) 539 final, 3.10.01, p.69.

1996. Previously there was no such stipulation, although in practice Member States organised evaluations at the request of the Commission using independent evaluators.

> Mid-term evaluation shall be carried out under the responsibility of the managing authority, in cooperation with the Commission and the Member State. It shall cover each Community support framework and each assistance. It shall be carried out by an independent assessor, be submitted to the Monitoring Committee for the Community support framework ... and then sent to the Commission, as a general rule three years after adoption of the Community support framework – Article 41(2).

> The Commission shall examine the relevance and quality of the evaluation on the basis of criteria defined beforehand by the Commission and the Member State in partnership, with a view to reviewing the assistance and allocating the reserve referred to in Article 44 – Article 41(3).

> As a continuation of mid-term evaluation, it shall be updated for each Community support framework and assistance and completed no later that 31 December 2005 in order to prepare for subsequent assistance operations – Article 41(4).

The Commission received a large number of mid-term evaluations of the 1993–1999 programmes mainly in 1997.[88]

Tourism Example of MTE

The mid-term evaluation of Ireland's tourism operational programme,[89] based on nine mid-term evaluations of individual operational programmes, is noteworthy in portraying a critical picture of the programme's effect.

> The Tourism OP is of medium size, accounting for £369 million, or over 8 per cent of SF spending. Against the background of a vigorous and sustained expansion in tourism output, there are two main challenges to a mid-term evaluation. First, understanding the degree to which this success is attributable to public spending programmes. ...

---

[88] See generally Commission, Mid-Term Review of Structural Interventions Objectives 1 and 6 (1994–99). For a list of evaluation reports, see Annex 3, p.35. Text available at http://europa.eu.int/comm/regional_policy/sources/docoffic/official/reports/pdf/ravi/texte_en.pdf.
[89] EU Structural Funds in Ireland: A Mid–Term Evaluation of the CSF 1994–99, ESRI Policy Research Series No. 31 Dublin (1997) ISBN No.0707001722 Honohan, P (Ed.), p.102 and pp.230–238.

Second, given the emerging problems of congestion, identifying the appropriate strategy for focusing future growth and management measures to relieve anticipated congestions without damaging the environment or otherwise causing adverse long-term repercussions on tourism demand. It should also be borne in mind that tourism benefits specifically from a number of tax concessions.

It also seems doubtful that the boom has been driven by the OP. Much of it has been in Dublin, where few facilities financed by the OP have come on stream, and there has been relatively little success in reducing the seasonal structure, though this was a key goal of the OP. Although tourism is job-intensive, the estimated cost-per-job created in tourism by the OP is, at £30,000, rather high. Furthermore, deadweight and negative externalities of a quite serious type seem to pervade the OP.

In addition to the Tourism OP itself, tourism–related spending is co-financed under about eight different OPs of CIs, and indeed, as noted by the MTE, tourism could be impacted by spending in almost any of the OPs or CIs. This has resulted in a scattershot approach to Tourism which is rightly criticised by the MTE.

Of the three sub-programmes, the first, TO1 – which helps with the funding of publicly owned facilities, including the major museum construction projects, national monuments, canals and national parks – comes in for criticism on the grounds that many of the projects being financed are more in the nature of conservation of local heritage rather than being likely to achieve a significant increase in tourist revenue. This judgment may be a little narrow, given the long-term focus of many of these projects, and the fact that a legitimate though non-tourism public purpose is being served by their completion. Indeed the MTE does not question the merits of the expenditure per se so much as the identification of associated tourist benefits.

TO2.1, the largest measure in the OP, is a grant facility for large 'flagship' projects. Such grants can be rationalised on the basis that there is a presumption of positive externalities in such projects not accruing to promoters. It has been envisaged that, apart from the proposed National Conference Centre, these projects would be located away from traditional tourist centres, but in many cases the projects being grant–aided are in areas already threatened with congestion: the externalities associated with these could be negative rather than positive.

Other measures under the Product Development sub–programme TO2 receive a mixed rating from the MTE. The danger of debasing the 'heritage town' designation under TO2.2 is noted; as are the problems of making the Angling measure TO2.3 effective, against a background of declining angler numbers and image problems. On the other hand the grant schemes for special interest holiday facilities and accommodation look like being greatly oversubscribed. However, it can be questioned whether the use of public funds is necessary for grant-aiding cruising, sailing and golf facilities which are privately profitable and whose externalities need not be positive. The MTE noted an absence of genuinely innovative products. If this sub–programme is being driven by an Ireland Inc. (italic) approach to the sector, that company looks seriously in need of a stronger strategic focus!

These passages reveal serious concerns about the effectiveness of the Irish tourism operational programme. It also provides indications as to what criteria are used to evaluate the use of Community funds and in that sense is a rich resource for future tourism plans and programmes. It would be interesting to make a comparative analysis of the Irish tourism programme/evaluation, and for example its Italian and Greek equivalents.

Ex–post evaluation

The purpose of ex-post evaluation is, by drawing on the evaluation results already available, to:

> cover the utilisation of resources and the effectiveness and efficiency of the assistance and its impact and … draw conclusions regarding policy on economic and social cohesion. It shall cover the factors contributing to the success or failure of implementation and the achievements and result, including their sustainability – Article 43(3).

It must be carried out by an independent evaluator within three years of the end of the programming period. As of the end of 2002 no evaluations were available from Community sources because many programmes did not finish until two years after the end of the last programming period and evaluations were still on-going.

CHAPTER CONCLUSION

The Treaty of Rome defines the purposes on which the vast amounts of regional aid are spent. Tourism remains a major beneficiary of this aid. Principles of sound financial management underlie the controls, checks and processes surrounding the use of Community regional aid. The principle of legal certainty underlies the extensive use by the Commission of guidelines to help states and parties follow correct programming procedures. For the future, the stronger evaluation and monitoring procedures introduced by the latest reform will provide more ample material to help evaluate the usefulness of tourism spending.

STUDENT TASKS

Undergraduate questions:

1. What are the aims of the Community cohesion policy?

2. Identify the Objective 1 and 2 regions in your state. What are main differences between Objective 1 and Objective 2 regions in the 2000–2006 programme?

3. Explain the principle of additionality.

4. Despite the improved evaluation and monitoring procedures governing the Structural Funds, tourism's role in regional development in Europe remains unclear. Comment.

Postgraduate questions:

1. EC cohesion policy is a guarantee for a strong and healthy tourism sector for Europe in the future.

   To what extent do you agree with this statement.

2. Discuss the current and potential role of the Committee of the Regions in promoting a regional policy.

3. "Rural tourism" as an opportunity for regional and local development and the role of Leader+ as a Community Initiative. Discuss.

CHAPTER 7

COMMUNITY CONSUMER PROTECTION AND TOURISM[1]

INTRODUCTION

This chapter examines the provisions of Community consumer law which affect tourists. Tourists are consumers of tourism products. When a tourist buys a tourism product, he/she suffers certain disadvantages. The tourist acts in a private capacity, while the product provider acts in a professional capacity. The product provider has the resources to study the market and tailor product, marketing and selling techniques to maximum advantage. The product provider makes many such contracts; the tourist usually makes only one per provider per trip. The individual tourist needs to buy the product more than the product provider needs to sell it.

The product provider has traditionally exploited the resulting economic inequality to adopt selling techniques and contract terms which can unfairly disadvantage the consumer. Typical tourism examples where this happened involve airline passenger contracts, package holiday contracts and timeshare contracts, although this has been changing as a result of the type of protection measure described in this chapter.

Community concerns with consumer and tourist protection are guided by the Treaty establishing the European Community (Rome Treaty) and have focused on, among other matters, consumer weaknesses resulting from marketing techniques, insufficient pre-contractual information, lack of clarity in defining the subject matter of a contract, and difficulties in rendering the product provider legally liable for problems which arise. Community responses to these problems have been varied and involve both policy and legal approaches. Most Community consumer measures affect all types of consumers, not just tourists:

Although there have been few measures directed specifically at the interests

---

[1] Susanne Storm, Marc Mc Donald.

of tourists, they do benefit significantly from measures designed to protect the interests of consumers generally.[2]

Among the few measures at Community level designed specifically with tourists in mind are the package holiday and timeshare directives, both of which are examined later in this chapter.

In a Green Paper in 2001[3] discussing the future direction of Community consumer policy the Commission categorised current consumer protection directives as follows:

> EU consumer protection directives fall into two broad categories: generally applicable directives and directives containing rules regarding specific sectors or selling methods. ...
>
> General Rules – Directive on Misleading Advertising, as amended by Directive on comparative advertising. Directive on price indications. Directive on unfair terms in consumer contracts. Directive on the sale of consumer goods and associated guarantees.
>
> Rules on sectors and selling methods – Directives on foodstuffs, cosmetics ... package travel, contracts negotiated away from business premises, consumer credit, distance selling contracts ... and timeshare. ...
>
> In addition, further EU legislation, which does not have consumer protection as its primary purpose, provides for some consumer protection. ... For example the e-commerce directive ... Furthermore, the Brussels Convention (now enshrined in an EU regulation) and the Rome Convention establish rules, in cases of a cross-border contractual dispute within the EU, to determine which Member State Court should hear the case (jurisdiction) and which Member State's law will apply to the contract (applicable law)...

To this can be added the directive on denied boarding compensation for airline passengers, which although in effect a consumer protection measure, comes under the responsibility of the Commission transport directorate-general. This directive forms part of a wider, increasingly important Community focus on improving the treatment of air passengers which it is convenient to deal with in

---

[2] Commission, Report on Community Measures affecting Tourism, COM (2001) 171 final, 28.3.01, p.26.

[3] Commission, Green Paper on European Union Consumer Protection, COM (2001) 531 final, 2.10.01, p.4.

this chapter.[4] Of the general directives on consumer protection, only one will be examined – the unfair contracts terms directive – since it holds significant potential for tourist protection on account of its broad sweep and immediate impact.

Tourists benefit under both general and sectoral approaches described above. A package traveller enjoys detailed protection under a sectoral law, and can also rely on a general law dealing with unfair contact terms where the specific law dos not go far enough.

Community activities in consumer protection have been channelled through a series of Action Plans since shortly before the introduction of strengthened Treaty references to consumer protection in 1992:

- First Action Plan 1990–1992.[5]
- Second Action Plan 1993–1995.[6]
- Third Action plan 1996–1998.[7]
- Fourth Action Plan 1999–2001.[8]

While the focus of these Plans has shifted over time, the following broad themes – mandated by the way the Treaty deals with consumer protection, as will be seen in the next section – have been pursued:

- improved health and safety of consumers;
- better information and education for consumers; and
- easier access to dispute settling procedures.

While each of these themes is of interest to tourists as well as other types of consumers, they are too broadly expressed to be further explored in the present context. However, specific elements of these themes can be found in two tourism directives dealing with package holiday and timeshare, particularly the pre-contractual provision of information.[9]

---

[4] Passenger safety issues, including tort law aspects such as personal injury and baggage loss/damage compensation issues are dealt with at p. 203 in the transport chapter, while delay and standard contract terms, issues are dealt with later in this chapter.

[5] Commission, COM(90) 98 final, 3.5.90.

[6] Commission, COM(93) 378 final, 28.7.93.

[7] Commission, COM(95) 519 final, 31.10.95.

[8] Commission, COM(1998) 696 final, 1.12.98.

[9] Another theme of Community consumer focus – protecting consumers against the use of improper distance selling techniques – is not so relevant to tourism, with the exception, as will be seen, of timeshare. The general Community measure in this area, Directive 97/7– OJ L 144/19, 4.6.97– on the protection of consumers in respect of distance contracts that is contracts made by distance communications, including letter, email, phone, fax, confers a

Future Community Consumer Policy

Some general remarks are appropriate in this introduction about the future direction of Community consumer policy since it bears on the way future Community measures may affect tourists.

Community consumer policy stands at a crossroads. Previously the focus has been mainly on specific consumer problems and specific responses to them. While this has brought some benefits to consumers, the Commission is not satisfied in light of the changing and fragmenting nature of the consumer marketplace, that the Community will be able to maintain the level of consumer protection required under the Treaty in a genuine internal market.

> Existing EU consumer protection directives, when compared to national regulation, do not constitute a comprehensive regulatory framework for business-consumer commercial practices, the central aim of consumer protection. While some areas have been effectively targeted, other key areas are not covered by EU rules, notably marketing practices linked to the contract, payment and after-sales services ... [Further, some] of the directives, notably the sector-specific ones, have developed as a very detailed response to specific identifiable problems at a particular moment in time. This approach combined with the long period between the proposal and implementation of EU measures ...has guaranteed a certain level of obsolescence as market practices have moved on. ... The time involved in modifying these directives to adapt them to technological development while attaining the same level of consumer protection compounds such inflexibility ... [Further, although] it is developing fast in many Member States, self regulation, through codes of conduct, is severely constrained at EU level. ... Self-regulation has been shown to be a potentially useful complement to regulation that can reduce the need for very detailed legislation and provide benefits for consumers.[10]

---

right to pre-contractual information, written confirmation of this information, a right to withdraw from the contract within seven working days without penalty or providing a reason, and a right to performance within a stipulated time. While tourist bookings for accommodation, flights and packages are distance contracts, Article 3(2) excludes from the Directive's protections "contracts for the provisions of accommodation, transport, catering or leisure services, where the supplier undertakes, when the contract is concluded, to provide these services on a specific date or within a specific period". This provision is broad enough to exclude most tourism bookings, except possibly the distance making of an open-ended accommodation contract with a hotel.

[10] Commission, Green Paper on European Union Consumer Protection, COM(2001) 531 final, 2.10.01, p. 5.

The Commission Green Paper in 2001 outlined how new forces, such as on-line transactions, and new commercial selling techniques, were shaping different consumer markets which the Community, in the absence of a general legal framework, could only tackle as and when the political will was there and in a slower fashion than national authorities. The key concern was that while national responses to emerging trends may satisfy national concerns, more divergent national responses threaten the reality of a genuine internal market, which is already subject to much divergence, both because of areas not covered by EU measures and because of divergences allowed under existing directives.

The key element of future Community legal response seems likely to be a broader targeting of unfair commercial practices, expressed as a business duty not to engage in unfair commercial practices which could result or lead to consumer detriment,[11] with reform of sector specific legislation, such as timeshare and package travel planned for the 2000–2006 period.[12]

Consumer Protection and Tourism

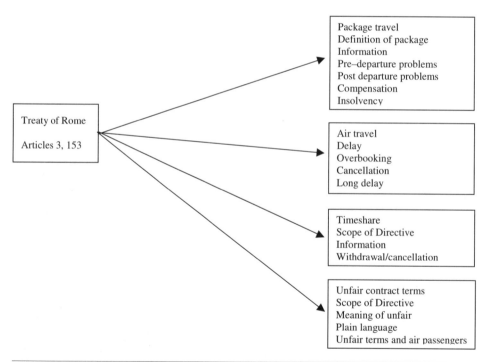

---

[11] Commission, Communication on follow-up to the Green Paper on EU consumer protection, COM(2002) 289 final, 11.6.02, p.8

[12] Commission, Communication on Consumer Policy Strategy 2002–2006, COM (2002) 208 final, 8.6.02, p.32

Learning Outcomes

After reading this chapter, the student should:

- be aware of how the Treaty of Rome shapes Community consumer protection and its impact on tourism,
- understand how Community consumer law addresses specific problems in tourism concerning package holidays, air travel and timeshare,
- appreciate how general consumer protection against the use of unfair contract terms applies to tourism contracts.

The above outcomes will be addressed through the following main headings:

The Treaty and Consumer Protection.
Package Travel.
Air Travel.
Timeshare.
Unfair Contract Terms.

THE TREATY AND CONSUMER PROTECTION

The legal competence of the Community to adopt measures to promote consumer protection is based on a series of provisions in the Treaty establishing the European Community (Treaty of Rome). The current version of the Treaty provides in Article 3:

> For the purposes set out in Article 2, the activities of the Community shall include … (t) a contribution to the strengthening of consumer protection.

Article 2, it will be recalled, fixes the creation of a common market as a primary goal of the Community. The Community therefore has competence in consumer matters in so far as it furthers the operation of the common market. For a long time this was the only basis for Community consumer action, but, as will be seen, this has now changed.

In line with the increasing importance of consumer protection during the 1980s and the realization that as a high-profile area it represents an opportunity for the Community to demonstrate its relevance to Union citizens, the Maastricht Treaty in 1992 inserted a new title on consumer protection into the Treaty of Rome. This was somewhat re-focused by the Amsterdam Treaty in 1997. Title XIV now identifies a hierarchy of objectives for Community consumer action – promoting consumer interests and ensuring a high level of consumer protection by contributing to the protection of:

> the health, safety and economic interests of consumers, as well as to promoting their right to information, education and to organise themselves in order to safeguard their interests – Article 153(1).

According to the Commission:

> The promotion of the health, safety and economic interests of consumers and of these three rights (to information, education and to organise themselves) are the fundamental objectives of EU consumer policy. Promoting these three rights is central to giving consumers a more powerful voice.[13]

Article 153(3) offers a choice of means by which these objectives can be attained:

- measures under Article 153(3)(a) designed to ensure completion of the internal market.
- measures which "support, supplement and monitor the policy pursued by the Member States" – Article 153(3)(b).

Both types of measure must be enacted using the co–decision procedure provided for in Article 251.

Thus, while Article 153(1) determines the focus or objective of Community activity, Article 153(3) provides the necessary legal rationale and thus shapes the contours or ambition of what can be done. Accordingly:

- measures under Article 153(3)(a) – justified by the internal market – are under the exclusive competence of the Community, are potentially very wide ranging and are not subject to the subsidiarity principle,
- measures under Article 153(3)(b) – designed to support and supplement Member States policy in consumer protection – can be adopted independently of the internal market, yet suffer from being an area of shared competence with the Member States and any proposed measures must be put to the subsidiarity test. Because of the need for a clear Community added benefit to any action in an area of shared competence, measures are subject to a greater scrutiny.

Despite being subject to subsidiarity, the insertion of Article 153(3)(b) into the Rome Treaty was warmly welcomed, providing a basis for the much expanded

---

[13] Commission Communication, Consumer Policy Action Plan 1999–2001, COM (1998) 696 final, 1.12.98, p.6.

Community involvement with consumer protection during the 1990's. According to the Commission, this Treaty provision:

> clearly requires the European Community to deal with the broad range of consumer issues, not just those related to the Internal Market project.[14]

Further, the use of the term 'measures' particularly as applicable to Article 153(3)(b) should be noted. Before 1997 the word used in the Treaty was "actions". The change is important, as "actions" are taken in the practical sphere and may take the form of Community research programmes and Commission Action Plans, whereas "measures" are legal steps in the form of regulations, directives, and decisions and thus permit Community legislative measures which are independent of the internal market.

Two further elements of the Rome Treaty should be briefly noted. Firstly, Community action must also ensure that consumer protection requirements are:

> taken into account in defining and implementing other Community policies and activities – Article 153(2).

Secondly, while Member State actions may impose higher levels of consumer protection than Community law requires, under Article153(5) these must still be compatible with the Treaty. This means that states can have stricter consumer laws if they wish, but divergences in levels of protection across the Community obviously carry the risk of inhibiting the genuine operation of the common market.

The general relationship between the Treaty, consumer protection and tourism can be seen in the following extract from a recent opinion in a package travel case by Advocate General Tizzano:[15]

> As is well known [the package holiday directive] forms part of the broad context of consumer protection policy which, over several decades, has undergone interesting developments not only in the Member States, but also at Community level. Originally based on sporadic and occasional measures adopted on the basis of [Article 94], Community action on consumer protection was subsequently given, first in the Single European Act and then in the Maastricht Treaty of 1992, express mention and a more transparent legal base in [Article 95], finally being incorporated independently as one of the Community policies. ... Thus in the course of

---

[14] Commission Communication, Priorities for Consumer policy, COM (95) 519 final, 31.10.95, p.2.

[15] *Leitner v. TUI* [2002] E.C.R. I–2631, para.2. See also p. 302.

time numerous important directives have been adopted, which have taken direct account of the need to protect consumers, in conjunction with directives geared to the implementation of the internal market and the progressive liberalization of the movement of goods and persons between the Member States.

So far consumer protection measures of specific benefit to tourists have been adopted within the context of the completion of the internal market. The standard justification for such measures is that national laws which fix varying rules and degrees of consumer protection impacting consumers as tourists can constitute both obstacles to the common market in tourism services and also distortions in competition among tourism service providers. The preamble to the Timeshare Directive typically expresses this justification:

> the disparities between national legislations ... are likely to create barriers to the proper operation of the internal market and distortions of completion and lead to the compartmentalization of national markets. [16]

But merely removing disparities could lead to the adoption of the lowest denominator as the basis for Community action. The requirement in Article 153(1) however that not alone must consumers be protected – thus simple removal is not enough – but a high level of consumer protection must be attained, prevents this. As will be seen, this has proved significant both in the construction of the contents of Community consumer measures directed at tourists, and also in the way any uncertainties surrounding such measures have been interpreted and resolved by the Court of Justice.

PACKAGE TRAVEL

Introduction

In the early 1980s the Commission surveyed the degree of consumer satisfaction with package holidays[17] and found significant levels of dissatisfaction. While the types of problems were not detailed it is common knowledge they included:

- failure of holiday to match brochure description,
- increases in contract price after booking,

---

[16] OJ L 280/83, 29.10.94.
[17] Commission Proposal for a Council Directive on Package Travel, including Package Holidays and Package Tours, COM (88) final, 21.3.88, p. 12.

- failure of tour operators to accept responsibility for problems caused by service suppliers, such as hotels,
- difficulties in obtaining compensation, and
- consumers stranded abroad after collapse of tour operator.

The Commission also surveyed Member State laws associated with package holidays and found considerable variations among them. Based on this the Commission concluded that the common market in tourism, of which package services is an essential part, was being distorted and that consumers were not obtaining the level of protection required under the Treaty. Therefore the basis existed for a harmonization measure designed to help complete the common market and ensure a high level of Community-wide consumer protection for package consumers.

For a variety of reasons, including the complexity of issues involved, the range of divergent interests and the need to strike a balance between tour operators/travel agents and consumers, it was not until 1990[18] that Directive 90/314[19] was finally agreed.[20] Since its passage the Directive has considerably succeeded in its deliberately broad objectives, though, as will be seen, at a cost. Vague provisions in the Directive which facilitate differing interpretations have figured not only in cases before the Court of Justice, but also in Commission efforts to secure a uniform application of the Directive and promote reform.

> The Directive's provision allow for a very large margin of interpretation for national legislators. Consequently, the approaches taken by the different Member States to transpose the Directive (and the level of protection of consumers' economic interests) differ considerably.[21]

---

[18] Until the Package Travel Directive was adopted in 1990, the 1970 International Convention on Travel Contracts and the 1979 OECD Council Recommendation on Package Holidays by Air dealt with the subject at the international level. The then twelve Member States each had very diverse national provisions for package holidays, including a civil law approach in Germany, administrative regulation in France, and a self–regulatory structure in the UK and Denmark. Belgium and Italy had adopted the 1970 International Convention on Travel Contracts. A description of the legal provisions of each Member State at the time of the Commission's submission of its first proposal to the Council is provided in the proposal – COM(88)41 final, 21.3.88, pp.2–10.

[19] OJ L 158/59, 23.6.90.

[20] The Danish, Greek, Italian and German delegations originally wanted only a recommendation. The legal base in Article 100a was questioned in the Council because of doubt whether the Directive could really be said to be part of the establishment of the internal market.

[21] Commission, Report on the Implementation of Directive 90/314/EEC on Package Travel and Holiday Tours in the Domestic Legislation of the EC Member States, SEC (1999) 1800 final, p.4.

The idea underlying the Directive is that the recreational opportunity offered by a holiday package is an important asset for the modern citizen for which compensation should be available when the opportunity is wrongfully denied. Historically, national laws were reluctant to award compensation for what can be called non-material or non-physical loss. But this reluctance has been abandoned as the numbers taking package holidays and the need to protect their recreational opportunities have increased. A recent Advocate-General opinion identified:

> a widespread trend, which has made varied progress in the different legal systems, towards a wider concept of liability for [non-material damage] and, more specifically, for damage arising out of a ruined holiday. This trend is linked to the overall development of the subject of liability, but also, from a more general point of view, to the rapid development of tourism and to the fact that holidays, travel and leisure breaks are no longer the privilege of a limited sector of society, but are a consumer product for a growing number of people to which they devote part of their savings and their holidays from work or school. The very fact that holidays have assumed a specific socio-economic role and have become so important for an individual's quality of life means that their full and effective enjoyment represents in itself an asset worth protecting.[22]

The legal basis in the Treaty for enacting the Directive, formerly Article 100a, now Article 95 is significant. Article 95(3) provides that when producing a proposal under this Article in relation, among other matters, to consumer protection, the Commission must "take as a base a high level of protection".

The consumer protection offered by the Directive will be examined under the following headings:

- Definition of package.
- Brochures and other information.
- Pre–departure problems.
- Post–departure problems.
- Compensation claims.
- Organiser/retailer insolvency.

---

[22] *Leitner v. TUI* [2002] E.C.R. I–2631, A-G's Opinion, para.43.

DEFINITION OF PACKAGE

The protections in the Directive apply to consumers of packages and are intended not only to prevent problems arising, but when they do, to enable a disappointed or injured holidaymaker obtain compensation for a ruined holiday. Liability for non-compliance with the Directive is generally, but not always imposed on the organiser, who equates with the tour operator, that is the person who other than occasionally organises and sells or offers packages for sale. As will be seen, the retailer, the travel agent, is also sometimes made responsible.

Package is the key concept and is defined in Article 2(1) of the Directive as follows:

> 'package' means the pre-arranged combination of not fewer than two of the following when sold or offered for sale at an inclusive price and when the service covers a period a period of more than twenty-four hours or includes overnight accommodation:
>
> (a) transport,
> (b) accommodation,
> (c) other tourist services not ancillary to transport or accommodation and accounting for a significant proportion of the package.
>
> The separate billing of various components of the same package shall not absolve the organiser or retailer from the obligations under this Directive.

The explanatory memo accompanying the original Commission proposal described the possible permutations of elements within a package. While travel is normally one of the components, it is not essential.

> The essence of package travel is that what is offered and accepted is a combination of not less than two elements. The combination commonly includes travel and accommodation in an hotel with all meals. But it may consist of travel and self-catering in a chalet or cottage, or, conceivably of travel to and from the holiday place, plus excursions to places of interest or pleasure from that holiday place, the consumer being responsible for providing his own accommodation and meals; or, in some circumstances (certain sporting holidays, for example) accommodation in, say, school buildings, with self-catering for meals, the organiser making available sporting equipment and instruction but no travel – it being part of the holiday arrangement that the holidaymakers arrange their own travel to and from the holiday place.[23]

---

[23] Commission Proposal for a Council Directive on package travel, including package holidays and package tours, COM (88) final, 21.3.88, p.10.

Pre–arranged

The combination must be pre-arranged, which includes, as would be expected, an off-the-shelf package, that is one prepared by a tour operator in advance of an individual request, and also as the Court of Justice recently held *in ClubTour v. Garrido*,[24] tailor-made packages, that is packages put together by a travel agent typically at the request of a consumer. The inclusion of tailor-made packages surprised some who had considered the directive applied only to off-the-shelf packages. However, as the Court of Justice's decision makes clear:

> There is nothing in [the definition of package] to suggest that holidays organised at the request and in accordance with the specifications of a consumer or a defined group of consumers cannot be considered as package holidays within the meaning of the Directive.[25]

The Court relied on a textual reading or analysis of the definition of package in reaching its conclusion, while the preceding opinion of the Advocate General[26] relied additionally on policy statements in the Directive's preamble and on the Rome Treaty requirement that adopted measures take a high degree of consumer protection.

While the effects of the decision in the ClubTour case may take some time to be appreciated, the Commission's thinking was already moving along similar lines.

> Within the definition of 'package' … the word 'pre-arranged' appears to be artificial, of unclear meaning and effect and could be eliminated. The consumers' need for protection may, in some circumstances, be the same with regard to tailor-made as with regard to other packages.[27]

"Pre-arranged" also emphasises another dimension of the definition of a package. An organiser's liability under the Directive only applies to whatever was arranged or committed to before the package contract was made and not to services

---

[24] [2002] E.C.R. I–4051.

[25] *Ibid.*, para.14.

[26] [2002] E.C.R. I–4051.

[27] Commission, Report on the Implementation of Directive 90/314/EEC on Package Travel and Holiday Tours in the Domestic Legislation of the EC Member States, SEC (1999) 1800 final, p.8. The decision in *AFS Finland* [1999] E.C.R. I–825 may also be seen as an example of the Court implicitly treating a tailor made package as coming within the definition of package, only, however, to still exclude it on the basis that a free stay with a family did not amount to accommodation within the definition.

contracted for afterwards. Case law in a number of states has dealt with issues of organiser liability for injuries to tourists who bought excursions from third parties while on package holidays, either through or independently of the organiser's representative. Courts in such states have resisted attempts to impose liability on organisers for such third party acts on the basis that the definition of package in the Directive only applies to those elements of a package agreed in the contract and not to optional excursions made while on the holiday. Since an organiser might arrange matters so that an excursion lies outside a package, a Court of Justice ruling on how to differentiate between pre- and post-departure excursions would be helpful.

Business Packages

The Directive also protects business packages. The title of the Directive refers to package travel, holidays and tours respectively and in the explanatory memo accompanying the original proposal the Commission declared it had:

> widened the scope of its work so as to cover not only package holidays but the whole field of package travel. Thus a package holiday to one destination is covered. A package tour to several destinations is covered. Conference travel, health travel, business or professional travel combined with leisure travel, are covered. The essential criterion is that the travelling consumer has contracted for a travel package. If he has, the rules … would apply.[28]

Further, Article 2(4) states that "Consumer means the person who takes or agrees to take the package." This indicates that the reason a person takes a package is irrelevant. According to the Advocate–General in *AFS Finland*:[29]

> The purpose of the Directive, it's wording and the preparatory work leading up to it, disclose nothing to suggest that its scope is limited exclusively to tourist services.

And further:

> The scope of the Directive's application cannot, therefore, be defined by reference the purpose of the travel.

---

[28] Commission Proposal for a Council Directive on Package Travel, including Package Holidays and Package Tours, COM (88) final, 21.3.88, p.13.
[29] *Supra*, pp.832, 833.

Overnight or 24 Hours

The package must include either an overnight stay or last at least 24 hours. The Commission recently highlighted the effect of the 24 hour cut-off point:

> For example, an arrangement consisting of a ticket for the Soccer World Cup Final and a return ticket for the same day could easily cost more than an average one week package tour. The need for consumer protection is comparable in these circumstances.[30]

Irrelevance of Destination

The protection of the Directive does not depend on the consumer's destination. This is clear from the words "sold or offered for sale" in the definition of a package which suggest that the destination or departure point does not matter. All that is required is that the package is sold or offered for sale within the Community. The consumer who buys a package for travel either outside or inside the Community and from a tour operator who is located either outside or inside the Community is equally protected.

Occasional Packages

The Directive ensures that only professional tour operators are caught by its provisions. It declares in Article 2(1) that organiser means "the person who, other than occasionally, organises packages." The Commission recently highlighted the vagueness of this. Among different national approaches, Ireland[31] has interpreted occasionally as excluding from the Directive a conference package organised by a professional etc association through an organizing committee, a package organised by a firm for its employees, a package organised by a community/voluntary association in connection with its general objectives and a package organised by an educational institution for its teachers and students.

---

[30] Commission, Report on the Implementation of Directive 90/314/EEC on Package Travel and Holiday Tours in the Domestic Legislation of the EC Member States, SEC (1999) 1800 final, p.10.

[31] Package Holidays and Travel Trade Act 1995 (Occasional Organisers) Regulations S.I. No. 271 of 1995.

BROCHURES

Package consumers rely heavily on holiday brochures.

> Descriptive matter about package travel is usually contained in brochures issued by organisers. It may equally be contained in newspapers or other periodicals. ... Wherever it appears, it must be stated so clearly and understandably that the customer, or prospective customer, can actually read it, grasp its meaning and not be misled.[32]

To protect consumers against misleading information and to try to decrease the likelihood of misunderstanding as to what exactly is being offered by the organiser, the Directive takes two approaches:

- it imposes a duty to include certain information in the brochure (where one is used), and allows Member States make either the "retailer or organiser" liable for its inaccuracies – Article 3(2). It also requires more journey-oriented information (travel route details, organiser/retailers local representative details, insurance information, specific child travel information) to be supplied "in good time before the start of the journey" – Article 4(1)(b),

- it stipulates information which must be included in the package contract, says the contract must be in writing or other comprehensible and accessible form and given to the consumer before the contract is concluded. It also requires Member States to make the "organiser and/or retailer party to the contract" liable for compliance with the contract – Article 5(1).

The information to be provided in the brochure and contract is broadly similar (although in the contract it must be tailored to the specific person) – price, destination, details of travel route, transport and accommodation, meal plan, passport, visa and health formalities.

PACKAGE PROBLEMS

Pre–departure Problems

Two broad categories of problem can arise after a package contract is made and before departure:

- the consumer may change his/her mind and no longer wish to travel whether

---

[32] Commission Proposal for a Directive, p.16.

because of unavoidable reasons such as illness, close bereavement or other less meritorious ones,

- the organiser may want to change some of the contract terms because he/she miscalculated the profit margin, or because of increased prices from his suppliers, or increased airport charges, exchange rates etc or because some promised elements of the package cannot now be delivered, such as the promised hotel, location, departure/returning airport etc.

Transferring the Package

Under Article 4(3) the consumer who "is prevented from proceeding with the package" is given an entitlement, on reasonable notice to the organiser,[33] to transfer the package to another person who satisfies any conditions applicable to the package. Both consumer and substitute package user then become jointly liable for the contact price and costs associated with the transfer.

The original Commission proposal made the transfer entitlement conditional on "serious reasons (such as sickness, bereavement)". This was dropped after the Economic and Social Committee commented as follows:[34]

> This paragraph provides for the transfer of bookings from one consumer to another for certain specified 'serious reasons' (such as illness and bereavement). ... However, the committee is of the opinion that it should be possible to transfer bookings from one tourists/consumer to another provided that all additional costs are compensated for.

Whether the current Directive is as flexible as this remains to be seen since it still uses the term "prevented" which implies that the pre-condition to the transfer entitlement should be a cause beyond the control of the consumer.

The entitlement is one of transfer, not sale. If a consumer sought to "sell" a package to another person, say it was obtained at a sale price, under the guise of this entitlement, it is likely he/she would in most Member States be treated as acting as a travel agent without official authorisation and the contract might also be legally unenforceable.

---

[33] In its survey of implementation of the Directive the Commission termed this an imprecise provision and found wide variations in how it was interpreted by the Member States, ranging from any time before departure to 3 weeks – Report on the Implementation of the Directive, p.5.

[34] ECSC, Opinion on the proposal for a Council Directive on Package Travel, including Package Holidays and Package Tours, OJ C 102/28, 24.4.89.

Consumer Cancellation

The Directive does not deal with consumer cancellation of a package contract, though it does deal with organiser cancellation, as is seen below. Where a consumer cancels Member state rules dealing with the power of an organiser to impose cancellation charges will in all likelihood then apply. The fairness of these charges will, however, be subject to another Community consumer protection measure, the Unfair Contract Terms Directive.[35] The Commission recently highlighted this omission in the Directive.

> The Directive makes no provision for the case where the consumer withdraws without good reason from the travel contract. In practice, travel contracts contain 'penalty clauses' that specify penalties of up to 100% of the package price (depending on when the withdrawal is effected). Yet such penalties should be limited to a reasonable extent, corresponding to the damage caused by such behaviour .... There is no justification for the consumer, in the case where the contact is not executed due to the fault of the organiser, will receive compensation only for proven damage, while the tour operator needs not to prove any damage in order to obtain a 'penalty' payment in the case of unjustified withdrawal by the consumer.[36]

Tour operators use sliding scales to calculate consumer cancellation fees. At the behest of the Commission a group of package travel legal experts recommended the following principles regarding such scales:[37]

- The fees contained within any scale should not be higher than agreed by industry and consumer groups or public authorities in those States where this system is used, unless such agreements explicitly allow for exceptions.
- The fees should follow the principle of "liquidated damages" in other states. In other words, the operator must make a fair, reasonable and genuine pre-estimate of the loss it is likely to suffer if the consumer cancels at a given period before his planned departure.
- Operators may also use a system where cancellation charges are individually assessed. In such cases, any method of calculation used by the operator must be fair, reasonable and genuine.

---

[35] See p. 326.

[36] Commission, Report on the Implementation of the Directive, p.11.

[37] Round Table on Package Travel Contracts, Conclusions of the Expert Group, 13.2.01, p.5. Text available at http://www.europa.eu.int/comm/consumers/policy/developments/pack_trav/pack_trav03_en.pdf.

– In all cases, the operator must set out its cancellation terms in an
unambiguous and transparent manner.

Price Alterations

Surcharging, that is raising the price after the contract is made, was a common
feature of package holiday contracts before the Directive was made. Article
4(4) now greatly limits this in two ways. Firstly,

> During the last twenty days prior to the departure date stipulated, the price
> stated in the contract shall not be increased.

Secondly, before the last twenty days, surcharging is only allowed (if the contract
allows it) for a narrow range of reasons which lie beyond the organiser's control,
viz.,

– transportation costs, including the cost of fuel,

– dues, taxes or fees chargeable for certain services, such as landing taxes
or embarkation or disembarkation fees at ports and airports,

– the exchange rate applied to the particular package – Article 4(4)(a).

Agreeing on these limits to price increases was a controversial matter and the
present rules differ from the Commission's original proposal. That would have
allowed price increases up to 2% of the package price for the above reasons,
coupled with a consumer choice of either no increase at all in the last 30 days
before departure or no increase in the 3 months after the contract was made, but
not necessarily before departure.[38]

Other Organiser Alterations

The Package Travel Directive offers significant protection to the consumer
against the organiser making alterations to the contract after the contract has
been made. Under Article 4(5) if before departure the organiser "significantly
alters any of the essential terms" of the contract, such as the price,[39] the consumer
must be notified as quickly as possible and has the right:

---

[38] Commission, Proposal for a Council Directive on Package Travel, including Package Holidays
and Package Tours, OJ C 96/3, 12.4.88.

[39] The original Commission proposal was that the price change must be at least 10% of the
contract price – OJ C 96/7, 12.4.88. Its replacement by "significant" probably suggests the
Commission regarded 10% as a significant price change. Even a 5% change could be
significant if it meant the consumer could no longer afford the package.

- either to withdraw from the contract without penalty,

- or accept a rider to the contract specifying the alterations made and their impact on the price.

If the consumer withdraws from the contract he/she has a further series of protections:

- he/she can accept a substitute package offered by the organiser (if the organiser is able to offer one and repayment of the price difference, if any),

- or he/she must be repaid all sums paid under the contract.

In either case, the consumer is also entitled to compensation for non–performance of the contract if appropriate – Article 4(6) – from either the organiser or retailer, depending on which the Member State chooses to make liable. The amount of compensation is examined later.

Delayed Departure

The Directive does not specifically indicate whether its protection applies in the event of a delay in departure, say, from the airport. Delays could force an organiser to alter the destination or duration or even cancel the package. Do the Directive's protections apply in such a case? The solution to this question depends on the correct interpretation of the Directive's words and particularly the word "departure". The term is used on its own in the relevant provision – Article 4(5) – which is vague (it could mean either the date or actual departure), while elsewhere in the Directive reference is made to the "date of departure" and "dates, times and points of departure." Given that the Treaty requires a high level of consumer protection, it seems likely the Directive's protections do apply to changes made by a tour operator arising from delayed flight departure. The Commission's original proposal dealt with the matter explicitly when it listed as one of the circumstances which would trigger the Directive's protections:

> an unreasonable delay in departure, howsoever caused, otherwise than by his own fault.[40]

Yet the Economic and Social Committee criticised this as being imprecise and expressed the opinion:

> Possibly a delay in excess of 24 hours would be sufficient to justify

---

[40] OJ C 96/7, 12.4.88.

withdrawal from the contract while delays of between 12 and 24 hours might be subject of monetary compensation.[41]

Organiser Cancellation

If instead of significantly altering essential contract terms, an organiser chooses to cancel the agreed package before departure, a consumer enjoys the same rights as with alteration, that is he/she can accept a substitute package offered by the organiser or be repaid the money paid with, in either case, a right to compensation for breach of the contract, except in two instances:

• cancellation because the organiser was unable to make up the stipulated minimum number of people needed for the package,

• cancellation due to *force majeure* (excluding overbooking), that is:

> unusual and unforeseeable circumstances beyond the control of the party by whom it is pleaded, the consequences of which could not have been avoided even if all due care had been exercised – Article 4(6).

Post-departure Problems

There are two types of legal response envisaged by the Directive to post departure problems with a package:

• responses dealing with problems which arise while the package is on–going, that is, for example, while the person is still abroad on the package, and

• responses dealing with the problems on return home.

Only the former will be dealt with now. The latter concerns claims for compensation and, along with compensation claims which arise for pre-departure problems, can more conveniently be dealt with later.

   The Directive offers two protections for problems which arise when the consumer has departed on the package:

• a right to have suitable alternative arrangements made, or alternatively a right to be brought home early at no extra cost to the consumer, and

• independently of this, a right to prompt assistance where difficulties arise which cannot be attributed to the organiser.

---

[41] ECS, Opinion on the proposal for a Council Directive on Package Travel, including Package Holidays and Package Tours, OJ C 102/29, 24.4.89.

Right to Alternative Arrangements

The right to be offered a suitable alternative or if this cannot be or is not done, the right to be brought home, is dependant, in the first instance, on there being a present/future failure by the organiser to provide a significant proportion of the services contracted for. The cause of the failure, that is whether the organiser is to blame or not and whether the event was foreseeable or not, does not matter. Significant is the key word here, which it would seem should be objectively interpreted, taking account of the difference between what was promised in the brochure and contract and what is/can be delivered. The degree to which the consumer's ulterior motives or expectations will be disappointed is not the issue as regards whether the difference is significant. It is merely a factual matter of the degree of difference between what was promised and what will be provided.

Organisers will usually want to avoid the more expensive option of bringing the consumer home before the end of the package. However, any alternative offered must be reasonably suitable to the consumer, and not what the organiser believes is suitable, because Article 4(7) allows the consumer reject the alternative "for good reasons". Thus, the consumer's reasonable expectations and wishes do matter and must be taken into account by the organiser and may make the possibility of finding a suitable alternative more difficult.

Right to Prompt Assistance

The consumer right to be offered an alternative or be brought home early arises regardless of the reason why the organiser cannot provide a significant proportion of the services contracted for. However, the second consumer right to prompt assistance in relation to post-departure problems only arises where the reason why a substantial part of the package cannot be provided is beyond the organiser's control, that is:

- such failures are attributable to a third party unconnected with the provision of the services contracted for, and are unforeseeable or unavoidable,

- such failures are due to a case of *force majeure* … or to an event which the organiser and/or retailer or the supplier of services, even with all due care, could not foresee or forestall – Article 5(2).

A likely scenario where this right might arise is when a tour party is trapped in a hotel or on an island by civil unrest or torrential rain or an earthquake. The pro-active level of assistance offered should probably attempt to alleviate the duration and nature of the discomfort and anxiety caused by the event and also provide medical assistance where needed and if possible. However, the precise extent of the organiser's duty must await a definitive ruling from the Court of Justice.

The Directive does not say what the consequences of a failure by an organiser to respect the consumer's rights in relation to a post-departure problem should be. This appears to allow Member States to declare any breaches to be subject to an award of damages or a criminal sanction or both.

Organiser's Liability for Suppliers

One of the major innovations of the Package Travel Directive is to make the organiser legally responsible for the acts of his/her package suppliers. Thus, under Article 5(1) an organiser is liable not only for his/her own performance but also for that of, say, the airline, the coach operator, the hotel, the tour guide and other suppliers of contracted services. The tendency before the Directive was for organisers to reject liability for the acts of their suppliers. Since the Directive's enactment, consumers disappointed with their package will usually have someone in their own jurisdiction to sue, if they need to. Where the organiser is located outside the consumer's jurisdiction, the retailer is also now often made liable as well.

The desire to make the organiser liable to the consumer, however, also had to take account of the fairness of making the organiser liable for all supplier inspired consumer loss connected with the contract. Thus, as will be seen shortly, the organiser will seldom be liable for all the loss, only part of it.

Basis of Organiser's Liability

Article 5(2) makes the organiser liable for damage following the failure to properly perform the contract unless the failure is due neither to the organiser or supplier's fault because the fault is attributable:

- to the consumer,
- a third party unconnected with the contract and the failure was unforeseeable and unavoidable, or
- to *force majeure*, or other event which even with all due care could not have been foreseen or forestalled.

This appears to impose a rebuttable presumption of fault on the organiser where there is a failure to perform the contract with possible defences limited to the three listed scenarios (the indented defences) which cover so much of the possible excuses it is difficult to imagine any others for which the organiser could not be blamed. It is in effect a type of strict liability under which a consumer does not have to prove organiser fault.

However, there is need for caution in this area of law. Consumer loss can consist of either failure to meet the contract promises or physical/property injury. Some legal opinion appears to consider, despite what Article 5(2) appears to say, that different bases of liability attach to each type of loss. The view that has emerged is that the basis of liability for not keeping contract promises is strict liability which does not require a consumer to prove organiser fault, while the basis of liability for personal injuries is fault liability which does require a consumer to prove organiser fault.

The explanation for this surprising legal view appears to be as follows. To the extent that the Directive allows it, both the organiser and consumer are free to agree package contract terms. An organiser might thus promise only to make reasonable efforts/take reasonable care to do something. If a consumer wanted to claim compensation for breach of such a promise, it would be necessary to prove a lack of reasonable effort/care, in effect and apparently contrary to what Article 5(2) appears to say, prove organiser fault. The key issue however is whether the Directive does allow an organiser promise only reasonable behaviour. Of some importance in this regard is the fact that the Directive lists the mandatory elements of a package contract – Article 4(2) and the Directive's Annex. A mandatory element in a contract must be performed, a promise to make a reasonable effort to perform it would not be enough. This is reason to suppose that an organiser's freedom to promise only reasonable efforts/care at least as regards list matters is restricted significantly. Further, since Community law requires a purposive approach to be taken to the interpretation of the Directive, the appropriate performance term for a package contract may well be a term that the package is fit for the purpose for which it is intended, rather than a term that reasonable care will be taken. This too would restrict the use of promises based on reasonable efforts/care and thus frustrate organiser efforts to force a consumer prove organiser fault as a condition to making a case for compensation. It would duly follow then that there are not two bases of liability for different types of consumer loss, only one, strict liability as set out in Article 5(2) with its narrow indented defences.

Overall, however, it is not possible to be definitive in this area and a ruling from the Court of Justice would be welcome.

Consumer Compensation

Under the Directive compensation is awardable to consumers who suffer damage in connection with a breach of package contract.[42] Damage can comprise

---

[42] Compensation is payable in proportion to actual loss. If compensation has already been paid for delay in the air transport part of the package, it would not be payable again for the same delay under the Package Travel Directives.

material/physical and non-material/non-physical damage. Material/physical damage, such as physical injury or property loss or damage, is clearly compensatable under the Directive because it is mentioned in it. Non-material damage, such as disappointment and loss of recreational opportunity, although not explicitly mentioned, is also covered.

In *Leitner v. TUI*,[43] an Austrian case, a girl lost the second week of her package holiday while she recovered from food poisoning in the first week. Austrian law did not allow for compensation to be awarded for non-material loss. However, the Court of Justice held such loss was recoverable under the Directive and that Austria had failed to fulfil its obligations in not providing for it.

Compensation for loss of recreational opportunity and associated anguish and upset is difficult to quantify and can err on the side of being generous since the destruction of precious holiday opportunity can appear serious. Hence Article 5(2) of the Directive, in balancing the imposition of liability, at least initially, allows three circumstances where an organiser can limit the amount of compensation to be paid:

- where it is written in the contract and is not unreasonable,
- where certain international air/ferry/hotel conventions already allow it,
- where a consumer fails to communicate a complaint about a perceived contract failure to the organiser/retailer and supplier,

"in writing or any other appropriate form at the earliest opportunity" – Article 5(4). Since this obligation is usually treated as a contract term, its breach by a consumer will ultimately lead to a reduction in the amount of compensation received.

The first two circumstances merit further comment. In its 1999 survey of how Member States implemented the requirement that any limit must not be unreasonableis, the Commission commented that:

Here again, the views on which limitation would have to be considered 'unreasonable' seem to differ considerably. While some Member States have simply not transposed the provision (thus applying the general rules of their tort law) or have taken over the provision of the Directive, others have issued more detailed provisions. The Commission, being in charge of the control of application of the Directive, would for its part consider

---

[43] [2002] E.C.R. I–2631.

'unreasonable' [applicable] in cases of gross negligence; this policy appears to be in keeping with the general rules of tort law in all Member States.[44]

If the Commission is correct the compensation limits of five/three and twice (for adults) the package cost in Portugal, Germany and Ireland respectively, regardless of how the organiser may have acted, may be open to question. Probably they should allow for no limit where the organiser acted with gross negligence.

The second way that organisers can limit their liability is based on the existence of international conventions which allow airlines, ferries/cruise ships and hotels reduce their liability for injury and property loss to their customers when they are directly sued. Since the Directive makes the organiser liable for the acts of the airline/ferry/hotel supplier of services to the package contract, it was considered unfair to make the organiser liable, where the breach was caused by the supplier, for more than the supplier would be liable for if it was sued. Thus, the Directive:

> allows compensation to be limited in accordance with the international conventions governing such services – Article 5(2).

Until the recent reform of some of these conventions[45] this wording represented an exception to the requirement that the Directive offer a high level of protection to consumers since the convention limits themselves were quite low and in some cases even unreasonable.

Organiser/Retailer Insolvency

Organisers, especially smaller ones, are vulnerable to changes in the demand for holiday and business packages and can collapse leaving unpaid hotels and airlines who refused to honour unpaid bookings. Consumers who have booked and paid for their holiday but not yet departed can also suffer loss when the collapse occurs.

To provide protection against these possibilities, Article 7 of the Package Travel Directive requires:

> The organiser and/or retailer party to the contract shall provide sufficient

---

[44] Report on the Implementation of Directive 90/14/EEC on Package Travel and Holiday Tours in the Domestic Legislation of the EC Member States, SEC (1999) 1800 final, p.6.

[45] For airlines, see p. 204. For ferries/cruise ships see p. 220.

evidence of security for the refund of money paid over and for the repatriation of the consumer in the event of insolvency.[46]

Proper implementation of this has proved the most controversial part of the Directive. According to the Commission, Article 7:

> left the largest margin of interpretation and has therefore been transposed in very different ways by the various Member States. The European Court of Justice have made a number of decision with reference to Article 7.
> [47]
> ...

The original Commission proposal[48] for dealing with organiser collapse involved compulsory insurance and a reserve fund for circumstances where the insurance cover was inadequate. The insurance would have dealt with claims in relation to contract performance and the reserve fund with any insolvency. The insurance requirement was deleted in later stages, possibly because when inability to meet consumer claims for faulty performance pushed an organiser into insolvency, the protection under Article 7 would apply anyway.

Among others, Germany and Austria failed to properly implement Article 7 within the required timeframe. In separate proceedings referred by national courts to the Court of Justice – *Dillenkofer v. Germany*[49] and *Recbburger v. Austria*[50] – the Court held both states to be liable for losses suffered by citizens who suffered from organiser collapse. Neither state had ensured adequate security was available, as Article 7 required, and the Court applied the principle that states can be liable for citizen loss flowing directly from state failure to implement a directive designed to offer protection to individuals.

Proper implementation of Article 7 requires Member States to supervise the package market to determine if adequate levels of security are maintained. According to the Commission:[51]

The organiser's/retailer's duty to provide security for the event of his

---

[46] Note unpaid hotels and other suppliers of services are not protected by the Directive against the insolvent organiser. Many, especially in the tourist receiving states, feel they should be.
[47] Commission, Report on the Implementation, p. 3.
[48] OJ C 96/8, 12.4.88.
[49] [1996] E.C.R. I–4845.
[50] [1999] E.C.R. I–3499.
[51] *Ibid.*, p. 5.

insolvency, require public authorities to undertake steady efforts to supervise the market and to enforce the law. Many Member States have therefore instituted a licensing system under which each travel organiser/ retailer needs to fulfil certain requirements in order to obtain a licence that would allow him pursue his business. In other Member States, some organisers/retailers need to hold a licence whereas others do not. In this context the Commission would point out that the provisions of the Directive must be applied without any discrimination to all travel organisers/retailers, not only to those who are in possession of a valid licence or who would be obliged to hold one.

Case law provides some guidance on two of the central features of Article 7:
- what consumer losses should the organiser's 'adequate security' cover when the holidaymaker is stranded abroad?
- what is an adequate level of security?

In *VKI v. OK*,[52] an Austrian case from 1998, the insurer of an insolvent organiser refused to reimburse holidaymakers who having paid the tour operator before departure then had to pay their hotel expenses after the collapse. The resulting dispute centered on the meaning of the word 'repatriation' in the Directive and whether the organiser's security had to cover hotel bills paid by the stranded holidaymakers, or covered only flight home and taxi to the airport. The Court of Justice ruled[53] that Article 7 must be interpreted:

> as covering, as security for the refund of money paid over, a situation in which the purchaser of a package who has paid the travel organiser for the costs of his accommodation before travelling on his holiday is compelled, following the travel organiser's insolvency, to pay the hotelier for his accommodation in order to be able to leave the hotel and return home.

Calculating an adequate level of security is not easy. Some states rely on a percentage of the previous/anticipated level of the organiser's/retailer's turnover. This approach carries the risk, depending on the % amounts involved, that it might not be enough where significant increases in business makes calculations based on previous turnover insufficient.

---

[52] [1998] E.C.R. I–2949.
[53] *Ibid.*, p. 2965.

In *Rechberger v. Austria*[54] the Court of Justice ruled that Austria had failed to properly implement the Directive because it set % amounts (not less than 5%) that did not offer enough security:

> having regard to the fact that the sum secured is calculated on the basis of the turnover achieved by a given agency during the preceding year ... the specific arrangements ... were inadequate given that the [Austrian] Regulation only requires a limited guarantee both in terms of the amount of cover and the basis on which that cover is calculated. That system therefore appears structurally incapable of catering for events ... such as a significant increase in the number of bookings in relation to ... the turnover for the previous year.[55]

In fact, no matter what % is set, it seems clear the legal obligation is that there must be sufficient money available to recompense consumers. The precise ways in which other Member States have provided for adequate security and the Commission's view as to whether these satisfy Article 7 is detailed in Annex II of the Commission Implementation Report.[56]

Among the principles summarised by the Commission for ensuring adequate security is provided by organisers/retailers are:

> The guarantor (be it an insurance company, a financial institute, a trustee or a joint guarantee fund) should take over unlimited liability. The amount to be refunded must not be limited to any maximum refund or maximum portion.

> Security must provided by a guarantor who himself is not exposed to the risks consequent on insolvency. ...

> The security, whatever its nature, should be quickly available. ...[57]

Conclusion

The Commission and the Court of Justice have indicated that the Package Travel Directive should be interpreted in the light of the policy reasoning in the Directive's preamble and also the Treaty of Rome requirement that a high level of protection is offered to consumers. This inevitably justifies a broad

---

[54] [1999] E.C.R. I–3499.
[55] *Ibid.*, p. 3543.
[56] Pages 26–41.
[57] *Ibid.*, p.19.

interpretation of the Directive and attempts to rely on general expressions used in the Directive to claim a narrower scope for the protection of consumers of packages seem unlikely to succeed. Future reforms of the Directive seem likely to broaden its scope.

AIR TRAVEL

Air travel is not the only means of tourist movement but it is a major one and has arguably been the object of more Community attention than other forms of transport. And while the Commission has recognised that passengers encounter real difficulties with other forms of transport which should be addressed,[58] the primary focus at present rests with air travel.

Despite the advantages accruing from the liberalization of passenger air travel in the European Community,[59] dissatisfaction with air travel impacting tourists and other travellers has increased. According to the Commission:

> In the European Union today, more people than ever are flying for both business and pleasure. Moreover, many of them are doing so at historically low prices, taking advantage of the bargain fares and new routes that are being offered as competition hots up between airlines inside the liberalised EU market.
>
> Yet the Commission, along with the European Parliament and the national administrations, receives a constant steam of complaints from European citizens who are disappointed with the service they have received. In a number of areas, it seems that the air transport system is not living up to the passengers' expectations.
>
> Naturally, in an open and competitive market, our first reaction must be to let passengers themselves solve the problem by 'voting with their feet' and switching airlines or transport mode. Over the long term this will always be the most effective sanction of all. …
>
> However, there are some instances where the passenger cannot send a message by taking their business elsewhere. Certain business practices, contractual conditions and service standards are common to many, if not all airlines. Problems related to these issues cannot be avoided by switching between different carriers. Many of these problems are related partially or completely to other subjects than airlines, like, for instance, airports, ground

[58] Commission, Communication, Protection for Air Passengers the European Union, COM(2000) 365 final, 21.6.00, p.7.

[59] See p. 200.

handling companies. ... Moreover, standards can slip across a whole industry if competition becomes very harsh indeed.[60]

A variety of reasons explain the weak bargaining position of air passengers:

> In fact a passenger is in a weak negotiating position compared to the airline. ... He or she is subject to conditions of carriage and to business practices decided by the airline ... but will frequently be unaware of the exact terms and have little alternative to accepting them even if dissatisfied. The customer's position is further weakened by the obligation to pay for the service, before actually taking the flight. Here transport differs from other services, of which only part of the price is paid before the service is provided, leaving the customer some bargaining power if it does not come up to expectations. Finally, a passenger depends heavily on the efficiency and good will of the airline when things go wrong, for example when flights are delayed or cancelled and baggage lost or damaged. He or she will probably be unable to make other agreements because of financial commitments already made, the difficulty of finding alternative flights or the sheer impracticality of using other forms of transport. ...[61]

Many of the problems affecting passenger air travel in the Community while not new, are getting worse, and the Community already has a range of legal measures to deal with certain issues.

> The Amsterdam Treaty gives a new priority to the protection of consumers. In air transport, this means passengers. To some extent their interests have already been addressed through specific legislation on compensation in the event of denied boarding, improved levels of air carrier liability for passengers and the EC Code of Conduct for computer reservations systems (CRSs). ... In addition, much of the general Community legislation on consumer protection applies directly to the air transport sector, covering issues such as unfair contract terms in consumer contracts, general product safety, data protection, comparative and misleading advertising and package holidays.[62]

The Commission has recently concluded that in order to redress the current imbalance in consumer rights in relation to airlines, new initiatives are required on a range of fronts, including the following of specific consumer/tourist interest:

---

[60] Commission, *Air Passenger Rights in the European Union, A Consultation Document on Consumer Protection in Air Transport*, 2000, p.3.
[61] Commission, Communication, *supra*, p.6.
[62] *Ibid.*, p.4.

- fairer contract terms.[63]
- protection in relation to delayed flights.
- airline performance reports.[64]
- complaints.[65]

The remainder of this section will concentrate on one of these issues – delayed/cancelled flights.[66]

DELAY

Delayed departure of passenger flights is the biggest single issue facing Community air transport. Delay occurs for a multitude of reasons related to weather, air traffic management, airport capacity, airline technical and operational matters, the behaviour of other passengers and other airlines and extraneous causes.

> In the wake of the alarming situation of congestion in air traffic … [It] is recognised that responsibility for air traffic delays is shared, although today one half of these are due to the congestion in the airspace by reasons of the efficiency of the current European air traffic management system. Carrier operators and airports are equally responsible for the other half.[67]

It is not easy to create balanced legal remedies for delayed tourist passengers. It is not simply a matter of imposing responsibility on the airline since, as is clear from the above extract, the airline is not always responsible. As against this the passenger often deals only with the airline, has no ready means of finding and dealing with the real cause of the delay and is in a vulnerable position, away from home in an unfamiliar airport, cut of from normal support networks.

Possible responses, whether legal or voluntary (as in a code of conduct) to delay can take a number of forms:

- court awarded compensation for all the consequences of delay.
- fixed immediate compensation for inconvenience.

---

[63] See p. 335.
[64] Commission, Communication, supra, p.18; Commission Consultation Paper on a Community Air Passenger Report on Service Quality Indicators, 30.11.00.
[65] Commission, Communication, *supra*, p.19.
[66] Other air passenger travel issues relating to personal injury and damaged /lost luggage are dealt with at p. 203.
[67] Commission, Consultation Paper on a Community Air Passenger Report on service quality indicators, 30.11.00, p.4.

- reimbursement.
- rerouting sooner/later.
- passenger care during delay period.

So far only a limited range of these remedies are legally available, though current Commission proposals will see a significant expansion in their availability.

Court Awarded Compensation for Consequences of Delay

Passengers have always had a legal right to claim compensation, not for delay, but for the consequences of delay from airlines. This right is based, since 1933 on an international convention – the Warsaw Convention,[68] to be replaced in the future by the Montreal Convention.[69] All Community Member States are parties to the Warsaw Convention and have implemented it into their domestic laws. However, the drawback with the Convention is that it deals with delay in a traditional legal manner. Any claim must be processed through legal channels, using lawyers and courts often long after the delay occurred. This does not help the passenger deal with the immediate consequences of the delay. The airline can avoid responsibility by showing it took "all necessary measures to avoid the consequences of delay." A substantial and difficult body of case law has built up over the interpretation of this provision, including a disinclination to award compensation for minor delay on the assumption that no particular loss follows minor delay. Generally, it is by no means easy for passengers to succeed in winning court awarded compensation for delay. Not surprisingly, most delayed passengers do not pursue a legal claim and put up with the inconvenience.

Community Response

Recognising the limitations of this framework, the Community has sought to develop a different framework within which a range of more immediate and passenger-friendly measures, legal and non-legal, would become available. However, it has had to move slowly in face of Member State and airline concerns over measures which might impact on airline competitiveness.

The Community's initial legal response in 1991[70] focused on just one type of delay – delay caused by airline overbooking. However, this had limited effect

---

[68] Convention for the Unification of Certain Rules Relating to International Carriage by Air, 12.10.29.

[69] Convention for the Unification of Certain Rules Relating to International Carriage by Air, 29.6.99.

[70] Regulation 298/91 establishing common rules for a denied-boarding compensation system in scheduled air transport, OJ L 36/5, 8.2.91.

and did not stop an excessive use of overbooking by airlines. Complaints also continued from passengers about other types of delay caused by flight cancellations and capacity constraints associated with increased passenger numbers. In the absence of satisfactory voluntary action from the airlines and an inadequate competitive environment, a new legal response was required.

The Commission's initial desire to make airlines primarily liable for all delays and to let them pass any liabilities onto the real cause of the problem, was however frustrated.

> The obvious solution would be for the airline to assist and compensate the passenger and then reclaim from other service providers when it itself was not at fault. At the present time, however, this would encounter two difficulties. First, identification of the cause of a delay may be difficult particularly when it is an effect of earlier delays. Second, a chain of contracts is lacking between airlines, airports, air traffic managers and other service providers that would allow an airline reclaim costs.[71]

After a period of reflection and consultation, the Commission's response via an initial[72] and then an amended[73] proposal for a regulation was to significantly widen the types of delay for which consumers would be given defined and immediate rights (compensation, assistance, care), but also to maintain an appropriate balance between airlines and consumers so as not to damage the competitiveness of Community airlines. Three basic approaches, depending on the cause of the delay, are used:

- airlines must provide information to delayed passengers about their rights,
- compensation must be paid immediately to some delayed passengers,
- defined assistance and care rights must be provided to some delayed passengers.

The application of these protections will be looked at under the following headings:

> - denied boarding (overbooking),

---

[71] Commission, Communication on Protection for Air Passengers in the European Union, COM(2000) 365 final, 21.6.2000, p.17.

[72] Commission, Proposal for a Regulation of the European Parliament and of the Council establishing common rules on compensation and assistance to air passengers in the event of denied boarding and of cancellation or long delay, COM(2001) 784 final, 21.12.01.

[73] Commission, Amended Proposal, COM(2002) 717 final, 4.12.02. The Commission also accepted amendments to its amended proposal contained in the Council's common position (15855/1/02, Rev 1, 18.3.03 – Commission Communication SEC (2003) 361 final, 25.3.03. The article numbers, in the text above, are those used in the Council's common position.

- cancellations,
- long delay.

The protections will apply to all passengers[74] on scheduled and chartered flights departing from a Community airport and on flights on Community airlines originating from a third country outside the Community and finishing inside the Community, unless the passengers received benefits/compensation or assistance in the third country. The protections will also apply to consumers of packages using flights booked by organisers. Package consumers do not have contracts with airlines and current protection under the Package Travel Directive does not provide the type of immediate remedies that the proposal will offer.

To ensure that passengers are aware of their rights an airline must display at the check-in desk a notice telling delayed (overbooked/cancelled/2 hour delay) passengers to ask for a notice (which must be supplied) stating their rights. To ensure airlines properly apply the new passenger protections each state must under Article 16 appoint a body to receive and investigate any complaints about the delay protections. The role of this body is likely to become very significant.

Denied Boarding

When passengers are denied boarding due to overbooking airline fault is obvious and this is why it was the first and easiest type of delay to deal with. The reason airlines overbook is to be able to offer greater flexibility to the holders of expensive tickets.

> Overbooking is the result of the high degree of flexibility granted to passengers holding fully flexible tickets, i.e. having paid the full published economy, business or first class fare. They have the right not to present themselves for the flight for which they have a confirmed reservation without losing the right to use the ticket without any additional charges on another flight to the same destination.

> The high degree of flexibility has, however, created the so-called problem 'no-show' passengers. For various reasons a certain number of passengers book seats and do not claim them. It is usual international practice that airlines that understandably do not want to risk finding empty seats as a result of 'no-shows' accept a certain degree of overbooking. This behaviour,

---

[74] Except passengers travelling for free or on restricted access reduced fares, but not frequent flyers – Article 3(3). Responsibility for fulfilling the obligations of the proposed regulation will rest with the operating carrier – not the contracting carrier – SEC (2003) 361 final, p. 2.

however, implies the risk that the number of passengers holding confirmed reservations and presenting themselves within the usual time-limit for check-in will exceed occasionally the number of available seats on that flight. … One could … argue that solutions should be left to the market. … More competition will normally generate an improved quality of service. … It cannot be excluded, however, that certain air carriers might tend to neglect quality of the service considerations in areas in which transparency is widely lacking i.e. the behaviour of an individual air carrier in overbooking situations. Under these circumstances the public intervention is required in order to safeguard the interests of passengers.[75]

Under the proposed regulation certain passengers must have priority as regards not being denied boarding – a person with reduced mobility, an accompanying person or a designated service dog or an unaccompanied child – Article 11. Reduced mobility includes anyone with a physical, intellectual, age or other condition whose transport needs require special attention – Article 11, though an airline could still deny boarding, possibly for safety reasons.

When an airline reasonably expects to deny boarding it must call for volunteers to surrender their confirmed reservations in exchange for benefits under conditions to be agreed between the passenger and the air carrier/tour operator- Article 4(1).[76]

If volunteers come forward they are entitled, in addition to whatever compensation package they agree with the airline, to the assistance and care rights described below. Only when not enough volunteers come forward can airlines then lawfully deny boarding. Passengers unwillingly denied boarding are then entitled to the compensation, assistance and care rights.

The proposed mandatory and immediately payable compensation amounts vary depending on the distance to the destination (which includes the final destination where directly connecting flights are part of the ticket) on the ticket:

(a) EUR 250 for all flights of 1000 kilometres or less;

(b) EUR 400 for all intra-Community flights of more than 1500 kilometres, and for all other flights between 1500 and 3500 kilometres;

(c) EUR 600 for all flights not falling under (a) or (b) – Article 7(1).

These amounts must be paid in cash (or bank order/cheque/electronically) unless

---

[75] Commission Proposal, p.2.

[76] If an airline up or down grades in order to avoid an overbooking situation, it cannot charge for the upgrade and must reimburse (50% or 75% of the ticket price depending on the flight distance) for the downgrade – Article 10.

the passenger agrees and signs in writing to an alternative – Article 7(3). They can be reduced by half when, under Article 7(2), the passenger arrival time on a re-routed flight is no later than 2 hours for flights of less than 3,500 kilometres or 4 hours for flights of at least 3,500 kilometres.

The proposed compensation amounts are not as high as the Commission would have liked.[77] They are intended to reflect a balance between attempting to discourage airlines from excessive overbooking and preventing passengers from seeking too much when considering whether to volunteer for denied boarding.

> The Commission has tried to set rates that compensate passengers and deter operators from excessive overbooking. ... Such levels should not prevent airlines from overbooking in order simply to fill seats that otherwise would remain empty ... operators would pay the fixed rate infrequently, so long as they did not overbook exaggeratedly and were effective in finding volunteers.[78]

Thus, the level of denied boarding compensation is intended to provide airlines with an incentive to offer enough compensation to induce enough volunteers to come forward so that the airline can avoid denying boarding against anyone's will. If a possible volunteer holds out for the fixed rate, he/she runs:

> the risk that other passengers will accept a lesser offer in adequate numbers to eliminate overbooking. In that case, they would receive no compensation but would travel in the ordinary way.[79]

In opting to develop a volunteer system it is clear the Commission was influenced by the successful operation of such a system in the US.[80]

Besides compensation, those who volunteer or are unwillingly denied boarding are given two important protections – rights to assistance and care – both of which reflect the view that since the airline is responsible for the delay, it should look after those it delays. Neither right need, however, be made immediately available to the passenger, unlike the compensation right, though presumably, the two rights must be provided in a reasonable relation to the denied boarding.

The **assistance right** deals with getting the passenger to his/her destination and is set out in Article 8(1) which states:

---

[77] Commission, Communication SEC (2003) 361 final, 25.3.03, p. 2.
[78] Commission, Proposal, p.5.
[79] *Supra.*
[80] Commission Proposal, p.4.

passengers shall be offered the choice between:

(a) reimbursement within seven days ... of the full cost of the ticket ... for [any] journey not made together with, when relevant, a return flight at the earliest opportunity to the point of departure,

(b) re-routing, under comparable transport conditions, ... at the earliest opportunity, or

(c) re-routing ... at a later date at the passenger's convenience, subject to availability.

If the re-routing involves departure/return to another airport in the same town, city or region the airline must bear the additional costs of travel – Article 8(3).

The **care right** deals with catering for passengers needs while waiting for a later flight and is set out in Article 9(1) which states:

passengers shall be offered free of charge:

(a) meals and refreshments in a reasonable relation to the waiting time;

(b) hotel accommodation in cases where a stay of one or more nights ... or when a stay additional to that intended by the passenger becomes necessary;

(c) transport between the airport and place of accommodation. ...

In addition, passengers shall be offered free of charge two telephone calls, telex or fax messages or e-mails.

Delay Due to Flight Cancellation

The proposed regulation will create entirely new passenger rights (assistance/ care/compensation) to deal with the consequences of flight cancellation by an airline. However, a major restriction on their availability is that the care and compensation rights do not apply where the airline can show that the cancellation was:

caused by extraordinary circumstances which could not have been avoided even if all reasonable measures had been taken – Article 5(1) and (3).

Recital 14 of the regulation's Preamble (according to Council's common position) provides some examples of possible extraordinary circumstances:

political instability, meteorological conditions incompatible with the operation of the flight concerned, security risks, unexpected flight safety shortcomings and strikes that affect the operation of an operating air carrier..

It is important to note that these examples may, but do not necessarily, constitute extraordinary circumstances. Each case will depend on its facts and seems likely to be determined by the body designated to hear complaints and enforce the Regulation. Strikes and bad weather especially might not constitute extraordinary circumstances because, quite simply, they might not be extraordinary. Care and compensation rights can still potentially apply to cancellations caused by unextraordinary strikes and bad but not unextraordinary weather, while the assistance right (reimbursement/re-routing) will apply in all cases.

Even where extraordinary circumstances do not arise, the compensation right can, however, still be restricted. Whether this happens will depend both on when the passenger is told of the cancellation and whether on any offered re-routing will enable the passenger to still depart for/arrive at his/her destination within the following timeframe:

- 7-14 days cancellation notice – 2 hours before/4hours after scheduled departure/arrival times
- less than 7 days cancellation notice – 1 hour before/2 hours after scheduled departure/arrival times.

Thus, the airline has an incentive to respond well to the cancellation challenge and avoid paying cancellation compensation. If a flight is cancelled after passengers have checked-in and the reason is technical problems within the airline's control, the airline will have to offer the assistance and care rights. If the re-routed passengers arrive at their final destination, say, two and half hours later than the scheduled time, compensation is also payable, though the amount will vary according to the flight distance, as indicated earlier in Article 7.

The rationale for creating the new rights for passengers of cancelled flights is the unfairness of the airline effectively abandoning them after it cancels a fight.

> In the Commission's view, it is unacceptable for airlines to leave passengers stranded for many hours, where they have undertaken to use their best efforts to carry them with reasonable dispatch and have accepted payment to provide such a service.[81]

Re-routing at the earliest opportunity under "comparable transport conditions" is likely to be the preferred choice of most passengers affected by cancelled flights, that is where the airline cannot plead force majeure. The meaning of this phrase (Recital 13 of the Preamble in the Council's common position uses

---

[81] Commission, Communication on Protection for Air Passengers in the European Union, COM (2000) 365 final, 21.6.00, p.17.

"satisfactory conditions") is likely to be closely examined to see whether, for example, a low cost carrier who has cancelled must put the passenger on a higher cost carrier on the same route, or whether transport by bus, rail or ferry could be considered a comparable transport condition. However, the choice of type of assistance is the consumers. In any event, the airport body charged with receiving/investigating complaints is likely to determine what a comparable condition of transport, in a give case, is.

Long Delay

Under Article 6 of the proposed regulation passengers affected by long delays must always be offered the assistance right and must also be offered the care right except in the latter case where the airline can prove the delay is caused by extraordinary circumstances, etc.

Long delay is the key idea. Passengers affected by short delays will not be granted any of the proposed passenger protections. Their only recourse will be the airlines voluntary care programme or the traditional court based route under the Warsaw/Montreal Conventions.

Long delay passengers under the proposed Article 6 are those the airline reasonably expects to be delayed for more than 2 hours on flights up to 3,500 kilometres or for more than 4 hours on flights of 3,500 kilometres or more.

TIMESHARE

Introduction

Many EU citizens who take their holidays in other Member States, decide, once they have been attracted by the climate, the quality of life and the low cost of living, to buy a house or a flat there as a holiday or retirement home. Other citizens mainly from the UK and some other northern States, who do not want to fully own a holiday property, are attracted to the option of buying a right to occupy a holiday property for a defined period, known as timeshare or holiday/vacation ownership, usually for one week per year. This section focuses only on the latter.

Under a timeshare arrangement a consumer pays a capital sum to acquire an occupancy right and an annual fee for maintenance and services. The consumer also usually joins an exchange organisation through which, for a fee, they can swap their timeshare right with others in different holiday locations around the world.[82]

---

[82] For general information on the timeshare industry, see http://www.timeshare.org.uk/.

Many different legal issues can arise in a timeshare transaction – the legal nature of the occupancy right (a property, contract or statutory right), the extent of the physical property, rights of support, access, use of common amenity areas such as swimming pools etc). All have to be addressed. Some states have created a specific statutory framework for timeshare. Others use existing legal mechanisms such as a trust, a company etc within which occupancy rights operate. It is also necessary to deal with the timeshare managers obligations.

So far the Community has involved itself with just one particular aspect of timeshare, the marketing of timeshare properties. Timeshare marketing has attracted criticism due to the high-pressure sales techniques sometimes used by sellers. Before 1994 four Member States had enacted consumer protection legislation regarding timeshare contracts, each with different content and, in the Commission's view, none with sufficient levels of protection. The resulting legal diversity distorted the significant common market in timeshare holidays. Legal diversity also had the potential to cause serious difficulties in law enforcement as complex questions of private international law can arise in a cross-border claim.

Thus, the Council enacted Directive 94/47[83] on the protection of purchasers in respect of certain aspects of contracts relating to the purchase of the right to use immovable properties on a timeshare basis (timeshare directive). Its primary focus is to improve the transparency of the timeshare transaction affecting immoveable property located within the territory of Member States – Article 9. The idea is to ensure that the consumer is aware of the deal being offered. The Directive does not define the nature of a timeshare contract, or create a comprehensive legal structure for timeshare or attempt a complete harmonisation of all rules applicable to timeshare. Further, under the rules of private international law parties to timeshare contracts remain free to choose the state and applicable law for dealing with their legal disputes. The Directive is quite narrow in what it attempts to do and this, as will be seen, is one of its perceived failings.

The consumer protections offered by the Timeshare Directive fall under the following headings:

- Scope of the Directive.
- Provision of information.
- Withdrawal/cancellation.
- Payments.

---

[83] OJ L 280/83, 29.10.94.

Reference will also be made to:
- the implementation of the Directive, and the
- CLAB[84] cases on unfair terms in timeshare contracts.

Scope of Timeshare Directive

Under Articles 1 and 2 the consumer protections provided in the Directive only kick in when:
- there is a contract relating directly or indirectly to the purchase of the right to use a building/part of a building for accommodation on a timeshare basis.
- the contract lasts at least three years and the occupancy right created by the contract involves accommodation and the occupancy period lasts at least one week:

  [The Directive] has provided two different periods of time regulating its scope of application: the contract between the purchaser and the vendor must be concluded for a period of at least three years. The contract must allow the purchaser to use the property for a specified period during the year of no less than one week's duration. There is no upper limit in the Directive for the duration of the contract.[85]

- the purchaser of the timeshare must be a natural person (not a company etc) and must not act in a professional capacity, though obviously the seller can.

Thus, the Directive catches the typical arrangement under which a series of purchaser-consumers acquire consecutive rights to occupy a holiday apartment in a resort for a limited period. Attempts made before it was passed to extend the scope of the Directive to include purchasers who were incorporated as legal persons, such as companies etc. were rejected. The Council thought this was a matter better suited for legislation by the Member States.

Provision of Information

The provision of information about the timeshare contract and property is one of the key protections of the Directive. The idea behind it is that the more information provided to the consumer the less likely that high-pressure sales techniques will result in an unsuitable purchase. Article 3 lays down that the

---

[84] For an explanation of CLAB, see p. 323.
[85] Commission Report on the Application of Directive 94/47/EC (Timeshare Directive) SEC (1999) 1795 final, 26.10.99, p.10.

vendor must provide any person requesting information on the immovable property or properties with:

> a document, which, in addition to a general description of the property ... shall provide at least brief and accurate information.

on certain minimum items referred to in the Annex of the Directive. These items briefly concern:

- the identity and domicile of the parties concerned.
- the exact nature of the right which is the subject of the contract.
- an accurate description of the property and its location.
- whether or not the property is under construction.

The document must also give details of how the consumer can obtain further information about the contemplated purchase.

Further, under Article 4, the timeshare contract itself, which must be in writing, must include at least the items referred to in the Annex. Article 4 also determines the language in which both the contract and the document referred to in Article 3 are to be drawn up – the language of the Member State where the purchaser is either a resident or a national as long as it is an official language of the Community. It is the purchaser's choice which language it should be.

Withdrawal/Cancellation

The Timeshare Directive, unlike the Package Travel Directive, combines the transparency and information requirements in Articles 3 and 4, with provisions in Article 5 for a cooling-off period. Within this period of 10 days from signing the contract the consumer is entitled to withdraw from the contract without giving any reason. Further, if the contract does not contain the information specified in the Annex to the Directive, the consumer has a right to cancel the contract any time within three months of signing. In other words, the Timeshare Directive provides the purchaser with two kinds of protection after the contract has been made – Article 5(2) defines the manner in which the withdrawal and cancellation right should be exercised and Article 5(3) defines the circumstances in which the purchaser may have to pay any withdrawal expenses, while no cancellation expenses are payable.

If the information stipulated in the Annex is not provided before the contact is signed, but is provided within the three months' withdrawal period, the purchaser's 10 days withdrawal period starts from when the information is provided. If, on the other hand, the three months period elapses without the information being provided by the vendor, the purchaser's 10 days withdrawal period starts the day after the end of the three-month period – Article 5(1) third indent.

As a condition of exercising the right of withdrawal or cancellation, the consumer must notify the person designated in the contract for the purpose of receiving such notification. The notification must be dispatched before the expiry of the deadline –Article 5(2).

Advance Payments, Credit Agreements, Limitation Clauses

To further protect the consumer, Article 6 of the Timeshare Directive prohibits advance payments before the end of the 10-day withdrawal period. Also, according to Article 7, any agreement covering credit granted to the purchaser by the vendor (and third parties) must be cancelled, if the purchaser withdraws from, or cancels the contract. Clauses in the contract, which limit the rights of the purchaser or the responsibilities of the vendor, do not bind the purchaser, according to Article 8.

Implementation of Timeshare Directive

In 1999 the Commission produced a report on how the Timeshare Directive has been implemented.[86] According to this report, Member States implemented the Directive in different ways. Some opted for the literal approach,[87] that is they adopted the Directive just as it is written. Others improved on aspects on the Directive (longer cooling-off period, improved consumer withdrawal rights, longer lasting seller guarantee obligations, integration of timeshare into more general holiday developments) using as a base their own prior timeshare legislation[88] or general consumer protection.[89]

> Only two States – Spain and Portugal – have created a specific legal framework for timeshare contacts.[90]

To some degree the Directive itself foresaw that Member States would implement the Directive differently. Article 11 allows states to enact more stringent consumer protection measures. However, the Commission examination of the

---

[86] Commission Report on the Application of Directive 94/47/EC (Timeshare Directive,) SEC (1999) 1795 final, 26.10.99.

[87] Denmark, Finland, the Netherlands, Ireland, Italy, Luxembourg, Sweden, Germany and Austria.

[88] Portugal, the UK, France and Greece.

[89] France, Belgium, Portugal and Spain.

[90] *Supra* p.9.

ways states implemented the Directive showed important variations in a range of issues such as the minimum duration of the timeshare period, the legal consequences for agreements of shorter duration, consequences for failure to comply with the requirements of the Directive, the languages in which the contract and information documents should be written and the location of timeshare properties protected under national implementations.

Thus, even after the introduction of the Directive, the legal position concerning consumer protection in timeshare contracts remains confused and fragmented.

The limited scope of the Directive was also highlighted as an issue of on-going concern. The Commission noted:[91]

> The problems experienced by consumers in their relations with timeshare developers and vendors have not disappeared with the adoption of [the] Directive. ... the Commission departments responsible for consumer policy have received a large number of individual complaints (24 % of the complaints received by the Commission in 1998), as well as many letters from MEPs ... the vast majority of cases reported ... concern a series of problems and situations, which Directive 94/47/EC cannot resolve as it stands.

> The cases reported mainly concern unilateral actions on the part of vendors who, following conclusion of the contract, modify or fail to perform their contractual obligations. This mainly concerns the imposition of annual charges on the purchaser different to those initially set out in the contract, the impossibility for purchasers to resell their timeshare although this right was stipulated, the failure of vendors to follow up reservations and failure to enrol purchasers in the envisaged exchange or resale systems. The purchaser's situation is made more precarious because often several companies are involved in managing the timeshare, although they are not formally parties to the initial contract. This situation makes it even more difficult for the purchaser to rely on his legal or contractual rights.

It seems obvious that what is needed is more of an all-round protection of consumers acquiring timeshares. However this must respect the subsidiarity principle.

> The fact is that the shortcomings of Directive 94/47/EC are also to be found in the bulk of the national legislations and hence adversely affect

---

[91] Commission Report on the Application of Directive 94/47/EC (Timeshare Directive) SEC (1999) 1795 final, p.23.

consumers. ... Bearing this in mind, and in the light of the subsidiarity principle, the question arises as to whether a new Community action, in the form of an amendment of the existing Directive, should be envisaged.[92]

Somewhat tentatively the Commission identified three areas where further Community action might be justified:

- altering the time stipulations in the Directive to make more categories of timeshare contract subject to the Directive consumer protections.
- extending existing protections through longer rights of withdrawal and longer seller financial guarantees more appropriate to the long term nature of a timeshare contract.
- allowing exemptions from the ban on advance timeshare contact payments.

Part of the reason for wanting to bring more types of timeshare within the Directive is the emergence of new marketing techniques.

> In the case of timeshares, new marketing techniques have been designed to ensure that in some circumstances they are excluded from the scope of the Directive and its key obligations. For example, some sellers are offering contracts for a period less than three years or stipulating an annual period of use of less than 7 days. In addition, time-share type contracts are being offered through insurance or membership of a club or through point schemes with the purpose of excluding such arrangements from the scope of the Directive.[93]

EXAMPLES OF UNFAIR TIMESHARE TERMS

In connection with the introduction of the Unfair Terms Directive in 1993,[94] the Commission established the CLAB database, a collection of national court judgments, administrative decisions, voluntary agreements, out-of-court settlements and arbitration decisions concerning unfair contract terms. The idea was to create an instrument for monitoring the practical enforcement of the Unfair Terms Directive By analysing the data contained in the CLAB database, the Commission hoped to reveal particular trends in Member States' jurisprudence. The CLAB cases below on timeshare contracts revolve around

---

[92] *Ibid.*, p.24.

[93] Commission Green Paper on European Union Consumer Protection COM (2001) 531 final, 2.10.01, p.5.

[94] OJ L 95/29. See p. 326.

three issues: transparency of the contract, the right to cancel, and failure to fulfil the contract by one party.

Excessive damages, lack of transparency, the principle of good faith

A German consumer withdrew from a timeshare contract for a holiday village in Austria and claimed a refund of his expenses in making the contract. The timeshare seller had a clause in the contract giving it the right to retain 25% of the entire contractual sum as compensation if the contract was terminated prematurely. This lump sum would have covered the use of the timeshare property for 24 years, and far exceeded the damage to be paid under normal circumstances. The contract was declared void because it provided an unfair disadvantage to the client.

> The principle of good faith required that the user of standard business terms and conditions described the rights and duties of his contractual partner clearly and understandably. The user violated this principle as he described the contractual relationship intentionally in an unclear way and in a mode which was hard to understand – all for the purpose of concealing risks and disadvantages and in order to influence the decision-making process of the client.[95]

Period of withdrawal, misleading contract terms

A German consumer bought a timeshare and later withdrew from the contract. The question in the case was whether his withdrawal was in breach of the contract. A period of one month to withdraw was applicable according to the contract if all the contractual duties were completely executed. One of these duties was for the seller of the timeshare to enter a permanent right of residence in the land register. The contract in question contained statements and terms, which led the customer to believe that he was entered into the land register, but this had not in fact been done. Instead, the customer had been entered into a private joint-register. Thus, the contract was not fulfilled, and the period of withdrawal had not expired.

> The basic lesson to be gained from this case is that misleading terms are void, and that the sales-agent's contractual duties are not executed through entering the client's name into the joint–register.[96]

---

[95] CLAB 239/249.
[96] CLAB 201.

Clarity, good faith, the balancing of mutual obligations

In a Spanish case, the dispute was over a term in a timeshare contract requiring submission of any dispute between the parties to the Courts and Tribunals of Geneva (Switzerland). As the timeshare seller was located in Gibraltar and the flats were located in Spain and offered to Spanish or other European consumers, the term was declared null and void.

> First, it was considered contrary to good faith and the right balancing of mutual obligations, as well as prejudicial to the consumer, who had to sue the professional abroad, implying a great economic expense and making his defence very difficult. In addition, the term was written on the reverse side of the contract, and was not signed by the parties. A term requiring express submission of the parties also demands the specific acceptance of both parties, and this was missing.[97]

Vague terms

In another Spanish case, the timeshare contract imposed a duty on the consumer to pay lump sums for the costs of obtaining the public deed and the maintenance of the timeshare property during the first year. This term was declared unfair because it was contrary to the principle of good faith contained in Articles 7.1 of the Spanish Civil Code and 57 of the Commercial Code. It imposed upon the consumer the duty to pay vague sums for uncertain services.[98]

Penalty for withdrawal, nationality discrimination

In a Spanish case the timeshare contract contained a "penalty clause" in case the user unilaterally withdrew from the contract. It gave the timeshare seller the right to retain 35% of the amounts paid by the user. The Spanish Court of Appeal declared the term null and void for three reasons:

(1) it was entirely legitimate for the customer to withdraw from the contract after reflection. Simultaneously, it was just as legitimate for the professional to establish a penalty for such cases, but this penalty must be in accordance with the law.

(2) the unilateral withdrawal from the contract by the user did not carry

---

[97] CLAB 268.
[98] CLAB 270–274.

> any fees for the professional, and in addition, the user has paid some fees without enjoying a day of holidays.
>
> (3) since the user was a German citizen, applying a 35% penalty to him and a 10% penalty to a Spanish citizen was nationality discrimination and contrary to the Treaty on the European Union as well as to Article 14 of the Spanish Constitution, which forbids discrimination on the basis of nationality. The Court of Appeal fixed the same 10% penalty for both types of customer.[99]

Conclusion

Among the comparable aims of both the Package Travel Directive and the Timeshare Directive is the promotion of market transparency. The fundamental idea is that the consumer's pre-bargaining position is enhanced if the level of information he/she has before making the contract is high. Under the Timeshare Directive the consumer has the additional post-bargaining protection of a right to withdraw. The Package Travel Directive contains no similar right, perhaps because there is not the same scope for unscrupulous commercial tactics with the sale of a one-week holiday compared with the sale of a one-week timeshare. Cross-border transactions are much more frequent in timeshare contracts than in package travel though the latter is becoming rather more frequent. The question is, does the legal intervention of the Package Travel and Timeshare Directives go far enough to achieve effective protection of the consumer? Is it not necessary to move beyond adjustment of the bargaining environment towards regulation of the terms of the bargain themselves? This is what the Unfair Terms Directive has done and this is what will be considered in the following section.

UNFAIR TERMS IN CONSUMER CONTRACTS

Introduction

Travellers and tourists frequently encounter prepared (printed standard form) contracts when making bookings. Such contracts often contain terms which are unfair from the consumer perspective in that they shift the burden of risk in the relationship from the supplier, who often has the best means of controlling it, to the consumer who does not. Among the more frequently used types of unfair term are terms which:

• exclude or limit the consumer's legal rights in the event of unsatisfactory

---

[99] CLAB 262.

performance by the supplier,

- impose disproportionate penalties if the consumer fails to perform,
- bind the consumer to terms which were not communicated to him before the contract was made, or
- exclude or hinder the consumer's right to take legal action or exercise another legal remedy.[100]

Contracts can also be written in legalistic complicated language which consumers fail to understand.

The European Community has an interest in preventing the use of unfair and unintelligible contract terms in consumer transactions. Their use threatens the operation of the common market and the Community is also obligated under the Treaty to offer high levels of consumer protection. If consumers cannot understand a contract in another Member State because of the way it is written, or if different levels of legal protection of consumers apply, this will discourage cross border purchases.[101]

The reasons for the extensive use of unfair contract terms lie in the very nature of modern society. According to the Commission in 1990:[102]

> The emergence of a society of mass production, distribution and consumption has resulted in the increasing formalisation of contracts and, particularly, in an increased use of pre–prepared contacts containing standard terms. ...

> As standard terns are drawn up without the consumer's participation, he is unable to assert his interests and ensure that they are reflected in the terms. Most consumers who enter into contracts made on standard terms do so in ignorance of their precise meaning. Frequently, even if the contract stipulates that signature by the consumer indicates that he understands and accepts all its terms, the consumer has in practise no real opportunity to study the terms, either because they have not been communicated to him in advance or are to be found elsewhere. Even if the consumer does

---

[100] Commission, Report on the implementation of Council Directive 93/13/EEC on Unfair Terms in Consumer Contracts, COM(2000) 248 final, 27.4.00, p.44.

[101] Even without the Directive, it is clear that the combination of the Rome Convention dealing with which states laws apply in an international contract dispute – OJ L 266/1, 9.10.80 – and the repealed Brussels Convention dealing with the state in which the legal case should be taken – now Council Regulation 44/2001, OJ L 121, 16.1.01 – would have offered some protection to consumers based in states which had unfair terms laws The problem would have remained for consumers in other Member States.

[102] Commission, Proposal for a Council Directive on unfair terms in consumer contracts, COM(90) 322 final, 14.9.90, p.5.

have the opportunity to study the terms, he will probably be unaware of the precise legal significance of the language used, and may therefore be misled as to the contract's true meaning.

The widespread use of standard terms both in travel and tourism contracts and elsewhere has a specific legal result. It makes an illusion of the universal legal principle that individuals should be free to negotiate the terms of their contracts, or in other words, that the law should give legal effect to terms freely agreed by parties to commercial transactions.

In the 1980s the legal differences between Member States regarding unfair terms grew increasingly significant and the Commission concluded that they threatened the establishment of the common market and created unequal treatment as between consumers in different markets. It also made it more difficult for consumers to purchase services across borders.

Differences between the laws of the Member States – even where they have adopted laws on unfair contract terms – have led and are likely to lead even more to unequal treatment of the Community's citizens. For example, in its decision of 20 January 1984 in the case of *Lufthansa v. Verbracherschutzwerein*, the [German Supreme Court] declared a number of terms in passenger tickets issued by Lufthansa invalid under German law: the terms involved were part of the standard terms of carriage and covered limitation of liability, reservation of the right for Lufthansa to rescind the contract, the right to alter flights, and onus of proof. It is striking that some of the terms condemned are derived from international agreements within IATA, an international association of airlines. The Court considered that Lufthansa's argument to the effect that the use of such terms is worldwide was irrelevant, because the national interests in effectively protecting the consumer is more important than international uniformity. The Court took the view that limitation of liability could not be upheld even though derived from the Warsaw Convention, which had been ratified by the Federal Republic. The origin of the limitation did not alter its character as a standard term of contract which was governed by the German Act [on unfair terms]. The terms judged invalid by the [German Supreme Court] have not been adjudicated upon in other Member States. Thus the situation could arise where a passenger who bought his ticket in Dusseldorf under German law would be carried under more favourable terms of contract than the person in an adjacent seat on the same fight who had bought his ticket in London under English law. This is an unacceptable situation in an aspiring common market.[103]

---

[103] *Ibid.*, p.8.

Three types of legal response were possible – harmonised laws for individual types of consumer contracts or for contract law generally or a general law targeting unfair terms and negativing their effects. Non-legislative means were also available and in fact have been used.[104] For pragmatic reasons the third option was the one chosen.

Directive 93/13/EEC on unfair terms in consumer contracts[105] (Unfair Terms Directive) was adopted in April 1993 and Member States were given until the end of 1994 to transpose it into domestic law. Like the Timeshare Directive, the Unfair Terms Directive is a minimum harmonisation measure. Under Article 9 Member States can retain or adopt higher levels of consumer protection. This means that differences in national laws will continue and possibly even increase.

The broad approach of the Unfair Terms Directive is to declare that unfair terms are not legally binding on consumers and to provide a means for identifying whether a term is unfair. An additional concern is to improve the transparency of consumer contracts by focusing on how understandable they are to consumers. Responsibility is placed on the consumer to allege and prove in legal proceedings that a contract term is unfair. Since individual consumers are generally unwilling to take legal proceedings, Article 7 of the Directive provides that:

> organisations having a legitimate interest under national law in protecting consumers, may take action ... for a decision as to whether contractual terms drawn up for general use are unfair ...[106]

Since 1996 the Commission has subsidised cases taken by consumer associations combating unfair contract terms in areas relevant to tourism, such as car rental, timeshare and holiday services. The results of these actions were positive as the professionals concerned consented either to modify their contract terms or to negotiate changes to them.[107] The protections offered by the Unfair Terms Directive fall under the following headings:

- The scope of the Directive.
- The effect and meaning of unfair.
- Plain and intelligible language.
- The impact of the Directive.
- Cases from the CLAB database.

---

[104] *Ibid.*, pp.9 and 42.

[105] OJ L 95/29, 21.4.93.

[106] The Commission has raised the question whether this competence to seek injunctions restraining the use of questionable terms might be extended to the use of unclear consumer contract terms – Commission, Report on the implementation of Council Directive 93/13/EEC on Unfair Terms in Consumer Contracts, COM(2000) 248 final, 27.4.00, p.19.

[107] *Ibid.*, p.9.

SCOPE OF THE UNFAIR TERMS DIRECTIVE

The legal protections offered by the Directive are limited to contracts involving a consumer and a seller or supplier. Consumer is defined in Article 2(b) as:

> any natural person ... acting for purposes outside his trade, business or profession

while seller or supplier is defined in Article 2(c) as:

> any natural or legal person ... acting for purposes relating to his trade, business or profession whether publicly or privately owned.

Thus, a business person who buys an airline ticket might not be protected by the Directive, while a tourist who does the same is. In this the Directive uses the same distinction as the Timeshare Directive. By contrast, the Package Travel Directive extends its protections to whoever buys a package – business person or tourist. However, it is also possible to differentiate in the definition between principal and incidental purposes, to claim that the regulation only covers the former and that a person who purchases a plane ticket to travel to a business meeting is not acting for purposes relating to his trade.

The legal protections contained in the Directive also do not apply to consumer contract terms, which according to Article 1(2) of the Directive:

> reflect mandatory statutory or regulatory provisions and the provisions or principles of international conventions to which the Member States or the Community are party, particularly in the transport area ...

This has important legal implications for tourism. Many legal aspects of tourism activities, especially issues of liability for personal injury, loss/damage to property, and sometimes delay are indeed subject to international conventions which have been enacted into domestic law by Member States. The main conventions are the Warsaw Convention dealing with international air travel,[108] the Athens Convention dealing with international sea travel,[109] the Berne Convention (CIV) dealing with intentional rail travel[110] and the Paris Convention

---

[108] For text, see web page of the International Civil Aviation Organization at http://www.icao.int/ cgi/goto_leb.pl?icao/en/leb/treaty.htm. See also p. 203.

[109] For text, see web page of the International Maritime Organization at http://www.imo.org/ home.asp.

[110] For text, see http://www.otif.org.

dealing with hotel residents.[111] The general effect of these conventions is to limit the amount of compensation travellers can obtain for personal injury and property damage. Although some of these have recently been or are about to be reformed,[112] the effect of Article 1(2) is that the fairness of terms in air, sea and hotel contracts which are subject to these conventions cannot be challenged under the Unfair Terms Directive.

There is little doubt that this represents a significant defect in the Directive. These conventions were generally created to reduce, not increase, consumer protection. Article 1(2) may have been a pragmatic response to the need to avoid wholesale renegotiation of conventions which are in most cases open for world-wide signature. Now that the reformed conventions offer considerably improved protections for travellers, the question arises whether Article 1(2) should be retained. In any case, Member States can if they wish, under the Unfair Terms Directive, subject the operation of these conventions to local unfair terms laws and this in fact is what has happened in at least one state – Germany.[113]

A further exclusion for the scope of the Directive concerns individually negotiated terms. Under Article 3(2), contract terms which have been individually negotiated do not fall within the Directive. An individually negotiated term is one which is not drafted in advance by the seller/supplier so that the consumer has been unable to influence its substance (typically the prepared standard contract). The Directive also deals with the situation where the contract is partly pre-formulated and partly individually negotiated: If an overall assessment puts it down as a pre-formulated standard contract, the Directive applies. Article 3(2) places the burden of proof on the seller. It is for him/her to prove that a standard term has been individually negotiated.[114]

Effect and Meaning of Unfair

If a term in a prepared written consumer contract is unfair, then under Article 6(1), it:

> shall ... not be binding on the consumer and ... the contract shall continue

---

[111] For text, see web page of Council of Europe at http://conventions.coe.int/treaty/EN/cadreprincipal.htm.

[112] See pp. 204, 213 and 220.

[113] See p. 328.

[114] The Commission had questioned whether the distinction between individually and non-individually negotiated terms is worth preserving because it encourages attempts to declare that all terms in a contract to be individually negotiated – Commission, Report on the implementation of Council Directive 93/13/EEC on Unfair Terms in Consumer Contracts, COM(2000) 248 final, 27.4.00, p.14.

to bind both parties upon those terms if it capable of continuing in existence without the unfair terms.

The key issue is whether a term is unfair. According to Article 3(1), a contract term is regarded as unfair:

> if, contrary to the requirement of good faith, it causes a significant imbalance in the parties' rights and obligations arising under the contract, to the detriment of the consumer.

This links "unfairness" with "good faith": a contract term which is unfair cannot be made in good faith. However, it is not obvious what mentioning "good faith" brings to the definition which is not already covered by fairness. Lack of good faith and unfairness seem equally likely to be presumed from the really key requirement – the creation of a significant imbalance in the parties' rights and obligations arising under the contract to the detriment of the consumer.

Whether the consumer has to prove unfairness or the supplier has to prove fairness is not clear because the Directive is not explicit, although it would seem the onus rests on the consumer to prove that a term is unfair. Article 4 (1) indicates how unfairness is to be determined.

> the unfairness of a contractual term shall be assessed, taking into account the nature of the goods or services [covered by] the contract ... and ... all the circumstances attending the conclusion of the contract and ... all the other terms of the contract ...

This means that fairness must be assessed in each case, taking into consideration all the circumstances surrounding the making of the contract and its content. Whether this matters much in the typical case of an average tourist booking a flight or hiring a car seems doubtful. With the exception of special requirements, individual circumstances in travel bookings seem unlikely to vary much. Under Article 4(2) two central circumstances cannot be considered in the assessment of fairness–

> the definition of the main subject matter of the contract [or] the adequacy of the price...

This probably means that the value of the bargain itself, that is the fairness of the price in relation what is purchased, cannot be challenged under the Directive, though price and subject matter of contract may nevertheless be taken into account in assessing the fairness of other terms, such as the means of calculating the price.

One way this impacts on tourists concerns travel insurance contracts. A tourist who wrongly believes travel insurance covers a particular risk cannot claim that the insurance contract was unfair simply because the risk was not covered. The risks covered are the main subject of an insurance contract and are linked to the price of the cover.[115] Questions about their fairness lie outside this law.

To supplement the Directive's guidance on how the fairness or unfairness of a contract term should be assessed, an Annex to the Directive provides a sample non-exhaustive list of terms, which may be regarded as unfair. The list is indicative only which means that the inclusion of a term in the Annex in a contract does not make it unfair, only that, under Article 3(3), it may well be, but an assessment will still have to be carried out.

The Annex lists seventeen terms with some clarifications and definitions of their scope. The types of unfair contract terms listed can be divided into three groups:

- terms which reflect unilateral decision-making by the seller or supplier against which the consumer has no remedy.
- terms which involve a lack of proportionality between the obligations imposed on the consumer and on the seller/supplier.
- contracts lacking information, which should have been supplied, had the seller/ supplied not been making improper use of his superior bargaining strength.

Air travel contracts have historically included terms along these lines. Among other things, they have tried to allow airlines to unilaterally alter departure/ arrival times and locations and type of aircraft used, to impose price increases after the contract is made and oblige the traveller to pay them, to impose high cancellation fees with little consequences for the airline if it cancels, or to impose short time periods within which complaints/claims must be made. As will be seen, the Commission will propose a specific Community law to deal with these kind of terms.

PLAIN AND INTELLIGIBLE LANGUAGE

The Unfair Terms Directive also tries to improve the transparency of consumer contracts. Article 5 provides that written contract terms:

> must always be drafted in plain, intelligible language.

---

[115] The Commission has questioned whether this exclusion should be retained on the basis of the interpretive difficulties in defining the main subject matter of contract, insurance contracts being a good example – *Ibid.*, p.15.

If there is a doubt about the meaning of a term, under the same provision, the interpretation most favourable to the consumer must be chosen. This accords with the generally accepted rule of interpretation of contracts: an unclear contract term must be interpreted to the detriment of the party who wrote it and to the advantage of the party who had no influence over its preparation.

The obligation to provide intelligible written contracts has had a major impact on the travel and tourist industry. In the past contracts offered by tour operators were notoriously difficult even for lawyers to interpret. As a result of Article 5 this has changed and tour operator contracts, usually contained in their brochures, are generally carefully written so that ordinary consumers can understand what they mean. Air travel contracts are however different and will be looked at later.

Requiring consumer contracts to be intelligible only really advances transparency where there is a complimentary obligation to provide the consumer with the terms of the contract in advance. As has been noted earlier in this chapter, such obligations already apply to certain tourist contracts – package travel and timeshare – but do not apply as a general rule to all consumer contracts. In the tourism context the pre-eminent example of a consumer contract where there is no obligation to provide the terms in advance is air travel contracts which are rarely seen by travellers. While, as will be seen later, a new Community law for air travel is under active consideration, the Commission has also questioned whether Article 5 might be improved by a new obligation to provide more advance information to consumers.[116]

Impact of the Directive

The Commission produced a report in 2000 on the implementation of the Unfair Terms Directive[117] and the following section which is based on that, focus' only on the impact of the Directive on the travel and tourism industry. Generally, the Commission was disconcerted to discover:

> that, despite the endeavours of the Community ... and the national authorities, balanced contractual relations are anything but the rule, that unfair terms are widely used, and that new types of unfair terms arise by the day.[118]

---

[116] *Ibid.*, p.18.

[117] Commission, Report on the implementation of Council Directive 93/13/EEC on Unfair Terms in Consumer Contracts, COM(2000) 248 final, 27.4.00.

[118] *Ibid.*, p.13.

Among the measures canvassed by the Commission for improving the situation are:

- strengthening the powers of national courts to deal with unfair terms, possibly using accelerated procedures, and greater use of criminal sanctions,[119]
- widening the legal effects of terms found unfair so as to cover more than just the parties, strengthening the use of negotiated agreements between trade and consumer bodies over the use of contracts terms,
- creating a role at Community level for the elimination of unfair terms derived from international type contracts, such as apply in air travel, and
- more sector specific laws.

Specific market studies were commissioned by the Commission to monitor the implementation of the Directive and continued usage of unfair terms. Among the sectors studied were the tourist sector generally, passenger air transport, timeshare and car rental. Indicative of just how unfairly consumers can be treated was the difficulty the researchers had in actually obtaining copies of contract terms.

> This study examined general terms and conditions in brochures and contracts offered by holiday organisers and agents, with regard to different tourist sectors (rental of holiday accommodation, timeshares, car rental, cruises and other services) in the 18 Member States of the EEA. A total of 1,773 contracts and brochures were examined and 356 general terms or conditions were considered unfair, of which 87 on the basis of the Directive's general criterion within the meaning of Article 3(1). Of the 356 terms investigated, 101 concerned contractual liability (this being the most problematic area); such terms are to be found notably in Belgian, Spanish, Portuguese, Irish, Swiss and Norwegian contracts. Another 56 terms concerned enforceability and the formation of the contract (although a considerable number of terms of this kind were found in Danish, Finnish, Irish, UK and Italian contracts, none were found in the Dutch and Norwegian contracts), 50 concerned the annulment of the contract and 47 the alteration of the contract price (but no term of this kind was found in the Austrian contractual terms and conditions). It should be noted that a large number of terms designed to eliminate or discourage reliance on

---

[119] The only case so far to reach the Court of Justice – *Oceano Grupo Editorial v. Quintero* [2000] E.C.R. I–4941, not a tourism case – dealt with the role of the courts in dealing with unfair terms The Court ruled that a national court did not have to wait for a party to raise a claim that a term is unfair, but could raise and rule on the issue itself.

procedures or remedies were identified in the UK, Belgian and Austrian contracts.[120]

The Commission's general conclusion was that the studies:

> not only demonstrated the ubiquity of unfair terms in standard–form contracts but also the enormous difficulty of getting hold of the contractual terms before concluding a contract or independently of entering into such a contract.[121]

UNFAIR TERMS AND AIR PASSENGERS

The widespread use of unfair terms in passenger air transport contracts is a current particular concern of the Commission and merits separate examination. In a communication in 2000[122] the Commission referred to an earlier study[123] which focused on:

> the contractual terms and conditions offered by 24 airline companies (of which 21 are based in the Member States) catering to the Union's airspace but also a series of texts adopted by the International Air Transport Association (IATA) in this field (Resolutions 724,724a and 745) and to general terms and conditions of transport (notably Recommendation 1724).

> The study revealed a significant number of terms which could be defined as unfair and which are mainly based on the IATA texts.

> To eliminate unfair terms in this economic sector, the study argues that the Union should issue guidelines as to the application of Directive 93/13/EC to the general terms and conditions of airline companies. These guidelines would concern not only the substance of the general terms and conditions but also the way in which they are communicated to passengers. ...[124]

Guidelines, however, carry no force, and would not now be seen as sufficient

---

[120] Commission, Report on the implementation of Council Directive 93/13/EEC on Unfair Terms in Consumer Contracts, COM(2000) 248 final, 27.4.00, p.46.

[121] *Ibid.*, p.9.

[122] Communication on the Protection of Air Passengers in the European Union, COM(2000) 365 final, 21.6.00. Text available at http://www.europa.eu.int/comm/transport/themes/air/english/library/prot_passager_en.pdf .

[123] *Ibid.*, p.41.

[124] *Ibid.*, p.41.

guarantee that unfair terms will not be used by airlines. The Commission in fact appears to have lost patience that the airline industry and is now advocating Community legislation.

Part of the reason why unfair terms have been so prevalent in air travel and why IATA has not proved more amenable to altering its recommendations to member airlines is that it is a worldwide body which must act on behalf of airlines based outside as well as inside the Community. The fact that no legal challenges to the fairness of airline contracts of carriage have reached the Court of Justice has not helped in stimulating reform.

A number of national consumer protection authorities have challenged IATA recommended terms, with varying degrees of effectiveness.[125] These challenges only serve to highlight the fragmentation on the internal market which individual national responses produce.

With the exclusion of delay issues,[126] the issues in air passenger air contracts which the Commission has highlighted as giving rise to fairness concerns[127] include:

- airline freedom to alter departure/arrival times and flight craft after issue of ticket,
- the ban on the transfer of tickets,
- the ban on the use of the later coupons on a ticket if the earlier ones are not used in sequence,
- airline freedom to raise prices after the contract is made,
- general lack of clarity, intelligibility and transparency in the presentation/ availability of contract information,
- airline liability under a code-share agreement,
- cancellation/no-show charges,
- greater facilitation of travellers with reduced mobility.

Recently the Commission followed up on its 2000 communication with a consultation paper[128] highlighting the specific legal issues involved in air

---

[125] Commission Consultation paper on airline's contracts with passengers, June 7, 2002, p.3. Text available at http://www.europa.eu.int/comm/transport/air/contrat-cons_en.pdf. The UK consumer protection body has been particularly active in this area. See Office of Fair Trading, Airline Flight Contracts, Iata's recommended general conditions of carriage (RP 1724) UK action under EC Directive 93/13 on unfair contract terms – explanatory note, September 2000. Text available at http://www.oft.gov.uk/html/new/airline.htm.

[126] See p. 309.

[127] See generally Commission, Consultation Paper, *ibid.*, pp.8–21.

[128] Commission, Consultation paper on Airline's Contracts with Passengers, 7.6.02, p.3. Text available at http://www.europa.eu.int/comm/transport/air/contrat–cons_en.pdf.

passenger contracts and possible ways of addressing them. As a result of this the general parameters of the Commission's eventual proposals seem clear.

> While protecting air passengers, the Community should avoid over-regulation. Its legislation on contracts should establish information requirements designed to render contracts clear, complete and easily available, create certain rights so as better to balance the interests of passengers and of airlines, and specify the rights of people with reduced mobility. However, the legislation should leave a sufficient area of contractual freedom so as not to hamper competition. It should regulate some aspects of the relation between carriers and passengers but allow airlines to define other conditions, so long as they are fair. The text should not be over prescriptive nor necessarily cover all the subjects discussed in this paper.

A general comment on the Commission's plans in this area is that they unwittingly highlight the weaknesses of the Unfair Terms Directive. The Directive (and the implementing national legislation) has failed, at least until recently, to improve air passenger contracts. The Directive reflects a general approach to dealing with unfair terms, but relies too heavily on court and other actions to ensure compliance. It is a pity it took so long to realise that sectoral laws, such as the proposed air contract law, are more effective in combating unfair terms in consumer contracts.

TOURISM EXAMPLES OF UNFAIR TERMS

Analysis of the examples[129] below reveals the kinds of stratagems used by travel organisers to gain an upper hand in consumer contracts. Contract terms are written in a way, which takes advantage of the consumer's ignorance regarding contract law and defies the principle of good faith upon which the Unfair Terms Directive is based. The reaction of national courts to such contract terms has been overwhelmingly in accordance with the requirements of the Directive. In fact, in most cases, the national law has gone beyond the details of the Directive in order to consider and protect the interests of the consumer. The

---

[129] Taken from the CLAB database. For an explanation of CLAB, see p. 323. The database has several weaknesses. The cases only refer to the national implementing legislation, though a limited number of references to the Unfair Terms Directive are given also. The cases contain few references to the dates of decisions. There is little means of identifying these decisions. The future of the database is also uncertain; it was originally established only for a definite period which has expired.

cases serve to show that laws protecting the tourist as a consumer are much needed.

Clause excluding liability, unfairness

In an Italian case a consumer claimed compensation when his caravan was stolen from a camping site. The case was taken to the Italian Supreme Court. The manager of the camping site claimed no responsibility for the theft and referred to a clause in the contract with the traveller according to which the company – in the event of theft of vehicles or objects contained in them, – rejected all liability. The Court decided that such a clause was unfair and therefore invalid, on the grounds that it was not specifically approved in writing. "In this case Article 5 of the Unfair Contract Terms Directive was quoted".[130]

Travel organiser's information duties, exclusion of liability, alterations of the contract at the organiser's discretion

In a German case a consumer organization took a travel organiser to court over terms included in the standard contract used by his firm. One of the terms allowed the organiser to modify performance completely at its own discretion whether or not the modification was acceptable to the traveller. This term was considered to be unfair with reference to the Directive's Annex, paragraph (k), which states:

> that a term, which enables the seller or supplier to alter unilaterally without valid reason any characteristics of the product or service to be provided, is unfair.[131]

Damages for contract not fulfilled, limitations of liability

A German tour organiser was sued by a consumer organisation which objected to a clause requiring the client to submit all claims of alleged non–performance of the travel contract in written form. The court found that the term violated §651(g) of the German Civil Code, which states that the traveller is entitled to forward his claims without being met with any requirements as regards form. The offensive clause was declared void.

---

[130] CLAB 278.
[131] CLAB 256–258. It will be recalled that under the Package Travel Directive tour organisers are made legally liable for significant alternations to packages and this duty cannot be avoided. For independent travel, the Unfair Terms Directive may produce a similar result.

> The term was considered unfair under paragraph (q) of the Annex to the Directive, concerning terms which exclude or hinder the consumer's right to take legal action or exercise any other legal remedy.[132]

Increase in the price of the package

A German travel organiser used a term in standard business contracts allowing for the increase of the price of the package by up to 10% of the original price, in the event of a price increase of charges of administering bodies during a period of at least four months from the conclusion of the contract to the beginning of the tour. A consumer organization complained against the use of this term, as it gave the travel organiser "unilateral" ability to change prices. According to the court, the term was admissible without restrictions, had it referred to periods outside these four months. However, an increase in prices of more than 10% during the four months before departure was far beyond what the customer has to expect in the course of normal price developments. Thus, the term was in violation of §9 AGBG, and thus null and void. In this case paragraph (l) of the Annex was quoted:

> Clauses which provide for the price of goods or services to be determined at the time of delivery or allowing a seller of goods or supplier of services to increase their price without in either case giving the consumer the corresponding right to cancel the contract if the final price is too high in relation to the price agreed when the contract was concluded.[133]

Increase in the price of the package

In a Swedish case a slightly different view was taken. The court stated that price adjustment clauses can be fair if formulated properly (i.e. more narrowly), but the consumer should always be entitled to cancel in the event of a price increase, regardless of whether it is over 10% or below 10%. The contractual term should take into account the economic consequences of price adjustment for the consumer. Paragraph (l) of the Annex was again quoted.[134]

---

[132] CLAB 236. Similar possibly unfair terms include requiring any claim to be made via the travel agent or that a claim will be denied if not received within three days of return to the place of departure.

[133] CLAB 43.

[134] CLAB 94. The Package Travel Directive only controls price increases in the last 20 days before departure. Before then the general clause of the Unfair Terms Directive can be used to control price increases.

> **Alteration of travel destination, breach of contract, compensation, limitation of liability, burden of proof**
>
> A Danish family bought a holiday trip by bus to Yugoslavia. Just before the beginning of the bus ride, the travel agency announced that the Yugoslavian hotel was overbooked. The intended trip was cancelled, and the customers were given the option of travelling to Italy or remaining at home. Those that remained in Denmark would receive a full refund of the money they had paid. The family in question decided, under protest, to go to Italy. Upon their return home, they claimed compensation, as they had not arrived at the destination to which they had booked, the Italian hotel was of a lower standard, and the living expenses were higher than in Yugoslavia. The company refused payment, based on two terms, which limited the company's liability and placed the burden of proof on the customer. The family, despite the fact that they had agreed to go to Italy instead, won the case. The court decided that placing the burden of proof on the consumer was unfair under the circumstances and the change of destination was a material breach of contract. The travel agent had not proved that this breach was due to circumstances for which he was not liable, and the court ordered him to pay a small amount in damages (of 2000 DKK).[135]

CHAPTER CONCLUSION

There is little doubt that issues of consumer policy and protection are ancillary to the more central areas of Community law and policy, viz. the common market and competition. The 1992 introduction into the Treaty of Rome of a new Title on consumer protection and its single Article 153, does not seem to have changed the perspective significantly. Consumer protection remains little more than an indirect consequence of internal market policy rules.

Within this context consumer protection tries to encourage the "cross-border consumer." It was the intention that not only the worker, the self-employed and the service-provider would move freely within the Community but the consumer as well, as a recipient of services in general and of tourism services in particular. There is little doubt that the provisions described above greatly help in facilitating cross- border consumer/tourism activity. Future trends seem likely to continue the mix of general, specific and sectoral approaches to consumer protection. Experience in tourism suggests that only sectoral approaches, even with some built-in obsolescence, really work.

---

[135] CLAB 275, 276.

STUDENT TASKS

Undergraduate questions:

1. Select one area of law dealt with in this chapter and trace how the general themes of Community consumer policy are reflected in it.

2. Both the Package Travel Directive and the Timeshare Directive protect consumers by compelling the supply of information to the consumer before the contract is made.

Explain how this is done.

3. Discuss the definition of 'package' in the Package Travel Directive.

4. In your view, what are the most unfair terms in the CLAB database cases mentioned into the chapter? Why ? Why do you think such terms were used in the first place?

Postgraduate questions:

1. Explain why Member State implementation of the provisions in the Package Travel Directive dealing with organiser financial security in the event of a business failure have given rise to legal proceedings in the Court of Justice. Which state's provisions seems best designed to protect the consumer? Why?

2. Do you agree with the general approach used in the Unfair Terms Directive of banning all unfair terms, rather than banning specific terms found in specific consumer contracts? Why?

3. Do you agree with the reform analysis of the Commission regarding the possible defects in the Timeshare Directive? Why?

4. Write a submission to the Commission on a possible Community law dealing with air passenger contracts.

CHAPTER 8

COMMUNITY COMPETITION POLICY AND TOURISM[1]

INTRODUCTION

The Treaty establishing the European Community (Treaty of Rome) places the promotion and safeguarding of competition at the heart of the Community's economic functions. The creation of a common market carries the risk that competition in the cross border markets of the Community may be threatened by selfish behaviour intended to deny the benefits of market competition.

> Competition policy is one of the pillars of the European Commission's action in the economic field. This action is founded on the principle, enshrined in the Treaty, of 'an open market economy with free competition'. It acknowledges the fundamental role of the market and of competition in guaranteeing consumer welfare, in encouraging the optimum allocation of resources and in granting economic agents the appropriate incentives to pursue productive efficiency, quality and innovation. However, the principle of an open market economy does not imply an attitude of blind faith or, possibly, indifference towards the operation of market mechanisms; on the contrary, it requires constant vigilance aimed at preserving those mechanisms. This is particularly true in the present context of markets evolving at a fast pace and becoming increasingly integrated at global level.[2]

Community competition policy applies to tourism (and other areas of economic activity) and pursues five broad themes. It:
- prohibits anti-competitive agreements,
- permits agreements which promise useful market benefits,
- prohibits abuses of dominant positions,

---

[1] Ariane Portegies, Marc Mc Donald.
[2] Commission, 30th Report on Competition Policy 2000, SEC(2001) 694 final, p.21.

- controls mergers which threaten competition, and
- prohibits state aid to tourism undertakings.

Community competition policy operates through a large series of legal measures contained in the Treaty and in secondary legislation, both regulations and decisions. The text of Community competition laws can be accessed at:

www.europa.eu.int/comm/competition/index_en.html

The Commission plays a central role as regards Community competition law. Its activities include devising implementing rules, judging the application of rules to particular cases, allowing some anti-competitive agreements, prohibiting others and generally enforcing competition law. Commission scrutiny of possible anti-competitive behaviour follows certain common steps:

- identifying the relevant players and business operation under scrutiny,
- defining the markets in which the parties operate,
- assessing any anti-competitive impacts which the agreement/abuse of dominant position/proposed merger may have on those markets, and
- where necessary, identifying any counter balancing beneficial effects of the behaviour.

Market definition is a key initial step. The Treaty phrase 'common market' masks the existence of a huge number of specific markets for individual products. Within tourism the types of market identified by the Commission include:

- hotel services – different categories of hotels; owning and leasing hotels,
- restaurant services,
- catering services – contract and concession food services,
- tour operator's services – short and long haul package holiday destinations,
- air passenger services – scheduled and charter flights,
- ferry services,
- cruise services,
- car rental services – corporate and leisure markets,
- timeshare services,
- gaming services,
- travel/tourism intermediary services – marketing and promotion markets; management and franchise markets; accommodation/flights block booking/ procurement markets,
- computer reservation services – travel agent and tour operator markets; direct

reservation for airline/hotel/car rental markets, and

- airports– facility services; terminal services; in-flight catering, in-flight cleaning, baggage handling.

Much of the tourism focus of competition policy has been on the transport side of tourism, particularly passenger air transport and tour operations. Passenger air transport is a complex activity in which competitors frequently rely on each other when offering services. The Commission is frequently called on to adjudicate on airline cooperation to see if it might or might not be anti-competitive. Many of its decisions have significant implications for tourist travel.

The competitive behaviour of market players is not the only focus of Commission competition scrutiny. Interference by Member State governments in tourism markets by granting State aid (of varying types) is also dealt with. The Commission monitors State aid for companies in the transport and travel sector, particularly air passenger transport, as well as the activities of local or regional authorities wishing to provide aid for tourism undertakings as a means of promoting regional development.

The linkages between the topics covered in this chapter can be seen in the following diagram:

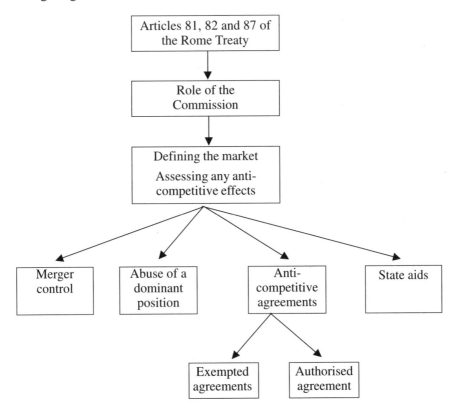

Learning outcomes:

After reading this chapter the student should:

- understand the role of market definition in competition analysis,
- appreciate the types of cooperative activity which are problematic/allowed under Community law,
- be able to discuss examples of competition law impact on tourism,
- understand why State aid to tourism is allowed in some cases and not others.

Based on the above, the following headings are used:

The Treaty and Competition.
Tourism Markets.
Agreements and Exemptions.
Abuse of Dominant Position.
Control of Tourism Mergers.
State Aid and Tourism.

THE TREATY AND COMPETITION

The principal aim of Community competition policy involves the creation "of a system ensuring that competition in the internal market is not distorted" – Article 3, Rome Treaty. An additional aim is to "strengthen the competitiveness of the Community industry".

Article 3 reflects the idea that market forces and not state intervention should drive market behaviour. Left alone, market competition should be able to contribute to economic efficiency by ensuring the competitive conduct of enterprises and ensuring consumers can buy goods and services on the best terms.

Two related aims of Community competition policy involve the protection of small and medium-sized enterprises (SMEs) and the fostering of larger Community undertakings which can compete on a global basis. In particular SMEs gain protection from the anti-competitive activities of larger dominant undertakings, while their own competitive behaviour is often excluded from Commission scrutiny. This particularly benefits tourism undertakings where 99% of enterprises are SMEs. Recently Community policy generally has attached an increasing importance to a healthy and dynamic SME sector as an instrument for tackling unemployment.

Treaty References to Competition

Articles 81 and 82[3] are the key provisions of the Rome Treaty which deal with competition between undertakings.[4] The former bans ant-competitive practises based on agreements and understandings, though it also allows some agreements where useful benefits can be identified. Article 82 prohibits abusive actions by dominant players in a market. The operation of both articles is discussed later and examples are given of their impact on tourism. Article 81 states that:

> The following shall be prohibited as incompatible with the common market: all agreements between undertakings, decisions by associations of undertakings and concerted practices which may affect trade between Member States and which have as their object or effect the prevention, restriction or distortion of competition within the common market, and in particular those which:
>
> (a) directly or indirectly fix purchase or selling prices or any other trading conditions
> (b) limit or control production, markets, technical development, or investment
> (c) share markets or sources of supply
> (d) apply dissimilar conditions to equivalent transactions with other trading parties, thereby placing them at a competitive disadvantage
> (e) make the conclusion of contracts subject to acceptance by the other parties of supplementary obligations which, by their nature or according to commercial usage, have no connection with the subject of such contracts.

Points (a) to (e) represent an indicative, not exhaustive, list. Practices not mentioned, but affecting trade between Member States and preventing, restricting or distorting competition, are also prohibited.

Under Article 81(3) agreements between competitors which contribute to promoting technical or economic progress, while allowing consumers a fair share of the resulting benefit and do not allow for the elimination of competition or impose unnecessary restrictions on the undertakings concerned, can be approved by the Commission.

The second major prohibition in the Treaty against anti-competitive behaviour

---

[3] Articles in the Rome Treaty were renumbered by changes made by the Amsterdam Treaty in 1999. Community documents pre-1999 refer to Articles 85 and 86.

[4] Article 87 dealing with State aid to undertakings is for convenience dealt with in the last section of this chapter.

concerns abuse of dominant position. Article 82 states that:

> Any abuse by one or more undertakings of a dominant position within the common market or in a substantial part of it shall be prohibited as incompatible with the common market in so far as it may affect trade between Member States.
>
> Such abuse may, in particular, consist in:
>
> (a) directly or indirectly imposing unfair purchase or selling prices or other unfair trading conditions
> (b) limiting production, markets or technical development to the prejudice of consumers
> (c) applying dissimilar conditions to equivalent transactions with other trading parties, thereby placing them at a competitive disadvantage
> (d) making the conclusion of contracts subject to acceptance by the other parties of supplementary obligations which, by their nature or according to commercial usage, have no connection with the subject of such contracts.

Article 82 does not, however, signal as clearly as might be wished that merger activity which might lead to a dominant position with the risk of abusive behaviour should also be controlled. For this reason the Council enacted Regulation 4064/89[5] on the control of concentrations with a Community dimension. This established the legal framework under which undertakings apply to the Commission for clearance for various merger agreements and the Commission evaluates and decides whether to prohibit or approve them (if necessary with conditions). As will be seen this has had a significant impact on merger activity in the tourism industry

The legal foundation of the central role of the Commission in competition matters lies in Article 85 of the Rome Treaty, which states that:

> the Commission shall ensure the application of the principles laid down in Articles 81 and 82. On application by a Member State or on its own initiative, and in cooperation with the competent authorities in the Member States, who shall give it their assistance, the Commission shall investigate cases of suspected infringement of these principles. If it finds that there has been an infringement, it shall propose appropriate measures to bring it to an end.
>
> If the infringement is not brought to an end, the Commission shall record

---

[5] OJ L 395/1, 30.12.89.

such infringement of the principles in a reasoned decision. The Commission may publish its decision and authorize Member States to take the measures, the conditions and details of which it shall determine, needed to remedy the situation.

TOURISM MARKETS

As already indicated Community competition (or anti-trust, to use the American term) policy is embedded in Articles 81 and 82 of the Treaty of Rome.

The first step which the Commission carries out in any competition enquiry is to identify the nature and extent of the commercial markets the relevant players operate in. Once the market is defined, the players and their respective shares can then be identified. Only when this is done is the Commission in a position to conduct a competitive assessment of whether, in the circumstances, the agreement or concentration or act of a dominant player, as the case may be, is likely to have noteworthy negative effects on competition.

Because market identification is common to all the Commission's competitive functions, it is appropriate at this point to set out what it involves before separately looking at anti-competitive agreements, exemptions, abuse of dominant position and merger control.

Defining the Relevant Market

Community literature refers to the market as the **relevant market**. Defining the relevant market is an important stage in competition analysis, since it provides the context in which the degree of competition between firms will be assessed. The market is defined from two dimensions – product and geographic. According to an interpretive notice designed to provide guidance on how the Commission applies competition law:

> The object of defining a market in both its product and geographic dimension is to identify those actual competitors of the undertakings involved that are capable of constraining their behaviour and of preventing them from behaving independently of an effective competition pressure.[6]

---

[6] OJ C 372/5, 9.12.97. According to the Commission (p.1) the value of setting out its approach in an interpretative Notice is: Increased transparency will result in companies and their advisors being able to better anticipate the possibility that the Commission would raise competition concerns in an individual case. Companies could, therefore, take such a possibility into account in their own internal decision making when contemplating for instance, acquisitions, the creation of joint ventures or the establishment of certain agreements. It is also intended that

Regarding product markets:

> A relevant product market comprises all those products and/or services which are regarded as interchangeable or substitutable by the consumer, by reason of the product's characteristics, their prices and their intended use

Thus, at the retail level a tourism product market consists usually of services which a tourist considers to be mutually interchangeable in a given geographic area, in particular, as regards use and price. The fact that the tourist can buy one service instead of another imposes an immediate and effective disciplinary force on the suppliers of a given product.

Regarding geographic markets:

> The relevant geographic market comprises the area in which the undertakings concerned are involved in the supply and demand of products or services, in which the conditions of competition are sufficiently homogenous and which can be distinguished from neighbouring areas because the conditions of competition are appreciably different in those areas.[7]

Geographic markets can be local, regional, national , international or even worldwide. Tourism products fit all these categories. While markets and their boundaries do not remain static and must be separately assessed in each case, the Commission sometimes finds that a market definition adopted in one case holds true in another. Markets too can be very specific. Any general tourism product like hotel accommodation can contain a variety of different markets depending on price, location, quality of service etc. The same applies to air transport, tour operators, travel agents. However, the Commission regularly avoids conclusively fixing the parameters of tourism markets because it is apparently difficult to be definitive about them. Instead, it conducts multiple competition assessments based on different market views. It also frequently concludes that whatever those parameters might be, no significant threat to competition arises.

---

companies should be in a better position to understand what sort of information the Commission considers relevant for the purpose of market definition.

[7] *Ibid.*, p.2.

Examples of Hotel Markets

Hilton/Scandic[8]

> The hotel businesses of Hilton and Scandic are to a very large extent complimentary. Whereas Hilton's traditional focus has been on the UK and major cities in continental Europe, Scandic's operation is based almost exclusively in the Nordic countries in which Hilton has only a single hotel. ... The notifying party states that the relevant product market is that for hotels, the competitive parameters of the market being determined by the combination of price, location and service quality offered by each hotel operating in the market ... However, it is not necessary to further delineate the relevant product market or the relevant geographical markets because, in all alternative market definitions considered, effective competition would not be significantly impeded.

The most detailed assessments of the hotel market were carried out in *Bass/ Saison*[9] where Bass bought the Intercontinental and Forum hotel chains and in *Accor/Vivendi*[10] where in partnership with others Accor bought the Libertel and Demeure hotel chains. The different hotel markets considered were based on distinctions between price/daily room rate, chain/franchised/ /independent hotels, city/local hotels, small/large hotels and even:

> the relevant market may therefore be one for all hotels (except perhaps the very cheapest and the most expensive) on the basis of a chain of substitutes.[11]

The grade of a hotel does not necessarily mean that it only competes with other hotels with the same grade.

> The market investigation has largely confirmed that even if significant price differences exist between the 'bottom' and the 'top' of the chain of stars (a 1 star hotel will rarely compete with a 4 stars hotel), a distinction relying exclusively on stars might be too rigid and does not reflect the actual substitutability between hotels, especially within hotel chains. Several sub-markets might be rather identified like 1 and 2 star hotels, 2 and 3 stars, 3 and 4 stars hotels, or 1, 2, 3 stars hotels and 2, 3, 4 stars hotels. ...[12]

---

[8] Case COMP/M.2451, 31.5.01, p.2.
[9] Case IV/M.1133, 23.3.98.
[10] Case IV/M.1596, 8.9.99.
[11] *Ibid.*, p.4.
[12] *Supra.*

> No conclusive view of the market was adopted in either case because under the various possibilities examined no competitive threat was identified.

In *Skanska/Securum*[13] both parties were involved in leasing hotels. The question was whether leasing hotels was a market on its own or merely part of a wider market of leasing buildings. The Commission ruled that:

> The leasing of hotels can be regarded as a separate market from the leasing of other buildings because of the special features required by hotel operators. It may be argued that there exist a certain degree of supply side substitutability, in that other kinds of real estate could be converted into hotels. However, this can only be relevant in a long term context and also requires high investments for the rebuilding and other requirements (as for sanitary and security demands and fire protection).

Examples of Tour Operator Markets

In a large number of cases the Commissions has identified the product and geographic markets for different types of leisure travel services, including markets for tour operations, travel agents, supply of airline seats for package holidays. The huge level of horizontal and vertical integration which has taken place in the tour operating industry in the last 15 years has seen the emergence of groups, originally tour operators, which have not only acquired competitors in other Member States but have also acquired suppliers both up stream (charter airlines) and downstream (travel agencies). When these groups make further acquisitions complex issues of market segmentations – both product and geographic – can arise.

Regarding travel agents the Commission accepted in a number of cases[14] that there are two product markets – business and leisure services and that the business market could be further divided into individual/group corporate, conference /exhibition. Regarding tour operators there are a number of possible markets – all holidays (including independent)/package holidays only, domestic/ foreign package holidays; within package holidays there may be a number of sub markets such as short/long haul, beach holidays, ski holidays, city breaks, destination markets and possibly even package holidays differentiated according

---

[13] Case IV/M 677, 8.1.96, p.2.

[14] *Thomas Cook/LTU/West LB*, Case IV/M.299, 14.7.92; *Havas Voyage/American Express*, Case IV/M.564; *Maersk/DKDS Travel,* Case IV/M.988, 4.11.97; *Wagon Lits/Carlson*, Case IV/ M.867, 7.3.97.

to type of transport used. The market for air seats as part of leisure travel services could be charter airline only or charter and scheduled airline.

In *Airtours/First Choice*[15] one vertically integrated UK tour operator sought to buy another. The Commission had to identify the different product and geographic markets of both to see if the deal would raise anti-competitive concerns. Possible market overlaps covered package holidays, travel agencies and airline seats. The Commission rejected Airtours views that (a) due to recent consumer trends the holiday market now consisted of independent as well as packaged holidays, and (b) that the foreign package holiday market should be regarded as a single entity. The Commission decided that the relevant holiday market consisted of package holidays alone and that the relevant distinction was between short and long-haul package holiday markets.[16] Regarding the travel agency services market, although other alternatives to travel agencies were identified (direct sales through tour operator shops, distance selling via the internet, telephone call centres, mail orders), the Commission held, after examining booking trends which indicated that the great majority of package sales were still made through in-person sales in a travel agency, that the relevant product market was that for travel agency services. Regarding airline seats for package holidays, both tour operators had their own charter airline and before assessing the competitive effect of the sale in that market the Commission decided that the relevant market for seats for package holidays was charter seats only and not scheduled seats as well:

> The major tour operators in the UK travel sector are vertically integrated, each with its own charter airline. However, in line with the Commission's normal approach in these matters, self-supply is not regarded as forming part of the relevant market. The market therefore consists only of sales to (and by) third-parties. ... Accordingly, the relevant market adopted for the purposes of the present decision as regards airline services, is that for the supply to tour operators of seats on charter flights to short-haul destinations. ...[17]

The Commission also decided that the relevant geographic markets were still national in character.

---

[15] Case IV/M.1524, 22.9.99. Reasoning followed in *Preussag/Thomson, supra* and *Preussag/Nouvelles Frontiere, supra*.

[16] *Ibid.*, p.9.

[17] *Ibid.*, p.13.

> The Commission has accepted in previous decisions that the markets within Europe for the supply of foreign package holidays are still essentially national in character. Tour operators, even those which sell holidays in several countries, generally produce and market their packages on a national basis – i.e. for the Community, with a point of departure in, and for sale to residents of, each Member State separately. Travel agents likewise market nationally. Charter airline services can also be regarded as national in character, as they fly out of and return to their country of origin and licensing and the demand for these services arises mainly from customers resident in the country of origin.[18]

Example of Air Passenger Services Markets

The relevant market for passenger air services depends principally on routes and their substitutability:

> In the air transport sector, the definition of the relevant market has to start from the route itself, or a bundle of routes to the extent that there is substitutability between them according to the features of each case. Other factors that could prove to be relevant are the structural conditions prevailing at airports and their capacity, as well as the impact of an extensive or high volume network in a given geographic are. The substitutability between routes depends on a number of factors such as the distance between the point of origin and the point of destination, the difference between the airports situated on each side of the route or the number of frequencies available on each route.[19]

> In *Lufthansa/SAS*[20] in 1996 the Commission ruled on a proposed alliance between two airlines involving among other things the setting up of a joint venture for air traffic between Germany and Scandinavia. In examining the relevant market the Commission looked at a range of alternatives:
>
> The Commission considers that the relevant markets in this instance

---

[18] Other Commission decisions on tour operator/travel agent market identification include *Kouni/ First Choice*; *West LB/Carlson/Thomas Cook*; *West LB/Thomas Cook*; *Wagons-Lits/Carlson*; *Thomas Cook/LTU/West LB*.

[19] Case IV/M.259, 27.1.92, p.5.

[20] Decision 96/180, OJ L 54/28, 5.3.96. Other cases where the Commission did not directly indicate its market analysis, but published notices as to possible conditions on which it might exempt airline alliance from Article 81(1) of the Treaty are British Airways/American Airways O JC 239/10, July 30, 1998; *Lufthansa/SAS/United Airlines* OJ C 239/5, 30.7.98.

are, first, the market for the scheduled air transport of passengers ... for each of the routes linking Scandinavia and Germany, including any hubs that might be situated at the end of such routes. ... The Commission takes the view that, in this instance, chartered air transport does not constitute a genuine alternative to scheduled air transport since the clientele consists essentially of business travellers. Such travellers need to travel to the main European cities to attend working meetings at agreed times and cannot therefore accept the inconvenience of charter flights, unlike passengers travelling in their leisure time. ... Theoretically, high-speed trains offer an alternative to air transport. Over medium distances, high-speed trains offer fast and regular services which mean that they are substitutable for air transport. ... However, the fact of the matter is that these alternative modes of transport are not applicable to any significant extent in this instance.

Example of Airport Facilities' Markets

The market for airports facilities, both for direct traffic and as a hub, was considered in *Flughafen Frankfurt/Main*,[21] which concerned Frankfurt Airport:

> the relevant service market is the provision of airport facilities, which allow aircraft to land and take off. These facilities are supplied by the airport operators, who charge fees in return. The relevant geographic market is Frankfurt

> An airline wishing to provide a point-to-point air transport service to or from a specific city or region – here the city is Frankfurt and its surrounding catchment area – cannot chose between different airports into which or from which to operate the service in question. There are no other international airports in the near vicinity of Frankfurt which could be considered substitutable for the provision of point-to-point air transport services to and from Frankfurt and its surrounding region. Beyond a certain distance, airports cannot realistically be considered to be substitutable in so far as point-to-point traffic is concerned. ... Competition between airports is significant only in so far as an airport constitutes a hub, i.e. a transfer point for connecting flights. ... In that context a competitive relationship exists between a number of large European airports for part of the overall traffic, i.e. non-direct traffic

---

[21] Decision 98/190, OJ L 72/30, 11.3.98.

using an airport as a transfer point. ... However, connecting traffic does not account for the total traffic at an airport, and the majority of such traffic will be traffic for which the airport in question is relevant as a point of origin or point of destination. ... Furthermore, the Commission consider that even with regard to non-direct traffic where a particular airport is used as a hub, the degree of substitutability is nevertheless limited to a small part of the total traffic at that airport. A larger degree of substitutability will exist for non-European airlines than for European airlines because the latter will tend to establish their hub in their country of origin.

Examples of Ferry/Cruise Markets

In *Costa Crociere*[22] the question was whether cruise holidays represented a separate market or were part of a larger leisure holiday market. Although there was some substitutability between cruises and other types of holidays in the medium-high price range, this was limited and the Commission concluded that the relevant market was the market for cruise holidays. The geographic market for cruises was national even though the cruises could take place anywhere.

> However, the definition of the market should be based on the area where conditions of competition are homogenous from the demand point of view, which implied that the definition should focus on the options available to consumers when making a reservation of a cruise or a package holiday in general. This is the area where cruise operators compete for customers, regardless of the final destination of the trip. In fact, a cruise operator providing a holiday in the Caribbean does not compete in the Caribbean itself but in those countries where that journey is offered to possible clients ... From this perspective, the market for cruses and package holidays as a whole seems to be national, or at least in the case of the Community.

In *P&O/Stena Line*[23] two ferry operators between the UK and France/Belgium proposed to consolidate their operations in a joint venture. To define the product markets, the Commission firstly identified two types of possible traveller (business and leisure travellers) and examined what

---

[22] Case IV/M.0334, 19.7.93.
[23] Decision 1999/421, OJ L 163/61, 29.6.99.

services (car shuttle – Le Shuttle – or high sped rail links – Eurostar – both operated through the Channel Tunnel or air links) the two types of traveller would regard as substitutable for ferry services. The Commission did not consider that business travellers would regard ferry or car shuttle through the Channel Tunnel as substitutable for either air transport or direct Tunnel high-speed rail links for reasons for speed and comfort. Since both ferries and Le Shuttle carried cars they were considered substitutable. The remaining question was whether Eurostar services operated in the same market for tourist travellers, including foot and vehicle travellers, as the ferry companies. The answer was no.

> It is ... only a limited category of tourist passenger for which Eurostar service may in practice be substitutable for those of ferries and Le Shuttle. For the larger proportion of customers the services will not be considered sufficiently substitutable for Eurostar to be considered as being within the same relevant market as the ferries and Le Shuttle.

Regarding the geographic market, the Commission concluded that while the North Sea (e.g. Hull/Felixstowe) and Western Channel (Portsmouth) routes to the continent were not substitutable for the Short Seas routes (Dover/Newhaven) because of the shorter crossing times available, the reverse applied because tourists from wider afield in the UK travelled to the south east English coast to cross the Channel because of the shorter crossing times. Thus,

> Tourist services on the North Sea routes should therefore be considered to operate within a relevant market consisting of North Sea and Short Sea routes (Calais/Dover, Dieppe/Newhaven).

ANTI-COMPETITIVE AGREEMENTS AND EXEMPTIONS

Once the Commission completes its market identification, it then considers the competitive effects of the activity in question. Article 81(1) of the Treaty of Rome, it will be recalled, prohibits agreements, decision and concerted practices which have as their object or effect the prevention, restriction or distortion of competition in the common market

Tourism Examples of Infringements of Article 81(1)

In *SAS/Maersk Air*[24] two airlines operating in and out of Denmark concluded a cooperation agreement which they notified to the Commission. The notification, however, did not reveal the full extent of anti-competitive cooperation between both airlines. It focused on code-sharing provision, and omitted the market-sharing agreement, which led to the withdrawal by Maersk Air from the Copenhagen-Stockholm route and SAS's exit from the Copenhagen-Venice and Frankfurt-Billund routes. The Commission, as will be seen further below, imposed large fines on both airlines.

> The agreements share markets between SAS and Maersk Air. Market-sharing agreements are expressly mentioned in Article 81(1)(c) as an example of the agreements that fall under Article 81(1). ... First, the parties concluded an overall market-sharing agreement, according to which SAS would not operate on Maersk Air's routes to/from Jutland and Maersk Air would not launch competing services from Copenhagen on the routes which SAS operated or wished to operate. Also the parties agreed to respect the share-out of the domestic routes. ... Second, the parties concluded specific market-sharing agreements regarding individual routes. In particular, the parties agreed that (a) Maersk Air would cease flying between Copenhagen and Stockholm as from 28 March 1999 and obtain compensation for its withdrawal; (b) as compensation, SAS would stop operating between Copenhagen and Venice at the end of March ... and Maersk Air would start operations on the route at the same moment; and (c) SAS would stop flying on the Billund-Frankfurt route in January 1999.

> By their very nature, these market-sharing agreements have the object of restricting competition. Therefore they are caught by the prohibition in Article 81(1).

In *International Union of Railways*[25] relating to the distribution of railway tickets by travel agents, the Commission declared that:

> the International Union of Railways has infringed the provisions of Article [81](1) of the EEC Treaty by adopting and circulating a leaflet on relations between railway companies and travel agents providing for a.o. setting a standard rate of commission, and the requirement that agents must not favour competing means of transport in their offers or advice to the public.

---

[24] OJ L 265/30, 5.10.01.
[25] Decision 568/92, OJ L 366/47, 15.12.92.

In *90 Tour Italia*[26] the Commission ruled that agreements between FIFA (governing body in world football) and various Italian organising committees and certain Italian travel agencies – under which 90 Tour Italia (a private company) was granted the exclusive supply of match tickets (ground entrance) for use as part of package tours to the 1990 World Cup in Italy and which made it impossible for other tour operators and travel agencies to find sources of supply other than 90 Tour Italia – infringed Article 81(1).

In *Greek Ferries*,[27] following a complaint from a member of the public, the Commission carried out investigations at the offices of ferry operators in Greece and Italy in July1994 and:

> concluded that ferry companies operating in Ancona, Bari, Brindisi – Greece routes participated in a price fixing cartel for several years. ... The parties engaged in regular, direct consultations aimed at fixing passenger fares.

Agreements between travel agents and tour operators which aim at preventing or restricting competition, are also incompatible with the common market. It has been emphasised that a travel agency is an independent intermediary providing a service distinct from that provided by the tour operator. Hence agreements which oblige travel agencies to charge the prices and tariffs set by tour operators for package tours or which prohibit the former from passing on to the customer the part of the commission they receive on the sale of holidays or from granting customers discounts, are incompatible with Article 81.

Punishments

The Commission can use either or both of two legal measures once anti-competitive behaviour is found – it can order it to stop and/or impose a fine. The first power is based on Article 3 of Regulation 117/62[28] (Article 4 of Regulation 3975/87[29] in the air transport sector) under which the Commission can "require the undertaking or associations of undertakings concerned to bring such infringement to an end".

The legal basis for imposing fines varies depending on the type of anti-

---

[26] Decision 92/521, OJ L 326/31, 12.11.92.
[27] Case IV/34.466, December 9, 1998; Competition Policy Newsletter, Number 1, February 1999, p.37.
[28] OJ L 13/204, 21.2.62.
[29] OJ L 374/1, 31.12.87.

competitive behaviour.[30] The same level of fines are provided for regarding anti-competitive agreements generally and in air transport, which is:

> 1000 to 1,000,000 ECUs, or sum in excess thereof but not exceeding 10% of the turnover in the preceding business year of each of the undertakings participating in the infringement, where, either intentionally or negligently ... they infringe Article [81(1)] or Article [82] ... In fixing the amount of the fine, regard shall be had both to the gravity and to the duration of the infringement.

In *Greek Ferries*[31] the Commission took into account the limited size of the relevant market and the limited impact of the price fixing agreement on this market. Furthermore, the undertakings cooperated with the Commission and this lead to significant reduction of fines.

In *SAS/ Maersk Air*[32] the Commission took into account the difference between the size of the two airlines, the need to set the fines at a level which ensures that they have a sufficiently deterrent effect, and the degree to which the parties cooperated with the Commission after the on-site inspections.

The Commission is also entitled to impose fines where undertakings, intentionally or negligently supply incorrect or misleading information, or information in an incomplete form during the investigations. In *KLM/Martinair*[33] the Commission imposed a fine of €40,000 on KLM for being grossly negligent in supplying incorrect information and withholding relevant information on the charter and scheduled services of a subsidiary.

Commission Investigation Powers

To carry out its duties, the Commission has the power to obtain all necessary information from the Governments and competent authorities of the Member States and from undertakings and associations of undertakings. For example it

---

[30] Article 15(2) Regulation 17/62 in case of anti-competitive agreements generally; Article 12(2), Regulation 3975/87 in case of air transport and Article 14 (2) of Regulation 4064/89 in case of ant-competitive concentrations.

[31] Case IV/34.466, 9.12.98.

[32] OJ L 269/33, 5.10.001.

[33] Case IV/M.1608, 14.10.99. See also Competition Policy Newsletter, Number 1, February 2000, p.26.

can send letters to undertakings and industry bodies seeking information and views about market definition and market share. If necessary, the Commission may also decide to conduct a general enquiry into specific sectors of the economy, whereby undertakings in the sector concerned may be obliged to supply the necessary information.

The Commission can also request competent authorities in Member States to undertake investigations which the Commission considers necessary. The officials of the Commission may assist the officials of such authorities in carrying out their duties. The investigation powers of the Commission are far-reaching as witnessed by Article 14(1) of Regulation 17/62 which states that:

> In carrying out the duties assigned to it… the Commission may undertake all necessary investigations into undertakings and associations of undertakings. To this end the officials authorised by the Commission are empowered:
>
> (a) to examine the books and other business records;
> (b) to make copies of or extracts from the books and business records;
> (c) to ask for oral explanations on the spot;
> (d) to enter any premises, land and means of transport of undertakings.

EXEMPTIONS

While the potential reach of the ban on anti-competitive behaviour in Article 81(1) of the Treaty of Rome is very broad, a number of means exist for narrowing its scope. These rest on either of two basic ideas – some agreements may actually serve some desirable overall economic purpose and some agreements because of their small or domestic scale might affect only national trade or have an insignificant effect on intra-Community trade.

Article 81(3) provides the means to implement these ideas since it allows Article 81(1) to be declared inapplicable to an agreement or category of agreements between undertakings, a joint decision or a concerted practice or category of concerted practices which:

> contributes to improving the production or distribution of goods or to promote technical or economical progress, while allowing consumers a fair share of the resulting benefit, which does not:
>
> (a) impose on the undertakings concerned restrictions which are not indispensable to the attainment of these objectives;
> (b) afford such undertakings the possibility of eliminating competition in respect of a substantial part of the *products in question*.

Article 81(1) can be declared inapplicable either by individual application and decision or by prior regulation intended to cover a range of similar type agreements. Article 83(2) requires the Community:

> to lay down detailed rules for the application of Article 81(3), taking into account the need to ensure effective supervision on the one hand, and to simplify administration to the greatest possible extent on the other.

On foot of this, Regulation 17/62[34] uses two key concepts to facilitate Commission decisions on individual applications – negative clearance and compulsory notification.

- Negative clearance – "Upon application by the undertakings concerned, the Commission may certify that ... there are no grounds under Article 85(1) or Article 86 of the Treaty for action on its part" – Article 2. Thus, an undertaking can apply for negative clearance where it is uncertain whether an agreement it has made might be caught by the prohibition. It asks the Commission to certify that in its opinion there are no grounds for taking action. It is also possible, if negative clearance will not be given, to simultaneously apply for an exemption under Article 81(3). "The parties requested the Commission to find that their agreement does not infringe Article 85(1) of the EC Treaty, or in the alternative, that the conditions are met for granting exemption under Article 85(3). ..."[35]

- Compulsory Notification – "Agreements ... of the kind described in Article 85(1) .... and in respect of which the parties seek application of Article 85(3) must be notified to the Commission" – Article 41. This creates a system of compulsory notification which enables the Commission to judge compatibility with the common market. Agreements which are not notified are automatically void, and cannot be put to the test of Article 85(3) for exemption.

The Commission can and does also issue Notices to provide guidance on its interpretation of Community competition law and particularly regarding agreements not likely to affect competition in the common market.

Examples of notices, regulations and decisions relevant to tourism which allow anti-competitive acts will now be looked at.

---

[34] OJ L 13/204, 21.2.62. This does not apply to the air transport sector, but Regulation 3975/87, OJL 374/1, 31.12.87 applies similar rules to air transport. Regulation 17/62 will be replaced from 1.5.04 by Regulation 1/2003, OJ L 1/1, 4.1.03.

[35] *Lufthansa/SAS*, OJ L 54/28, 5.3.96.

Authorised Co-operation

In the Notice on horizontal co-operation agreements[36] the Commission outlined the framework for deciding if defined cooperation (including research and development, production and commercialisation – standardisation, advertising/promotion, selling/distribution) between competitors which affects the common market is permitted. The key issue is whether the positive effects/efficiency gains from co-operation in terms of impact on the market will outweigh any negative effects in terms of consumer benefit. Much depends on the market impact of the co-operation. In the case of hotels where the market share tends to be low such agreements are less likely to cause competition worries, while co-operation agreements among competing airlines and tour operators where market share can be significant, will require closer analysis to see if either Article 81(1) is infringed and, if it is, whether the co-operation promises benefits in accordance with Article 81(3).

Two types of co-operation – joint advertising and the use of common labels – are particularly relevant to the tourism industry. According to a previous Commission Notice[37]:

> Joint advertising is designed to draw the buyer's attention to the products of an industry or to a common brand; as such it does not restrict competition between the participating enterprises. However, if the participating enterprises are partly or wholly prevented ... from themselves advertising ... there may be a restraint of competition.

> Agreements having as their sole object the use of a common label to designate a certain quality, where the label is available to all competitors on the same conditions ... Such associations for the joint use of a quality label do not restrict competition if other competitors, whose products objectively meet the stipulated quality requirements, can use the label on the same conditions as the members. Nor do the obligations to accept quality control of the products provided with the label, to issue uniform instructions for use, or to use the label for the products meeting the quality standards constitute restraints of competition.

Agreements of Minor Importance

In the Notice on agreements of minor importance,[38] the Commission declared that agreements having no appreciable effect either on competition within the

---

[36] OJ C 3/2, 6.1.01.
[37] OJ C 75/3, 29.7.68.
[38] OJ C 368/13, 22.12.01.

common market, known as the '*de minimis*' rule, are not caught by Article 81(1), although such cooperation may still be subject to national competition laws.

The Notice lays down market-share thresholds by which undertakings themselves can judge whether they come within the exemption. The Notice differentiates market-share threshold according to type of agreement. If the aggregate market share of the undertakings involved does not exceed:

- 10% for agreements between competitors (travel operator/travel agent), or

- 15% for agreements between non-competitors (tour operator/travel agent)

the Commission will not consider it caught by Article 81(1).

The higher % for agreements between non-competitors is based on the presumption that an anti-competitive practice committed within vertically linked companies has a less serious impact on competition in a market.

However, the Commission will not treat "hard core" restrictions (price fixing, market sharing) as exempt from Article 81(1).

SME Co-operation

In the same Notice on agreements of minor importance, the Commission specifically excluded agreements between small and medium sized enterprises (SMEs)[39] from its enforcement of the application of Article 81(1). This is particularly beneficial to SMEs as it avoids the laborious procedure of notification-negative clearance:

> agreements between small and medium-sized undertakings, as defined in ... the Commission Recommendation 96/280/EC are rarely capable of appreciably affecting trade between Member States and competition within the common market.

In *Relais et Chateaux*[40] an association of independent hotel owners, Relais & Chateaux, notified its basic statute and internal regulations containing the admission criteria for new members to the Commission. The association was established in 1954 and is an independently owned chain of 364 hotels and 49 restaurants in the 3, 4 and 5 star categories. They share a common trademark.

---

[39] The Commission recommendation concerning the definition of SMEs (OJ L 107, 30.4.96) proposes the following thresholds: firms whose annual turnover and balance-sheet total do not exceed ECU 40 million and 27 million respectively and in either case have a maximum of 250 employees.

[40] Case IV/36180, Competition Policy Newsletter, Number 1, February 1988, p.49.

According to its regulations, membership of R&C prevented a hotel from joining any other hotel chain, although members of R&C were still free to work together with organisations offering say specific services (reservation and distribution services for example) or with tourism offices. A member could terminate its membership annually.

The Commission considered the position of R&C and the effects of the agreement, not only on the hotel market, but also on the market of intermediaries in hotel and restaurant marketing. The Commission considered that the agreements notified would not affect trade between Member States significantly, because it was made between SMEs as defined in Community law and noted that this conclusion reflected the views expressed in the Notice on Agreements of Minor Importance.

However, SME co-operation may be subject to national competition rules.

Exempting Regulations

It will be recalled that Article 83 of the Rome Treaty permits the making of regulations to allow for exemptions from the ban on anti-competitive agreements. A number of regulations, supplemented by Commission guidance notices, have created general or block exemptions for defined types of anti-competitive actions on the ground that the benefits of competition restrictions outweigh the disadvantages of loss of competition. The Guidance Notices in particular are intended to help businesses determine if their actions come within the exemptions.

Airline Consultation

In the air transport sector the Council has conferred power on the Commission[41] to remove defined agreements from the scope of the basic prohibition in Article 81(1). In Regulation 1617/93[42] the Commission exercised this power and made three block exemptions covering IATA passenger tariff conferences (where competing airlines meet periodically to fix prices with a view to facilitating interlining[43]) as well as airline consultations regarding slot allocation and airport

---

[41] In Regulation 3976/87, OJ L 374/9, 31.12.87.

[42] OJ L 155/18, 26.6.93 as amended most recently by Regulation 1105/2002. Consolidated text available at http://europa.eu.int/eur-lex/en/consleg/pdf/1993/en_1993R1617_do_001.pdf.

[43] Interlining arises where a passenger has a ticket for a trip on more than one airline. See generally Commission, DG Competition Consultation Paper – IATA Passenger Tariff Conferences, February 2001. Available at http://www.europa.eu.int/comm/competition/ antitrust/air_transport/interlining/consultation_paper_iata_tariff_conferences.pdf.

scheduling. Article 1 declares that:

> Article [81(3)] of the Treaty shall not apply to agreements between undertakings in the air transport sector ... which have as their purpose one or ore of the following: the holding of consultations on tariffs for the carriage of passengers, with their baggage, on scheduled air services between Community airports; slot allocation and airport scheduling in so far as they concern air services between airports in the Community.

The reasons for this exemption are apparent from the Regulation Preamble.

> Consultations on passenger ... tariffs may contribute to the generalised acceptance of interlinable fares and rates to the benefit of air carriers as well as air transport users. ... Arrangements on slot allocations at airport and airport scheduling can improve the utilization of airport capacity and airspace, facilitate air-traffic control and help to spread the supply of air transport services from the airport.

All three block exemptions last until end June 2005.

Computer Reservation Systems

The operation of computer reservation systems (CRSs) has rapidly become central to passenger transport, particularly air transport, and has raised concerns regarding possible anti-competitive effects. Such concerns arise from competitors cooperating to establish such systems and from possible abuse of dominant positions in the way information is presented so as to favour particular undertakings or the availability of special fares on computer screens. CRSs, however, can also be hugely beneficial for suppliers and consumers of travel products. Thus, the Commission made Regulation 3652/93[44] which grants a block exemption for agreements between enterprises collaborating in the development or operation of CRSs for air transport. The Regulation allows, under strict conditions, co-operation between enterprises to develop and run computer reservation systems and to impose exclusive rights and obligations on distributors.

Regulation 2299/89[45] compliments this exemption by focusing not on the partners to such a system but on ensuring fairness in the way the system is used.

---

[44] OJ L 333/37, 31.12.93.

[45] OJ L 220/1, 29.7.89 as amended. Consolidated text available at http://europa.eu.int/eur-lex/en/consleg/main/1989/en_1989R2299_index.html.

The anti-competitive dangers in the way such systems interact with travel agents and air carriers are significant –

> denial of access to the systems or discrimination in the provision, loading or display of data or unreasonable conditions imposed on participants or subscribers can seriously disadvantage air carriers, travel agents and ultimately consumers.[46]

Instead of granting a block exemption regarding agreements covering CRS use, Regulation 2299/89 subjects the relationship between the CRS owners/operators and subscribers (generally travel agents) to a code of conduct. (This Code does not apply to travel websites which deal only with consumers, because although a website is technically a CRS, the Code focuses only on business-to-business dealings). The rationale for the Code of Conduct is summarised in the Preamble as follows:

> A mandatory code of conduct applicable to all computerised reservation systems and/or distribution facilities offered for use and/or used in the Community could ensure that such systems are used in a non-discriminatory and transparent way, subject to certain safeguards, so avoiding their misuse while reinforcing undistorted competition between air carriers and between computerised reservation systems and thereby protecting the interest of consumers

The Code applies to any CRS 'used in the territory of the Community' (Article 1) irrespective of where the flight airports are and, among other things, requires a CRS to allow any air carrier the opportunity to participate, on an equal and non-discriminatory basis, in its distribution facilities, forbids attaching any unreasonable conditions to a CRS contract with a participating carrier, forbids imposing irrelevant supplementary conditions or preventing a carrier from also using another system, forbids an air carrier joint owner of a CRS from refusing to let a rival CRS distribute the same information and products as its CRS. An Annex sets out ranking rules regarding flight display options in order to ensure that the way the information is presented on a computer screen is not unfair or discriminatory.

Article 8(1) of the Code prohibits a parent carrier from directly or indirectly

---

[46] *Supra*, Preamble. For a closed proceeding involving a complaint that Air France had discriminated against an American CRS - Sabre – by not supplying it with it with the same comprehensive and timely flight information as Air France provided to Amadeus (which it partly owned) and not providing the same technical facilities such as on-line confirmation of bookings – see, Press Release IP/00/835, 25.7.00.

linking the use of a specific CRS by a subscriber with receipt of any commission for the sale of air transport.

> In *Electronic Ticketing*,[47] the Commission ruled that Lufthansa was in breach of the CRS Code of Conduct by offering travel agents incentives to issue electronic tickets via START Amadeus (a CRS in which it was a part owner) while not enabling a rival CRS, SABRE, to do the same.

Franchising

Franchising is widely used to establish retail networks for the distribution of products. It involves a franchisor granting a licence to a franchisee (retailer) for the use of property rights in trade marks/signs and know-how and related training and commercial assistance. The franchisee acquires the use of an established and presumably successful retail system and in return pays a range of use and assistance fees depending on the type of franchise. In the tourism industry franchising appears to be principally used in hotels, fast food catering and some passenger air transport.

Franchising can have both positive and negative effects on competition in a marketplace. On the one hand:

> Franchise agreements ... normally improve the distribution of goods and/ or the provision of services as they give franchisors the possibility of establishing a uniform network with limited investments, which may assist the entry of new competitors on the market, particularly in the case of small and medium-sized undertakings, thus increasing interbrand competition. They also allow independent traders to set up outlets more rapidly and with higher chance of success than if they had to do so without the franchiser's experience and assistance. They have therefore the possibility of competing more efficiently with large distribution undertakings. ... As a rule, franchise agreements also allow consumers and other end users a fair share of the resulting benefit. ...[48]

On the other hand, franchise agreements normally contain a range of restrictions on both parties, especially the franchisee, which may hinder their commercial freedom during or even after the agreement. These restrictions may confer benefits exclusively on the franchisor and ultimately deprive the consumer of the benefits of franchising. Among restrictions which can be found in franchise

---

[47] Decision 618/99, OJ L 244/56, 16.9.99.
[48] Preamble to earlier franchise Regulation 4087/88 OJ L 359, 28.12.88, no longer in force.

agreements are restrictions which limit the franchisee and franchisor in setting up competing outlets, require the purchase of supplies from designated sources, and limit the use which can be made of the franchise know-how.

The Community approach to the competition impact of franchising is to encourage its positive effects, while controlling such franchise forms or terms which prevent consumers gaining the benefits of franchising. Thus, the Commission enacted Regulation 2790/99[49] which applies to vertical agreements (agreements between different parties in the distribution chain e.g. retailer/ wholesaler) including franchise agreements and which automatically exempt types of franchise agreements and types of franchise conditions from the ban on anti-competitive agreements in Article 81(1) of the Rome Treaty. The Commission has published guidelines on how this exemption should be operated.[50]

Only franchise agreements where the franchisor's market share does not exceed 30% can potentially benefit from the exemption. This figure is chosen on the basis that a greater market share by the franchiser raises the risk that there might not be enough competition in that market for the advantages of the franchise to outweigh the loss of competition involved in any restriction on the franchisee.

Where the transfer of know-how is the more important element in a franchise agreement, vertical restraints will more easily fulfil the conditions for exemption.

Generally, restraints which are necessary to protect the uniformity of the franchise and the integrity of the trade mark/know-how property rights to be used under the franchise, are covered by the exemption. These could include the franchisee obligation not to engage directly or indirectly in a similar business or acquire a controlling influence in a competing business, to respect the confidentiality of the know-how being used and to communicate experience gained from using the franchise.

> A non-compete obligation on the goods or services purchased by the franchisee falls outside Article 81(1) when the obligation is necessary to protect the common identity and reputation of the franchised network.[51]

Equally, restraints which require a franchisee to purchase supplies from defined sources may benefit from the exemption if they can be shown as necessary to maintain the integrity of the franchise.

---

[49] OJ L 336/21, 29.12.99.
[50] OJ C 291/1, 13.10.00.
[51] *Ibid.*, p.40.

Airlines and Travel Agents

In IATA Passenger Agency Programme[52] the Commission declared Article 81(1) inapplicable to the IATA Passenger Agency Programme (PAP) because the agreements in question:

> contribute to improving the production and distribution of goods and to promoting technical and economic progress, while allowing customers a fair share of the resulting benefit. They neither impose, on the undertakings concerned, restrictions which are not indispensable to the attainment of these objectives nor do they afford the undertakings the possibility of eliminating competition in respect of a substantial part of the products in the common market.

PAP represented an agreement among IATA airlines to create a system whereby airlines appoint retail intermediaries to sell tickets to the public in a professional manner. In seeking its exemption IATA argued that the main objective of the programme was to ensure that travel agency outlets selling on behalf of IATA members were competent and professional, provided dependable and impartial service to the public and appointing airlines, and handled the airline's monies and documents with integrity. After a lengthy analysis of the agreements contained in the IATA resolution, the Commission concluded that the agreements fell within Article 81(1) since they restrict competition and affect trade between Member States, but granted an exemption on the basis of the greater public benefit provided by the programme.

However, the Commission granted the exemption only until March 20, 1998. Presently the Commission is examining a request for renewal of the exemption.[53]

In *Lufthansa/SAS*[54] two airlines notified a planned agreement to the Commission in May 1995 in order to obtain exemption under Article [81(3)] of the Treaty. The Commission granted the exemption because the agreement was considered to contribute to economic progress by establishing a European network, reducing costs and benefiting consumers. Only on the issue of elimination of competition were a few conditions imposed to safeguard against the risk.[55]

---

[52] Decision 91/480. OJ L 258/18, 16.9.91.

[53] See speech in March 2002 by head of transport unit, Competition Directorate General available at http://europa.eu.int/comm/competition/speeches/text/sp2002_009_en.pdf.

[54] OJ L 54/28, 5.3.96.

[55] Another case where Lufthansa had to agree to give up slots and modify its future reaction to

ABUSE OF A DOMINANT POSITION IN A TOURISM MARKET

Article 82 of the Treaty of Rome, it will be recalled, prohibits any abuse of a dominant position, which impacts on competition in a market. It does not prohibit the obtaining of a dominant position, only its abuse. This reflects the view that, while the concentration of small and medium-sized enterprises into larger units is in principle desirable and should be encouraged – since it leads to a strengthened business environment – excessive concentration if allowed is undesirable. Undertakings in a dominant market position may be tempted to use their market power to influence trading conditions to the detriment of competitors and consumers. While the Commission has responsibility for observance of this prohibition, unlike Article 81 dealing with anti-competitive agreements, it cannot grant exemptions from abusive practises, no matter the benefit which might be claimed to result.

Proving an abuse exists requires close investigation of a market, for which the Commission has extensive powers. Detecting anti-competitive behaviour under Article 82 is more difficult than under Article 81 since undertakings evidently do not notify the Commission of their abusive behaviour (they hide it) and will only be suspected where complaints are made by the victims of the abuse or the Commission instigates its own investigation.

The legal analysis used to determine whether an abuse has taken place involves establishing a number of elements:

- the market,
- the activity in the common market or a substantial part of it,
- the dominant position,
- the abuse,
- the effect of the abuse on trade within the common market.

Establishing a Dominant Position

A dominant market position can be achieved in either of two ways – by on-going growth/acquisition or by statutory monopoly. The latter, which has existed

---

new entrant competition is *Lufthansa/Austrian Airlines*, Case COMP/37.730, 5.7.02, where in order to gain an exemption until end 2005 both parties has to "make available a maximum of 40 percent of the slots they operate in any given city-pair to any new comer". If they reduce prices in the future due to a new competitor on a route "they will be obliged to apply the same fare reduction, in percentage terms, on three other Austrian-German city-pairs on which they do not face competition" – Press Release, IP/02/1008.

to a significant degree in the tourism sector in relation to airports[56] and sea ports, arises where legislation has conferred either exclusive provision of a service on an undertaking or has conferred the exclusive right to grant entitlement to others to proved services. In *Flughafen Frankfurt/Main*[57] concerning the owner/operator of Frankfurt airport, the Commission stated:

> The Court of Justice has held ... that Article [82] applies to an undertaking holding a dominant position on a particular market, even where that position is due not to the activity of the undertaking itself, but to the fact that by reason of provisions laid down by law there can be no competition or only very limited competition on that market. ... FAG holds a monopoly on the market for the provision of airport facilities at Frankfurt Airport. It holds a dominant position within a substantial part of the common market.

Effect on Trade between Member States

The final step in the legal assessment of abusive dominance, which it is convenient to deal with now, concerns the effect of the abuse on trade between Member States. In tourism cases, especially involving transport modes, it will not be difficult to establish the necessary effect on trade between Member States.

Internal travel within a Member State is not generally relevant to competition analysis, as illustrated in *P&O/Stena Line*[58] where the Commission ignored the competitive effects of a proposed joint venture between two ferry operators on tourist travel between Northern Ireland and Great Britain.

> In view of the low proportion and amount of inter-State traffic using the [NI/GB] routes it can be concluded that there is no appreciable effect on inter-State traffic.

Treaty Examples

The main step in the legal assessment of Article 82 cases is the determination of actual abuse of a dominant position. It is worth repeating the examples of abuse offered in Article 82:

---

[56] The level of landing fees and related charges imposed by airport authorities is a consequence of a dominant position, although the Commission has dealt with them more as a restriction on airline freedom to provide services. See XXXth Report on Competition Policy, 2000, European Commission Directorate for Competition.
[57] OJ L 72/41, 11.3.98.
[58] Decision 98/190, OJ L 163/70, 29.6.99.

(a) … imposing unfair purchase or selling prices or other unfair trading conditions; (b) limiting production, market or technical developments…; (c) applying dissimilar conditions to equivalent transactions with other trading parties …; (d) making the conclusion of contracts subject to acceptance by the other parties of supplementary obligations which have no connection with such contracts.

Tourism Examples of Abusive Behaviour

In *Port of Roscoff*[59] an Irish ferry operator who wished to start a ferry service between Ireland and Brittany, France complained that the operator of the only port in Brittany, CCI Morlaix, which could handle ferry traffic was refusing it access. Brittany Ferries was the only ferry company operating out of the port at the time.

The Commission found that, *prima facie*, CCI Morlaix had abused its dominant position as the operator of the port of Roscoff in Brittany by its unjustified refusal to give ICG access to the facilities of Roscoff.

In *Alpha Flight Services/Aeroports de Paris*[60] the Commission ruled that Aeroports de Paris abused its dominant position as manager of the Paris airports by imposing discriminatory commercial fees on suppliers /users of ground/self handling services relating to aircraft catering and cleaning.

In *Ilmailulaitos/Luftfartverket*[61] the Commission ruled that the Finnish civil aviation authority had abused a dominant position in the market for landing and take-off services in five Finish airports by imposing higher landing charges for intra-EEA flights than for domestic flights.[62]

---

[59] Competition Policy Newsletter Number 5, Summer 1995, p.12. For a case involving an abuse of a dominant positron in imposing discriminatory piloting charges for a passenger ferry service between Corsica and Genoa, see *Corsica Ferreis v. CPPG* [1993] E.C.R. I – 1783. See also p. 214.

[60] OJ L 230/10, 11.8.98.

[61] OJ L 69/24, 16.3.99.

[62] For similar Commission decisions involving discriminatory airport landing charges at Portuguese and Spanish airports, see Decision 99/1999, OJ L 69/31, 16.3.99 and Decision 521/2000, OJ L 208/36, 18.8.00 respectively. See also Competition Policy Newsletter, October 2000, p.40.

In *Flughafen Frankfurt/Main (FAG)*[63] where the owner/operator of Frankfurt airport refused to allow other operators provide ramp-side services, the Commission ruled that FAG had:

> abused its dominant position in breach of Article 82 of the EC Treaty by denying, without objective justification, potential third party handlers access to the ramp and airport users the right to self-handle, thereby reserving for itself the market for the provision of ramp-handling services at Frankfurt airport. This finding does not apply to the eastern part of Pier B, from Gate B2 to Gate B42, nor to Pier C up to Gate C15, where FAG's monopoly is objectively justifiable.

In *Virgin/British Airways*[64] the Commission fined British Airways (BA) EUR 6.8 million and ruled that BA had abused a dominant position in the UK market for air transport by operating travel agent commission systems which discriminated between travel agents. According to a Commission press release:[65]

> For at least the past seven years BA has been offering travel agents extra commission payments in return for their meeting or exceeding their previous year's sales agency services. This makes the travel agents loyal to BA, discouraging them from selling travel agency services to other airlines and has created an illegal barrier to airlines that wish to compete against BA on the UK markets for air transport. ...

> The initial complaint in this case was provoked by BA introducing a scheme for larger travel agents to gain extra income if they increased their sales of BA tickets. A supplementary complaint was introduced when BA reduced its standard rate of commission to 7% for all sales, and introduced a scheme for all travel agents whereby they could increase this commission rate. ...

> Such commissions are equivalent to a 'loyalty discount' i.e. a discount based not on cost savings but on loyalty of the type consistently condemned as an exclusionary abuse of a dominant position in the past. It is well established community law that a dominant supplier cannot give incentives to its customers and distributors to be loyal to it, so foreclosing the market from the dominant firm's competitors.

---

[63] OJ L 72/30, 11.3.98.
[64] Decision 74/2000, OJ L 30/1, 4.2.00.
[65] IP/99/504, 14.7.99.

In *EasyJet/KLM*[66] EasyJet filed a complaint with the Commission in 1996, when KLM lowered its prices on its Amsterdam-London route to 95 DFL (pre-Euro Dutch currency), after EasyJet introduced an all time low tariff of 99 DFL on the same route. According to EasyJet, KLM was abusing a dominant position a route by offering a price below its operating costs. The Commission initiated legal proceedings a few months later, and asked KLM to justify its price decrease because it suspected KLM had abused its dominant position to eliminate EasyJet from the market. KLM argued that the low tariffs reflected a policy of boosting transfers on Schipol to long-haul flights. Thus the costs of the short-haul route could not be seen separately from the long-haul flights and were an essential part of KLM's strategy. The Commission decided that if KLM could not prove it was not making losses on the A-L route, it would have to raise its prices immediately, even before the Commission could publish its final decision on this case KLM stopped its practice.

In *Football World Cup 1998*[67] the Commission ruled that the organising committee for the 1998 World Cup finals in France had abused its dominant position in the market for match tickets by imposing onerous ticketing conditions on persons outside France who wanted to buy match tickets.

CONTROL OF TOURISM MERGERS

Articles 81 and 82 of the Treaty of Rome, while applicable to mergers/concentrations, are not considered sufficient to cover all operations related to the Community's competition policy. Article 82 prohibits abuse of a dominant position, but does not impede the existence or creation of a dominant position. The Treaty itself does not require authorization of the Commission for a merger/concentration transaction which may lead to the creation of a dominant position. As demonstrated in the previous section, this means that the Commission can only control mergers/concentrations on an *a posteriori* basis. The Commission is then also dependent on the complaints of others (competitors and/or third parties involved) to be able to investigate the case. To deal with what might seem like a gap in the Treaty:

a new legal instrument should therefore be created in the form of a Regu-

---

[66] *de Volkskrant*, 16.8.97.
[67] Decision 12/2000, OJ L 5/55, 8.1.00.

lation to permit effective monitoring of all concentrations from the point of view of their effect on the structure of competition in the Community and to be the only instrument applicable to such concentrations.[68]

Thus the Council enacted Regulation 4064/89,[69] which has proved to be of major importance in preventing the creation of dominant positions in the common market. It has been widely applied in the tourism sector, particularly as regard merger and related activity in the air passenger and tour operator/ travel agent markets.

Regulation 4064/89 creates a system of notification, examination, approval or disapproval of all acquisition and merger activity above a certain size, which has potential Community-wide effects on competition in the different markets. To steer clear of unintentionally over controlling anti-competitive agreements, it was considered necessary:

> to exclude from the scope of this Regulation those operations which have as their object or effect the coordination of the competitive behaviour of independent undertakings, since such operations fall to be examined under the appropriate provision of Regulations implementing Article [81] or Article [82].[70]

If a concentration is found to have a Community dimension which would significantly impede competition in the common market, Article 2 of Regulation 4064/89 requires the Commission to declare it void.

> A concentration which creates or strengthens a dominant position as a result of which effective competition would be significantly impeded in the common market or in a substantial part of it shall be declared incompatible with the common market.

Regulation 4064/89 is thus based on a number of key concepts:
- concentration.
- community dimension.
- identification of product and geographic markets.
- assessment of competition effects.

---

[68] Preamble to Regulation 4064/89.
[69] OJ L 395/1, 30.12.89 as amended. Consolidated text available at http://europa.eu.int/eur-lex/en/consleg/pdf/1989/en_1989R4064_do_001.pdf.
[70] Preamble to Council Regulation 4064/89, OJ L 395/1, 30.12.89.

Leaving aside market definition which has already been addressed, the remaining concepts will now be briefly explained and a series of tourism examples provided. However, the procedure for dealing with proposed concentrations should first be noted.

Procedure

Once notified of a proposed merger, the Commission has at the most one month to decide either:

- the concentration is not within the Regulation,
- the concentration is within the Regulation but it "does not raise serious doubts as to its compatibility with the common market" – Article 6(1)(b),
- the concentration is within the Regulation and the Commission does have serious doubts as to its compatibility; in this case the Commission "shall decide to initiate proceedings" – Article 6(1)(c).

The first two parts of the procedure are known as Phase I. The Commission grants authorization to the vast majority of notified concentrations[71] because the initial examination reveals little doubts as to compatibility, or else the parties have accepted/suggested modifications to the concentration which remove any serious compatibility doubts.

Phase 2 of the procedure arises when the Commission decides to initiate proceedings under Article 6(1)(c) because it has serious doubts about compatibility. This proceeding consists of an investigation to determine the facts and the parties' arguments, including possibly a hearing,[72] and must be closed by means of decision which can either declare compatibly, compatibility with conditions or incompatibility. If the concentration has already been implemented the Commission can require its undoing. Incompatibility decisions must be made within four months of initiating proceedings.

In carrying out its investigation into market share and likely anti-competitive effects, the Commission has extensive powers, under Article 11 of Regulation 4064/89, to require information from governments, competent authorities and undertakings and associations of undertakings. This is used to gain information about the market and market share.[73]

---

[71] Some examples of Phase I cases are *Swissair/Sabena*, OJ L 239, 7.10.95; Sunworld/Thomas Cook, Competition Policy Newsletter, Volume 2, Number 2, Autumn/Winter 1996 and the clearance of a concentration in the British railway sector Competition Policy Newsletter, Volume 2, Number 3, Autumn/Winter 1996.

[72] See generally Regulation 447/98, OJ L 61/1, 2.3.98.

[73] For how this operated during the aborted takeover of Martinair by KLM see *de Volkskrant*, 28.5.99.

CONCENTRATION

Three different situations are identified in Article 3 of Regulation 4064/89 as giving rise to a concentration:

- where two or more previously independent undertakings merge – Article 3(1)(a),

- where one or more persons already controlling one undertaking acquires direct or indirect control of the whole or part of another – Article 3(1)(b),

- where undertakings create a joint venture "performing on a lasting basis all the functions of an autonomous economic entity, which does not give rise to coordination of the competitive behaviour of the parties amongst themselves or between them and the joint venture" – Article 3(2)(b).[74]

Concentrations are also defined "in such a manner as to cover only operations bringing about a durable change in the structure of the undertakings concerned".[75]

Concentrations are thus arrangements whereby through acquisitions and mergers, the structure of undertakings and of the market change in a durable way. Acquisitions can be partial or total. Concentrations may have positive impacts like economies of scale, improved profitability or an increased benefit to the consumer. All these are objectives of the Community's industrial policy encouraging the international competitiveness of Community undertakings. However, concentrations can also exceed certain limits, for example by leading to a monopoly situation restricting competition in such a way that goes against consumers' interests.

While airline alliances are a significant feature of the contemporary tourism industry, they generally do not involve mergers. Code sharing, depending of course on degree, usually falls within the Notice on authorised cooperation and Regulation 1617/93 discussed earlier. If, however, the Commission considers airline cooperation to be sufficiently comprehensive and integrative to fall under the merger regulation, then it will be treated accordingly.

---

[74] See generally Commission Notice on the concept of full function joint ventures OJ C 66/1, 2.3.98.

[75] See generally Commission Notice on the concept of concentration, OJ C 66/5, 2.3.98.

Examples of Mergers

In *Granada Compass* "a new company, Granada Compass Plc, will be put in place above both Granada and Compass companies. Shareholders will receive shares in the new company in lieu of their present shareholding".[76]

In *Kouni/First Choice* "the operation will consist of two steps: first a new UK company, listed in the London and Swiss Stock exchanges will be formed (Koumi Holdings Plc). The new company will then make a take-over offer for Koumi under Swiss laws and a take-over offer for First Choice under the UK's City Code on Takeovers and Mergers".[77]

Examples of Acquisitions

In *Preussag/Nouvelles Frontieres* "NF is currently controlled by Mr Jacques Maillot, the company's founder and majority shareholder. Preussag has an obligation to acquire 34.9% of NF's capital and voting rights before 31.3.2002. It will nevertheless assume joint control as of 15.11.2000 through a shareholders agreement which will, in particular, give it veto rights over NF's business plan. The notified operation, therefore, constitutes a concentration within the meaning of Article 3(1)(b) of the Merger Regulation".[78]

In *Thomson/Fritidsresor* the operation involved "the acquisition by Thomson of 100% of Fritidsresor' shares from its three major institutional shareholders … and smaller shareholders … for a cash consideration".[79]

In *West LB/Thomas Cook* the termination of a shareholders agreement between West LB and another shareholder would give West LB sole control of Thomas Cook.

> This acquisition of sole as opposed to joint control represents a change in the quality of decisive influence exercised by West LB and brings

---

[76] Case COMP/M.1972, 29.6.00, p.2.

[77] Case IV/M.1502, 6.5.99 at p.2. Compass subsequently demerged from Granada and in Compass/Selecta Case IV/M.2373, 8.5.01 acquired by direct public bid the remaining shareholding in Selecta which did not already control.

[78] Case COMP/M.2186, 14.11.00.See also *Preussag/Thomson*, Case COMP/M.2002, 26.7.00 – public bid. Other merger cases featuring Thomas Cook are *C&N Touristic/Thomas Cook Holdings*, 9.2.2001, IP/01/188; *Thomas Cook/LTU/WEST LB*, Case IV/M.229, 14.7.92.

[79] Case IV/M.1088, 4.2.98 at p.2.

about a lasting change in the structure of both undertakings. The acquisition of sole control therefore constitutes a concentration within the meaning of Article 3(1) of the Regulation.[80]

In *Bass/Saison* Bass acquired the Intercontinental and Forum hotel businesses' by acquiring control "of the whole of the issued share capital of Saison ... by way of acquisition of shares".[81]

Examples of Joint Ventures

Article 3(2) of Regulation 1310/97 provides that for so-called full-function joint ventures:

> in addition to the dominance test set out in Article 2 ... it should be provided that the Commission apply the criteria of Article [81(1)] and (3) of the Treaty to such joint ventures, to the extent that their creation has as its direct consequence an appreciable restriction of competition between under-takings that remain independent.

This provision reflects the sometimes difficult to distinguish line between agreement between undertakings cases, and concentration cases. Among joint ventures in tourism ruled on by the Commission are:

In *Marsk/DFDS Travel* two Danish based companies established a new travel agency active primarily in business travel. Both parent companies had 50% of the new company with the board appointed 50/50 by the parents. While each parent remained active upstream in the air and sea transport markets, the Commission did not see that this would permit coordination of competitive behaviour between the parents in the upstream market.

> The purchases made by the joint venture from its parents will not constitute a significant part of the joint venture's purchases [and will] not be the main customer of its parents'. Moreover, it would be exceptional that a business travel ticket sold by the joint venture would

---

[80] Case IV/M.350, 30.6.93 at p.2. An acquisition by Thomas Cook ruled on by the Commission is *Thomas Cook/Sunworld*, Case IV/M.785, 7.8.96.

[81] Case IV/M.1133, 23.3.98. Other hotel acquisitions are *Accor/Blackstone/Colony/Vivendi*, Case IV/M.1596, 8.9.99; *Hilton/Scandic*, Case IV/M.2451, 31.5.01 – public bid; *Nomura/ Le Meridien Hotels*, Case IV/M.2464, 3.7.01; *Morgan Grenfell/Whitbread*, Case IV/M.2395, 8.5.01 – acquisition of part of Whitbread 'by way of purchase of shares in newly created company' – p.1.

combine the transport means of both parents. ... Finally, airline tickets and ferry tickets appear in general not to be substitutable ... Based on the above, the joint venture cannot be seen as an instrument for producing or reinforcing coordination between the parents in the upstream market. The joint venture will, therefore, perform on a lasting basis all the functions of an autonomous economic entity. ...[82]

In *Leisure Plan* "the joint venture involves the incorporation of a joint venture company, LPI, with its shares to be held in equal proportions by LeisurePlan, Thomas Cook and Philips Media. LPI will be active in the development and marketing worldwide of a multimedia travel information planning and booking system which is a point-of-sale tool for professional providers of travel services such as travel agents. ... With the contribution to LPI by LeisurePlan of all its travel related assets ... and by the contribution to LPI by Thomas Cook and Philip Media of an appropriate amount of liquid capital, LPI will have the means to perform on a lasting basis all the functions of an autonomous economic entity".[83]

In *West LB/Carlson/Thomas Cook* a joint venture was established which combined the UK travel operations of Cook and Carlson:

Preussag will be the majority shareholder ... but Carlson and West LB, whilst minority shareholders, will enjoy veto rights over so-called 'reserved matters' which go beyond normal minority protection ... Therefore Thomas Cook will be jointly controlled by Preussag, West LB and Carlson ... and will have the resources (assets, staff, management and finance) necessary to perform on a lasting basis all the functions of an autonomous economic entity.[84]

---

[82] Case IV/M.988, 4.11.97 at p.2. Another joint venture in business travel services is *Wagons-Lits/Carlson*, Case IV/M.867, 7.3.97.

[83] Case IV/M.662, 21.12.95.

[84] Case IV/M.1341, 8.3.99.

In *LSG//SKYCHEFS* a new company was set up to which Skychefs transferred it's holding in an airline catering business and a Lufthansa subsidiary LSG would acquire half of the shares. Because the new company would perform on a lasting basis all the functions of an autonomous entity and would not rely to any significant extent on sales to parent company Lufthansa, "the proposed operation constitutes a concentration within the meaning of Article 3(1)(b) of the Merger Regulation".[85]

In *Skanska/ Securum*, both companies were involved in leasing and operating hotels. Securum bought 50% of Pandex a subsidiary of Skanska.

> Following the operation the parties will transfer to the joint venture their hotel businesses in Sweden. ... Their joint venture will be jointly controlled by the parent companies. They are equally represented on the board and the appointment of the management of the joint venture, as well as alterations to the business plan, requires unanimity of the parent companies.[86]

In *BA/TAT* BA acquired 49.9% of a subsidiary of TAT, with a time-limited option to purchase the balance. A shareholders agreement indicated that both BA and TAT would exercise joint control. Further, the parent TAT would withdraw from the air transport market, transferring all its activities to the subsidiary and BA would become more involved in the operation of the TAT subsidiary. The Commission ruled the that object of the deal was not to coordinate the competitive behaviour of both parties and although the joint venture would cone to an end in six and a half years, it could still be regarded as performing on a lasting basis all the functions of an autonomous entity because the subsidiary operated in a sector facing rapid change.[87]

---

[85] Case IV/M.1268, 9.11.98. A subsequent transaction whereby LSG acquired through purchase 100% of the voting securities in OFSI (which jointly controlled SkyChefs with LSG) as cleared by the Commission in Case COMP/M.2190, 1.6.01. Other cleared catering mergers are *Sodexho/Abela(II)*, Case COMP/M.2466, 8.6.01.

[86] Case IV/M.677, 8.1.96.

[87] Case IV/M.259, 27.11.92.

COMMUNITY DIMENSION

In order for a concentration to be subject to Community competition law it must have a Community dimension, that is it is must involve a minimum scale as defined in criteria set out in Regulation 4064/89. Concentrations below this figure are generally the concern of national competition authorities. There are two alternate tests of Community dimension.

- Under Article 2(1):

  A concentration has a Community dimension where:

  (a) the combined aggregate worldwide turnover of all the undertakings concerned is more than ECU 5000 million; and
  (b) the aggregate Community-wide turnover of each of at least two of the undertakings concerned is more than ECU 350 million, unless each of the undertakings concerned achieves more than two-thirds of its aggregate Community-wide turnover within one and the same Member State.

- Under Article 2(3):

  A concentration … has a Community dimension where:

  (a) the combined aggregate world-wide turnover of all the undertakings concerned is more than ECU 2500 million;
  (b) in each of at least three Member States, the combined aggregate turnover of all the undertakings concerned is more that ECU 100 million;
  (c) in each of at least three Member States included for the purpose of point (b), the aggregated turnover of each of at least two of the undertakings concerned is more that ECU 25 million; and
  (d) the aggregate Community-wide turnover of each of at least two of the undertakings concerned is more that ECU 100 million;

  unless each of the undertakings concerned achieves more than two-thirds of its aggregate Community-wide turnover within one and the same Member State.[88]

Turnover is the key concept in calculating threshold figures under both tests and both Article 5 of Regulation 4064/89 and the Commission Notice on the

---

[88] Council Regulation No 1310/97, OJ L 180, 9.7.97.

calculation of turnover[89] should be consulted for the detailed rules of how the calculations should be made. Since in the tourism cases under review only the set of dimension criteria in Article 2(1) figured, this alone will be dealt with.

Turnover is calculated according to worldwide, Community and national criteria and includes figures for any larger groups which any of the parties belong to. The third requirement is a negative one. A concentration falls outside Commission merger scrutiny only if all of the parties realise more than the two-thirds figure in the same state. Where the other tests are satisfied and thus the financial scale of the transaction is very large, it seems unlikely that such figures would be realised in the one state. Thus, if more than one state is involved under this latter part of Article, the concentration will have a Community dimension.

In *Bass/Saison*,[90] a hotel concentration case, "Bass and Saison have a combined aggregate worldwide turnover in excess of ECU 5.000 million (Bass, ECU 7,3338; and Saison, ECU 1,885 million). Each of them has a Community-wide turnover in excess of ECU 250 million (Bass, ECU 6.559 million; and Saison ECU 559 million), but Saison does not achieve more than two-thirds of its aggregate Community-wide turnover within one and the same Member State. The notified operation therefore has a Community dimension".

In *Preussag/Nouvelles Frontieres*,[91] the parties satisfied the first two tests and regarding the third "Preussag did not achieve more than two-thirds of its aggregate Community-wide turnover within one and the same Member State, although NF did so within France". The concentration still had a Community dimension because Preussag did not also achieve two thirds of its Community-wide turnover in France.

In *West LB/Carlson/Thomas Cook/Preussag*[92] Thomas Cook was the subject of a concentration involving three other parties. Regarding Community-wide turnover, the Commission had to be satisfied that only two and not the three parties, achieved the 250 million figure and also that each of the three parties did not achieve more than two-thirds of its Community-wide turnover in the same Member State.

---

[89] OJ C 66/25, 2.3.98.
[90] OJ C 156/11, 21.5.98.
[91] Case COMP/M.2186, 14.11.00, p.2.
[92] Case IV/M.1341, 8.3.99.

ASSESSMENT OF COMPETITIVE EFFECTS

The basic statement of how the likely impact of a concentration on competition in the common market should be assessed is set out in Article 2(1) of Regulation 4064/89.

> Concentrations within the scope of this Regulation shall be appraised in accordance with the following provisions with a view to establishing whether or not they are compatible with the common market. In making this appraisal, the Commission shall take into account:
>
> (a) the need to maintain and develop effective competition within the common market in view of, among other things, the structure of all the markets concerned and the actual or potential competition from undertakings located either within or out with the Community;
> (b) the market position of the undertakings concerned and their economic and financial power, the alternatives available to suppliers and users, their access to supplies or markets, any legal or other barriers to entry, supply and demand trends for the relevant goods and services, the interests of the intermediate and ultimate consumers, and the development of technical and economic progress provided that is to consumers advantage and does not form an obstacle to competition

The likely competitive effect of a concentration depends in part on how the relevant market is defined. Since the Commission often declines to be definitive about market parameters, its assessment about competitive effect is conducted on a series of different hypothesis as to what the market is.

One of the first steps in determining competitive effect is to consider whether the parties are operating in the same market. Clearly if they are not, as where the products belong to entirely different categories, as in *Nomura/Le Meridien*[93] where an investment bank acquired control of a chain of hotels, or where they both operate in tourism/leisure but in different product markets, as in *Kuoni/ First Choice*[94] where in a merger of travel services, only one party was involved in business travel, or in different geographic markets as in *Thomson/*

---

[93] Case COMP/M.2464, 3.7.01.

[94] Case IV/M.1502, 6.5.99. In *Accor/Dorint*, COMP/M 2997, 23.12.02, Accor acquired a controlling stake in a German hotel chain. In some cities, Accor operated budget hotels while Dorint operated higher segment hotels, and in others where their hotels operated in the same market, the combined market share was moderate.

Fritidsresor[95] where one tour operator was active in the UK while the other was active in Scandinavia, then it is easier to conclude the concentration will not have worrying competition effects. Equally, if the parties create a joint venture intending to create a new product and thus create a new market for which at present there are imperfect substitutes, the only competition concerns might relate to upstream or downstream effects.[96]

Once market overlaps are identified, the Commission then identifies relative market shares with a view to seeing whether the concentration will create or strengthen a dominant position in the market and enable the parties to act independently of market pressures. If the combined post-concentration market shares of the parties are small, say up to 15/20%, the Commission is unlikely to have any competition worries. The Commission had no worries in *Hilton/Scandic*[97] where the concentration would have given a combined market share of 27% in the Copenhagen hotel 2 to 4 star market because other hotels were present in that market and able to offer competition. Where the combined shares will be greater than this a closer market examination will be necessary.

Closer market examination will focus on the nature of the market and especially its recent history. If a market is already significantly concentrated within a few major players and significant differences exist in market share between the large and small players, any concentration between the major players will raise competition fears. But whether a merger will actually be refused depends on each case and on there being a significant likelihood of collective dominance.

Collective dominance arises not only where there are a few main players in a market, but where they are able to sell at above competitive prices, safeguard their market positions and have no incentive to overly compete with each other, and all this without any contact with each other.

> three conditions are necessary for a finding of collective dominance. ... First, each [large player] must have the ability to know how the other members are behaving ... it is not enough for each member ... to be aware that interdependent market conduct is profitable ... but each ... must also have a means of knowing whether the other operators are adopting the same strategy and whether they are maintaining it ... second, the situation of tacit coordination must be sustainable over time. ... [Here this means that each player is aware that] highly competitive action on its part designed to increase market share would provoke identical actions by others, so

---

[95] Case IV/M.1088, 4.2.98.
[96] *LeisurePlan*, Case IV/M.662, 21.12.95.
[97] Case COMP/M.2451, 31.5.01.

that it would derive no benefit from its initiative ... third, to prove the existence of a collective dominant position to the requisite legal standard ... [it must be shown that] the foreseeable reaction of current and future competitors ... and consumers would not jeopardise the results expected from the [tacit coordination].[98]

Collective dominance can be difficult to identify.

In *Airtours/First Choice*,[99] the Commission thought it had identified it when it refused to approve a proposed merger between two of the four main players in the UK short haul foreign package holiday market. The merger of both would have produced a post-merger share of 34%, while the post-merger share of the three remaining players would have been 83%. The Commission analysis of market trends highlighted a range of factors including substantial barriers to market entry, a high degree of market transparency (ability to follow how competitor's market strategy is evolving), similar cost structure and commercial links and insignificant buyer power. The Commission deemed these likely to reinforce a tendency towards collective dominance in the future.

On appeal the Court of First Instance[100] disagreed and annulled the Commission decision, concluding that the same evidence was not strong enough to support the view that the merger would be likely to create a collective dominant position.

If a market is expanding and new entrants have recently begun operations in it, this may be an important indicator that competition is already healthy and might tolerate the concentration under review, as in *Accor/Vivendi*[101] where the Commission cited the expanding nature of the French hotel market in approving the acquisition of hotels by a consortium led by Accor. Similarly, if entry costs remain low or conversely if they are high but other potential players have the resources to enter it or develop a small existing market share, as in *Costa Crociere* where barriers to entry in the cruise market do not seem to be very high, at least for well-established tour operators with a wide distribution network and sufficient financial resources, that may also suggest the concentration will have an insignificant effect on the market. Likewise in another cruise market merger,

---

[98] *Airtours v. Commission*, Case T–342/99, 6.6.02, para.62.
[99] Case IV/M.1524, 22.9.99.
[100] *Airtours v. Commission*, Case T–342/99, 6.6.02.
[101] Case IV/M.1596, 8.9.99. See also *Compass/Selecta*, Case IV/M.2373, 8.5.01.

Carnival/P&O Princess,[102] the Commission's initial competition concerns about a post merger UK market share of about a third, were allayed when closer market examination showed the recent arrival of new competitors in the market, the ability of rivals to shift capacity from elsewhere to the UK market and the combined factors of a growing market and new capacity coming on-stream. The Commission noted:

> the high recent and projected growth rate in cruise markets would, in itself, constitute a significant constraint on the incumbent cruise operators as high growth rates provide an incentive for new operators to enter the market.

Degree of market share post concentration, while an important factor, is not conclusive. If one of the parties already has a high market share and the concentration will only increase it marginally or not at all, then the competitive effect may be insignificant, as in *Costa Crociere*[103] where in the Italian cruise holiday market before the acquisition one of the parties held 55% while the other was not active there. Even if a post-concentration market would be divided between a few main players it is still possible the Commission might not regard the concentration as having significant effects because barriers to entry may remain low and new players could still enter the market.[104] The fact that competition in a market is strong will outweigh many factors including the fact that a buyer may be able to put large financial resources behind the acquisition, as in *West LB/Thomas Cook*[105] where a bank bought a diverse leisure travel group.

Modifying the Deal

Where the Commission has concerns about the competitive effects of a concentration parties can volunteer, or the Commission can suggest, modifications to the deal, which would calm or remove the Commission's worries. The Commission is careful to tie such modifications into any favourable ruling it gives.

---

[102] COMP/M.2706, 24.7.02; Press Release IP/021/1141.
[103] Case IV/M.0334, 19.7.93.
[104] As in *Sodexho/Abela*, Case COMP/M.2466, 8.6.01.
[105] Case IV/M.350, 30.6.93.

> In *Preussag/Thomson*[106] Preussag already owned one of the four major players in the UK short haul foreign package holiday market, Thomas Cook, and proposed acquiring another, Thomson.
>
> > The Commission's investigation in the present case has indicated ... serious doubts as to the creation of a collective dominant position in the UK market ... between the major vertically integrated tour operators ... The transaction would therefore have required in-depth investigation. In order to resolve these doubts, in the course of the proceedings Preussag submitted an undertaking ... to divest its interest in TC [Thomas Cook] ... After appropriate investigation, the Commission has concluded that, subject to full compliance with the divestment undertaking, the notified concentration will not create a dominant position in the relevant market.[107]

In an airline alliance the Commission can look for promises that airport slots will be given up and future competitive behaviour modified to facilitate new route competitors.

> In *KLM/Alitalia*[108] the Commission approved a joint venture between two airlines subject to undertakings to facilitate the entry of new competitors on two hub-to-hub routes Amsterdam – Milan and Amsterdam – Rome where the Commission raised serous concerns about the impact of the concentration on competition in the common market. The conditions related to:
>
> * making slots available to existing/new entrants,
> * reducing flight frequencies if a new entrant started operations,
> * promising to enter interlining agreements with new entrants,
> * promising to allow new entrants participate in frequent flyer programmes, and
> * a commitment to refrain from tying travel agents and corporate customers with loyalty schemes.[109]

---

[106] Case COMP/M.2002, 26.7.00.

[107] In the *Airtours/First Choice* case *op cit.*, an undertaking was rejected because it would not have removed the Commission's competition concerns.

[108] Case JV.19, 11.8.99. See also *United Airlines/US Airways*, Case COMP/M.2041; Competition Policy Newsletter Number 2 – June 2001, p.47.

[109] In other *KLM* cases – *KLM/Martinair* Case No. IV/M. 1328, 1.2.99, OJ L 395/1, 30.12.99. Competition Policy Newsletter, Number 2, June 1999, p. 30 and Case IV/M.1608, 14.12.99; Competition Policy Newsletter Number 1, February 2000, p 26 – KLM twice notified the Commission of a planned acquisition of Martinair and twice withdrew the notification, the

However, surrendering slots does not in itself produce new market entrants and other approaches which tie the exemptions into the appearance of new competitors are under consideration:

> these remedies have not proved particularly effective in restoring new competitors. ... For example, on the routes operated by Lufthansa/SAS[110] where these remedies were imposed there are still no other airlines competing. [For the future it may be that] the exemption decision should only be granted [when] market entry by a new competitor on certain key routes actually takes place.[111]

STATE AID AND TOURISM

Introduction

Member State governments and public bodies, such as national tourism authorities, have in the past frequently intervened in the operation of tourism markets and provided State aid not only to undertakings in difficulty, but also where there is a scarcity of investment capital. Whether as part of national, regional or local policy, whether the beneficiaries were state owned airlines, ferries, hotels or local tourism enterprises, State aid has been endemic. Among the types of State aid granted were investment grants, subsidized loans, training subventions, tax reductions/ deferrals/allowances/exemptions, loan guarantees, state equity participation, social security reductions and undervaluing state assets in sales to private undertakings.

It has however become increasingly recognised, because of the obvious potential of such aid for threatening the operation of the common market, that this form of aid is subject to Community law, and specifically to Article 87 of the Rome Treaty. Article 87(1) bans State aid and links the ban to preserving competition in the common market.

> Save as otherwise provided in this Treaty, any aid granted by a Member State or through State resources in any form whatsoever which distorts or

---

first time because of an information issue – the Commission fined KLM EURO 40,000 for supplying misleading information, and the second because it appeared the Commission would disapprove of the acquisition. The acquisition of Martinair would have lead to two-thirds market share of the "Mediterranean market", and 75% of the rest of the European market as well on Dutch routes especially ones from Schipol as well as the acquisition of an excessive number of slots at Schipol airport – de Volkskrant, 28/31.5.99.

[110] See p. 370.

[111] See fn. 53.

threatens to distort competition by favouring certain undertakings … shall, insofar as it affects trade between Member States, be incompatible with the common market.

This ban applies, at least in theory, to State aid to tourism enterprises, despite their general small-scale.

It is the well-established view of the Commission that tourism is not necessarily confined to national markets. [State aid to tourism] may therefore threaten or distort competition and affect trade between Member States in the meaning of Article 87 (1) EC. This is so because the aid gives an advantage to the undertakings benefiting from the scheme, which in turn changes the market conditions to the detriment of their competitors in [the same] and other Member States.[112]

The two main areas where State aid has had an impact on tourism and which are examined later are:

• State aid to national airlines, and

• regional aid for the purpose of directly or indirectly developing tourism.

State aid needs to be distinguished from state investment generally which is not caught by the Article 87 ban. Investment in infrastructure or public goods, such as heritage protection or promotion, which benefits the entire local community, and not a specific enterprise or sector, is not treated as State aid.

Responsibility for ensuring observance of the ban on State aid is conferred by Article 88(1) on the Commission. Regulation 659/99[113] creates the framework within which the Commission deals with State aid. Member States are obliged to notify the Commission of proposed State aid (individual or a scheme) and await a Commission decision which can allow or refuse the proposed aid.

The Treaty of Rome also recognizes that not all forms of State aid should be banned. Aid can serve useful social and economic purposes. Restrictions on the broad scope of the ban in Article 87(1) relevant to tourism will be examined under the following headings:

• minimal aid, SMEs and training, and

• exceptional circumstances, economic development, and specific activities.

---

[112] Commission, State Aid 436/2001 – Ireland "Tourism and Recreational Angling Grant Scheme", C(2002)139, 21.1.02, p.3.

[113] OJ L 83/1, 27.3.99.

Minimal Aid, SMEs and Training

Small-scale State aid is unlikely to affect trade between states and is not prohibited under Article 87. Under Regulation 69/01[114] State aid to tourism enterprises of under •100,000 over three years is exempt from the Treaty ban.

Equally, State aid to SMEs[115] is generally not considered likely to distort competition to an unacceptable degree. This is because of the benefits to be derived from this sector are potentially significant. The Commission has declared that State aid below certain thresholds, granted either individually or through schemes, to SMEs is not caught by the Article 87(1) ban and is also exempt from the obligation, described below, which requires the Commission's prior approval for State aid schemes. Article 4 of Regulation 96/01 lays down the permitted aid intensities (amount of State aid as a percentage of a project's eligible costs) of State aid and these include 15% for small enterprises and 7.5% for medium ones, though increased thresholds are permitted in areas which qualify for regional aid.

State aid for training in tourism enterprises has also been declared by regulation[116] to be compatible with the common market and is permitted. Individual or sector specific training aid for tourism enterprises benefit from this exemption. The permitted aid intensities vary depending on the size of the enterprises, whether it is located in an area approved for regional aid, whether the training is general (generally useable) or specific (useable for specific employer) and whether the workers are disadvantaged.

Exceptional Circumstances, Economic Development and Specific Activities

Article 87(2) and (3) of the Rome Treaty sets out two lists of circumstances in which State aid can be permitted. The first list indicates aid which is considered automatically compatible with the common market, and the second indicates aid which may be considered compatible depending on the circumstances. Both lists are considered in more detail below. The Treaty allows for the making of regulations fixing the conditions and categories of permitted State aid – Article 89.

The Commission has responsibility for approving State aid which falls within

---

[114] Regulation 69/01, OJ L 10/30, 12.1.01.

[115] Regulation 280/96 – OJ L 107/4, 30.4.96 – generally defines small and medium sized enterprises as having less than 250 employees, have an annual turnover of not more than €40 million or an annual balance sheet not more than €27 million and satisfy independence criteria set out in an Annex.

[116] Regulation 68/01, OJ L 10/20, 13.1.01.

the second list. Member States are obliged to notify the Commission of 'plans to grant or alter aid' – Article 88(3). Commission approval/disapproval depends on compatibility with the common market. The detailed rules for enabling the Commission carry out its State aid functions are set out in Regulation 659/99.[117]

Assessing State aid is a more complex exercise than determining anti-competitive behaviour among private undertakings, as larger issues than purely economic ones may be at stake. Further, it has always been difficult for the Commission to secure compliance with the ban on State aid because the infringers are governments, not private undertakings. Thus, the Treaty approach, and by consequence, the Commission's and the Court of Justice's, seems more lenient than in cases of concentration or dominance.

State aid for tourism is a small part of overall State aid in the Community. In 2000 tourism State aid accounted for only €212 million out of a total Community figure of €82,373 billion. Only in three states (Austria, Italy and Portugal) did State aid amount to 1% of overall State aid.[118] Details of Community State aid decisions are available at:

> http://www.europa.eu.int/comm/competition/state_aid/register/ii/by_sector_tourism.html

Aid in the first list, set out in Article 87(2), is aid which has a social character, and is granted to individual consumers, and also:

> aid to make good the damage caused by natural disasters or exceptional circumstances – Article 87(2)(b).

The hijacking and crashing of airplanes in North-Eastern US on September 11, 2001 was considered an exceptional circumstance. Following this attack air flights over US airspace were suspended for four days, there was a withdrawal by airline insurers of cover for war and terrorism risks and there were huge increases in the cost of remaining insurance cover. Cover was even withdrawn from airports and related services. The assistance airlines sought from their governments was intended to cover these unexpected operating costs and as such had a capacity to distort competition. According to the Commission:[119]

---

[117] OJ L 83/1, 27.3.99.

[118] Commission State aid scoreboard, available at http://www.europa.eu.int/comm/competition/state_aid/scoreboard/stat_tables.html .

[119] Commission, The repercussions of the terrorist attacks in the United States and the air transport industry, COM (2001) 574 final, 10.10.01, p.7.

As operating aid is in principle prohibited the Commission considers that the provisions of Article 87(2)(b) fit the problem facing the airlines. It is of the opinion that, given their unforeseeable nature, the number of victims and the impact on the world economy, the events of 11 September 2001 were exceptional circumstances within the meaning of Article 87(2)(b). ... [These provisions] may apply to two types of damage resulting from the events of 11 September 2001 ... measures to compensate for the costs to airlines of American airspace being closed for four days ... [and] the assumption of the extra cost of insurance.[120]

Article 87(3) sets out the second list of potentially permitted State aid:

(a) aid to promote the economic development of areas where the standard of living is abnormally low or where there is serious underemployment,

(b) aid to promote the execution of an important project of common European interest or to remedy a serious disturbance in the economy of a Member State,

(c) aid to facilitate the development of certain economic activities or of certain economic areas, where such aid does not adversely affect trading conditions to an extent contrary to the common interest [...],

(d) aid to promote culture and heritage conservation where such aid does not affect trading conditions and competition in the Community to an extent that is contrary to the common interest , and

(e) such other categories of aid as may be specified by decision of the Council acting by a qualified majority on a proposal from the Commission.

As will be seen, categories (a) and (c) are the main categories of interest to tourism.

STATE AID FOR AIRLINES

State aid for national carriers used to be commonplace.[121] State aid to airlines more obviously affects the common market both because airline activity is

---

[120] Member state were still obliged to seek Commission approval for aid granted and the Commission was careful to ensure the aid was not extended to other capital problems facing European airlines – see, e.g. Press Releases IP/01/1883, 20.1.01; IP/02/333, 27.2.02; IP/02/981, 2.7.02.

[121] See Commission, Report on the evaluation of aid schemes established in favour of Community air carriers, SEC (92) 431 final, 19.3.92.

inherently cross border and many of the Community's airlines have been or still are state owned.

However, since the completion of the air transport liberalisation programme in 1992 such aid is becoming scarce, and approvals by the Commission even more so. In 1994 the Commission published guidelines on its approach to enforcing the Treaty rules regarding State aid and air transport.[122] According to these the goal of Community policy is the increased competitiveness of European airlines, which can only be achieved by proper financial management. This means that state investment in a national carrier (state owned or not) is not prohibited if it is proposed as a normal commercial transaction, that is if the investment would be made by a normal market investor. For example, regarding capital injections:

> The market economy investor principle will normally be satisfied where the structure and future prospects for the company are such that a normal return, by way of dividend or capital appreciation by reference to a comparable private enterprise, can be expected within a reasonable period.[123]

If the funding is considered State aid, the Commission will then assess it according to the exceptions allowed for in Article 87(3). Under (3)(c):

> The Commission ... will continue with its policy to allow, in exceptional cases, State aid given in connection with a restructuring programme; and in particular, if the aid is given, at least partly, for social purposes facilitating the adoption of the workforce to a higher level of productivity, (early retirement schemes).[124]

The aid mist also form part of a comprehensive restructuring programme intended to restore the airline's health. The State aid programme must also be implemented in such a way as to not give undue advantages to the airline supported by the aid. This explains a number of conditions which are attached to the clearances of State aid, namely freezing or reducing capacities, fleet or frequencies.

In Decision 653/94[125] the Commission approved French State aid for Air

---

[122] Commission, Application of Articles 92 and 93 [now 87,88] of the EC Treaty to State aids in the aviation sector, 94/C 350/07; OJ C 350/5, 10.12.94.

[123] *Ibid.*, at para.28.

[124] *Ibid.*, at para.38.

[125] OJ L 254/73, 30.9.94.

France, and though it was annulled by the Court of First Instance[126] on grounds of "insufficient reasoning" the Commission provided such reasoning in Decision 197/99[127] and reaffirmed its earlier decision.

Today the restructuring programmes of state owned air carriers are closely monitored both by the Commission and by privately owned air carriers and new State aids are not cleared "except for truly exceptional and unforeseeable circumstances."[128]

STATE AID FOR REGIONAL TOURISM

The Commission approach to regional State aid is influenced by its Guidelines on National Regional Aid.[129] These indicate, among other things, that State aid to regions is allowable only 'to develop less-favoured regions by supporting productive investment and job creation in a sustainable manner.' Such aid should be 'used sparingly', should not generally be given as an ad hoc payment to a single firm or be confined to a single area of activity because its effects on competition may be too great and its regional effects too limited. The aid recipients' contribution should be at least 25%, the aid cannot generally be combined with other forms of State aid, it must respect rules on aid intensities (the aid as a percentage of the investment) and should be directed towards initial investment, not operating costs.

Although tourism represents a single sector, State aid within the framework of regional funding for tourism purposes, i.e. investment aid for construction, modernization or improvement of tourism facilities generally, do not raise objections from the Commission.

> The Commission recognizes, in line with its constant practice, that the tourism sector in general has a particularly positive effect on regional development.[130]

Whether State aid to low-cost airlines in the form of reduced landing fees at airports in regions in need of development and any related aid is permitted

---

[126] *BA v. Commission* [1998] E.C.R. II–2405.

[127] OJ L 63/66, 12.3.99.

[128] "Competition Policy in the Air Transport Sector," Speech by Commissioner Karel Van Miert, Royal Aeronautical Society, March 9, 1998, London.

[129] OJ C 74/9, 10.3.98.

[130] Commission, State aid 832/2000 – Ireland "Capital Allowances Depreciation Regime for Hotels", C (2002), 15.1.02, para.17.

State aid remains to be seen. Most of the State aid schemes in favour of tourism concern small-scale projects. These projects may be small either in terms of the overall amount of aid granted or in terms of the size of the beneficiary enterprises.

In *Capital Allowance Depreciation Regime for Hotels*[131] Ireland sought clearance for a favourable tax exemption scheme for hotels.

> The notified scheme foresees an accelerated tax depreciation for the trade of hotel keeping if compared to other sectors of the economy. This has the effect of a tax exemption for hotels as the Irish authorities have waived this right to receive certain tax payments from hotels. Ireland has thus conferred upon them an economic advantage. Consequently, that advantage was accorded through the use of state resources and makes hotels more competitive in the tourism sector As the tourism sector is an industry competing on an EU wide level, the tax exemption will influence trade patterns between Member States. Therefore, Article 87(1) EC applies.

The Commission approved the scheme until 2006 on the basis of its conformity with the Guidelines.

In *Regional Aid Schemes in the Tourism Sector*[132] in 2001 the Commission approved two tourism aid schemes proposed by the Irish government, the first providing grant assistance of €77million for creating major tourist attractions/clusters of smaller tourist attractions and the second of •46 million for developing niche tourist product sectors, like cycling, equestrian centres, marine and heath tourism. The overall objective of both schemes was to develop the tourism product in an environmental and sustainable way that widened the spatial spread of tourism within Ireland. After holding that the schemes fell within the Article 87(1) ban, the Commission also held that both fell within Article 87(3)(a) and (c) and respected the Guidelines on national regional aid.

---

[131] *Ibid.*, at para.14.
[132] Commission, State aid 710/2000, C (2001) 2990, 7.11.01.

In *Terra Mitica Theme Park, Benidorm, Spain*[133] the Commission examined whether aspects of the sale of a theme park from a public authority to a private company, involved notifiable State aid. In all respects except one (95% reduction of municipal building tax) it found no evidence of State aid.

> The Commission established that the reduction was indeed granted, and found that it constitutes State aid which should have been notified to the Commission in advance. It considered, however, that the aid is compatible with the EC Treaty under Article 87(3)(a) in view of its very low aid intensity and the fact that the park contributes effectively the development of a backward region.

Further data on the range of State aid schemes approved by the Commission for tourism is available in the periodic Commission reports on Community measures affecting tourism.[134]

CHAPTER CONCLUSION

The surprisingly extensive volume of legal measures and decisions detailed in this chapter illustrate the relevance of Community competition law to tourism. Much competitive activity in the tourism industry benefits from various exemptions and the main daily relevance of competition law to European tourism concerns illegal acts, large scale mergers and compliance with exemption conditions. One area of continuing importance involves ensuring that airlines do not abuse their dominant position in the market for distributing their products through incentive schemes for travel agents or the operation of computer reservation systems. Community competition policy tries to ensure that tourists receive a fair share of its benefits. Tourist appear to have benefited from the integrations which have taken place among the larger players in the tour operator and airline services markets Community competition policy is not, however, an isolated area of Community competence, though in ignoring how its success leads to increased pressures on the environment, it acts as though it is.

---

[133] Press Release IP/02/1195, 5.8.02.
[134] See, e.g. SEC (2000) 3000, 15.3.02, p.50.

STUDENT TASKS

Undergraduate questions:

1. Formulate in your own words the main objectives of European competition policy.

2. Describe the main legal instruments used to control and monitor either anti-competitive behaviour or abusive dominant market behaviour among tourism service providers.

3. Do you agree with the wide range of exemptions under Community law to the ban on anti-competitive behaviour? Why?

4. Describe the analytical steps followed by the Commission when determining if a notified concentration will be approved.

Postgraduate questions:

1. Identify a firm or group of firms in your country that is/are currently dealing with the European Commission and the national competition authorities. What stage in the procedure are they? What are the expected outcomes/decisions?

2. Identify an example of state aid to tourism in your country and examine whether it is compatible with Community law.

3. How can developments in the air transport sector in the last decade regarding competition policy be described? What implications do they have both for small and large airline companies? For airports?

CHAPTER 9

COMMUNITY ENVIRONMENTAL POLICY AND TOURISM[1]

INTRODUCTION

The environment is one of the major assets or public goods which tourism relies on. Tourists use and value the recreational amenity of mountain, island and coastal regions, and the leisure amenity of urban and archaeological areas. Tourists seek out wilderness and remote regions for their recuperative and aesthetic amenity.

Tourism, however, also uses the environment as the basis for its infrastructure needs, that is for the provision of capacity to facilitate tourists, especially mass tourism, such as airports, roads, trails, marinas, ski lilts, hotels, golf clubs, resorts, water and waste systems etc. Tourism infrastructure places considerable demands on local environments. The demands often involve using virgin space to provide for new transient communities of vacationers. Many regions where tourists holiday are remote from existing centres of population, possess little existing infrastructure and require considerable alternation to cope with mass tourism. There can be particular difficulty in adequately coping with the water and waste demands of tourism.

Tourism infrastructure can also bring benefits to an area. It can encourage economic regeneration, improve employment and ensure the flow of national and Community funding to help preserve environmental, archaeological and cultural attractions. According to the European Environment Agency (EEA)[2] in 1995, tourism and recreation:

> bring income and jobs, increased understanding of other cultures, preservation of cultural and natural heritage and investment in infrastructure, which in turn brings social and cultural benefits. On the other hand, some forms

---

[1] Marc Mc Donald, Arantza Arruti.

[2] EEA, Europe's Environment. The Dobris Assessment EEA, 1995, p.489. Chapter 25, pp.489 – 501 contains a useful account of tourism pressures on Europe's environment. See also EEA, Europe's Environment: The Second Assessment, EEA, 1998, p.30.

of tourism, and some recreational activities, can cause destruction of habitats, degradation of landscapes and competition for scarce resources and services, such as land, freshwater, energy and sewage treatment. In addition host populations may suffer the loss of their traditions and become overdependent on tourism incomes.

The specific negative environmental impacts of tourism are varied. According to an EEA study in 2001:[3]

Tourism is responsible for a large share of air and road traffic, and consumption of energy by tourist infrastructure adds further emissions of greenhouse gases and acidifying substances. In France for example, 5–7% of greenhouse gas emissions are due to tourism, mainly because 80% of domestic tourist travel is by private car.

Hotels appear to be the most ecologically acceptable form of accommodation. However, energy consumption in a one star hotel is 157kWh, in a two star 230 kWh and in a four star hotel 380 kWh. ... Hotels, swimming pools and golf courses can put critical pressure on water resources, particularly in regions such as the Mediterranean where resources are scarce. Tourists typically consume around 300 litres (luxury tourism 880 litres) and generate 180 litres of wastewater per day. Tourism contributes about 7% of pollution in the Mediterranean. Annual waste generation per capita at coastal holiday resorts in France is 100 kg higher than the national average. ...

An important characteristic of tourism is its concentration in particular areas. In France, for example, the most visited country in the world, 4.5% of municipalities ... receive about half the total number of tourists. Some coastal areas, particularly around the Mediterranean, are under extreme pressure from such large numbers. ... One study ... suggests that three quarters of the sand dunes between Spain and Sicily have disappeared as a result of urbanisation linked to tourism development.

In mountain regions, too, tourism can bring economic benefits to otherwise poor communities, but at significant environmental cost. Walking and mountain biking can lead to erosion and wear and tear of paths. The building of cable cars and ski lifts, and in particular the laying out of new ski runs, has resulted in extensive clearing of forests. Most visitors to ski resorts are day trippers arriving by car, leading to traffic congestion, overcrowding and litter problems.

---

[3] EEA, Environmental Signals 2001 – regular indicator report, EEA, 2001, p.27

Nonetheless, these negative impacts are generally quite specific and local and in a comparative sense, less significant than the environmental impacts of other economic activities, as the following EEA table indicates:[4]

Table 9.1

	Energy	Transport	Industry	Agriculture and Forestry	Tourism
GLOBAL SCALE					
Climate Change	<<<	<<<	>>>	<	=
Ozone depletion	=	=	<<<	=	=
TRANSBOUNDARY SCALE					
Acidification	<<<	<<<	<<<	<<<	=
Other air pollution	<	<<<	<<<	=	=
REGIONAL SCALE					
Waste Management	<<<	<	<<<	=	<
Inland Water Quality	<	=	<<<	<<<	<
Urban Environment	<	<<<	<	=	<
Risk	<<<	<	<<<	<	=
Coastal zones and marine	<	<<<	<	<<<	<<<
IMPACT					
Nature and Bio-diversity	<	<	<	<<<	<

Legend: = Nil or insignificant; < Some impact; <<< Substantial impact

Tourism thus has substantial environmental impacts on coastal and mountain regions and a lesser though noticeable impact on nature, inland water quality and urban environment.[5]

---

[4] Adapted from EEA, Environment in the European Union 1995. Report for the Review of the Fifth Environmental Action Programme, EEA, 1995, p.15.

[5] Acknowledging the difficulty of quantifying tourism pressure on the environment, Eurostat has suggested, using statistical analysis that "the difference between the regions with the highest tourism density and those with the lowest density do suggest a causal link between the pressure of tourism on the one hand and a high level of electricity consumption and waste emission on the other". – Eurostat, Statistics in Focus, Theme 4 – 40/2002, Tourism and the Environment, p.6.

Community literature or policy discussion is rich in its focus on the negative impacts of tourism on the environment (as the above excerpts suggest) and possible ways of relieving them.

In general Community literature on tourism pressures on the environment reflects certain basic preoccupations:

- improving knowledge of the nature and extent of tourism pressure on the environment and developing better indicators for measuring these pressures,
- developing best practices/codes of conduct and exchange/disseminating information on better ways for dealing with these pressures,
- improving screening of development proposals/frameworks (in order to better assess environmental sustainability) through measures such as environmental impact assessment and strategic environmental assessment,
- greater integration of environmental concerns into all relevant social and economic policies, and
- facilitating citizen involvement in environmental protection through access to information, and greater participation in decision-making.

These preoccupations operate at different levels – the citizen, the site, the social, and the global. While each is important, it is the issue of integration which has come to be seen as the really key issue by the European Community and, as will be seen, around which the whole concept of sustainable development and sustainable tourism has emerged.

The dissonance between Community policy discussion on tourism impacts on the environment and the paucity of specific legal responses is no accident and can be partly explained as follows. Like many areas of Community involvement in the environment, Community activities take place at one remove from the locus of decision-making affecting environmental quality – the local/ regional authority. Consequently, the principle of subsidiarity prevents the Community from taking action unless the effects are cross-border and Community action can address them better than national action. The Commission itself has candidly acknowledged its limited role.

But, in a practical reflection of the principle of subsidiarity and the spirit of shared responsibility, it is mainly at levels other than that of the Community that the real work of reconciling tourism activity and development and the guardianship of nature and cultural assets must be brought into a sustainable balance, i.e. by Member States, regional and local authorities, the tourism industry itself and individual tourists. ... Only in certain specific cases – as where a complaint is made that a member-state has failed to properly transpose a directive into national law, or where it is claimed that a local project partly funded by money from the ERDF has not respected Community law – can the Commission become directly involved. ...

[Thus on] the basis of the Treaty on the European Union (Article 3b), the Community will take action, in accordance with the principle of subsidiarity, only if and insofar as the objectives of the proposed action cannot be sufficiently achieved by the Member states themselves and can therefore, by reason of the scale or the effects of proposed action, be better achieved by the Community. [6]

Because of the specific way tourism impacts on the environment, and also because of the way tourism is dealt with by the Rome Treaty, few measures of the large body of Community environmental legislation[7] directly address specific tourism impacts on the environment. However, a number of Community environmental laws indirectly affect tourism,[8] some more than others, such as Directive on Bathing Water Quality[9] and Directive 91/71 on Urban Waste Water Treatment.[10]

However, it is no surprise that the type of Community environmental laws which mainly affect tourism are essentially land use measures. As tourism greedily uses land and alters landscapes, Community legal responses try to provide frameworks and inputs which improve the environmental quality of decision-making at local/regional/national level.

In the complex interplay of different forces and pressures which give rise to environmental problems, the role of land-use planning and management is crucial. This covers a wide range of decisions, usually made at local and regional level, determining the character and intensity of land-uses and activities which may often have a major impact on environmental conditions. Such impacts may be direct for example by way of destruction of habitats and landscapes or indirect such as influencing the generation of additional traffic and hence contributing to congestion, air pollution and greenhouse gases. These impacts are of particular concern in urban

---

[6] Community Programme of policy and action in relation to the environment and sustainable development (5th EAP) OJ C 138/16/17, 17.5.93.
[7] http://www.europa.eu.int/eur–lex/en/lif/ind/en_analytical_index_15.html.
[8] For a summary of wider Community initiatives impacting tourism and the environment, see Commission, Community Measures affecting Tourism (1997/99), COM (2001) 171 final, March 28.3.01, pp.28–30.
[9] OJ L 31/1, 5.2.76.
[10] OJ L 135/40, 30.5.91. Consolidated text available at http://europa.eu.int/eur–lex/en/consleg/main/1991/en_1991L0271_index.html.

and coastal areas where the greater pressure and conflict for land use and development is taking place.[11]

The Community environmental laws which will be examined in this chapter are:

- Directive 85/337 on the environment impact assessment of certain public and private projects[12] and Directive 01/42 on the assessment of the effects of certain plans and programmes on the environment,[13] both of which are framework measures which seek to ensure improved decision-making by local/regional/national authorities by requiring full account be taken of sustainability considerations.

- Article 41(2)(b) of Regulation 99/1260[14] dealing with integrating environmental considerations into the spending of Community funds under regional policy.

- Directive 92/443 on the conservation of natural habitats and of wild fauna and flora,[15] which exceptionally gives an albeit indirect but significant role to the Community in influencing the types of tourism and other activities Member States can allow in large parts of their territories which are of European conservation importance.

---

[11] Commission, Communication on the sixth environmental action programme of the European Community, COM(2001) 31 final, 24.1.01, p.21.
[12] OJ L 175/40, 5.7.85 as amended by Directive 97/11, OJ L 73/5, 14.3.97.
[12] OJ L 197/30, 21.7.01.
[13] OJ L 197/30, 21.7.01.
[14] OJ L 161/1, 26.6.99.
[15] OJ L 206/7, 22.7.92.

Environmental Protection and Tourism

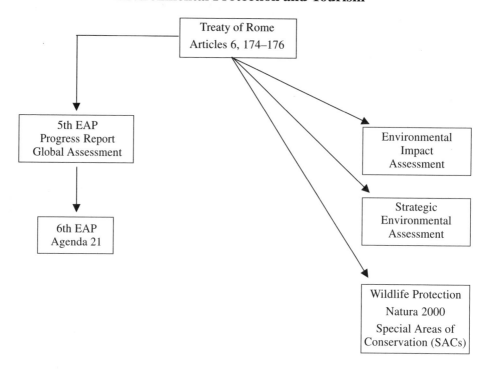

Learning Outcomes:

After reading this chapter, the student should:
- understand the underlying legal basis of Community involvement in environmental matters and the framework for implementing that involvement,
- be aware of the important role the Environmental Action Programmes in general and the 5th/6th EAPs in particular play in the design, definition and implementation of the objectives and principles of Community environmental approaches to tourism,
- be aware of the way in which selected legal measures are relied upon by the Community to diminish the negative environmental impacts of tourism development, and
- acquire insight into how the Community tries to integrate environmental considerations into regional policy and how Agenda 21 tries to advance sustainability.

These learning outcomes will be addressed through the following main headings:

The Treaty and the Environment.
Tourism in the 5th /6th Environmental Action Programmes.
Environmental Impact Assessment.
Strategic Environmental Assessment.
Habitat Protection.

THE TREATY AND THE ENVIRONMENT

When the Treaty establishing the European Community (Treaty of Rome) was written in 1957, few saw the need to provide a common policy on the environment or indeed to provide for tourism impacts on the environment. It was not that there was not anything wrong with the environment, but the focus of those who devised the Treaty was on regeneration and economic integration and consequently the notion of "environment" or "environment protection" simply did not register.

Mounting fears over the consequences of industrial development ultimately lead to the recognition at a conference of the Community Heads of State or Government held in Paris in October 1972 that the environment is a finite resource and that attention must be paid to environmental protection. While this recognition provided the impetus for some Community action in the area, it was not until the adoption of the Single European Act in 1986 that formal recognition was given in the Treaty to environmental concerns. However, it was only in 1992, after the adoption of the Maastricht changes to the Treaty of Rome, that the basis of Community involvement in environmental matters was given the status of a 'policy', though it was still not and may perhaps never be a 'common policy' due to the requirements of subsidiarity.

Since 1973 the Community has been active in environmental matters. A large body of legal and policy measures (regulations, directives, decisions, conventions, action programmes etc.) has been adopted.[16] Few deal directly by name with tourism, although as will be seen some do, while most can and do bear on the quality of the environment in which tourism operates.

Currently, the fundamental provisions of the Rome Treaty place environmental concerns at the core of Community actions.

The Community shall have as its task...to promote throughout the

---

[16] Community environment legal measures are available at http://www.europa.eu.int/eur–lex/en/lif/ind/en_analytical_index_15.html.

Community a harmonious, balanced and sustainable development of economic activities, sustainable and non-inflationary growth ... a high level of protection and improvement of the quality of the environment – Article 2.

Article 3 then provides that:

the activities of the Community shall include ... (l) a policy in the sphere of the environment.

These provisions are amplified somewhat in Title XIX, Articles 174 to 176 of the Treaty, which are entirely given over to environmental matters and reflect the current priority given to this area. Article 174(1) identifies certain objectives of Community policy on the environment:

– preserving, protecting and improving the quality of the environment;

– protecting human health;

– prudent and rational utilisation of natural resources; and

– promoting measures at international level to deal with regional or world-wide environmental problems.

The principles of Community policy intended to help achieve these objectives are set out in Article 174(2) which states that:

Community policy on the environment shall aim at a high level of protection taking into account the diversity of situations in the various regions of the Community. It shall be based on the precautionary principle and on the principles that preventive action should be taken, that environmental damage should as a priority be rectified at source and that the polluter should pay.

In this context, harmonisation measures answering environmental protection requirements shall include, where appropriate, a safeguard clause allowing Member States to take provisional measures, for non-economic environmental reasons, subject to a Community inspection procedure.

These principles are the guiding force for Community environmental action and their influence can be seen in the policy and legal approaches discussed in this chapter.

The crucial principle of integrating environmental concerns into all Community policies (a repeatedly identified but seemingly intractable problem) is now distinctly set out in Article 6 (before Maastricht it was merely part of the Title on the environment) which states:

Environmental protection requirements must be integrated into the definition and implementation of Community policies and activities referred to in Article 3, in particular with a view to promoting sustainable development.

It is easy enough to see that this means that environmental protection must be built into all Community policies and actions which affect tourism so as to produce a sustainable tourism. However, following through on this has not been easy and consolidating the political will to take, where necessary, unpalatable measures has, as will be seen, proved almost impossible.

Action Programmes

Action programmes are one of the primary means identified in the Treaty by which the Community is empowered to take focused measures relating to environmental protection. Since 1973, 5 Environmental Action Programmes have been approved by the Community and the Member States. The duration of these programmes has increased over time:

- 1st Environmental Action Programme 1973–1976,[17]
- 2nd Environmental Action Programme 1977–1981,[18]
- 3rd Environmental Action Programme 1982–1986,[19]
- 4th Environmental Action Programme 1987–1992,[20]
- 5th Environmental Action Programme 1993–2000,[21]
- 6th Environmental Action Programme 2001–2010.[22]

The current legal basis for these programmes is Article 175(3) which states that:

In other areas, general action programmes setting out priority objectives to be attained shall be adopted by the Council, acting in accordance with the procedure referred to in Article 251 and after consulting the Economic and Social Committee and the Committee of the Regions.

---

[17] OJ C 112/3, 20.12.73.
[18] OJ C 139/3, 13.6.77.
[19] OJ C 46/3, 17.2.83.
[20] OJ C 328/5, 7.12.87.
[21] OJ C 138/5, 17.5.93.
[22] Commission, Communication on the sixth environmental action programme of the European Community, COM(2001) 31 final, 24.1.01.

The Council, acting under the terms of paragraph 1 or paragraph 2 according to the case, shall adopt the measures necessary for the implementation of these programmes.

Thus, the Treaty identifies two dimensions to an action programme – priority objectives and measures to implement the programmes. It is clear that the Council has ownership of an action programme, though the onus rests on the Commission to draw it up and secure its implementation. Interestingly, the Council is not obliged to ensure the priority objectives are actually achieved, only that it correctly analyses the problems, identifies the appropriate measures and adopts them. Thereafter, while the Commission must carry out the measures adopted, no one is, in a sense, to blame if the objectives are not achieved. The fact that the Treaty specifically refers to general action programmes possibly means that until the Treaty is changed, these, and not other types of approach, must remain the means of realising Community goals in environmental protection.

The 1st EAP is generally considered the most important, mainly because it was in this programme that the basic principles and objectives of general Community environment policy were first defined.[23] However, it was not until the 5th EAP was adopted that priorities and measures dealing with tourism impacts on the environment tourism were specifically provided for.

For this reason and also because the Commission conducted a progress review on the operation of this programme which, among other things, dealt explicitly with environmental impacts of tourism, the remainder of this part will focus only on the 5th and 6th EAPs.

TOURISM IN THE 5TH AND 6TH ENVIRONMENTAL ACTION PROGRAMMES

The 5th EAP adopted in 1993 for the period 1993–2000, titled "Towards Sustainability – a European programme of policy and action in relation to the environment and sustainable development",[24] was in many ways intended to signal a shift in the Community approach to environmental degradation. Locating the cause of degradation in current patterns of consumption, and proposing a wider range of policy instruments than before, the EAP sought to switch the focus of efforts from combating types of pollution to themes/sectors and agents/ activities impacting the environment. It outlined long-term objectives/ performance targets/actions in varying degrees of clarity, detail and ambition.

---

[23] The 4th EAP merely acknowledged that "the impact of tourism on the environment and *vice–versa* is a matter of great concern" – OJ C 328/13, 7.12.87.

[24] OJ C 138/11, 17.5.93.

Tourism was one of the sectors chosen for particular focus. When explaining its choice of sectors, the Commission perhaps unwittingly revealed a contradiction at the heart of the Programme's perspective on tourism. On the one hand:

> These are sectors where the Community as such has a unique role to play and where a Community approach is the most efficient level at which to tackle the problems these sectors cause or face. They are also chosen because of the particularly significant impacts that they have or could have on the environment as a whole and because by their nature, they have crucial roles to play in the attempt to achieve sustainable development.[25]

And on the other;

> it is mainly at levels other than that of the Community that the real work of reconciling tourism activity and development and the guardianship of nature and cultural assets must be brought into a sustainable balance, i.e. by Member States, regional and local authorities, the tourism industry itself and individual tourists.[26]

The major innovative feature of the 5th EAP was its focus of the concept of sustainable development as the greater goal of Community environment policy and its attempts to spell out what this might mean in relation to development impacts on the environment.

> As used in the Programme, the word 'sustainable' is intended to reflect a policy and strategy for continued economic and social development without detriment to the environment. … The Report of the World Commission on Environment and Development (Brundtland) defined sustainable development as 'development which meets the needs of the present without compromising the ability of the future generations to meet their own needs.'[27]

If taken seriously sustainable development will involve painful social change which the Resolution of the Council of Ministers approving the 5th EAP appeared to acknowledge when it noted:

---

[25] *Ibid.,* p.14.
[26] *Ibid.,* p.16.
[27] *Ibid.,* Executive Summary para.5.

that many current forms of activity and development are not environ-mentally sustainable and [endorsed], accordingly, the general objectives of progressively orientating human activity and development toward sustainable form ... [and agreed] that the achievement of sustainable development calls for significant changes in current patterns of development, production, consumption and behaviour.[28]

Tourism Focus of 5ᵗʰ EAP

In presenting its analysis in 1993 of tourism impact on the environment, the 5ᵗʰ EAP firstly noted the leisure and economic benefits of tourism for the individual. Tourism, it declared:

> is an important element in the social and economic life of the Community. It reflects the legitimate aspirations of the individual to enjoy new places and absorb different cultures as well as to benefit from activities or relaxation away from the normal home or work setting. It is also an important economic asset to many regions and cities ...and has a special contribution to make to the economic and social cohesion of the peripheral regions. Tourism represents a good example of the fundamental link which exists between economic development and environment, with all the attendant benefits, tensions and potential conflicts. If well planned and managed, tourism, regional development and environmental protection can go hand in hand.[29]

But, the Commission noted, demand for tourism was increasing, and not evenly, across the Community:

> The increase is much more than average in the southern part of the EC. In the Alpine regions tourism has risen sharply to about 50 million people every year. As income levels and leisure time increase over the next decade, substantial growth is anticipated. This will have its effect over the whole of Europe with an emphasis on coastal and mountain zones, with the Mediterranean region taking a large share. Income increases are expected to trigger more second holidays, which may be short but are expected to take place in environmentally high quality surroundings.[30]

The 5ᵗʰ EAP was forthright about these pressures in the Mediterranean area:

---

[28] *Ibid.,* p.2.
[29] *Ibid.,* p.37.
[30] *Supra.*

the number of tourists in the Mediterranean region could grow to as many as 380–760 million per year in 2025, depending on economic growth rates. This development would be in addition to predicted demographic changes in the area. 160 million of these tourists in the year 2000 and 260 million in the year 2025 would visit Mediterranean coastal areas, as compared to 55 million in 1984 and around 100 million in 1990 Estimates ... indicate that up to 90% of any increase could accrue to Community Member States in the region. Such increases would require double the occupation of space by the year 2000 alone; the solid waste and waste water generated could more than triple by the year 2025.

These developments will have major implications for the environment, imposing tremendous pressures on habitats, transport facilities, coastal and mountain land, energy and water resources, and waste-water treatment facilities, particularly at periods of peak demand. The coastal zones especially will face severe problems.[31]

The 5th EAP identified the broad elements of a plan for dealing with these pressures.

It will be necessary therefore to develop national and regional integrated management plans for coastal and mountain areas. ... Elements in these strategies which directly relate to the interaction of tourism and the environment would be controls on land use, the setting of strict rules on new constructions and the fight against illegal housing, management of private traffic flows to and in the tourist areas, diversification of tourism, strict implementation and enforcement of environmental standards on noise, drinking water, bathing water, waste water and air emissions (including emissions in the hinterland of the tourist areas), creation of buffer zones around sensitive areas such as wetlands and dunes, better dispersion of summer holidays, awareness building and education of local people and tourists, and education and professional training of people involved in the management of the areas concerned.[32]

In summary according to the Commission:

It is essential to place future growth of tourism within the framework of sustainability.[33]

---

[31] *Ibid.,* p.39.
[32] *Supra.*
[33] *Supra.*

Following this, the 5th EAP identified three main lines of action[34] needed to achieve an environmentally friendly sustainable tourism:

– diversification of tourism activities, including better management of the phenomenon of mass tourism, and encouragement of different types of tourism;

– quality of tourist services, including information and awareness-building, and visitor management and facilities;

– tourist behaviour, including media campaigns, codes of behaviour and choice of transport.

These ideas were developed in a tabular format which:

> gives an overview of the elements of a strategy on tourism, indicating which instruments need to be developed within what time-frame and by which combination of actors and target group.[35]

---

[34] Executive Summary OJ C 138/16, 17.5.93, para.30.
[35] *Ibid.,* p.39.

Table 9.2: Tourism

Objectives	Measures up to 2000	Instruments	Time-frame	Actors
Type of Tourism	Better management of of mass tourism	Improved control on land use	1993 onwards	LAs
		Strict rules for new constructions	idem	LAs
	National and regional integrated	Management of traffic flows to, in and from tourism areas	idem	MS+LAs
	Management plans for coastal and	Visitor management; exchange of expertise	1992–93	Idem
	Mountain areas	Pilot models of sustainable tourism	idem	Idem
		Strict implementation and enforcement of environmental standards on noise, drinking water, bathing water, waste-water treatment and air emissions	ongoing	MS+LAs + EC
		Creation of buffer zones around sensitive areas	1993 onwards	MS+LAs
Behaviour of Tourists	Building environmental awareness	Development and promotion of code of conduct	1993–95	MS+LAs
	Liberalization of air and coach	Multi-media campaigns and conferences	idem	Tourist ind.+EC
	Transport – TGV network	EC transport policy and national transport policies	1993 onwards	EC+MS
	Increase of marginal costs of use of private car and promotion of alternative transport	Economic incentives such as CO_2 / energy fax and road pricing and encouraged use of public transport	1993 1993 onwards	EC+MS MS+ECs
	Better dispersion of holidays	Cooperation and exchange of information	before 1998	MS+EC+ Tourist ind.
		National plan + regional plans	before 1995	LAs+MS+ EC
	Diversification of tourism (including Rural Rural and cultural tourism)	European Regional Development Fund	idem	LAs+MS+ EC
		EC tourism action plan	idem	LAs+MS+ EC
		EC tourism Advisory Committee	idem	LAs+MS+ EC

LA: refers to actions at local and regional authority level, MS: refers to actions at Member State level, EC: refers to actions at Community level

Objectives	Measures up to 2000	Instruments	Time-frame	Actors
Quality of Tourism Services	Promotion of new forms of tourism which care for environment	Brochures	1993 onwards	Ind. +LAs
		Professional training	idem	Idem
	Careful selection of accommodation	Pilot projects	idem	Idem
	Building of environ-mental awareness of people involved in management of tourist areas	Professional training and education/exchange of best practice	idem	MS+LAs +EC+Ind.
	Building of environ-mental awareness of local people and tourist services			

LA: refers to actions at local and regional authority level, MS: refers to actions at Member State level, EC: refers to actions at Community level

Various strategies for tourism were then summarised.[36]

Table 9.3: Programme framework for selected target sectors

	Sectoral Impacts	Resources	Behaviour
Tourism	Sustainable tourism, land-use, infrastructure	Protection of coastal zones and natural, Man-made or built amenities	Broader consumer choice
	– drinking water	– desertification	– broader choice of options
	– bathing water	– cultural heritage	– better information
	– waste management	– forest fires	– better seasonal spreads of tourism
	– sustainable mobility	– natural trails	

NB: The instruments indicated above are not exclusive to the sectors in which they appear, they have been inserted in the sectors in respect of which they have the most obvious potential.

It is notable that the list of instruments in Table 9.2 did not include imposing tourism taxes, which although even now a controversial idea, was identified as a possible approach by the Economic and Social Committee in an Opinion on the proposed EAP:[37]

---

[36] *Ibid.*, p.39. This an edited extract from Table 6. Other sectors of activity have been omitted.
[37] ESC, Opinion on the proposal for resolution of the Council of the European Communities

Taxes levied on tourism might also be used for environmental purposes.

PROGRESS REPORT

In 1996 the Commission produced a mid term review[38] of the operation of the 5th EAP. The review confirmed the continuing robustness of tourism demand and the emergence of some new trends.

> According to the Dobris Assessment based on data from the World Tourism Organisation, by 2000, tourism is likely to become the largest single economic activity in the EU. … In 1993, the number of tourist arrivals in Europe was 296.5 millions … this is expected to continue.

> While the most popular countries for travel in 1993 were France, Spain, Italy and the UK, tourism in Greece and in Eastern Europe is growing very rapidly due to lower prices for accommodation, the lower cost of living etc. Other trends are, that more tourists from the South will visit the North; that tourists will avoid visiting areas with serious environmental problems; and that air and private car travel will become even more popular. The driving factors behind these trends are financial (the average citizen is becoming better off and consequently has more disposable income), an increase in leisure time, and changes in expectations and population structures. …

The Review also noted continuing increased use of land for tourism purposes in the Alps (ski resorts), the Mediterranean coast (hotels, camping resorts, beaches) and the North Sea coast, but acknowledged an information gap about the precise environmental impacts of tourism developments.

> However, very little information on the environmental impact of tourism is available at either EU or Member State level. Given the site nature of such impact, tourism indicators tend to focus on the underlying economic causes of environmental pressures.

The findings of the Progress Report were presented under two headings – actions

---

on a Community programme of policy and action in relation to the environment and sustainable development OJ C 287/37, 4.11.92.

[38] Progress Report from the Commission on the Implementation of the European Community Programme of Policy and Action in relation to the Environment and Sustainable Development Towards Sustainability COM(95) 624 final, 10.1.96. The passages quoted over the following pages derive from pp. 46–50.

at EU and Member State level, though many of the State actions in fact described local actions.

At EU level, it is not surprising that the Progress Report could point to very little since the Commission had promised so little in the 5th EAP. Financial support for a number of tourism pilot projects was cited, along with the Commission Green paper on the Role of the Union in Tourism, a paper which in retrospect signalled the downgrading of direct Community interest in the tourism.[39]

Actions at Member State Level

At Member State level the report catalogued a lengthy list of tourism actions that had been undertaken.

> Member States are currently attempting to control mass tourism so as to preserve the environments upon which tourism thrives. Constraints on the over-exploitation of nature areas serve to ensure that new recreation developments only take place in multi-use designated areas. Examples of this include the number of berths available for the construction of marinas, access to pleasure boating areas (e.g. in Waddenzee), and maximum length for forest in the Netherlands. Portugal and Austria recently completed studies on the impact of tourism on the environment, and in tourism and initiatives for nature and environment protection respectively.

> To preserve sensitive areas from exploitation or mass tourism, several member States ... have created buffer zones around such areas. In Germany and Sweden, buffer zones around sensitive areas may be created on the assessment of needs, for example, the creation of nature reserves. The national ecological network in the Netherlands provides for the development of ecological corridors around core zones, and for an equilibrium between the development of agriculture, forestry, nature, landscape and outdoor recreation retaining the area's specific character over 20 years. Ireland has published guidelines on the balance between forestry practices and agriculture, and forestry practice and fishing.

As far was transport was concerned, taking into account geographic factors,

> in Finland the car remains the most convenient transport means to cover large distances. ... Austria has developed a system of traffic management by promoting traffic free tourism, soft mobility in tourist communes, Länder

---

[39] See p. 67.

level requirements, and trains to ski resorts. Germany has adopted local transport principles focusing in decreasing traffic.

Among actions to promote sustainable tourism noted in the Progress Report:

> in Germany, incentives are given for sustainable rural tourism through quality labels, prizes for clean villages, and the creation of nature parks ... governments are publishing educational materials, brochures, etc., on a variety of tourism related topics, e.g., brochures on waste management in coastal zones and practical nature conservation (Finland); brochures by professional organizations and guidelines on concepts of sustainable tourism that can be applied to individual management practices, 'Guest opinion on Austria', a periodical opinion poll of tourists (Austria), information material from communes and federations (Germany), and a 'Green audit kit' providing guidance to tourism businesses on becoming more environment-friendly (UK).

The Commission also noted efforts at Member State level to encourage change in the attitudes of tourists.

> Efforts to develop and promote a tourism code of conduct have been taken by Finland and the United Kingdom. In the UK, the government supports initiatives to develop environmental codes of conduct ... [in 1992, the British Holiday and Home Parks Association, The Caravan Club, the Camping and Caravanning Club, the Camping and Outdoor Leisure Association, and the National Caravan Council adopted a Parks Industry Environmental Code as a guide to caravan park and campsite owners on sustainable land-use practices and greener tourism. The code promotes proper attention to sympathetic park layout, location and design, the use of environment-friendly products and design, efficient and sensitive management, energy conservation, the use of biodegradable material, and material recycling...] In Finland, codes of conduct have been prepared for particular target groups such as national park visitors, i.e., hikers, leisure boaters, etc. Italy is currently preparing a 'tourist's code' of behaviour and the publication of the 'Charter of Touring and Environment Ethics'.

Limits of Actions

The impression of progress which this lengthy catalogue of measures gives is, however, misleading. The Progress Report frankly acknowledged that Member State policies with respect to the environmental impact of tourism:

have little effect on the number of tourists or the surface area they use

and further that:

trends indicate continued growth in air and road transport as well as in tourism activities, signifying increase strain on the environment.

In overall terms, the inability of both the 5th EAP and the Progress Report to advance policies for addressing increasing tourism pressures on the environment seemed to result from:

- a lack of precise information about the extent of current impacts – in turn caused by the absence of sufficient indicators of environmental pressure caused by tourism,
- a lack of sufficient information at local level of the nature and extent of these pressures, and
- the inability of the Community to focus on the root causes of increasing tourism and react accordingly.

The Commission, however, continued to believe that improved integration of environmental considerations into Member State tourism policies remained the best way forward and even suggested the following future priority actions:

A. Integration

- public authorities in the Member States should work together to better integrate environmental considerations into their tourism policy at the most appropriate level;
- public authorities in the Member States need to develop integrated land-use planning at local or regional level;
- public authorities in the Member States need to implement stricter control measures on land-use;
- at EU level approaches to sustainable development in the tourism sector need to be strengthened, building on suggestions in the Green Paper on Tourism and using principal instruments such as the Structural and Cohesion Funds, to support Member States in their efforts to protect the quality of the environment, to change attitudes and approaches and to promote sustainable development;

B. Protection of sensitive areas

– Member States need to develop frameworks for the protection of the environment particularly in sensitive areas such as the Mediterranean, the Baltic, the Alps and coastal zones;

C. Information of tourists

– public authorities in the Member States and the tourist industry should make available to the public better information on the state of the environment in order to enable public pressure to act as a driver towards sustainable tourism; the success of the Blue Flag initiative demonstrates the importance of the public's role;

D. Management of tourist flow

– public authorities in the Member States and the tourist industry need to examine the carrying capacity of tourist sites and take appropriate measures to manage tourists flows to the lasting benefit of the sector and the environment. The LIFE programme can be used to demonstrate the benefits of more sustainable approaches.

No one could disagree with these suggestions, especially the suggestion of strict control over land-use. But the key point to note about many of these suggestions is that the Community had no power (due to the subsidiarity principle) to ensure they happened.

A debate ensued among the various Community institutions following publication of the Progress Report. It culminated in a decision of Parliament and Council[40] which reaffirmed the general approach and strategy of the 5th EAP, and established both general and tourism priorities for moving forward. Parliament and the Council jointly undertook:[41]

> to examine, *inter alia*, in the light of the Commission proposal of 25 March 1997 on the assessment of the effect of certain plans and programmes on the environment, how the environmental impact of policies, plans and programmes in the Community and, where relevant, Commission proposals for programmes and Community legislation can be assessed.

---

[40] Decision 98/2179 of the European Parliament and of the Council of 24 September 1998 on the review of the European Community programme of policy and action in relation to the environment and sustainable development "Towards sustainability" OJ L 275, 10.10.98.

[41] The following extracts are from pp.5–7.

Among general priority objectives the Decision identified the need for action:

> (a) to improve the legal framework for environmental policy by adopting more coherent, comprehensive and integrated approaches to specific sectors, where appropriate by simplifying legislative and administrative procedures and by using framework directives ... to promote the incorporation of the issue of "environment and tourism", where appropriate, into international agreements ... (g) to speed up efforts, at Community and member State level, to deal effectively with breaches of Community environmental legislation in accordance with the Treaty, in particular Articles 155 and 171 hereof.

In relation to tourism, the Decision identified the following modest priorities for action:

> (a) to provide for regular exchanges of information on the impact on the environment of tourism practices;
> (b) to support awareness campaigns in order to promote environment-friendly use of tourism resources;
> (c) to promote the implementation of innovative good practices in the field of sustainable tourism development, including by means of pilot projects in the framework of existing financial instruments and by applying the 'polluter pays` principle;
> (d) to ensure that the Structural Funds contribute to sustainable forms of tourism in accordance with:
>
>> • the requirements of the Structural Fund regulations, including any provisions for the appraisal of the environmental impact of operations,
>> • any other relevant Community legislation, such as measures concerning Environmental Impact Assessment (EIA);

Many of these are 'soft' policy options which hold little hope of effecting significant change regarding tourism impacts on the environment.

END OF 5TH EAP AND BEGINNING OF 6TH EAP

Global Assessment

Towards the end of the period covered by the 5th EAP the Commission produced another report, this time a 'global assessment' on the implementation of the 5th EAP. It did this partly because the Decision of the Parliament and Council on the Review of the 5th EAP requested it and partly:

> with the intention to launch a debate with the other Institutions, stakeholders and citizens on the priorities for a 6th Programme to be put forward in 2000.[42]

Unfortunately, the Global Assessment did not review progress in the five sectoral areas, including tourism, identified in the 5th EAP. Rather it concentrated on assessing progress on a variety of general environmental issues, such as climate change, waste urban environment etc. Of the issues covered, it is perhaps the issue of coastal zones which is most directly related to tourism. Here the review and prognosis was not optimistic.

> Many coastal zones are densely populated and under intense pressure from urban development, industry, transport and tourism. The activities also impact heavily on the quality of the marine environment. At the same time coastal zones continue an important part of Europe's natural and cultural heritage.
>
> The Community has during the 5th Programme period undertaken an Integrated Coastal zone Management Demonstration Programme to show ways to address coastal zone issues. The question is how this Programme should be followed up.
>
> There continues to be urgency in this area since 80% of coasts are at risk from different pressures, and in particular they are suffering from increasing urbanisation.

The effective implementation of environmental legislation remained as real a concern of the Global Assessment as it had been of the mid term review.

> The Communication on the state of implementation of Community law, published by the Commission in 1996, showed however that implementation of Community law on the environment was often unsatisfactory ... The main reasons for this currently unsatisfactory situation are to be found in the legal and technical complexity of the legislation and the difficulty of balancing the interest of the stakeholders concerned. ... In considering future policy we have to remind ourselves that the first step

---

[42] Commission, Europe's Environment: What directions for the future? The Global Assessment of the European Community Programme of Policy and Action in relation to the environment and sustainable development, 'Towards Sustainability', COM (99) 543 final, 24.11.99. The following extracts are taken from pp. 2–22.

for improving the environment on the ground is the full implementation of what has been adopted already …it is crucial not least for the creditability of Community environmental policy as a whole.

Overall, the Commission frankly admitted the failings of the 5th EAP:

> Although the 5th Programme raised awareness of the need for stakeholders, citizens and decision-makers in other sectors to actively pursue environmental objectives, less progress has been made overall in changing economic and societal trends which are harmful to the environment. The commitment by other sectors and by Member States to the Programme is partial, and the patterns of production and consumption in our countries prevent us from achieving a clean and safe environment … The outlook is that new environmental standards will not keep pace with the growing demand for example for transport, consumer goods or tourism.

As for future strategy:

> Besides the implementation and where needed the strengthening of existing measures and the development of new measures to address emerging problems under a 6th Environment Action Programme, reinforced integration of environmental concerns into other policies and the stronger involvement of citizens and stakeholders in the process aiming at commitment and responsibility are the keys towards sustainable development

The stress on reinforced integration and greater citizen involvement is significant because it reflects the limitations of Community involvement. Integration of environmental matters into Community policies is an administrative issue for the Community and citizen involvement acts almost as a substitute for Community involvement. Moreover, the fact that there is no Community tourism policy and that any action must respect the subsidiarity principle means that real integration of environmental concerns into tourism matters cannot take place. Only a tourism policy could provide the focus (and legal authority) for actions which could go beyond facilitating the working of the common market and attempt to deal systematically with the environmental pressures of tourism. As the EEA remarked recently:[43]

> The lack of an EC policy on tourism makes developing a coherent framework to tackle [environmental problems resulting from ever increasing tourism demand and the variable nature of that demand] more difficult.

---

[43] EEA, Environmental Signals 2001, EEA, 2001.

Comments such as this are among the first to imply that the reason for attempting to develop a Community tourism policy should not be the better facilitation of the tourism industry, but the better protection of the tourism environment.

Other Perspectives

Other perspectives on the effect of the 5th EAP are available in surveys conducted during the preparation of the Global Assessment of the views of various environmental stakeholders – sectors; groups/NGOs/governments/institutions – canvassed by the Commission while preparing the Global Assessment.[44] They provide a useful flavour of other opinion on the 5th EAP, although recorded in note form. In general they reflect concerns and opinions reflected in previous commentary in this section.

- The momentum of the 5th EAP has been "undermined by the Member States preoccupation during the 1990's with competitiveness and subsidiarity The use of EU finance (especially through the CAP and Structural Funds) should have been identified as a key theme.[45] … The CAP and Structural Funds together account for 80% of the EU budget, yet are subject to inadequate environmental screening".[46]

- Other remarks get closer to the key fundamentals. "Others argue, however, that a future programme should adopt a broader 'three-dimensional approach', addressing social and economic issues as well as environmental in a full sustainable development programme".[47]

- An EU Sustainable Development Plan?

  - A combined approach should be pursued.

  - There should be a Sixth Environmental Action Programme to take forward policies and measures which are the responsibility of DG XI and to advance the application of Article 6 of the Amsterdam Treaty.

  - At the same time, foundations should be laid for the development of an EU Sustainable Development Programme integrating environmental, economic and social concerns. It should be built around the 6th EAP. An EU SD Programme should be the responsibility of a new Sustainable Development Task Force attached to the Commission President. The

---

[44] Commission Services Staff Working Paper, Key Developments in the implementation of the 5th Environment Action Programme. Accompanying document to the Global Assessment, SEC (1999) 191, 24.11.99; Views of Sectoral Groups/NGO's p.1.

[45] *Ibid.*, 2.

[46] *Ibid.*, 4.

[47] *Ibid.*, 5.

successful development of an EU SD programme will require stronger inter DG co-ordinating mechanisms and extensive staff training.[48]

Improved integration was a clear wish:[49]

> Clear integration objectives – an EAP for the entire EU, not only DG XI and MS Ministries of Environment.

6th EAP

The 6th EAP[50] to run from 2001 to 2010 is less directly relevant to tourism than the 5th EAP. The proposal identified a series of priority environmental areas (climate change, nature and bio-diversity, environment and health, sustainability of natural resource and waste) and priority environmental actions (including better implementation of environmental legislation, better integration of environmental concerns into other areas and greening of land use planning and management).

Tourism is explicitly identified as a cause of environmental depletion, though in a significant departure from the 5th EAP, little or no targeted and programmatic tourism actions are promised. The overall picture is bleak:

> Forecasts suggest that, with current policies and socio-economic trends, many of the pressures that give rise to [certain persistent environmental problems including climate change, loss of bio-diversity and natural habitats, soil loss and degradation] such as transport, energy use, tourist activities, land-take for infrastructure, etc, will worsen over the coming decade.[51]

Although tourism pressure on the environment is not identified as a priority area for action, it is important to note that future Community action regarding the environmental pressures of tourism is also being driven by the on-going implementation of the United Nations' inspired strategy – Agenda 21 – for promoting sustainable development, including tourism development.

---

[48] Working Group B Tourism, Coastal Zones, Urban, Spatial Planning. Retrospective 1992–1999.

[49] Contributions to the Global Assessment, p.5.

[50] Decision 1600/2002 laying down the Sixth Community Environment Action Programme, OJ L 242/1, 10.9.02. See also Commission, Communication on the sixth environmental action programme of the European Community, COM(2001) 31 final, 24.1.01; OJ C 154E/218, 29.5.01.

[51] Commission Communication, p.10.

Agenda 21 and Sustainable Tourism

Agenda 21is a brand name inspired by the UN to describe the process of filtering down to all levels of economic, social and governmental activity the prioritising of principles of sustainable development. In the tourism context this involves at Community level[52]

- Consumer oriented awareness –raising
- Multi-stakeholder partnership and networks
- Governance and policy integration at each level
- Stakeholder commitment, capacity building, and good practice to sustainability
- Multi-stakeholder monitoring and reporting

Given the influence of the subsidiarity principle on Community involvement in environmental matters, the Community has a limited role to play in this.

> The principle responsibility certainly lies at the individual, local and regional levels.[53]

Legal approaches play a minimal role in achieving the objectives of Agenda 21 and essentially involve doing better what is or should already be done. This mainly involves:

- improved compliance with Community environmental law,
- highlighting successful compliance examples,
- more focused use of Structural Funds, and
- improved impact assessment and stakeholder consultation on the law-making process.

Individual responsiveness to moral exhortation forms an important part of the strategy. 'Some change of stakeholder behaviour and the achievement of sustainable tourism objectives can occur with voluntary instruments on the basis of potentially convincing argument' though it is also recognised that "actors in the market place are reluctant to reverse behaviour unilaterally".[54] Only when this approach fails will the use of regulatory instruments be examined.

---

[52] Commission DG Enterprise Tourism Unit, Agenda 21- Sustainability in the European Tourism Sector – A Discussion Document, prepared for the European Tourism Forum, 10.12.02, p.5.

[53] Commission DG Enterprise Tourism Unit, Agenda 21- Sustainability in the European Tourism Sector – A Background Document, prepared for the European Tourism Forum, 10.12.02, p.23.

[54] *Supra.*

This softly softy approach by the Commission is no doubt attributable to the lack of political and indeed popular support for more forthright law based approaches to combating negative tourism impacts on the environment. As mapped out by the Commission the implementation of Agenda 21 objectives in the Community will be a slow, intense, consultative and participatory process. In many ways it is an ideal approach for dealing with a structural issue when time is not a problem. Much of the Community sourced material in this chapter, however, suggests that time is a problem.

Both the 6th EAP and Agenda 21 concur in highlighting the importance of improved enforcement of Community environmental legislation as a means of advancing sustainability. It is appropriate in this last section to examine the main pieces of Community land-use legislation, which impact on tourism and provide a framework for sustainability.

ENVIRONMENTAL IMPACT ASSESSMENT

The idea behind environmental impact assessment (EIA) is straightforward. Many tourism and other projects have negative environmental impacts because decision-makers failed to think clearly beforehand about a project's potentially adverse impacts, whether they could be avoided and indeed whether the project was worth the impacts.

Directive 85/337 on the environmental impact assessment of projects[55] is an attempt to force advance and systematic consideration of potential environmental impacts, firstly, by listing a wide range of projects which in some cases must and in other cases may be made subject to a prior assessment by the developer of specified impacts, and secondly by listing how the assessment should be carried out. Annex I of the Directive lists projects where an assessment must be carried out and Annex II lists projects where states have a discretion. Prior assessment means the assessment must be carried out before any formal planning or other development consent is given and its results properly considered. However, the requirement to carry out the assessment is procedural only in that once the assessment is carried out and taken into account, permission for a project may still be given. Arguably the Directive could have gone on to provide that consent should not be given where the assessment indicates defined levels of negative impact.

Article 2(1) is the key provision in Directive 85/337 and it is important to note that its general scope supersedes some later more specific provisions in the Directive.

---

[55] OJ L 175/40, 5.5.85. Consolidated text available at http://europa.eu.int/eur–lex/en/consleg/pdf/1985/en_1985L0337_do_001.pdf.

Member States shall adopt all measures necessary to ensure that, before consent is given, projects likely to have significant effects on the environment by virtue, *inter alia*, of their nature, size or location are made subject to a requirement for development consent and an assessment with regard to their effects. These projects are defined in Article 4.

Article 3 defines what the assessment must do.

The environmental impact assessment shall identify, describe and assess in an appropriate manner, in light of each individual case and in accordance with Articles 4 to 11, the direct and indirect effects of a project on the following factors:

– human beings, fauna and flora;
– soil, water, air, climate and the landscape;
– material assets and the cultural heritage;
– the interaction between the factors mentioned [above].

Scenery or visual amenity are important tourism assets, and while not mentioned, probably come within landscape and/or cultural heritage, but not material assets.

A planning consent authority should clearly not accept a deficient assessment since it will mean that the Directive was not complied with. In tourism terms a factor of particular significance in an assessment is whether tourism has already altered the existing landscape. If it has, then baring exceptional circumstances, the assessment is unlikely to reveal unacceptably negative environmental effects.

Article 4 divides the types of assessable projects into the two categories already mentioned. Article 4(2) provides:

for projects listed in Annex II, the Member States shall determine through

(a) a case-by-case examination, or
(b) thresholds or criteria set by the Member State,

whether the project shall be made subject to an assessment in accordance with Articles 5 to 10.

Article 4(3) provides that the selection criteria to be taken into account in using the case-by-case or threshold approach are set out in Annex III. Selection criteria are detailed under various headings – characteristics of projects, location of projects and characteristics of potential impact. Under the second heading, some of the selection criteria have clear relevance to tourism developments:

Annex III

Selection Criteria referred to in Article 4(3) ... Location of projects

The environmental sensitivity of geographical areas likely to be affected by projects must be considered, having regard, in particular, to:

- the existing land use,

- the relative abundance, quality and regenerative capacity of natural resources in the area,

the absorption capacity of the natural environment, paying particular attention to the following areas: (a) wetlands; (b) coastal zones; (c) mountain and forest areas; (d) nature reserves and parks; (e) areas classified or protected under Member States' legislation;

- special protection areas designated by Member States pursuant to Directive 79/409/EEC and 92/43/EEC; (f) areas in which the environmental quality standards laid down in Community legislation have already been exceeded; (g) densely populated areas; (h) landscapes of historical, cultural or archaeological significance.

No tourism projects are mentioned in Annex I, though the original Annex II list included a few. Annex II was substantially enlarged in 1997 and it now lists the following projects under a specific tourism heading:

(a) Ski-runs, ski-lifts and cable-cars and associated developments;

(b) Marinas;

(c) Holiday villages and hotel complexes outside urban areas and associated developments;

(d) Permanent camp sites and caravan sites;

(e) Theme parks.

The general effect of the insertion in 1997 of Article 4(3) in Directive 85/337 is to severely limit Member State discretion in taking a threshold approach to deciding when an environmental assessment for an Annex II project is needed. Prior to this the Commission had to take proceedings[56] in the Court of Justice against a number of states for failure to properly implement the Directive. The difficulty arose from the fact that Member States interpreted the power granted in Article 4(2) to lay down thresholds as meaning that any development below

---

[56] IP/193, 28.2.00.

that threshold was exempt from the need to require an assessment. Since some states set quite high thresholds the result was that smaller projects were exempt and the cumulative effect of a number of smaller projects in the same area was not assessed.

In *Commission v. Ireland*[57] in 1999 Ireland stipulated space thresholds only for projects involving intensive agricultural use (100ha), initial afforestation (70ha), land reclamation (100 ha) and peat extraction (50 ha) when implementing Annex II. Assessment below these figures was not required. This approach was criticised[58] by the Court of Justice.

As far as the objection to thresholds is concerned, although the second subparagraph of Article 4(2) of the Directive confers on Member States a measure of discretion to specify certain types of projects which are to be subject to an assessment or to establish the criteria or thresholds applicable, the limits of that discretion lie in the obligation set out in Article 2(1) that projects likely, by virtue, *inter alia*, of their nature, size or location, to have significant effects on the environment are to be subject to an impact assessment. ...

Thus, a Member State which established criteria or thresholds taking account only of the size of projects, without also taking their nature and location into consideration, would exceed the limits of its discretion under Articles 2(1) and 4(2) of the Directive.

Even a small-scale project can have significant effects on the environment if it is in a location where the environmental factors set out in Article 3 of the Directive, such as fauna and flora, soil, water, climate or cultural heritage, are sensitive to the slightest alteration.

Similarly, a project is likely to have significant effects where, by reason of its nature, there is a risk that it will cause a substantial or irreversible change in those environmental factors, irrespective of its size.

In order to demonstrate that Ireland has failed to fulfil its obligations in this regard, the Commission has put forward several convincing examples of projects which, whilst considered solely in relation to their size, may none the less have significant effects on the environment by reason of their nature or location.

The most significant example is afforestation because, when carried out

---

[57] [1999] E.C.R. I–5901.
[58] *Ibid.*, p. 5950.

> in areas of active blanket bog, it entails, by its nature and location, the destruction of the bog ecosystem and the irreversible loss of biotopes that are original, rare and of great scientific interest. In itself, it may also cause the acidification or eutrophication of waters.

Thus, it is clear that the overriding requirement for Member States in deciding when an assessment is needed is whether as a matter of likely fact a particular project may have significant environmental impacts due to its nature, size or location. The ability to set thresholds is intended as a mere guide to when impacts may be more likely to occur than not, but projects below the threshold may still require an assessment. Many tourism projects, especially those located in environmentally sensitive areas and almost regardless of the scale of the project will probably require assessment under the Directive.

In 1993[59] the Commission noted some thresholds used by Member States for projects related to tourism:

holiday villages and hotel complexes:

- Flanders set a size threshold of 20 hectares,
- Denmark set a minimum of 75 rooms

marinas:

- Flanders set a threshold of 500 of fixed docking places (more of a focus on size and not location or nature),
- Portugal differentiated between river, river estuary marinas and sea coast and for the latter established a threshold of 'more than 250 places, boats up to 6 metres long but 7% of the places can be for bigger boats,'
- Spain utilised the freedom to enact more stringent legislation than required by the Directive and has subjected all marina developments to a mandatory assessment.

Flanders required assessments for the erection of a tourist or recreational facility which may attract an average traffic flow of 1,000 vehicles per day of operation, or which covers an area of 50 hectares or more.[60]

---

[59] Commission, Report on the Implementation of Directive 85/337/EEC on the Assessment of the effects of certain public and private projects on the environment, COM (93) 28 final – Vol. 13, 2.4.93, pp.38/62/221/234.

[60] *Ibid.*, p.39.

STRATEGIC ENVIRONMENTAL ASSESSMENT

The second major piece of Community land-use legislation with the potential to significantly impact on tourism, and only fully effective from 2004, is Directive 2001/42[61] on the assessment of the effects of certain plans and programmes on the environment, also known as strategic environmental assessment (SEA). Assessment under this Directive is different from an assessment under Directive 85/337 in that it focuses on the assessment of the plans and programmes (under which individual project consents are given, rather than the individual projects themselves) which are prepared or adopted at local, regional or national level under statutory authority for defined industries and activities.

Among the defined industries are forestry, transport, tourism and among the defined activities is town and country planning or land use.

Thus, plans prepared for tourism operational programmes, local authority Development Plans and all framework plans focused on tourism must be made subject to this prior assessment. In other words, future frameworks within which development consents may be given relating to tourism must themselves be scrutinised from an environmental impact perspective. The reasoning is hopefully clear. If the framework itself is properly balanced between development and environmental sustainability consents given are more likely to ensure sustainability. Equally, if the framework itself is skewed in favour of development, even with an environmental impact assessment of an individual project carried out under Directive 85/337, an environmentally sustainable outcome is less likely.

The overall object of Directive 2001/42, according to Article 1, is to use the environmental assessment of plans and programmes:

> to provide for a high level of protection of the environment and to contribute to the integration of environmental considerations into the preparation and adoption of plans and programmes with a view to promoting sustainable development ...

In seeking to achieve this objective the Directive pursues a number of themes. It:

- defines when an SEA must be carried out – "during the preparation of a plan

---

[61] OJ L 197/30, 21.7.01. Member states have until July 21, 2004 to implement the Directive. See generally Commission, SEA and the Integration of the environment into strategic decision–making, May 2001, available at http://www.europa.eu.int/comm/environment/eia/sea–studies–and–reports/sea_integration_main.pdf. See also the Commission's Initial Proposal, COM(1996) 511 final, 4.12.96.

or programme and before its adoption or submission to the legislative procedure" – Article 4(1),

- defines the procedures and consultation to be followed before adoption of a plan/programme. The first step in the assessment is the production of an environmental report in which the likely significant effects on the environment of implementing the plan or programme and reasonable assumptions are identified, described and evaluated. Thereafter the draft plan and the environmental report must be made available to the public as part of a consultation process. Following this, and any transboundry consultation where necessary, the report, the opinions expressed during the consultation process and also from any transboundry consultation.

  > shall be taken into account during the preparation of the plan or programme and before its adoption … – Article 8

- establishes the criteria in Annex II for determining the likely significant environmental effects of plans and programmes,

- defines the criteria for drawing up the environmental report used as part of the SEA.

The contrasting purposes of an SEA and an EIA have been described as follows:

> An SEA of a plan will aim to assess the broad environmental and sustainability [implications (positive and negative) of a large number of initiatives which can vary in type (e.g. from a transport network to a research programme for universities). It will anticipate development proposals instead of reacting to them (as in the case of EIA). This enables a more comprehensive protection of the environment which is focused on promoting sustainable development as much as preventing negative environmental impacts.]

> An EIA of a single project (e.g. a tourism complex) will aim to identify the specific impacts on the ground, as much as possible in quantitative terms. It is intended as a tool which helps decision makers to establish whether a single project will have negative impacts on the local environment. As a result, it gives significant importance to practical mitigation and compensation solutions. While at SEA level, these are often discussed in terms of broad policy alternatives.[62]

---

[62] Commission, *A Handbook on Environmental Assessment of Regional Development plans and EU Structural Funds Programmes*, September 1999, p.20.

Although Member States have until 2004 to implement Directive 2001/42, from a tourism perspective, the controversial parts seem likely to be:

- Article 3(3) under which Member States can exempt from the need for assessment plans which relate to the use of small areas at local level and also minor modifications to plans where they determine the plans are not likely to have significant environmental effects.

- Article 6 under which Member States are entitled to identify the public which has the right to be consulted for its views on draft plans or programmes, although this discretion is limited by Article 6(4) which expressly lists 'relevant non-governmental organisations, such as those promoting environmental protection' as likely bodies with the right to be consulted.

STRATEGIC ENVIRONMENTAL ASSESSMENT AND REGIONAL DEVELOPMENT

Activities sponsored by the Community can negatively impact on the environment. Large numbers of development projects are part funded by the Community under regional programmes. Even with the best intentions, these can degrade environmental quality. While these projects have to obtain local planning consent and are also often subject to an EIA, Community law also requires that sustainability considerations be integrated into Community programmes such as community support frameworks (CSF), operational programmes (OP) and single programming documents (SPD).[63]

This arises under two legal grounds. Firstly Article 6 of the Treaty of Rome, it will be recalled, requires:

> Environmental protection requirements must be integrated into the definition and implementation of Community policies and activities referred to in Article 3, in particular with a view to promoting sustainable development.

Secondly, in the context of the Structural Funds, this is emphasised in a number of places in Regulation 1260/99 laying down general provisions on the Structural Funds,[64] but particularly Article 41(2)(b) which in dealing with the mandatory evaluation of programmes as they are prepared for submission to the Commission requires:

---

[63] These instruments are dealt with at p. 266.
[64] OJ L 161/1, 26.6.99.

> The ex-ante evaluation shall give a description, quantified as far as possible, of the existing environmental situation and an estimate of the expected impact of the strategy and assistance on the environmental situation.

This provision is necessary because the Directive on strategic environmental assessment, considered above, does not automatically apply to regional policy funding programmes. It only applies to frameworks within which development consents are given. Commission agreement on an CSF/OP/SPD is not a development consent. However, strategic environmental assessment (which assess broad development strategies against broad environmental considerations) is the appropriate type of assessment for such Community programmes, rather an environmental impact assessment, which is site specific and appropriate for assessing local impacts.

The importance of proper integration of the results of a strategic environmental assessment into Community programmes is stressed in the following passage:

> Structural Fund programming is a logical framework involving a number phases: the preparation of a plan, the adoption of an agreed programming document (CSF or SPD), an implementation programme and finally an evaluation of the impact of interventions on the basis of agreed objectives and indicators (social, economic and environmental). All these phases are strongly inter-linked. It is therefore necessary to ensure that the potential environmental impacts identified at the plan preparation stage are carefully accounted for during the entire planning process.

> The SEA process requires that full attention is given to environmental and sustainable development issues from the very first stage of Structural Fund programming: i.e. the preparation of the Regional Development Plan. This is intended to ensure that the results and information obtained will benefit the next planning levels, reducing the consuming conflicts between environmental and economic objectives.[65]

An SEA operates by firstly profiling the environmental position in the target region and the interaction with the target economic sectors. It then assesses the environmental implications of the development priorities identified in the programme and identifies possible alternative ways of matching the economic/social objectives with sustainable development. A set of environmental indicators will also be established with which the on-going implementation of the

---

[65] Commission, *A Handbook on Environmental Assessment of Regional Development plans and EU Structural Funds Programmes*, September 1999, p.20.

programme can be assessed. Finally the adoption of the programme should take full account of the assessment and the indicators.

HABITAT PROTECTION

Tourists frequent areas which contain important wildlife, whether habitats, flora or fauna. If tourism impacts in these areas are not properly managed, and this can include prohibiting as well as restricting and channelling tourist access, negative wildlife impacts will follow. Wildlife areas are also often isolated, under-populated, and scenically attractive, and thus aesthetically and visually appealing to tourists. Although Member States operate national systems of wildlife protection which impose some restraint on tourism impacts in these areas, Community action focuses on, wildlife of European importance and tries to protect, particularly endangered, species and landforms. While the object of Community intervention in wildlife protection is not the protection of landscapes from or even for tourists, it is clear that Community intervention can have both effects.

The primary instrument of Community involvement in habitat protection is Directive 92/43 on the conservation of natural habitats and of wild fauna and flora.[66] In this section it is proposed to briefly outline the contents of this Directive and highlight its relevance to tourism. The Commission maintains an extensive website devoted to this Directive at:

http://www.europa.eu.int/comm/environment/nature/themes.htm.

Directive 92/43 requires Member States to establish special areas of conservation (SACs) within their territories under the brand title "Natura 2000" to protect wildlife of Community-wide importance. The object of the creation and maintenance of such areas, according to Article 2(2), is:

> to maintain or restore, at favourable conservation status, natural habitats and species of wild fauna and flora of Community interest.

In seeking to achieve this conservation status, the Directive pursues four main themes. It:

• establishes in a series of annexes the criteria for defining whether an area holds the wildlife necessary to require the establishment of an SAC,

---

[66] OJ L 206/7, 22.7.92. Consolidated text available at http://europa.eu.int/eur–lex/en/consleg/pdf/1992/en_1992L0043_do_001.pdf.

- lays down the steps to be followed in establishing an SAC,
- defines the various levels of legal protection which Member States must provide for an SAC,
- defines the circumstances in which, despite SAC status, plans and projects which might adversely affect the conservation status, may still proceed.

Before looking more closely at these themes, note should be taken of the great ambition of this Directive. As of the beginning of 2002 there are approximately 11,500 proposed SACs covering 413,000 km2 of the Community covering approximately 13% of the Community surface. Each SAC has to be vetted and approved at Commission level before designation takes place. Afterwards the Commission is responsible for ensuring that all SACs are properly protected and managed at Member State level. This offers the opportunity for a wide degree of Commission intervention in local matters. Moreover the creation and observance of SACs is potentially controversial since it involves land and traditional rights owners accepting restrictions over their activities. Many SACs encompass living communities where tourism, recreation, hunting, agriculture and forestry and other industries have traditionally been pursued. The task of reconciling these interests is not easy.

The scale of direct Commission involvement is worth noting. Every act of designation or redesignation (where the boundary of an SAC is redrawn perhaps to facilitate some development or change in wildlife patterns) and every unauthorised act impacting an SAC is a matter of Community law about which environmental activists can be expected to be vigilant. Overall, the Habitats Directive is a striking and unusual example of direct Community involvement in local matters unhindered by the subsidiarity principle. In actually controlling land-use in certain cases, it goes beyond both the EIA and the SEA directives.

Criteria for Establishing SACs

Directive 92/43 divides the Community into five bio geographical regions – Atlantic, Continental, Alpine, Mediterranean and Macronesian – and lists:

- in Annex I a range of habitat types which broadly speaking must be in danger of disappearance or present outstanding examples of typical characteristics of one of the five biogeograhpical regions,
- in Annex II the types of species which must be endangered, vulnerable, rare or for other reasons require particular attention.

The application of these criteria to any site is a matter of judgment and, not surprisingly, this has proved a controversial aspect of the Directive. However, the ultimate test for designation as an SAC under the Directive is whether an area:

> contributes significantly to the maintenance or restoration at a favourable conservation status of a natural habitat types in Annex I or of a species in Annex II ... and/or contributes significantly to the maintenance of biological diversity within the biographic region or regions concerned – Article 1.

Among the habitats listed in Annex I are defined types of open sea and tidal area, sea cliffs and beaches, sand dunes, marshes, running waters, heaths, fens and bogs, grasslands, forests, rocky slopes and habitats. Among the species listed in Annex II are bears and wolves. The entire area in which defined species, such as bears and wolves, may roam does not, however, have to be designated as an SAC. The Directive states in Article 1:

> For animal species ranging over wide areas sites of Community importance shall correspond to the places within the natural range of such species which present the physical or biological factors essential to their life and reproduction.

Similarly, for sea species which range over wide areas:

> Such sites will be proposed only where there is a clearly identifiable area representing the physical and biological factors essential to their life and reproduction – Article 4(1).

Creating/Changing SACs

There are no SACs currently in existence. Due to the lengthy timetable envisaged by the Directive none are expected to be formally created before 2004. However, the Directive creates various intermediate deadlines which have already passed and triggered significant levels of protection for potential SACs. Because of the complexity of issues involved and a degree of popular opposition, Member States have had difficulties in meeting these deadlines. Consequently, the Commission has secured judgment in the Court of Justice against a number of states over implementation delays.[67] Such failures arise in part because of

---

[67] France, Germany and Ireland were held by the Court of Justice on the same day, September 11, 2001, and in virtually identical terms, to have failed to meet their obligations under the Directive to forward list of sites and prescribed information relating to those sites by the deadlines – *Commission v. France* [2001] E.C.R. I–5831; *Commission v. Germany* [2001] E.C.R. I–5811; *Commission v. Ireland* [2001] E.C.R. I–5757.

disputes over site designation arising in turn from the reluctance of land and traditional rights owners to accept the restrictions which designation will involve.

Article 4 establishes the procedure to be followed leading to the designation of an area as an SAC. Considerable legal importance attaches to this procedure, firstly because any one wishing to oppose designation can only resist it by challenging a site's importance on scientific grounds and no other, and secondly by claiming the designation procedure was not properly complied with.

The designation procedure is as follows:

- the Member State proposes a list of sites to the Commission with stipulated information,

- the Commission examines the data and in conjunction with the Member State and after following a specific procedure (which also provides for including further sites not initially forwarded by a state) establishes a draft list of what the Directive terms "sites of Community importance",[68]

- the Member State then formally designates the site as an SAC.

This procedure is still on-going.

The Legal Protection of SACs

Article 6 is the key provision specifying the obligations of Member States in ensuring an adequate level of protection for an SAC.[69] The obligations can be categorised as site specific and site general. Site specific essentially means ensuring a site does not get worse – "take appropriate steps to avoid … the deterioration of natural habitats and the habitat of species". The Directive imposes this obligation even before formal designation takes place. Site specific also means, that once formal designation takes place, the Member State.

> shall establish the necessary conservation measures including, if need be, appropriate management plans specifically designed for the site … and appropriate statutory, administrative or contractual measures – Article 6(1).

This is clearly a demanding obligation which States may easily fail to meet. It

---

[68] e.g. Commission Decision adopting the list of sites of Community importance for the Macronesuian biographical region, OJ L 5/16, 9.1.02. The list was approved by Spain and Portugal.

[69] See generally Commission, Managing Natura 2000 Sites – The provisions of Article 6 of the 'Habitats' Directive 92/43, Luxembourg 2000; Commission, Assessment of Plans and Projects Significantly affecting Natura 2000 Sites – Methodological Guidance on the provisions of Article 6(3) and Article 6(4) of the 'Habitats ' Directive, May 2002. Text available at http://www.europa.eu.int/comm/environment/nature/natura_2000_assess_en.pdf.

will require considerable on-going commitment and resources to satisfy. Site general means that Member States must ensure that proposed plans or projects

> likely to have a significant effect ... either individually or in combination with other plans or projects, shall be subject to appropriate assessment of its implications for the site in view of the sites conservation objectives – Article 6(3).

This means in effect that a Member State must operate a control system over activities potentially affecting sites under which permission must be sought in advance for a plan or project. The choice as to how a Member State structures the system, whether a new permission system is needed or whether an existing system comprising town and country planning can be used, is left to the Member States. No information is yet available as to how Member States have implemented this requirement.

As to how the system should operate:

> In the light of the conclusions of the assessment of the implications for the site ... the competent national authorities shall agree to the plan or project only after having ascertained that it will not adversely affect the integrity of the site concerned and, if appropriate, after having obtained the opinion of the general public – Article 6(3).

This provision is highly significant and shows that this Directive goes further than Directive 85/337 dealing with environmental impact assessment in declaring that if the assessment is negative then permission must be refused.

ASSESSING PLANS OR PROJECTS AFFECTING SAC

While designation generally means that Member States must ensure that no activities which threaten the integrity of the site are permitted, provision is also made for exceptional plans or projects which might damage an SAC but which for major reasons of public interest should be allowed. Defining the circumstances in which this may happen in a way which does not open the door to abuse or expansive interpretation is critically important.

The Directive envisages two different situations – where the site hosts a priority habitat/species and where it does not. If it hosts a non-priority site the project can be allowed for:

> imperative reasons of overriding public interest including those of social or economic nature – Article 6(4).

If it hosts a priority site the project can only be allowed for a narrower range of public interest reasons relating to:

> human health or public safety, to beneficial consequences of primary importance for the environment, or, further to an opinion from the Commission, to other imperative reasons of overriding public interest – Article 6(4).

Infrastructure projects and particularly roads seem likely to come within the exceptions.

While these exceptions are broadly expressed, they are circumscribed by the cumulative effect of strong terms like "overriding" and "imperative" and also by the need for public value. Privately beneficial projects will not be permitted destroy an SAC. It is worth recalling, however, that it only becomes necessary to claim that one of these exceptions applies when the integrity of a site would be adversely affected. There is probably considerable scope for debate in any instance whether an impact affects the integrity of a site or, whether it is a minor or neutral impact as opposed to an adverse one.

Where a Member State allows a project proceed under the above exceptions, it must still respect two requirements set out in Article 6(4) – all compensatory measures must taken to ensure that the coherence of the overall Natura 2000 network is protected and the Commission must be informed of these measures. Further, a Member State is still subject to the overriding policy of the Directive which is to ensure European bio-diversity through conservation. It seems likely that this is the yardstick which the Commission will use for judging compatibility with the Directive.

The following Commission flow chart[70] indicates the sequencing of steps to be followed by public bodies when assessing plans or projects likely to affect an SAC.

---

[70] Taken from Commission, Assessment of Plans and Projects Significantly affecting Natura 2000 Sites – Methodological Guidance on the provisions of Article 6(3) and Article 6(4) of the 'Habitats ' Directive, November 2001, p.7.

CONSIDERATION OF A PLAN OR PROJECT (PP) AFFECTING A
NATURA 2000 SITE

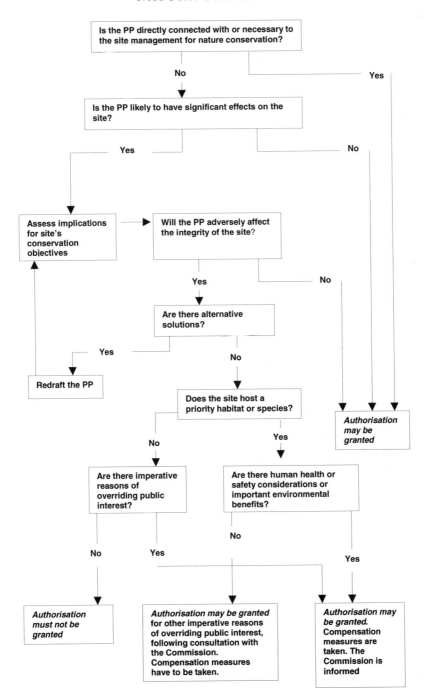

In the absence of Community-wide data it is difficult to comment on how the Directive's potentially controversial provisions allowing inroads on SACs have been operated by Member States.

Examples of Current Management Approaches

The proper implementation of the Habitats Directive will probably require a more systematic approach to site management of tourism impacts than has historically been the case. Management plans which seek to reconcile leisure, tourism and occupational needs with nature conservation will, among other things, need to provide for means to restrict uses, whether the restrictions are legally based or visitor management based.

Already in some states there are areas which will become SACs which have experience of trying to manage the diverse uses made of such areas.[71]

Finland – Tammisaari Archipelago National Park as part of Natura 2000 site, Finland

> Located in the western part of the archipelago of Uusimaa Province, the Tammisaari National Park ... is a group of islands extending from the open marine area right across to the island of Algo. The National Park is part of a much larger Natura 2000 area.

> The area is under pressure from different types of users: the large number of boars on the busy boat route between Helsinki and Hanko, guests or owners of summer cottages who use the site for outdoor recreational and owners with building rights. ... In order to manage visitor impact, facilities are provided in the less sensitive areas. Restricted and closed areas are not equipped with any facilities to discourage visitors. Due to the presence of many rare and endangered bird species, access to islands and islets in the marine zone is prohibited during spring and summer. However, visitors are permitted to land on restricted areas on weekdays when a guide is present. The Park visitor centre is situated on the mainland in order to avoid too much boat traffic and to allow people easy access to information without taking a boat out.

---

[71] Taken from Commission, Sustainable Tourism and Natura 2000 – Guidelines, initiatives and good practises in Europe, Good practise in action, September 2001, p. 227. Text available at http://www.europa.eu.int/comm/environment/nature/sust_tourism_gpract.pdf.

Germany

[In] the Steinhuder Meer Nature Park, located in the north of Germany near Hanover ... the core and most attractive part of the park is the Steinhuder Meer (30km2), the biggest lake in north-western Germany. ... The lake, parts of the lakesides and the adjoining bogs are an important bird habitat ... and the site will be integrated into the Natura 2000 network.

The Steinhuder Meer is also the most attractive recreational area for the conurbation of Hanover (1 million people). On the nice summer weekends up to 50,0000 people visit the area. The main sports and recreational activities are water sports, biking and hiking. ... In order to protect nature and offer attractive facilities for visitors for recreation, the park ... has established a zoning system. All recreational and tourism facilities are concentrated in two areas and the more sensitive parts of the lakeside are strictly prohibited. ... The park's visitor management system is based around limiting access to nature without banning it completely. A circular path around the lake has been built ... concentrating people in certain areas. ... In order to avoid disturbance of the birds by water sports on the lake, similar measures have been taken. Practising water sports is now only allowed from 1 April to 31 October. Certain parts of the lake have been designated nature protection areas, and access to these parts is prevented by buoy chains.

Overall, legal challenges to Member State implementation of Directive 92/43 seem likely to form a considerable volume of litigation before the Court of Justice in the years to come. Conflict appears likely over the following legal issues:

- compliance with the Directive's procedures.
- redrawing of SAC boundaries.
- interpretation of the public interest reasons for justifying inroads on an SAC.

CHAPTER CONCLUSION

While the negative impacts of tourism on the environment are well catalogued by the Community, direct Community legal and policy involvement to counteract these effects remains limited. The greater hope for effective Community involvement lies with fuller observance and enforcement of Community laws which lay down legislative frameworks which Member States must implement. However, ideal enforcement will never exist and frameworks often provide only a mechanism within which policy conflicts over land use between environment and tourism are decided on a case-by-case basis. Bad decisions can and will still be made, though at least regarding wildlife of European importance the Community can directly influence land-use decisions. Whether the Community should seek greater involvement in land-use decision-making especially concerning scenery, landscapes and heritage of European, even world, importance is worth examining. The wider questions and their legal implications – whether Community policy should seek to channel ever expanding tourism demand into less destructive modes or even reverse policies which increase demand or advance new polices which target the social factors which determine tourist demand and what role law might play in all this – are not currently on the agenda. If anything, the focus is the other way, on increasing tourist demand through more innovative and entrepreneurial approaches to developing tourism businesses, encouraging competitiveness and channelling regional aid to tourism. The belief that sustainable tourism is not, in many instances, a contradiction in terms, remains robust.

STUDENTS TASKS

Undergraduate questions:

1. Discuss the types of pressures on the environment which the Community considers are associated with tourism.

2. Assess whether the 5th EAP has achieved its objectives regarding tourism pressures on the environment.

3. Taking as a reference the 5th EAP, what kind of actions would you propose in order to change the behaviour of tourists to minimise environmental pressures?

4. Explain the procedure to be followed before development consent for a project adversely impacting on an SAC can be given.

Postgraduate questions:

1. Improved integration of environmental concerns into other Community policies continues to be a major challenge facing the Community.

Express a view on why this challenge has not been met?

2. Identify two proposed special conservation areas in your region and assess how the protection of the relevant type of wildlife in those areas will impact on tourism.

3. Take any plan or programme which affects a tourism area which you are familiar with and which is subject to Directive 2001/42, and assess what difference the Directive will have on tourism in that area.

4. In general terms, how do you think an environmental action programme should deal with tourism pressures on the environment?

INDEX

SA

343.
078
91
EUR